Discover
Scotland

Contents

Throughout this book, we use these icons to highlight special recommendations:

 The Best...
Lists for everything from bars to wildlife – to make sure you don't miss out

 Don't Miss
A must-see – don't go home until you've been there

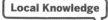 Local experts reveal their top picks and secret highlights

 Detour
Special places a little off the beaten track

 If you like...
Lesser-known alternatives to world-famous attractions

These icons help you quickly identify reviews in the text and on the map:

Sights

Eating

Drinking

Sleeping

Information

This edition written and researched by

Neil Wilson
Andy Symington

p255 Inverness &
the Highlands

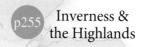

Stirling &
p157 Northeast Scotland

p213
Skye & the Islands

Glasgow &
Loch Lomond p117   p51 Edinburgh

Contents

Contents

On the Road

In Focus

Survival Guide

This Is Scotland

Like a fine malt whisky, Scotland is a connoisseur's delight. It's an intoxicating blend of stunning scenery and sophisticated cities, of salt-tanged sea air and dark peaty waters, of wry humour and generous hospitality. It's a land with a rich, multilayered history that reveals its true depth and complex flavours only to those who savour it slowly.

Every corner of the Scottish landscape seems steeped in the past. A deserted croft on an island shore, a moor that was once a battlefield, a cave that once sheltered Bonnie Prince Charlie. History feels very close here, lurking over your shoulder as you explore the echoing halls of ancient castles, stately homes and royal palaces.

Scotland has made a contribution to Western civilization out of all proportion to its size. The long list of influential Scottish scientists, philosophers, writers, explorers and inventors would fill a separate book – it was Scots who gave the world steamships, television, the telephone and countless other world-changing inventions. Oh, and golf, too. The country's museums and art galleries are richly rewarding.

The Highlands and islands are one of Europe's last great wildernesses. Their high peaks, wooded valleys and deep-sea lochs are a wildlife haven where you can see golden eagles soaring above the mountains and red deer foraging in the glens, spot otters frolicking along the kelp-fringed shores of Skye and watch minke whales breaching through shoals of mackerel off the coast of Mull.

Edinburgh, the festival city, is one of the world's favourite party towns, but it's also rich in history and culture. Glasgow offers stunning galleries, great pubs and a foot-stomping live-music scene, while Inverness combines a gorgeous riverside setting with superb dining. You could spend a lifetime savouring Scotland, but we've distilled it down to the quintessential experiences. Discover it your way.

> ❝ Scotland reveals its true depth only to those who savour it slowly ❞

The ruins of Urquhart Castle (p280), on the edge of Loch Ness
PHOTOGRAPHER: PATRICK HORTON

Scotland

Shetland Islands (see Inset)

North Sea

Fair Isle

ELEVATION

	1000m
	700m
	500m
	300m
	200m
	100m
	0

Shetland Islands

ATLANTIC OCEAN

North Sea

Hermaness
Unst
Uyea
Ulsta
Toft
Shetland Islands
Isle of Noss
Lerwick
Mousa
Hillswick
Foula

0	40 km
0	20 miles

To Shetland Islands (see inset)

Orkney Islands ⑦

North Ronaldsay
Egilsay
Stronsay
Kirkwall
South Ronaldsay
John O'Groats
Hoy
Dunnet Head
Wick
Stromness
Scrabster
Thurso
Lybster
Strathy Point
Helmsdale

N

0	100 km
0	50 miles

Butt of Lewis

Cape Wrath
Durness
Bettyhill
Tongue
Melvich
Ben Hope (927m)

Kinlochbervie
Handa
Lochinver
Ben More Assynt (998m)

Brora
Golspie
Dornoch
Portmahomack

Elgin ⑫
Moray Firth
Invergordon
Nairn
Inverness ③
Grantown-on-Spey
Black Isle
Dingwall
Strathpeffer

Bonar Bridge
Ben More (1084m)

Ullapool
An Teallach (1062m) ②①
Beinn Dearg

Enard Bay

Stornoway

Isle of Lewis (Leòdhais)

North Harris

Tarbert
Isle of Harris

Shiant Islands

The Minch

Rona
Uig
Trotternish
Raasay
Portree ②
Dunvegan ⑤ ⑧
Isle of Skye
Cuillin Hills
Egol
Sleat
Isle of Canna
Isle of Rum
Isle of Eigg
Isle of Muck

Sea of the Hebrides

Kyleakin
Kyle of Lochalsh
Knoydart Peninsula
Five Sisters (1068m)
Mallaig
Lochailort
Glen Affric

The Little Minch

North Uist (Uibhist A Tuath)
Lochmaddy

South Uist (Uibhist A Deas)

Lochboisdale

Barra (Barraigh)

Berneray (Bearnaraigh)

Coll

Monadhliath Mountains
Aviemore
Fort Augustus
Kingussie
Newtonmore
Monadh (855m)
Cairngorm Mountains
Strathdon

Fort William ⑬
Ben Nevis (1344m)
Glencoe ⑭
Kinlochleven

Huntly

Fraserburgh
Rattray Bay
Peterhead

Banff

Aberdeen

⑨
⑳
Monroe
Braemar ㉒
Grampian Mountains ⑲
Stonehaven
Brechin
Montrose

Pitlochry

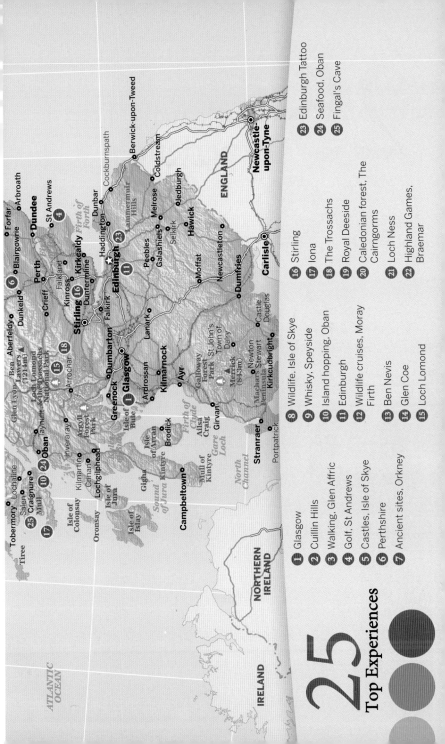

25 Top Experiences

1. Glasgow
2. Cuillin Hills
3. Walking, Glen Affric
4. Golf, St Andrews
5. Castles, Isle of Skye
6. Perthshire
7. Ancient sites, Orkney
8. Wildlife, Isle of Skye
9. Whisky, Speyside
10. Island hopping, Oban
11. Edinburgh
12. Wildlife cruises, Moray Firth
13. Ben Nevis
14. Glen Coe
15. Loch Lomond
16. Stirling
17. Iona
18. The Trossachs
19. Royal Deeside
20. Caledonian forest, The Cairngorms
21. Loch Ness
22. Highland Games, Braemar
23. Edinburgh Tattoo
24. Seafood, Oban
25. Fingal's Cave

25 Scotland's Top Experiences

Glasgow

Scotland's biggest city (p117) lacks Edinburgh's classical beauty, but more than makes up for it with a barrelful of things to do and a warmth and energy that leave every visitor impressed. It's edgy and contemporary, a great spot to browse art galleries – Kelvingrove (p140) and the Burrell Collection (p148) are among the best in the country. Add to that what's perhaps Britain's best pub culture, and one of the world's best live-music scenes, and the only thing to do is live it. Kelvingrove Art Gallery & Museum

OLF/IMAGEBROKER ©

Cuillin Hills

In a country famous for stunning scenery, Skye's Cuillin Hills (p234) take top prize. Their near-alpine craggy peaks offer knife-edge ridges, jagged pinnacles, scree-filled gullies and acres of naked rock. A paradise for experienced mountaineers, the higher reaches are off-limits to most walkers, but there are easy trails through the glens and into the corries, where walkers can soak up the views and share the landscape with red deer and golden eagles.

Walking

The best way to really get inside landscapes like Glen Affric (p283) is to walk them. Despite the midges and drizzle, walking here is a pleasure, with numerous short- and long-distance trails, hills and mountains begging to be tramped. Mild winters mean it's a year-round option, and the real bonus is the vibrant walking community here: you'll forge friendships on hillsides and, flushed and muddy, over a dram in a country pub or cosy Highland bothy at the end of the trail.

The Best...
Places for Food

EDINBURGH
Sophisticated and atmospheric restaurants, some Michelin-starred. (p96)

GLASGOW
Huge range of cuisines in one of the best food cities in Scotland. (p139)

INVERNESS
Has developed an excellent dining scene in recent years, with some outstanding restaurants. (p272)

OBAN
Probably has more top-notch seafood restaurants than any other town in Scotland. (p242)

ISLE OF SKYE
Funky cafes, fish restaurants, and fine dining at Three Chimneys. (p237)

The Best...
Art Galleries

KELVINGROVE ART GALLERY & MUSEUM
Glasgow's great cathedral of culture, home to Dali's notorious *Christ of St John on the Cross.* (p140)

NATIONAL GALLERY OF SCOTLAND
The national collection includes the *Three Graces* by Antonio Canova. (p81)

BURRELL COLLECTION
Breathtaking private collection bequeathed to the city of Glasgow. (p148)

SCOTTISH NATIONAL PORTRAIT GALLERY
An intriguing look at Scottish history through the medium of portraiture. (p88)

MARTIN MOOS

Golf

4

Scotland invented the game of golf and is still revered as its spiritual home by hackers and champions alike. Links courses are the classic experience here – bumpy coastal affairs where the rough is heather and machair and the main enemy is the wind, which can make a disaster of a promising round in an instant. St Andrews (p186), the historic Fife university town, is golf's headquarters, and an alluring destination for anyone who loves the sport. The Old Course, St Andrews

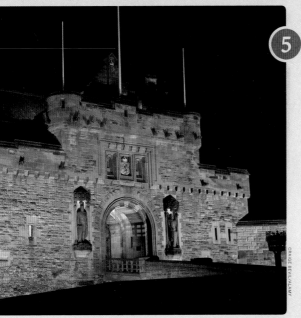

CRAIG BREVIL/ALAMY

Castles

5

Whether you're after desolate stone fortresses looming in the mist (like Eilean Donan, p229), noble keeps towering over historic towns or luxurious palaces set in expansive grounds, Scotland has a full range of castles, reflecting a turbulent history and tense relations with its southern neighbour. Most have stories of plots, intrigues, imprisonments and treachery; a worryingly high percentage have a phantom rumoured to stalk their parapets. Edinburgh Castle

Perthshire

Blue-grey lochs shimmer, swaths of woodland clothe the hills and majestic glens scythe into remote wildernesses. Picturesque towns like Pitlochry (p201) bloom with flowers, distilleries emit tempting malty odours, and sheep graze in impossibly green meadows. Here in Perthshire, the heart of the country, there's a feeling of the bounty of nature that no other place in Scotland can replicate.

Loch Tummel, near Pitlochry

Ancient Sites

Visiting ancient sites, it's sometimes difficult to really feel the gulf of years or sense a connection with the people that built them – but Scotland's superb prehistoric remains have an immediate impact. Few better glimpses of Stone Age life exist than Skara Brae (p278) on Orkney, and the incredible cairns and chambered tombs scattered across that archipelago are equally impressive. Mysterious standing stones, muscular broch towers and richly symbolic Pictish stones mean that the distant past is a constant presence throughout the country. Skara Brae

Wildlife

Sparsely populated, and with large areas of wilderness, Scotland is an important sanctuary for all sorts of land, air and sea-based creatures. Amazing birdwatching is on offer throughout the country, with the white-tailed sea eagles of Skye and Mull (p250) the highlight. Capercaillie, corn-crakes, puffins, ospreys, golden eagles and red kites are other feathered drawcards, while red deer roam the heath-ered uplands, pine martens and wildcats stalk the forests, and dolphins, whales, otters and orcas splash about in the northern waters. Atlantic Puffin

The Best...
Museums

NATIONAL MUSEUM OF SCOTLAND
Its historic treasures include the famous Lewis chessmen. (p83)

KELVINGROVE MUSEUM
Offers everything from a Spitfire plane to an Egyptian sarcophagus. (p140)

HIGHLAND FOLK MUSEUM
An open-air museum of traditional rural buildings. (p287)

SKYE MUSEUM OF ISLAND LIFE
Turf-roofed crofters' cottages re-create farming life in the 1800s. (p238)

ROYAL YACHT *BRITANNIA*
A floating museum of the royal family's former holiday yacht. (p90)

Whisky

Scotland's national drink – from the Gaelic *uisge bagh*, meaning 'water of life' – has been distilled here for more than 500 years. More than 100 distilleries are still in operation, producing hundreds of varieties of single malt – learning to distinguish the smoky, peaty whiskies of Islay, say, from the flowery, sherried malts of Speyside (p210) has become a hugely popular pastime. Many distilleries offer guided tours rounded off with a tasting session, and ticking off the local varieties is a great way to explore the whisky-making regions.

The Best...
Hiking

GLEN COE
Scotland's spiritual home of hill-walking, with low-level hikes, too. (p288)

ISLE OF SKYE
A challenging destination for ambitious walkers, with long and technically demanding routes. (p226)

THE CAIRNGORMS
Everything from easy strolls around Loch Morlich to strenuous climbs onto the high tops. (p281)

ROYAL DEESIDE
Lovely low-level walks on river banks and through native woods. (p204)

BEN NEVIS
Britain's highest peak: the ultimate for summit baggers. (p300)

10
Island Hopping

Much of the unique character of western and northern Scotland comes down to the expansive vistas of sea and islands – there are more than 700 islands off Scotland's coast, of which almost 100 are inhabited. A network of ferry services links these islands to the mainland and each other, and buying an Island Rover ticket (unlimited ferry travel for 15 days) provides a fascinating way to explore. Oban (p239), the 'gateway to the isles', has ferries to no fewer than seven different islands. Oban Harbour

Edinburgh

Scotland's capital (p51) may be famous for its festivals, but there's much more to it than that. Edinburgh is a city of many moods, worth visiting out of season for sights such as the castle silhouetted against a blue spring sky, with a yellow haze of daffodils misting the slopes below the esplanade; or a chill December morning with the haar (fog) snagging the spires of the Old Town, the dark mouths of the wynds more mysterious than ever, rain on the cobblestones and a warm glow beckoning from the window of a pub. The Royal Mile

11

KARL BLACKWELL

Wildlife Cruises

Scotland is one of the best places in Europe for seeing marine wildlife. In high season (July and August) many cruise operators on the west coast can almost guarantee sightings of minke whales and porpoises, and the Moray Firth (p269) is famous for its resident population of bottlenose dolphins. Basking sharks – at up to 12m, the biggest fish to be found in British waters – are also commonly sighted. Tobermory (p247) and Armadale (p229) on Skye are top departure points.

EOIN CLARKE

Climbing Ben Nevis

The allure of Britain's highest peak is strong – around 100,000 people a year set off up the summit trail, though not all will make it to the top. Nevertheless, the highest Munro of them all is within the ability of anyone who's reasonably fit. Treat Ben Nevis (p300) with respect and your reward (weather permitting) will be a truly magnificent view and a great sense of achievement. Real walking enthusiasts can warm up by hiking the 95-mile West Highland Way first.

Glen Coe

Scotland's most famous glen (p288) combines those two essential qualities of the Highland landscape – dramatic scenery and deep history. The peacefulness and beauty of this valley today belie the fact that it was the scene of a ruthless 17th-century massacre (p293), when the local MacDonalds were murdered by soldiers of the Campbell clan. Some of the glen's finest walks – to the Lost Valley, for example – follow the routes used by clansmen and women trying to flee their attackers, where many perished in the snow.

The Best...
Seafood Restaurants

CAFÉ FISH
Fresh shellfish straight off the boat and a view of Tobermory harbour. (p248)

WATERFRONT
Their motto: 'From pier to pan as fast as we can'. (p242)

LOCHBAY SEAFOOD RESTAURANT
Cosy farmhouse kitchen-style restaurant overlooking a Skye sealoch. (p237)

FISHERS BISTRO
One of Edinburgh's oldest and best seafood places. (p100)

SEAFOOD RESTAURANT
Impeccable cuisine with a panoramic view of the West Sands. (p193)

The Best...
Wildlife Watching

ISLE OF MULL
Eagles overhead and porpoises and whales in the waters below. (p250)

LOCH GARTEN
Get a close-up view of ospreys in the nest. (p287)

ISLE OF SKYE
An otter hotspot. (p335)

MORAY FIRTH
Home to Scotland's only resident pod of bottlenose dolphins. (p269)

THE CAIRNGORMS
Good chance of spotting red deer. (p281)

HIGHLAND WILDLIFE PARK
See rare species such as Scottish wildcat. (p287)

Loch Lomond

Despite being less than an hour's drive from the bustle and sprawl of Glasgow, the bonnie banks and bonnie braes (hills) of Loch Lomond (p150) – immortalised in the words of one of Scotland's best-known songs – comprise one of the most scenic parts of the country. At the heart of Scotland's first national park, the loch begins as a broad, island-peppered lake in the south, its shores clothed in bluebell woods, narrowing in the north to a fjord-like trench ringed by 900m-high mountains.

FEARGUS COONEY

Stirling

For centuries Stirling (p170) sat astride the route taken by English armies invading from the south. Its crag-top castle commanded the crossing of the River Forth at Stirling Bridge – site of a famous victory for William Wallace in 1297 – and was a favourite residence of kings James IV and James V. Stirling Castle is every bit as much a must-see as Edinburgh – some would say more so – along with the nearby historical attractions of Bannockburn battlefield and the National Wallace Monument. Stirling Castle

Iona

Legend has it that when St Columba left Ireland in AD 563 to found a mission in Scotland, he kept sailing until he found a spot where he could no longer see his homeland on the horizon. It was the little jewel of Iona (p251) – Scotland's most sacred island, and one of its most beautiful, with lush green pastures, pink granite rocks, white-sand beaches and turquoise waters. The Iona Community continues the spiritual calling in an abbey on the site of Columba's first chapel.
Pillar carving, Iona Abbey

The Trossachs

The Trossachs (p177) is as famous for its literary links as it is for its picture-postcard scenery – it was here that Sir Walter Scott set his epic poem *The Lady in the Lake,* and his historic novel *Rob Roy*. While Loch Lomond is at its scenic best in spring and early summer, when blue-bell woods and rhododendron blooms add colour to the scene, the Trossachs comes alive in autumn, when the turning leaves bring a blaze of fire and gold to the native woods of oak, birch and ash.

The Best...
Castles

STIRLING CASTLE
Historic fortress with Great Hall and sumptuous Royal Palace. (p170)

URQUHART CASTLE
Wonderfully atmospheric ruins with brilliant view over Loch Ness. (p280)

EDINBURGH CASTLE
The biggest and bold-est, home to the Stone of Destiny and the Scottish crown jewels. (p65)

EILEAN DONAN CASTLE
Impossibly picturesque tower house perched on a sea-girt islet. (p229)

BALMORAL CASTLE
A profusion of Scottish Baronial turrets with that all-important royal con-nection. (p209)

The Best...
Scenery

GLEN AFFRIC
Classic Highland scene of lochs, heather, high peaks and pine woods. (p283)

THE TROSSACHS
Compact and bijou combination of woods and water. (p177)

ISLE OF SKYE
Jagged peaks, wild waterfalls and expansive sea views. (p226)

GLEN COE
Steep cliffs and brooding mountains crowd around a glen of breathtaking beauty. (p288)

ARISAIG
Wide open vistas of sea and mountain, superb sunsets over Eigg and Rum. (p302)

Royal Deeside

The long valley of the River Dee stretches from its headwaters in the heart of the Cairngorms mountains to the oil-industry port of Aberdeen. Its picturesque upper reaches, ringed by rock-girt mountains and fringed with native pine woods, has been known as Royal Deeside (p204) ever since Queen Victoria fell in love with Balmoral Castle – it has been the royal family's summer retreat since the mid-19th century. Nearby is the delightful village of Ballater, its shopfronts adorned with royal crests boasting their status as 'suppliers to Her Majesty'. Balmoral Castle

STEPHEN DOREY/ALAMY

CHRISTINE WHITEHEAD/ALAMY

20 Caledonian Pine Forest

In the wake of the last ice age, 10,000 years ago, much of the land that is now Scotland was covered in extensive forests of Scots pine, birch, oak and rowan. Known as the Caledonian Forest, it has been mostly wiped out by thousands of years of human attrition – chopped down for fuel and timber. Only about 1% of the original forest remains, but what does is truly beautiful. The largest area of forest, at Rothiemurchus Estate (p282) in the Cairngorms, harbours rare wildlife including capercaillie, crossbill and wildcat.

Loch Ness

In a land rich in legends, there are few that match the international reach of the Loch Ness monster, which is famous the world over. While the monster legend may be what draws you to Loch Ness (p276) in the first place, once you're there you'll realise that it's a hauntingly beautiful place, rich in historic sites such as Urquhart Castle and Fort Augustus, and close to some of Scotland's finest scenery in the shape of gorgeous Glen Affric.

Highland Games

The archetypal event of the Scottish summer, Highland Games – such as the Braemar Gathering (p208) – started with after-battle celebrations and strength trials by warring clansmen. Traditional events – shot-putting, hammer-throwing and caber-tossing – have been joined today by bagpipes and Highland dancing, and even hill-running races and 100m sprints. The atmosphere is that of a family-friendly village fair, with plenty to see and do.

Edinburgh Military Tattoo

Of all the varied festival events that take place in Edinburgh in August, few are as enduringly popular as the Military Tattoo (p113). It's an entertaining and often breathtaking extravaganza of marching bands, dancers, motorcycle display teams, acrobats and military set pieces performed by service men and women from British, Commonwealth and other armed forces from around the world. Held annually on the castle esplanade since 1950, it regularly sells out in advance with more than 200,000 people attending each year.

The Best...
Places to Stay

WITCHERY BY THE CASTLE
Divine decadence with a Gothic touch. (p88)

MONACHYLE MHOR
Relaxed luxury Perthshire hideaway with superb food. (p184)

ROCPOOL RESERVE
Boutique chic comes to Inverness. (p270)

AULD KIRK
Atmospheric accommodation in a converted church in Ballater. (p205)

TORAVAIG HOUSE HOTEL
Country house in Skye is the quintessence of Highland hospitality. (p229)

LIME TREE
More like an art gallery with bedrooms. (p293)

Seafood

One of the great pleasures of a visit to Scotland is the opportunity to indulge in the rich harvest of the sea. The cold, clear waters around the Scottish coast provide some of the most sought-after seafood in Europe, with much of it being whisked straight from the quayside to waiting restaurant tables from London to Lisbon. Fortunately there are plenty of places to sample this bounty right here, with Oban (p239) topping the list of towns with more than their fair share of seafood restaurants.

The Best...
Scenic Drives

A939 COCKBRIDGE TO TOMINTOUL
Swooping, whooping rollercoaster of a ride over the Grampian grouse moors. (p169)

FORT WILLIAM TO MALLAIG
The Road to the Isles provides classic views of Glenfinnan and offshore islands. (p300)

SALEN TO ARDNAMUCHAN POINT
Mostly twisting single-track, at best in early summer when rhododendrons are in bloom. (p298)

A82 GLASGOW TO FORT WILLIAM
Includes Loch Lomond and Glen Coe, with the vast expanse of Rannoch Moor in between. (p150)

Fingal's Cave

The surge and echo of Atlantic waves in the dark recesses of Fingal's Cave on the Isle of Staffa (p253) inspired the composer Felix Mendehlsson to pen his enduringly popular *Hebrides Overture*. Since then, thousands of visitors have braved the step from a rocking boat onto Staffa's slippery landing place and clambered among the soaring basaltic columns that frame this impressive sea-filled cavern to experience that same magical blend of sight and sound.

Scotland's
Top Itineraries

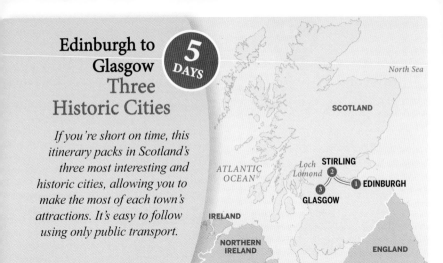

Edinburgh to Glasgow
5 DAYS
Three Historic Cities

If you're short on time, this itinerary packs in Scotland's three most interesting and historic cities, allowing you to make the most of each town's attractions. It's easy to follow using only public transport.

North Sea

SCOTLAND

ATLANTIC OCEAN

Loch Lomond **STIRLING** ②

① EDINBURGH

③ **GLASGOW**

IRELAND

NORTHERN IRELAND

ENGLAND

① Edinburgh (p64)

You'll need two days to do justice to the Scottish capital, taking in **Edinburgh Castle**, strolling down the **Royal Mile**, touring the halls of the **Palace of Holyroodhouse** and heading down to Leith to board the **Royal Yacht Britannia**. Put aside an afternoon to visit the beautiful and mysterious **Rosslyn Chapel**, made famous by the movie *The Da Vinci Code*. There's great shopping along Princes St and George St, and some of Scotland's best restaurants too.

EDINBURGH ⊃ STIRLING

🚗 **45 minutes** Along the M9. 🚆 **One hour** From Edinburgh Waverley or Haymarket direct to Stirling.

② Stirling (p170)

One day will give you enough time to visit **Stirling Castle** – many people think this picturesque fortress is even more interesting and evocative than Edinburgh Castle – and **Bannockburn**, the battlefield where Robert the Bruce led the Scots to victory over the English in 1314.

There's the **Wallace Monument** too, a tribute to the freedom fighter immortalised in the movie *Braveheart*. No need to overnight here – head on to Glasgow at the end of the day.

STIRLING ⊃ GLASGOW

🚗 **45 minutes** Via the M80. 🚆 **40 minutes** Frequent services from Stirling to Glasgow Queen St.

③ Glasgow (p128)

Culture vultures will need two days to absorb all that Scotland's biggest city has to offer – **Kelvingrove Art Gallery & Museum** and the **Burrell Collection** are both world class and will occupy you for a full day. Then there's the **Hunterian Gallery** and the **Mackintosh House**, and the museums along the Clyde. But if one day of art appreciation is enough, you could spend your final day on a trip to the bonnie banks of **Loch Lomond**, less than an hour away by car or train.

Canongate Tolbooth (p75) on the Royal Mile, Edinburgh
PHOTOGRAPHER: JONATHAN SMITH

Edinburgh to Inverness
Tayside to Speyside

Another shortish route, this time forging north through the heart of the Highlands, taking in Blair Castle in the valley of the River Tay, and Aviemore on the banks of the Spey, before reaching the Highland capital, Inverness.

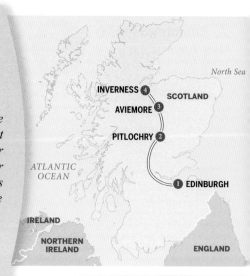

❶ Edinburgh (p64)

Again, as with the first itinerary, allow yourself two days to make the most of **Edinburgh** and **Rosslyn Chapel**.

. . . .

EDINBURGH ⊙ PITLOCHRY

🚗 **One hour 45 minutes** Via Forth Road Bridge, M90 and A9 via Scone Palace (p188). 🚆 **One hour 50 minutes** Direct from Edinburgh Waverley or Haymarket.

. . . .

❷ Pitlochry (p201)

If you're travelling by car, you can stop off at **Scone Palace** on your way north to visit the ancient coronation place of Scottish kings, and see the place where the **Stone of Destiny** (on display in Edinburgh Castle) was stolen in 1297 by the English King Edward. Plan to overnight at Pitlochry, giving yourself time to visit nearby sights such as **Blair Castle**, home to the Duke of Atholl and Britain's only private standing army, and **Killiecrankie**, site of an important battle during the 18th-century Jacobite rebellions; it's a name feted in many Scottish folk songs of the era.

. . . .

PITLOCHRY ⊙ AVIEMORE

🚗 **One hour 20 minutes** Along the A9 via Newtonmore (p287). 🚆 **One hour** Direct trains every two hours or so.

. . . .

❸ Aviemore (p281)

Day four sees you at Aviemore and ready to explore the **Cairngorms National Park**. You'll only have time for two or three sights – we recommend you head to **Loch Morlich** for a short hike, a visit to the **Cairngorm Reindeer Centre**, and (if the weather is clear) a trip on the **Cairngorm Mountain Railway** which will take you to the 1000m-high summit plateau. If you're driving, you can visit the **Highland Folk Museum** at Newtonmore on your way from Pitlochry.

. . . .

AVIEMORE ⊙ INVERNESS

🚗 **40 minutes** Along the A9. 🚆 **40 minutes** Direct trains every two hours.

. . . .

❹ Inverness (p268)

It's only a short trip from Aviemore to the attractive Highland capital, Inverness. There are some excellent **restaurants** here where you can celebrate the end of your itinerary, but before you head for the dinner table make sure to take a dolphin-spotting boat trip with **Moray Firth Cruises**.

Reindeer being fed in winter, the Cairngorms (p281)
PHOTOGRAPHER: DAVID TIPLING

10 DAYS

Edinburgh to Skye
Over the Hills to Skye

This is a more leisurely trip, leading to the beautiful Isle of Skye by way of St Andrews (home of golf), Royal Deeside, the Speyside whisky distilleries and Loch Ness.

North Sea

PORTREE
6

INVERNESS
4

DRUMNADROCHIT
5

SCOTLAND

BALLATER
3

ST ANDREWS
2

EDINBURGH
1

ATLANTIC OCEAN

IRELAND

NORTHERN IRELAND

ENGLAND

① Edinburgh (p64)

Allow yourself two days to make the most of **Edinburgh** and **Rosslyn Chapel**.

EDINBURGH ➲ ST ANDREWS

🚗 **1½ hours** Via Forth Road Bridge and A92.
🚌🚃 **One hour** Direct trains from Edinburgh to Leuchars every 30 minutes; free connecting bus into St Andrews.

② St Andrews (p164)

History buffs can tour **St Andrews Castle** and the ruins of **St Andrews Cathedral**. Golf aficionados will want to play a round on the **Old Course**; alternatively, visit the **British Golf Museum**. Celebrate with a fancy dinner at the **Seafood Restaurant**.

ST ANDREWS ➲ BALLATER

🚗 **2½ hours** Tay Bridge to Dundee, then A90 and A928 to Glamis (p206); A94 and A93 to Braemar and Ballater. 🚌🚃 **Four to five hours** Train Leuchars to Aberdeen, then bus Aberdeen to Ballater; both services hourly.

③ Ballater (p205)

Having your own wheels is an advantage on the next two legs, allowing you to travel through the heart of the mountains; public transport means a detour via Aberdeen. Call in at **Glamis Castle**, but leave time to visit **Balmoral Castle** too before overnighting in the pretty Royal Deeside village of **Ballater**.

BALLATER ➲ INVERNESS

🚗 **Three hours** A939 and B-roads to Dufftown (p208), then A941 and A96 via Elgin to Inverness. 🚌🚃 **4½ hours** Bus Ballater to Aberdeen, then train Aberdeen to Inverness.

④ Inverness (p268)

The A939 Cockbridge to Tominoul road is one of the finest drives in Britain, leading to the **whisky distilleries** of Speyside. Take a distillery tour before continuing to Inverness for a slap-up dinner at **Contrast**.

INVERNESS ➲ DRUMNADROCHIT

🚗 **20 minutes** on the A82; one hour each way for a detour to Glen Affric (p283). 🚌 **30 minutes** Around six buses a day.

⑤ Drumnadrochit (p277)

Take a **Moray Firth Cruise** in the morning, then make the short trip to Drumnadrochit to visit the **Loch Ness Exhibition Centre** and **Urquhart Castle**, and take a cruise on the loch itself.

DRUMNADROCHIT ➲ PORTREE

🚗 **Three hours** Via A82, A887 and A87; add three or four hours for a detour to Glen Affric (p283). 🚌 **Three hours** Two direct buses a day.

⑥ Portree (p231)

Take a whole day for the scenic drive from Loch Ness to Skye, starting with a side trip to beautiful **Glen Affric**. That leaves two whole days to explore the wonders of the **Isle of Skye**.

Glamis Castle (p206)
PHOTOGRAPHER: JONATHAN SMITH

10 DAYS

Glasgow to Inverness
Island Hop to the Highlands

Leading via the scenic treasures of Loch Lomond, Mull and Glenfinnan to the Highland delights of the Cairngorms, this route combines an island adventure with a journey through Scotland's highest mountains.

North Sea

INVERNESS
6

SCOTLAND

5 AVIEMORE

FORT
WILLIAM
4

TOBERMORY 3

*ATLANTIC
OCEAN*

2

OBAN

1 GLASGOW

IRELAND

NORTHERN
IRELAND

ENGLAND

① Glasgow (p128)

Spend a day in Glasgow to visit **Kelvingrove Art Gallery and Museum** and the **Burrell Collection**.

GLASGOW ○ OBAN

🚗 **2½ hours** A82 via Loch Lomond (p150) and A85. 🚌 **Three hours** Three direct buses daily.

② Oban (p239)

The road north leads past **Loch Lomond**, and there will be time for a break at **Loch Lomond Shores** or **Luss**. Oban, the 'gateway to the isles' awaits, with a choice of several top-notch **seafood restaurants**.

OBAN ○ TOBERMORY

🚗 **Two hours** Ferry from Oban to Craignure, then A849/848; detour to Iona (p251) takes at least four hours. 🚢🚌 **Two hours** Ferry to Craignure then connecting bus; Iona can be visited on organised tour from Oban.

③ Tobermory (p247)

Be up in time for the first ferry to Mull, and head west to Fionnphort for a trip to the magical **Isle of Iona**. Plan to spend two nights in Tobermory so that you can explore the rest of Mull, including **Duart Castle** and the beach at **Calgary**.

TOBERMORY ○ FORT WILLIAM

🚗 **Three hours** Ferry to Kilchoan, then A861 and A830 via Glenfinnan (p301); detour to Ardnamurchan Point (p298) adds one hour. 🚌 Not possible by public transport.

④ Fort William (p291)

Take the ferry from Tobermory to Kilchoan, and detour west to **Ardnamurchan Point**, the most westerly point on the British mainland. From here a magnificent scenic drive leads back east via **Glenfinnan** to Fort William. While you're there, make a trip to lovely **Glen Nevis**, and set aside the following day to climb **Ben Nevis**.

FORT WILLIAM ○ AVIEMORE

🚗 **1½ hours** Via A86 and A9. 🚌 Not possible by public transport.

⑤ Aviemore (p281)

You'll be weary after your climb, so plan a midday start and allow two nights in Aviemore and the **Cairngorms National Park**. As well as **Loch Morlich** and the **Cairngorm Mountain Railway**, visit the **Highland Wildlife Park** at nearby Kincraig and the osprey reserve at **Loch Garten**.

AVIEMORE ○ INVERNESS

🚗 **40 minutes** Along the A9. 🚌 **40 minutes** Direct trains every two hours.

④ Inverness (p268)

It's only a short trip from Aviemore to Inverness, allowing time for a visit to nearby **Culloden** and/or a dolphin-spotting boat trip with **Moray Firth Cruises**.

Tobermory (p247), the Isle of Mull
PHOTOGRAPHER: MARTIN MOOS

Edinburgh to Glasgow
The Grand Highland Fling

This two-week tour takes in as many of Scotland's highlights as possible without rushing things. It's possible using public transport but that would take a bit longer – a car really is necessary to make the most of this trip.

① Edinburgh (p64)

Allow yourself two days to make the most of **Edinburgh** and **Rosslyn Chapel**.

EDINBURGH ⟶ ST ANDREWS

🚗 **1½ hours** Via Forth Road Bridge and A92. 🚆🚌 **One hour** Direct trains from Edinburgh to Leuchars every 30 minutes; free connecting bus to St Andrews.

② St Andrews (p186)

Tour **St Andrews Castle** and the ruins of **St Andrews Cathedral**, or play a round on the **Old Course**; alternatively, visit the **British Golf Museum**. Celebrate with a fancy dinner at the **Seafood Restaurant**.

ST ANDREWS ⟶ BALLATER

🚗 **2½ hours** Tay Bridge to Dundee, then A90 and A928 to Glamis (p206); A94 and A93 to Braemar and Ballater. 🚆🚌 **Four to five hours** Train Leuchars to Aberdeen, then bus Aberdeen to Ballater; both services hourly.

③ Ballater (p205)

This leg goes through the heart of the mountains. Call in at **Glamis Castle**, but be sure to also stop by **Balmoral Castle** before overnighting in the pretty village of **Ballater**.

BALLATER ⟶ INVERNESS

🚗 **Three hours** A939 and B-roads to Dufftown (p208), then A941 and A96 via Elgin to Inverness. 🚌🚆 **4½ hours** Bus Ballater to Aberdeen, then train Aberdeen to Inverness.

④ Inverness (p268)

The A939 Cockbridge to Tominoul road is one of the finest drives in Britain, leading to the **whisky distilleries** of Speyside. Take a distillery tour before continuing to Inverness for a slap-up dinner at one of its excellent **restaurants**.

INVERNESS ⟶ PORTREE

🚗 **3½ hours** Via A82, A887 and A87 via Drumnadrochit (p277). 🚌 **Four hours** Two direct buses a day.

Clocktower at Balmoral Castle (p209)
PHOTOGRAPHER: JONATHAN SMITH

FORT WILLIAM ➡ OBAN

🚗 1½ hours Via A82 and A85; add one hour for a detour to Glen Coe (p288). 🚌 1½ hours Direct buses twice a day.

⑦ Oban (p239)

Plan a day trip from Oban to **Iona** – you can take your own car on the ferry (Craignure to Fionnphort is only 35 miles, but allow 1½ hours each way) or take an organised tour.

OBAN ➡ GLASGOW

🚗 2½ hours A85 and A82 via Loch Lomond (p150). 🚌 Three hours Three direct buses daily.

⑧ Glasgow (p128)

The road south leads past **Loch Lomond**, and there will be time for a break at **Loch Lomond Shores** or **Luss**. That leaves two days to enjoy Glasgow's varied attractions.

⑤ Portree (p231)

Allow a full day for the scenic drive from Inverness to Skye, stopping at Drumnadrochit to visit the **Loch Ness Exhibition Centre**. Spend two nights in Portree, allowing time to visit **Dunvegan Castle** and the **Cuillin Hills**.

PORTREE ➡ FORT WILLIAM

🚗 Four hours Drive to Armadale, ferry to Mallaig, drive to Fort William via Glenfinnan (p301). 🚌🚶🚆 Four hours Bus to Armadale, ferry to Mallaig, train to Fort William; connections twice daily.

⑥ Fort William (p291)

Heading south from Portree, turn right past Bradford on the road to **Armadale**, where you take the ferry to **Mallaig**; the drive from here to Fort William is on the scenic **Road to the Isles**. Spend two nights in **Fort William**, allowing time to visit lovely **Glen Nevis**, and perhaps even to climb **Ben Nevis**.

Scotland Month By Month

Top Events

 Edinburgh Festival Fringe, August

 T in the Park, July

 Glasgow West End Festival, June

 Celtic Connections, January

 Braemar Gathering, September

 January

The nation shakes off its Hogmanay hangover and gets back to work, but only until Burns Night comes along. It's still cold and dark, but the skiing can be good.

Burns Night

Suppers all over the country (and the world for that matter) are held on 25 January to celebrate the birthday of national poet Robert Burns, with much eating of haggis, drinking of whisky and reciting of poetry.

Celtic Connections

Glasgow hosts the world's largest winter music festival, a celebration of Celtic music, dance and culture, with participants arriving from all over the globe. Held mid- to late January. See www.celticconnections.com.

Up-Helly-Aa

Half of Shetland dresses up with horned helmets and battleaxes in this spectacular re-enactment of a Viking fire festival, with a torchlit procession leading the burning of a full-size Viking longship. Held in Lerwick on the last Tuesday in January. See www.uphellyaa.org. (For transport info to Shetland, see p351.)

 February

The coldest month of the year is usually the best for hillwalking, ice-climbing and skiing. The days are getting longer now, and snowdrops begin to bloom.

Six Nations Rugby Tournament

Scotland, England, Wales, Ireland, France and Italy battle it out in this prestigious tourna-

(left) August Street performer at the Edinburgh Festival Fringe
PHOTOGRAPHER: JONATHAN SMITH

ment, held February to March; home games played at Murrayfield, Edinburgh. See www.rbs6nations.com.

Fort William Mountain Festival

The UK's 'Outdoor Capital' celebrates the peak of the winter season with ski and snowboard learning workshops, talks by famous climbers, kids' events and a festival of mountaineering films. See www.mountainfilmfestival.co.uk.

April

The bluebell woods on the shores of Loch Lomond bloom and ospreys arrive at their Loch Garten nest. Weather is improving, though heavy showers are still common.

Rugby Sevens

A series of weekend, seven-a-side rugby tournaments held in various towns throughout the Borders region in April and May, kicking off with Melrose in early April. Fast and furious rugby (sevens was invented here), crowded pubs and great craic. See www.melrose7s.com.

May

Wildflowers on the Hebridean machair, hawthorn hedges in bloom and cherry blossom in city parks – Scottish weather is often at its best in May.

Burns an' a' That

Ayrshire towns are the venues for performances of poetry and music, children's events, art exhibitions and more in celebrations of the Scottish bard. See www.burnsfestival.com.

Spirit of Speyside

Based in the Moray town of Dufftown, this festival of whisky, food and music involves five days of distillery tours, knocking back the 'water of life', cooking,

art and outdoor activities; held late April to early May in Moray and Speyside. See www.spiritofspeyside.com.

June

Argyllshire is ablaze with pink rhododendron blooms as the long summer evenings stretch on till 11pm. Borders towns are strung with bunting to mark gala days and Common Ridings.

Common Ridings

Following an age-old tradition that commemorates ancient conflict with England, horsemen and women ride the old boundaries of common lands, along with parades, marching bands and street parties. Held in various Border towns; Jedburgh (www.jethartcallantsfestival .com) is one of the biggest and best.

Glasgow Festivals

June is Glasgow's version of the Edinburgh festival, when the city hosts three major events – **West End Festival** (www.westendfestival.co.uk), Glasgow's biggest music and arts event; **Glasgow International Jazz Festival** (www.jazz fest.co.uk); and **Glasgow Mela** (www2 .seeglasgow.com/glasgowmela), a celebration of the city's Asian community.

July

School holidays begin, as does the busiest time of year for resort towns. High season for Shetland birdwatchers.

T in the Park

Held annually since 1994, and headlined by world-class acts such as The Who, REM, Eminem and Kasabian, this major music festival is Scotland's answer to Glastonbury; held over a mid-July weekend at Balado, by Kinross. See www .tinthepark.com.

August

Festival time in Edinburgh and the city is crammed with visitors. On the west coast, this is the peak month for sighting minke whales and basking sharks.

Edinburgh Festivals

You name it, Edinburgh has a festival event that covers it – books, art, theatre, music, comedy, dance, and the Military Tattoo (www.edintattoo.co.uk). The over-lapping International Festival and Fringe keep the city jumping from the first week in August to the first week in September. See www.edinburghfestivals.co.uk.

September

School holidays are over, midges are dying off, wild brambles are ripe for picking in the hedgerows, and the weather is often dry and mild – an excellent time of year for outdoor pursuits.

Braemar Gathering

The biggest and most famous High-land Games in the Scottish calendar, traditionally attended by members of the Royal Family. Highland dancing, caber-tossing and bagpipe-playing; held early

(below) **September** A pipe band marches through Braemar for the Highland Games **(right)**
December Christmas Ferris wheel, Edinburgh

PHOTOGRAPHER:
(BOTH PHOTOS)
JONATHAN
SMITH

September in Braemar, Royal Deeside. See www.braemargathering.org.

December

Darkness falls mid-afternoon as the shortest day approaches. The often cold and wet weather is relieved by Christmas and New Year festivities.

 Hogmanay

Christmas celebrations in Edinburgh (www.edinburghschristmas.com) culminate in a huge street party on Hogmanay (31 December). The fishing town of Stonehaven echoes an ancient, pre-Christian tradition with its procession of fireball-swinging locals who parade to the harbour and fling their blazing orbs into the sea (www.stonehavenfireballs.co.uk).

Get Inspired

Books

- **Waverley** (1814; Sir Walter Scott) Historic derring-do by the master.

- **A Scot's Quair** (1946; Lewis Grassic Gibbon) Vividly captures prewar rural life in the northeast.

- **The Prime of Miss Jean Brodie** (1962; Muriel Spark) Shrewd portrait of 1930s Edinburgh.

- **The Crow Road** (1992; Iain Banks) Warm, witty and moving family saga.

- **Exit Music** (2007; Ian Rankin) Crime novel exploring the darker side of modern Edinburgh.

Films

- **The 39 Steps** (1935; Alfred Hitchcock) Old-fashioned thriller.

- **Whisky Galore!** (1949; Alexander Mackendrick) Gentle comedy.

- **Gregory's Girl** (1981; Bill Forsyth) Teenage romance.

- **Rob Roy** (1995; Michael Caton-Jones) Historic legend.

- **Trainspotting** (1996; Danny Boyle) Gritty realism.

♫ Music

- **The Crossing** (1983) Only Big Country could make guitars sound like bagpipes.

- **This Is the Story** (1987) Debut album of folk-influenced, close-harmony pop from The Proclaimers.

- **The Cutter and the Clan** (1987) Celtic folk-rock from Gaelic-speaking Skye band Runrig.

- **Franz Ferdinand** (2004) Rousing guitar rock from Glasgow band Franz Ferdinand.

- **This Is the Life** (2007) Best-selling pop from 18-year-old Amy Macdonald.

Websites

- **VisitScotland** (www.visitscotland.com) Official Scottish Tourist Board site, online accommodation-booking service.

- **Lonely Planet** (www.lonelyplanet.com) Destination information, traveller forums, hotel bookings, guidebook shop.

- **Scotland's People** (www.scotlandspeople.gov.uk) A comprehensive online resource for exploring your Scottish ancestry.

Short on time?

This list will give you an instant insight into the country.

Read *Greenvoe* (1972), by George Mackay Brown, is a warm and poetic evocation of everyday life in an island community.

Watch *Local Hero* (1983), directed by Bill Forsyth, has it all: glorious scenery, wry wit and a streak of sentimentality.

Listen *Songs of Robert Burns* (2003) by Eddi Reader offers Burns' poetry and love songs by Scotland's finest vocalist.

Log on *Internet Guide to Scotland* (www.scotland-info.co.uk) is the best of several online tourist guides to Scotland.

Left: Steall Falls, Glen Nevis (p297);
Right: West Sands Beach, St Andrews (p188)

PHOTOGRAPHERS: (LEFT) MARTIN MOOS, (RIGHT) DGB/ALAMY

Need to Know

Currency
Pounds Sterling (£)

Language
English
Gaelic and Lallans

ATMs
Widely available, except in remote areas and islands.

Credit Cards
Widely accepted.

Visas
Generally not needed for stays under six months. Not in the Schengen Zone.

Mobile Phones
Mobile network uses GSM 900/1800. Local SIM cards can be used in European and Australian phones.

Wi-Fi
Hotspots aplenty in cities, available in most hotels and many B&Bs.

Internet Access
Internet cafes in most towns.

Driving
A good way to get around. Cars drive on the left; steering wheel is on the right.

Tipping
10–15% in restaurants (unless service charge already added); around 10% to taxi drivers in cities. Don't tip in pubs.

When to Go

Cool to mild summers, cold winters

Isle of Skye
GO May, Jun & Sep

Inverness
GO May–Sep

The Cairngorms
GO May–Sep

Fort William
GO May or Sep

Edinburgh
GO Aug

High Season
(Jul & Aug)
- Accommodations 10–20% more; pre-book for Edinburgh and popular resorts
- Warmest season, but often wet, too
- Midges worst in Highlands, islands
- Also applies to late December in Edinburgh

Shoulder
(May, Jun & Sep)
- Wildflowers bloom May to June
- Best chance of dry weather; no midges
- Daylight till 11pm in June

Low Season
(Oct–Apr)
- Many rural B&Bs and tourist attractions closed
- Snow on hills November to March at least
- December days get dark at 4pm
- Can be very cold and wet November to March

Advance Planning

- **Six months before** Book Edinburgh accommodation for August festival period; reserve a table for Witchery at the Castle restaurant.

- **Two months before** Book hotel or B&B accommodation; reserve tables in top restaurants; book car hire.

- **One month before** Book train tickets, make reservations for wildlife tours and boat trips if timing is crucial.

- **Two weeks before** Confirm opening times for visitor attractions.

Your Daily Budget

Budget <£30
- Dorm beds: £10-20
- Wild camping is free
- Cheap supermarkets for self-caterers
- Lots of free museums and galleries

Midrange £30–100
- Double room in midrange B&B: £50-90
- B&Bs often better value than midrange hotels
- Bar lunch: £10; midrange restaurant dinner: £25
- Car hire: £30 a day
- Petrol costs: around 12p per mile

Top End >£100
- Double room in top-end hotel: £120-250
- Dinner at top-end restaurant: £40-60
- Flights to islands: £60-120 each

What to Bring

- **Travel insurance documents** Just in case.
- **Insect repellent** In summer – be prepared for those pesky midges.
- **Waterproof jacket** Any time of year – Scottish weather can go through four seasons in one day.
- **Hiking boots** You will want to wander off the highway and onto the soggy Scottish hillsides.
- **Binoculars** You'll wish you had them when you spot that otter/golden eagle/red deer/minke whale.
- **Small day-pack** To carry waterproofs, binoculars, insect repellent etc.

Exchange Rates

Australia	A$1	£0.63
Canada	C$1	£0.65
Euro zone	€1	£0.83
Japan	¥100	£0.77
New Zealand	NZ$1	£0.49
USA	US$1	£0.64

For current exchange rates see www.xe.com.

Arriving in Scotland

o Edinburgh Airport

Buses To Edinburgh city centre every 10 to 15 minutes from 4.30am to midnight.

Night buses Every 30 minutes from 12.30am to 4am.

Taxis £15-20; about 20 minutes to the city centre.

o Glasgow Airport

Buses To Glasgow city centre every 10 to 15 minutes from 6am to 11pm.

Night buses Hourly 11pm to 4am, half-hourly 4am to 6pm.

Taxis £20-25; about 30 minutes to city centre.

Getting Around

- **Air** Can cut travel time significantly between Glasgow or Edinburgh and Inverness or the farther-flung islands (except Skye – nearest airport is Inverness).
- **Bus** Scottish Citylink coaches run frequent services between all the main tourist centres.
- **Train** Fast and comfortable for intercity travel, and scenic rail journeys to Oban, Mallaig and Kyle of Lochalsh.
- **Car** Having your own wheels is tops for speed and flexibility.

Accommodation

- **Youth Hostels** The budget traveller's choice; good network in all the right places.
- **B&Bs and Guesthouses** Usually the best value for money, friendly, well equipped and great breakfasts.
- **Hotels** Some great places in the cities, often average in the countryside; old Highland hotels are often full of character.

Be Forewarned

- **School holidays** Roads, accommodation, tourist attractions are all busier during Easter, summer and Christmas vacations.
- **Traffic congestion** Can be a serious problem in and around the larger cities at rush hour.
- **Midges** Tiny biting flies can make life misery in summer if you aren't prepared.

Edinburgh

Edinburgh is a city that just begs to be explored. From the vaults and wynds that riddle the Old Town to the Georgian elegance of the New Town, it's filled with quirky, come-hither nooks that tempt you to walk just a little bit further. And every corner turned reveals sudden views and unexpected vistas – green, sunlit hills; a glimpse of rust-red crags; a blue flash of distant sea.

But there's more to Edinburgh than sightseeing – there are top shops, world-class restaurants and a bacchanalia of bars to enjoy. This is a city of pub crawls and impromptu music sessions; mad-for-it clubbing and all-night parties; overindulgence, late nights and wandering home through cobbled streets at dawn.

All these superlatives come together in August at festival time, when it seems as if half the world descends on Edinburgh for one enormous party. If you can possibly manage it, join them.

Edinburgh Castle and Old Town (p64) from Arthur's Seat **51**

THE PEOPLE'S STORY

The People's Story museum (p75), Royal Mile, Edinburgh

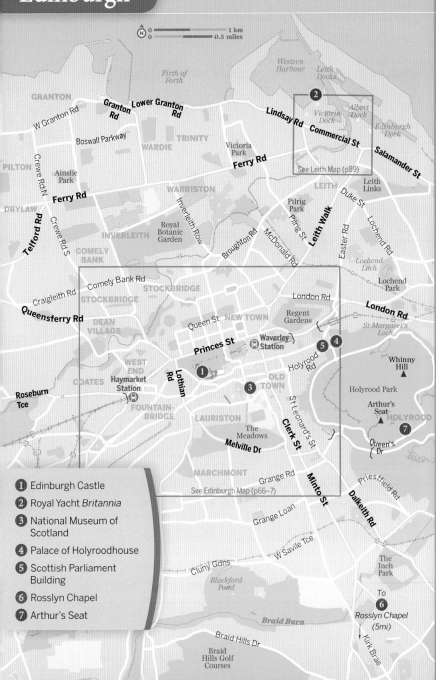

Edinburgh

0 — 1 km
0 — 0.5 miles

GRANTON
W Granton Rd
Granton Rd
Lower Granton Rd
Boswall Parkway
WARDIE
TRINITY
Firth of Forth
Western Harbour
Leith Docks
Albert Dock
Edinburgh Dock
Lindsay Rd
Commercial St
Salamander St

PILTON
Crewe Rd N
Ainslie Park
Ferry Rd
DRYLAW
Crewe Rd S
Telford Rd
WARRISTON
Inverleith Row
Victoria Park
Ferry Rd
LEITH
Leith Links
Duke St
Lochend Rd
 See Leith Map (p89)

INVERLEITH
Royal Botanic Garden
COMELY BANK
Pilrig Park
Pilrig St
Leith Walk
Easter Rd
Lochend Loch
Lochend Park

Craigleith Rd
Comely Bank Rd
STOCKBRIDGE
STOCKBRIDGE
Broughton Rd
McDonald Rd
London Rd

Queensferry Rd
DEAN VILLAGE
Queen St
NEW TOWN
Regent Gardens
London Rd
St Margaret's Loch

WEST END
COATES
Haymarket Station
Lothian Rd
Princes St
Waverley Station
Holyrood Rd
OLD TOWN
Whinny Hill
Holyrood Park
Arthur's Seat
HOLYROOD

Roseburn Tce
FOUNTAIN-BRIDGE
LAURISTON
The Meadows
Melville Dr
St Leonard's St
Clerk St
Queen's Dr

MARCHMONT
Grange Rd
Minto St
Dalkeith Rd
Priestfield Rd

See Edinburgh Map (p66–7)
Grange Loan
W Savile Tce
The Inch Park

Cluny Gdns
Blackford Pond
To
Rosslyn Chapel (5mi)
Kirk Brae

Braid Burn
Braid Hills Dr
Braid Hills Golf Courses

1 Edinburgh Castle
2 Royal Yacht *Britannia*
3 National Museum of Scotland
4 Palace of Holyroodhouse
5 Scottish Parliament Building
6 Rosslyn Chapel
7 Arthur's Seat

Edinburgh's Highlights

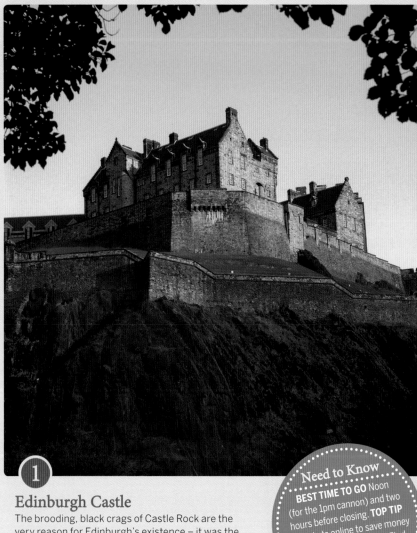

1 Edinburgh Castle

The brooding, black crags of Castle Rock are the very reason for Edinburgh's existence – it was the most easily defended hilltop on the invasion route from England. Crowning the crag with a profusion of battlements, Edinburgh Castle is now Scotland's most popular pay-to-enter tourist attraction.

Need to Know
BEST TIME TO GO Noon (for the 1pm cannon) and two hours before closing. TOP TIP Buy tickets online to save money and time. SECRET SPOT Find the cemetery for officers' dogs! For more, see p65.

Edinburgh Castle Don't Miss List

PETER YEOMAN, HISTORIC SCOTLAND'S
HEAD OF CULTURAL RESOURCES

1 HONOURS OF SCOTLAND

The Crown and Sceptre of Scotland and the Sword of State are glittering symbols of our nationhood. They were first used at the coronation of Mary, Queen of Scots in 1543 when she was only nine months old – Cardinal Beaton had to hold the crown to her tiny brow! The centuries-old regalia are displayed in the Royal Palace alongside the Stone of Destiny.

2 ST MARGARET'S CHAPEL

The oldest building in the castle is a wee gem, possibly part of a tower-keep built in the early 12th century to commemorate Scotland's royal saint, who died in the castle in 1093. The chapel's interior (pictured bottom left) is delightfully decorated with fine Romanesque architecture; if you get a peaceful moment you can really connect with the medieval kings who carried out their private devotions here.

3 MONS MEG

Step outside the chapel to be confronted by the great bombard Mons Meg (pictured top left), gifted to James II in 1457. This is a great vantage point for the One O' Clock Gun, fired daily (except Sunday) – causing many visitors to jump out of their skins! The views across the Georgian New Town to the Forth Estuary from here are truly magnificent.

4 DAVID'S TOWER

Deep beneath the Half Moon Battery lies David's Tower, built as a fancy residence for David II in 1371. Badly damaged in the siege of 1573, the tower became hidden in the foundations for the new battery, and was only rediscovered in 1912. The Honours of Scotland spent much of WWII here, hidden down a medieval loo!

5 CASTLE VAULTS

In 1720, 21 pirates captured in Argyll were thrown into the castle dungeons. They had all sailed with one of the most infamous pirate-captains of the Caribbean, 'Black Bart' Roberts. The following decades saw a busy time for this state prison, which was stuffed full of prisoners from the wars with America and France. The reconstructed cells allow you to experience something of the squalor!

55

Royal Yacht *Britannia*

The *Britannia* served as the royal family's floating home during their foreign travels until it was decommissioned in 1997. Now permanently moored at Ocean Terminal in Leith, the ship offers an intriguing insight into the queen's private tastes.

Need to Know

ROYAL EDINBURGH TICKET Admits to *Britannia*, Edinburgh Castle and Holyroodhouse, plus bus tours. **LOCATION** 25-minute bus ride from city centre. **LUNCH SPOT** Fishers Bistro (p100). **For more, see p90.**

Royal Yacht *Britannia*'s Don't Miss List

FIONA MAXWELL, BLUE BADGE TOUR GUIDE

1 ROYAL APARTMENTS

Don't expect a sumptuous royal residence – it's more like a comfortable country house, with simple furnishings and old-fashioned charm. Even the Queen's and duke's private apartments are not at all elaborate, with basic, 3ft-wide single beds! The only double bed is in the honeymoon suite, where Bill and Hillary Clinton slept during a state visit.

2 STATE ROOMS

The State Rooms are slightly grander, but still understated. The **Drawing Room** has chintz chair covers and a grand piano (firmly bolted to the floor); Noël Coward once tickled its keys while entertaining the royal family. The **Dining Room** is adorned with treasures gifted to the Queen during her travels. Check out the place settings: it took over three hours to lay the table for a state banquet – the space between each piece of cutlery was meticulously measured with a ruler!

3 CREW QUARTERS

You'll get a shock when you see the cramped conditions below deck where the non-commissioned sailors, and even some of the officers, slept in narrow bunk beds three tiers high. There was no space for peace or privacy; the only officer who had ensuite facilities was the admiral.

4 THE WOMBAT

There are some lovely traditions on the vessel, including that of the Wombat, still on view in the anteroom of the Wardroom – the officers would give the poor stuffed animal many a hammering during after-dinner batting games – and the coins placed beneath the foot of each of the three masts, in payment to the angels for guiding the vessel safely at sea.

5 ROYAL DECK TEAROOM

During your visit you can enjoy delicious home baking and tea served in bone china in the Royal Deck Tearoom, a recent innovation, while looking down on Prince Phillip's famous yacht *Bloodhound*, now lying alongside *Britannia*. On a clear day you have wonderful views across the Firth of Forth towards the hills of Fife.

57

National Museum of Scotland

The National Museum of Scotland (p83) charts the history of the country from geological beginnings to the present day. Highlights include the Monymusk Reliquary, a tiny silver casket dating from 750 (said to have been carried into battle with Robert the Bruce at Bannockburn in 1314), and the Lewis Chessmen, a set of charming 12th-century chess pieces made from walrus ivory.

Palace of Holyroodhouse

Mary, Queen of Scots spent six eventful years (1561–67) living at Holyroodhouse (p78), a 16th-century tower house that was extended to create a 17th-century royal palace, now Queen Elizabeth II's official residence in Scotland. Besides offering the chance to visit Mary's private bedchamber, the palace brims with fascinating antiques and artworks, and afterwards you'll have the opportunity to wander round Holyrood Park or climb Arthur's Seat.

KARL BLACKWELL

Scottish Parliament Building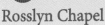

Edinburgh's most spectacular and controversial building, officially opened in 2004, houses Scotland's devolved parliament (p77). The strange forms of the unusual exterior are all symbolic in some way, from the oddly shaped windows on the west wall to the ground plan of the whole complex, which represents a 'flower of democracy rooted in Scottish soil' (best seen looking down from Salisbury Crags).

WILL SALTER

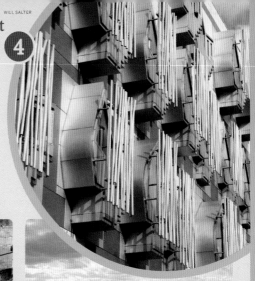

BRITAIN ON VIEW/PHOTOLIBRARY

Rosslyn Chapel

The success of Dan Brown's novel *The Da Vinci Code* and the subsequent Hollywood movie has seen a flood of visitors descend on Scotland's most beautiful and enigmatic church (p93). This 15th-century chapel, wreathed in ornate and mysterious stone carvings, has been the subject of Knights Templar and Holy Grail conspiracy theories for decades, and provides the setting for *The Da Vinci Code*'s dénouement.

Arthur's Seat

Hiking to the summit of this long-dormant volcano (p77) is an Edinburgh rite of passage, and you haven't really seen the city till you've done it. You'll be rewarded with a fantastic view that stretches from the Firth of Forth to the Pentland Hills, and the rocky summit makes a great spot for a picnic on one of those elusive sunny Scottish days.

Edinburgh's Best…

Wining & Dining

○ **Tower** (p97) Steaks and seafood in chic setting with castle view

○ **Outsider** (p97) Great bistro food in perennially popular Old Town location

○ **Ondine** (p97) Elegant modern dining room specialising in superb seafood

○ **Oloroso** (p99) Trendy rooftop restaurant with food to match the spectacular cityscape

○ **Martin Wishart** (p101) Scottish produce meets French cuisine in Michelin-starred magnificence

Viewpoints

○ **Edinburgh Castle** (p65) Grand views from the Esplanade and Mills Mount Battery

○ **Camera Obscura** (p69) Outlook Tower offers classic photo op for shot along Royal Mile rooftops

○ **Scott Monument** (p81) Lofty perch provides stunning view across gardens to Old Town skyline

○ **Nelson Monument** (p85) Picture-postcard scenes of Princes St, parliament building and Salisbury Crags

○ **Arthur's Seat** (p77) All-around city panorama from Firth of Forth to Pentland Hills

Spooky Spots

○ **Real Mary King's Close** (p73) Remarkable 17th-century street preserved beneath 18th-century building

○ **Greyfriars Kirkyard** (p77) Edinburgh's spookiest graveyard, best visited on night-time ghost tour

○ **South Bridge Vaults** (p85) Haunted stone cellars beneath Old Town streets

○ **Surgeons' Hall Museums** (p79) Grisly Burke and Hare exhibit includes pocketbook covered in human skin

Need to Know

Historic Sites

⚬ Palace of Holyroodhouse (p78) Mary, Queen of Scots' bedchamber, where her secretary (and lover?) was murdered

⚬ Edinburgh Castle (p65) Home to Scotland's crown jewels and the Stone of Destiny

⚬ Greyfriars Kirk (p77) Where the National Covenant was signed

⚬ Grassmarket (p79) Former place of execution

⚬ Heart of Midlothian (p73) Marks the spot of the Old Tolbooth jail, made famous in Walter Scott's novel

ADVANCE PLANNING

⚬ Six months before Book accommodation if you plan to visit during festival time (August) or Hogmanay (New Year); book tickets for the Military Tattoo

⚬ One month before Book accommodation for any other time of year; reserve a table at the Tower or Oloroso restaurants

⚬ Two weeks before Reserve a table at any other fine-dining restaurant

⚬ One week before Book a tour of the Real Mary King's Close (p73)

RESOURCES

⚬ Edinburgh & Lothians Tourist Board (www.edinburgh.org) Official tourism site, with listings of accommodation, sights, activities and events

⚬ Edinburgh Museums & Galleries (www.edinburghmuseums.org.uk) Information on city-owned museums and art galleries

⚬ Edinburgh Festivals (www.edinburghfestivals.co.uk) Full details on all of the city's official festivals

⚬ Edinburgh Bus Tours (www.edinburghtour.com) Offers a range of tours around the city; **Royal Edinburgh Ticket** (adult/child £40/20) gives two days' unlimited travel on sightseeing buses and admission to Edinburgh Castle, Palace of Holyroodhouse and Royal Yacht *Britannia*.

GETTING AROUND

⚬ From the Airport Airlink bus runs every 10 minutes during day, at least hourly through night; 30 minutes to city centre

⚬ Bus Good city bus network; real-time bus tracking info available as free iPhone app (EdinBus)

⚬ Car Parking in city centre is difficult; best to use public transport

⚬ On Foot Old Town is compact and easily explored on foot; however, be aware of steep hills and flights of steps

⚬ Train Frequent trains to Glasgow (every 15 minutes) and London (every 30 minutes)

Left: Nelson Monument, Calton Hill; **Above:** Holyrood Abbey, Palace of Holyroodhouse

Edinburgh Walking Tour

Much of what makes Edinburgh's Old Town so fascinating is its maze of narrow alleys. This walk explores a few of the many interesting nooks and crannies around the upper part of the Royal Mile.

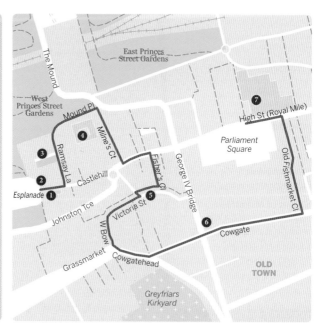

WALK FACTS
- **Start** Castle Esplanade
- **Finish** High St, Royal Mile
- **Distance** 0.75 miles
- **Duration** One to two hours

❶ Cannonball House

Begin at the Castle Esplanade and walk downhill towards the Royal Mile. The 17th-century house on the right, above the steps of North Castle Wynd, is known as **Cannonball House** because of the iron ball lodged in the wall (look between, and slightly below, the two largest windows). It was not fired in anger, but instead marks the gravitation height to which water would flow naturally from the city's first piped water supply.

❷ Witches Well

The rectangular building across the street was originally the reservoir that held the Old Town's water supply. On its west wall is the **Witches Well**, where a modern bronze fountain commemorates around 4000 people (mostly women) who were burned or strangled in Edinburgh on suspicion of witchcraft between 1479 and 1722.

❸ Ramsay Garden

Go past the reservoir and turn left down Ramsay Lane, and take a look at **Ramsay Garden**, one of the most desirable addresses in Edinburgh, where late-19th-century apartments were built around the nucleus of the octagonal Ramsay Lodge, once home to poet Allan Ramsay.

❹ New College

The cobbled street continues around to the right below student residences, to the twin towers of the **New College** – home to the University of Edinburgh's Faculty of Divinity. Nip into the courtyard to see the **statue of John Knox**.

⑤ Victoria Terrace

Turn right and climb up the stairs into Milne's Ct, a student residence. Exit onto Lawnmarket, cross the street (bearing left) and then turn right down Fisher's Close, which leads onto the delightful **Victoria Terrace**, poised above the cobbled curve of Victoria St. Wander right, enjoying the view, then descend the stairs at the foot of Upper Bow and continue downhill to the Grassmarket.

⑥ George IV Bridge

Turn left along the gloomy defile of the Cowgate. The first bridge you pass under is **George IV Bridge** (built 1829–34). Although you can see only one arch here, there are nine in total – one more is visible a block south at Merchant St, but the rest are hidden beneath and between the surrounding buildings, as are the haunted **vaults of South Bridge**, further west along Cowgate.

⑦ Real Mary King's Close

Beyond the bridge take the first left turn and climb up Old Fishmarket Close to emerge once more into the Royal Mile. Across the street to the left is the **Real Mary King's Close**, a guided tour of which offers a fascinating look into 16th- and 17th-century Edinburgh life.

Edinburgh in...

TWO DAYS

Start by visiting **Edinburgh Castle,** then follow our walking tour of the Old Town. After lunch, continue down the Royal Mile to the **Scottish parliament building** and the **Palace of Holyroodhouse**. You can work up an appetite by climbing **Arthur's Seat**, then satisfy your hunger with dinner at the **Tower restaurant** while you watch the sun set behind the castle. On day two spend the morning visiting **Real Mary King's Close** or the **Royal Museum of Scotland**, then catch the bus to **Leith** for a visit to the **Royal Yacht Britannia**. In the evening have dinner at one of Leith's many excellent restaurants, or scare yourself silly on a guided ghost tour.

FOUR DAYS

Two more days will give you time for a morning stroll around the **Royal Botanic Garden**, followed by a trip to the enigmatic and beautiful **Rosslyn Chapel**. Dinner at the **Cafe Royal Oyster Bar** could be had before or after your sunset walk to the summit of **Calton Hill**. On day four head out of town for a day trip to **Abbotsford**.

Victoria Terrace
PHOTOGRAPHER: JONATHAN SMITH

Discover Edinburgh

 Sights

Edinburgh's main attractions are concentrated in the city centre – on and around the Old Town's Royal Mile between the castle and Holyrood, and in New Town. A major exception is the Royal Yacht *Britannia,* which is in the redeveloped docklands district of Leith, 2 miles northeast of the centre.

If you tire of sightseeing, good areas for aimless wandering include the posh suburbs of Stockbridge and Morningside, the pretty riverside village of Cramond, and the winding footpaths of Calton Hill and Arthur's Seat.

Old Town

Edinburgh's Old Town stretches along a ridge to the east of the castle, and tumbles down Victoria St to the broad expanse of the Grassmarket. It's a jagged and jumbled maze of masonry riddled with closes (alleys) and wynds (narrow lanes), stairs and vaults, and cleft along its spine by the cobbled ravine of the Royal Mile.

Until the founding of New Town in the 18th century, old Edinburgh was an overcrowded and insanitary hive of humanity squeezed between the boggy ground of the Nor' Loch (North Loch, now drained and occupied by Princes Street Gardens) to the north and the city walls to the south and east. The only way for the town to expand was upwards, and the five- and six-storey tenements that were raised along the Royal Mile in the 16th and 17th centuries were the skyscrapers of their day, remarked upon with wonder by visiting writers such as Daniel Defoe. All classes

Victoria Street, Old Town
PHOTOGRAPHER: JONATHAN SMITH

of society, from beggars to magistrates, lived cheek by jowl in these urban ants' nests, the wealthy occupying the middle floors – high enough to be above the noise and stink of the streets, but not so high that climbing the stairs would be too tiring – while the poor squeezed into attics, basements, cellars and vaults amid the rats, rubbish and raw sewage.

The renovated Old Town tenements still support a thriving city-centre community, and today the street level is crammed with cafes, restaurants, bars, backpacker hostels and tacky souvenir shops. Few visitors wander beyond the main drag of the Royal Mile, but it's worth taking time to explore the countless closes that lead off the street into quiet courtyards, often with unexpected views of city, sea and hills.

THE ROYAL MILE

This mile-long street earned its regal nickname in the 16th century when it was used by the king to travel between the castle and the Palace of Holyroodhouse. There are five sections – the Castle Esplanade, Castlehill, Lawnmarket, High St and Canongate – whose names reflect their historical origins.

EDINBURGH CASTLE   Castle
(Map p72; www.edinburghcastle.gov.uk; Castlehill; adult/child incl audio guide £14/7.50; ⊙9.30am-6pm Apr-Sep, 9.30am-5pm Oct-Mar, last admission 45min before closing, closed 25 & 26 Dec)
The brooding, black crags of Castle Rock rising above the western end of Princes St are the very reason for Edinburgh's existence. This rocky hill was the most easily defended hilltop on the invasion route between England and central Scotland, a route followed by countless armies from the Roman legions of the 1st and 2nd centuries AD to the Jacobite troops of Bonnie Prince Charlie in 1745.

Edinburgh Castle has played a pivotal role in Scottish history, both as a royal residence – King Malcolm Canmore (r 1058–93) and Queen Margaret first made their home here in the 11th century – and as a military stronghold. The castle last saw military action in 1745; from then until the 1920s it served as the British army's main base in Scotland. Today it is one of Scotland's most atmospheric, most popular – and most expensive – tourist attractions.

The **Entrance Gateway**, flanked by statues of Robert the Bruce and William Wallace, opens to a cobbled lane that leads up beneath the 16th-century **Portcullis Gate** to the cannon ranged along the Argyle and Mills Mount Batteries. The battlements here have great views over New Town to the Firth of Forth.

At the far end of Mills Mount Battery is the famous **One O'Clock Gun**, where crowds gather to watch a gleaming WWII 25-pounder fire an ear-splitting time signal at exactly 1pm (every day except Sunday, Christmas Day and Good Friday).

South of Mills Mount, the road curls up leftwards through **Foog's Gate** to the highest part of Castle Rock, crowned by the tiny, Romanesque **St Margaret's Chapel**, the oldest surviving building in Edinburgh. It was probably built by David I or Alexander I in memory of their mother, Queen Margaret, sometime around 1130 (she was canonised in 1250). Beside the chapel stands **Mons Meg**, a giant 15th-century siege gun built at Mons (in what is now Belgium) in 1449.

The main group of buildings on the summit of Castle Rock are ranged around Crown Sq, dominated by the shrine of the **Scottish National War Memorial**. Opposite is the **Great Hall**, built for James IV (r 1488–1513) as a ceremonial hall and used as a meeting place for the Scottish parliament until 1639. Its most remarkable feature is the original, 16th-century hammer-beam roof.

The **Castle Vaults** beneath the Great Hall (entered from Crown Sq via the Prisons of War exhibit) were used variously as storerooms, bakeries and a prison. The vaults have been renovated to resemble 18th- and early-19th-century prisons, where graffiti carved by French and American prisoners can be seen on the ancient wooden doors.

Edinburgh

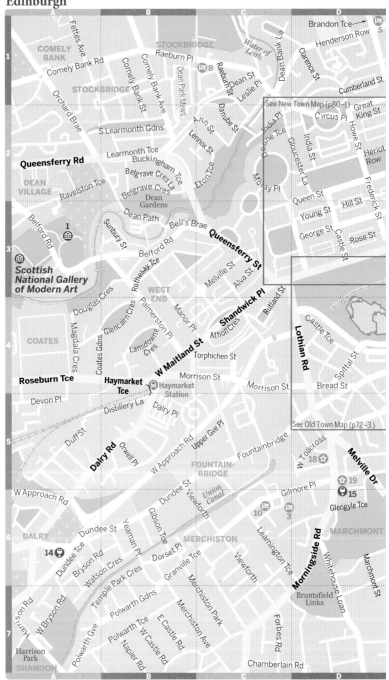

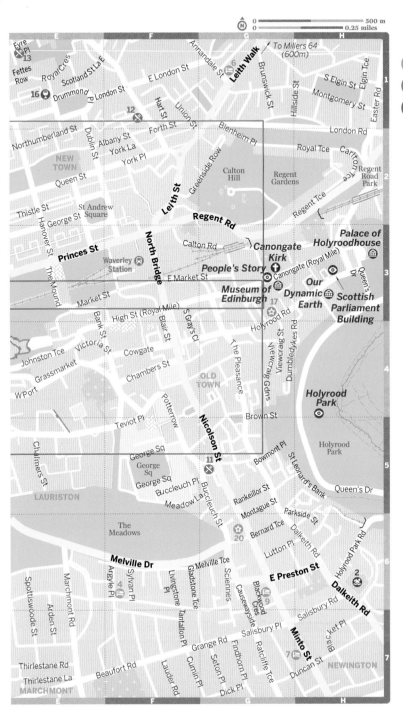

Edinburgh

On the eastern side of the square is the **Royal Palace**, built during the 15th and 16th centuries, where a series of historical tableaux leads to the highlight of the castle – a strongroom housing the **Honours of Scotland** (the Scottish crown jewels), the oldest surviving crown jewels in Europe. Locked away in a chest following the Act of Union in 1707, the crown (made in 1540 from the gold of Robert the Bruce's 14th-century coronet), sword and sceptre lay forgotten until they were unearthed at the instigation of the novelist Sir Walter Scott in 1818. Also on display here is the **Stone of Destiny** (see the boxed text, p77).

Among the neighbouring **Royal Apartments** is the bedchamber where Mary, Queen of Scots gave birth to her son James VI, who was to unite the crowns of Scotland and England in 1603.

NATIONAL WAR MUSEUM OF SCOTLAND
(Map p72; www.nms.ac.uk; admission incl in Edinburgh Castle ticket; ⊙9.45am-5.45pm Apr-Oct, 9.45am-4.45pm Nov-Mar) At the western end of the castle, to the left of the castle restaurant, a road leads down to the National War Museum of Scotland, which brings Scotland's military history vividly to life. The exhibits have been personalised by telling the stories of the original owners of the objects on display, making it easier to empathise with the experiences of war than any dry display of dusty weaponry ever could.

HIGHLAND TOLBOOTH KIRK　Church
(Map p72; Castlehill; admission free; ⊙9.30am-7pm) Edinburgh's tallest spire (71.7m) is at the foot of Castlehill and is a prominent feature of the Old Town's skyline. The interior has been refurbished and it now houses the **Hub** (www.thehub-edinburgh .com), the ticket office and information centre for the Edinburgh Festival. There's also a good cafe here.

SCOTCH WHISKY EXPERIENCE
　　　　　Whisky Exhibition
(Map p72; www.scotchwhiskyexperience.co.uk; 354 Castlehill; adult/child incl tour & tasting £11.50/5.95; ⊙10am-6.30pm Jun-Aug, 10am-6pm Sep-May; 📞) A short distance downhill from the Castle Esplanade, a former school houses this multimedia centre explaining the making of whisky from barley to bottle in a series of exhibits, demonstrations and tours that combine sight, sound and smell, including the world's largest collection of malt whis-

kies; look out for Peat the distillery cat! There's also a restaurant that serves traditional Scottish dishes with, where possible, a dash of whisky thrown in.

CAMERA OBSCURA   Camera Obscura
(Map p72; www.camera-obscura.co.uk; Castlehill; adult/child £9.25/6.25; ◷9.30am-7.30pm Jul & Aug, 9.30am-6pm Apr-Jun, Sep & Oct, 10am-5pm Nov-Mar) Edinburgh's 'camera obscura' is a curious 19th-century device – in constant use since 1853 – that uses lenses and mirrors to throw a live image of the city onto a large horizontal screen. The accompanying commentary is entertaining and the whole experience has a quirky charm, complemented by an intriguing exhibition dedicated to illusions of all kinds. Stairs lead up through various displays to the **Outlook Tower**, which offers great views over the city.

LAWNMARKET   Historic Street
Lawnmarket (a corruption of 'Landmarket', a market selling goods from the land outside the city) takes its name from the large cloth market that flourished here until the 18th century. This was the poshest part of the Old Town,

where many of its most distinguished citizens made their homes.

GLADSTONE'S LAND   Historic House
(Map p72; NTS; www.nts.org.uk; 477 Lawnmarket; adult/child £5.50/4.50; ◷10am-6.30pm Jul & Aug, 10am-5pm Apr-Jun, Sep & Oct) One of Edinburgh's most prominent 17th-century merchants was Thomas Gledstanes, who in 1617 purchased the tenement later known as Gladstone's Land. It contains fine painted ceilings, walls and beams, and some splendid furniture from the 17th and 18th centuries. The volunteer guides provide a wealth of anecdotes and a detailed history.

FREE **WRITERS' MUSEUM**
    Literature Museum
(Map p72; Lady Stair's Close, Lawnmarket; ◷10am-5pm Mon-Sat year-round, 2-5pm Sun Aug) Tucked down a close just east of Gladstone's Land you'll find Lady Stair's House (1622), home to this museum which contains manuscripts and memorabilia belonging to three of Scotland's most famous writers: Robert Burns, Sir Walter Scott and Robert Louis Stevenson.

The Royal Bank of Scotland, Highland Tolbooth Kirk and Camera Obscura

JONATHAN SMITH

Royal Mile

A Grand Day Out

Planning your own procession along the Royal Mile involves some tough decisions – it would be impossible to see everything in a single day, so it's wise to decide in advance what you don't want to miss and shape your visit around that. Remember to leave time for lunch, for exploring some of the Mile's countless side alleys and, during festival time, for enjoying the street theatre that is bound to be happening in High St.

The most pleasant way to reach the Castle Esplanade at the start of the Royal Mile is to hike up the zigzag path from the footbridge behind the Ross Bandstand in Princes Street Gardens (in springtime you'll be knee-deep in daffodils). Starting at Edinburgh Castle ❶ means that the rest of your walk is downhill. For a superb view up and down the length of the Mile, climb the Camera Obscura's Outlook Tower ❷ before visiting Gladstone's Land ❸ and St Giles Cathedral ❹ . If history's your thing, you'll want to add Real Mary King's

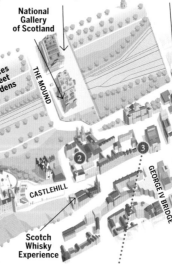

Royal Visits to the Royal Mile

1561: Mary, Queen of Scots arrives from France and holds an audience with John Knox.

1745: Bonnie Prince Charlie fails to capture Edinburgh Castle, and instead sets up court in Holyroodhouse.

2004: Queen Elizabeth II officially opens the Scottish Parliament building.

Royal Scottish Academy

Scott Monument

Heart of Midlothian

City Chambers

NORTH BRIDGE

National Gallery of Scotland

Edinburgh Castle
If you're pushed for time, visit the Great Hall, the Honours of Scotland and the Prisons of War exhibit. Head for the Half Moon Battery for a photo looking down the length of the Royal Mile.

Princes Street Gardens

THE MOUND

❶

❷ ❸ ❹ ❺

HIGH ST

CASTLEHILL

GEORGE IV BRIDGE

Scotch Whisky Experience

Lunch Break

Pie and a pint at **Royal Mile Tavern**; soup and a sandwich at **Always Sunday**; bistro nosh at **Café Marlayne**.

Gladstone's Land
The 1st floor houses a faithful recreation of how a wealthy Edinburgh merchant lived in the 17th century. Check out the beautiful Painted Bedchamber, with its ornately decorated walls and wooden ceilings.

Close **⑤**, John Knox House **⑥** and the Museum of Edinburgh **⑦** to your must-see list.

At the foot of the mile, choose between modern and ancient seats of power – the Scottish Parliament **⑧** or the Palace of Holyroodhouse **⑨**. Round off the day with an evening ascent of Arthur's Seat or, slightly less strenuously, Calton Hill. Both make great sunset viewpoints.

TAKING YOUR TIME

Minimum time needed for each attraction:

Edinburgh Castle: two hours

Gladstone's Land: 45 minutes

St Giles Cathedral: 30 minutes

Real Mary King's Close: one hour (tour)

Scottish Parliament: one hour (tour)

Palace of Holyroodhouse: one hour

Real Mary King's Close
The guided tour is heavy on ghost stories, but a highlight is standing in an original 17th-century room with tufts of horsehair poking from the crumbling plaster, and breathing in the ancient scent of stone, dust and history.

Canongate Kirk

CANONGATE

⑦

⑥

ST MARY'S ST

SOUTH BRIDGE

Tron Kirk

⑧

Our Dynamic Earth

⑨

Scottish Parliament
Don't have time for the guided tour? Pick up a *Discover the Scottish Parliament Building* leaflet from reception and take a self-guided tour of the exterior, then hike up to Salisbury Crags for a great view of the complex.

Palace of Holyroodhouse
Find the secret staircase joining Mary, Queen of Scots' bedchamber with that of her husband, Lord Darnley, who restrained the queen while his henchmen stabbed to death her secretary (and possible lover), David Rizzio.

St Giles Cathedral
Look out for the Burne-Jones stained-glass window (1873) at the west end, showing the crossing of the River Jordan, and the bronze memorial to Robert Louis Stevenson in the Moray Aisle.

Old Town

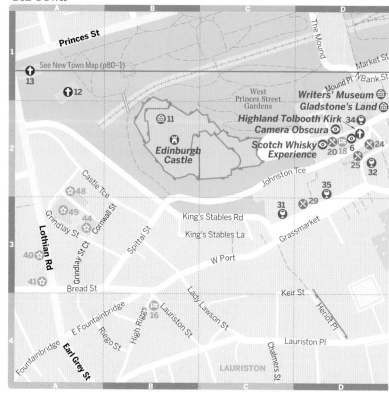

HIGH ST
Historic Street

High St, which stretches from George IV Bridge down to the Netherbow at St Mary's St, is the heart and soul of the Old Town, home to the city's main church, the Law Courts, the city council and – until 1707 – the Scottish parliament.

ST GILES CATHEDRAL
Church

(Map p72; www.stgilescathedral.org.uk; High St; £3 donation suggested; ⏰9am-7pm Mon-Fri, 9am-5pm Sat, 1-5pm Sun May-Sep, 9am-5pm Mon-Sat, 1-5pm Sun Oct-Apr) Dominating High St is the great grey bulk of St Giles Cathedral. Properly called the High Kirk of Edinburgh (it was only a true cathedral – the seat of a bishop – from 1633 to 1638 and from 1661 to 1689), St Giles Cathedral was named after the patron saint of cripples and beggars. A Norman-style church was built here in 1126 but was destroyed by English invaders in 1385; the only substantial remains are the central piers that support the tower.

The present church dates largely from the 15th century – the beautiful **crown spire** was completed in 1495 – but much of it was restored in the 19th century. The interior lacks grandeur but is rich in history: St Giles was at the heart of the Scottish Reformation, and John Knox served as minister here from 1559 to 1572. One of the most interesting corners of the kirk is the **Thistle Chapel**, built in 1911 for the Knights of the Most Ancient & Most Noble Order of the Thistle. The elaborately carved Gothic-style stalls have canopies topped with the helms and arms of the 16 knights – look out for the bagpipe-playing angel amid the vaulting.

72

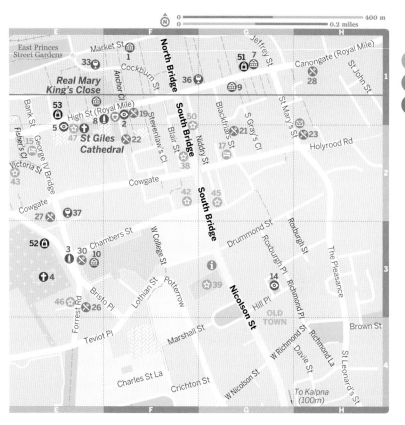

By the side of the street, outside the western door of St Giles, is a cobblestone **Heart of Midlothian** set into the paving. This marks the site of the Tolbooth. Built in the 15th century and demolished in the early 19th century, the Tolbooth served variously as a meeting place for parliament, the town council and the General Assembly of the Reformed Kirk, before becoming law courts and, finally, a notorious prison and place of execution. Passers-by traditionally spit on the heart for luck (don't stand downwind!).

At the other end of St Giles is the **Mercat Cross**, a 19th-century copy of the 1365 original, where merchants and traders met to transact business and royal proclamations were read.

REAL MARY KING'S CLOSE

Historic Building

(Map p72; 📞 0845 070 6255; www.realmarykings close.com; 2 Warriston's Close, Writers Ct, High St; adult/child £11/6; ⏰10am-9pm Apr-Jul, Sep & Oct, to 11pm Aug, 10am-5pm Sun-Thu & 10am-9pm Fri & Sat Nov-Mar) Across from St Giles is the **City Chambers**, originally built by John Adam (brother of Robert) between 1753 and 1761 to serve as the Royal Exchange – a covered meeting place for city merchants. However, the merchants preferred their old stamping ground in the street and the building became the city council offices in 1811.

Part of the Royal Exchange was built over the sealed-off remains of Mary King's Close, and the lower levels of this medieval Old Town alley have survived almost unchanged in the foundations of the City Chambers for 250 years.

73

Old Town

◉ Top Sights

◎ Sights

⊜ Sleeping

⊗ Eating

⊙ Drinking

⊗ Entertainment

⊜ Shopping

Now open to the public as the Real Mary King's Close, this spooky, subterranean labyrinth gives a fascinating insight into the daily life of 16th- and 17th-century Edinburgh. Costumed characters give tours through a 16th-century town house and the plague-stricken home of a 17th-century gravedigger. Advance booking recommended.

3D LOCH NESS EXPERIENCE Exhibition
(Map p72; www.3dlochness.com; 1 Parliament Sq; adult/child £5.95/3.95; ⊙9.30am-10pm Jul & Aug, 9.30am-8pm Apr-Jun, Sep & Oct, 10am-5pm Nov-Mar) The centrepiece of this exhibition dedicated to Scotland's most famous mythical beastie is a 3D documentary film (in five languages) exploring the various theories, eyewitness accounts and hoaxes surrounding the Loch Ness Monster (for more on Nessie, see the boxed text, p279). Plus, of course, a gift shop crammed with cheekily priced cuddly toys in the form of Nessie...

FREE **MUSEUM OF CHILDHOOD** Museum
(Map p72; 42 High St; ⊙10am-5pm Mon-Sat, 2-5pm Sun) Halfway down the

Royal Mile is 'the noisiest museum in the world'. Often filled with the chatter of excited children, it covers serious issues related to childhood – health, education, upbringing and so on – but also has an enormous collection of toys, dolls, games and books, recordings of school lessons from the 1930s, and film of kids playing street games in 1950s Edinburgh.

JOHN KNOX HOUSE   Historic House
(Map p72; www.scottishstorytellingcentre.co.uk; 43-45 High St; adult/child £4/1; ☺10am-6pm Mon-Sat year-round, noon-6pm Sun Jul & Aug)
The Royal Mile narrows at the foot of High St beside the jutting facade of John Knox House. This is the oldest surviving tenement in Edinburgh, dating from around 1490; John Knox, an influential church reformer and leader of the Protestant Reformation in Scotland, is thought to have lived here from 1561 to 1572. The labyrinthine interior has some beautiful painted-timber ceilings and an interesting display on Knox's life and work.

CANONGATE   Historic Street
Canongate, the stretch of the Royal Mile from Netherbow to Holyrood, takes its name from the Augustinian canons (monks) of Holyrood Abbey. From the 16th century it was home to aristocrats attracted to the Palace of Holyroodhouse. Originally governed by the monks, Canongate was an independent burgh separate from Edinburgh until 1856.

FREE **PEOPLE'S STORY**   Museum
(Map p66; 163 Canongate; ☺10am-5pm Mon-Sat year-round, 2-5pm Sun Aug) One of the surviving symbols of Canongate's former independence is the **Canongate Tolbooth**. Built in 1591, it served successively as a collection point for tolls (taxes), a council house, a courtroom and a jail. With its picturesque turrets and projecting clock, it's an interesting example of 16th-century architecture, and now houses a fascinating museum called the **People's Story**, which covers the life, work and pastimes of ordinary

The Stone of Destiny

On St Andrew's Day 1996 a block of sandstone with rusted iron hoops at either end was installed with much pomp and ceremony in Edinburgh Castle. For the previous 700 years it had lain in London, beneath the Coronation Chair in Westminster Abbey. Almost all English, and later British, monarchs from Edward II in 1307 to Elizabeth II in 1953 have parked their backsides firmly over this stone during their coronation ceremony.

The legendary Stone of Destiny – said to have originated in the Holy Land, and on which Scottish kings placed their feet during their coronation – was stolen from Scone Abbey near Perth by King Edward I of England in 1296. It was taken to London and there it remained for seven centuries (except for a brief removal to Gloucester during WWII air raids, and a three-month sojourn in Scotland after it was stolen by Scottish Nationalist students at Christmas in 1950), an enduring symbol of Scotland's subjugation by England.

The Stone of Destiny returned to the political limelight in 1996, when the then Scottish Secretary and Conservative Party MP, Michael Forsyth, arranged for the return of the sandstone block to Scotland. A blatant attempt to boost the flagging popularity of the Conservative Party in Scotland prior to a general election, Forsyth's publicity stunt failed miserably. The Scots said thanks very much for the stone and then, in May 1997, voted every Conservative MP in Scotland into oblivion.

WILL SALTER

Edinburgh folk from the 18th century to the present day.

FREE MUSEUM OF EDINBURGH
Museum

(Map p66; 142 Canongate; ⏲10am-5pm Mon-Sat year-round, 2-5pm Sun Aug) Across the street from the People's Story is Huntly House. Built in 1570, it now houses a museum covering the history of Edinburgh from prehistory to the present. Exhibits of national importance include an original copy of the National Covenant of 1638, but the big crowd-pleaser is the dog collar and feeding bowl that once belonged to **Greyfriars Bobby**, the city's most famous canine citizen.

CANONGATE KIRK
Church

(Map p66) Downhill from Huntly House is the attractive curved gable of the Canongate Kirk, built in 1688. The kirkyard contains the graves of several famous people, including the economist Adam Smith (1723–90), author of The Wealth of Nations, Mrs Agnes MacLehose (the 'Clarinda' of Robert Burns' love poems), and the 18th-century poet Robert Fergusson (1750–74). Fergusson was much admired by Robert Burns, who paid for

the gravestone and penned the epitaph – take a look at the inscription on the back.

OUR DYNAMIC EARTH
Multimedia Exhibition

(Map p66; www.dynamicearth.co.uk; Holyrood Rd; adult/child £10.50/7; ⏲10am-6pm Jul & Aug, 10am-5.30pm Apr-Jun, Sep & Oct, 10am-5pm Wed-Sun Nov-Mar, last admission 90min before closing; 👪) The modernistic white marquee pitched beneath Salisbury Crags marks Our Dynamic Earth, billed as an interactive, multimedia journey of discovery through Earth's history from the big bang to the present day. Hugely popular with kids of all ages, it's a slick extravaganza of whiz-bang special effects and 3D movies cleverly designed to fire up young minds with curiosity about all things geological and environmental. Its true purpose, of course, is to disgorge you into a gift shop where you can buy model dinosaurs and souvenir T-shirts.

HOLYROOD PARK
Park

(Map p66) In Holyrood Park Edinburgh is blessed with a little bit of wilderness in the heart of the city. The former hunting ground of Scottish monarchs, the park covers 263 hectares of varied landscape, including crags, moorland and loch. The highest point is the 251m summit of **Arthur's Seat**, the deeply eroded remnant of a long-extinct volcano. Holyrood park can be circumnavigated by car or bike along Queen's Dr (it is closed to motorised traffic on Sunday), and you can hike from Holyrood to the summit in around 45 minutes.

SOUTH OF THE ROYAL MILE

FREE **GREYFRIARS KIRK** Church
(Map p72; www.greyfriarskirk.com; Candlemaker Row; ☺10.30am-4.40pm Mon-Fri & 10.30am-2pm Sat, 1.30-3.30pm Thu only Nov-Mar) Candlemaker Row leads from the eastern end of the Grassmarket towards one of Edinburgh's most famous churches. **Greyfriars Kirk** was built on the site of a Franciscan friary and opened for worship on Christmas Day 1620. In 1638 the **National Covenant** was signed here, rejecting Charles I's attempts to impose episcopacy and a new

English prayer book, and affirming the independence of the Scottish Church. Many who signed were later executed at the Grassmarket and, in 1679, 1200 Covenanters were held prisoner in terrible conditions in the southwestern corner of the kirkyard. There's a small exhibition inside the church.

Surrounding the church, hemmed in by high walls and overlooked by the brooding presence of the castle, **Greyfriars Kirkyard** is one of Edinburgh's most evocative cemeteries, a peaceful green oasis dotted with elaborate monuments. Many famous Edinburgh names are buried here, including the poet Allan Ramsay (1686–1758), architect William Adam (1689–1748) and William Smellie (1740–95), the editor of the first edition of the *Encyclopedia Britannica*.

In July and August you can join a **guided tour** (free; donation suggested) of the kirkyard; check the website for times and dates. If you want

Scottish Parliament Building

The **Scottish parliament building** (Map p66; ☎0131-348 5200; www.scottish.parliament .uk; admission free; ☺9am-6.30pm Tue-Thu, 10am-5.30pm Mon & Fri in session, 10am-6pm Mon-Fri in recess Apr-Oct, 10am-4pm in recess Nov-Mar; 🔁), built on the site of a former brewery close to the Palace of Holyroodhouse, was officially opened by HM the Queen in October 2005.

The **Main Hall**, inside the public entrance, has a low, triple-arched ceiling of polished concrete, like a cave, or cellar, or castle vault. It is a dimly lit space, the starting point for a metaphorical journey from this relative darkness up to the **Debating Chamber** (sitting directly above the Main Hall), which is, in contrast, a palace of light – the light of democracy. This magnificent chamber is the centrepiece of the parliament, designed not to glorify but to humble the politicians who sit within it.

The public areas of the parliament building – the Main Hall, where there is an exhibition, a shop and cafe, and the **public gallery** in the Debating Chamber – are open to visitors (tickets needed for public gallery – see website for details). You can also take a free, one-hour **guided tour** (advance booking recommended) that includes a visit to the Debating Chamber, a committee room, the Garden Lobby and, when possible, the office of an MSP (Member of the Scottish Parliament). If you want to see the **parliament in session**, check the website to see when it will be sitting – business days are normally Tuesday to Thursday year-round.

JONATHAN SMITH

Don't Miss **Palace of Holyroodhouse**

This palace is the royal family's official residence in Scotland, but is most famous as the 16th-century home of the ill-fated **Mary, Queen of Scots**. The palace is closed to the public when the royal family is visiting and during state functions (usually in mid-May, and mid-June to early July; check the website for exact dates).

The guided tour leads you through a series of impressive royal apartments, ending in the **Great Gallery**. The 89 portraits of Scottish kings were commissioned by Charles II and supposedly record his unbroken lineage from Scota, the Egyptian pharaoh's daughter who discovered the infant Moses in a reed basket on the banks of the Nile.

But the highlight of the tour is **Mary, Queen of Scots' Bed Chamber**, home to the unfortunate Mary from 1561 to 1567, and connected by a secret stairway to her husband's bedchamber. It was here that her jealous first husband, Lord Darnley, restrained the pregnant queen while his henchmen murdered her secretary – and favourite – David Rizzio. A plaque in the neighbouring room marks the spot where he bled to death.

The exit from the palace leads into the ruins of Holyrood Abbey. In summer you can join a **guided tour** of the ruins (included with your admission fee); the rest of the year you can explore them on your own. King David I founded the abbey here in the shadow of Salisbury Crags in 1128. It was probably named after a fragment of the True Cross (rood is an old Scots word for cross), said to have been brought to Scotland by his mother, St Margaret. Most of the surviving ruins date from the 12th and 13th centuries.

THINGS YOU NEED TO KNOW

Map p66; www.royalcollection.org.uk; Canongate; adult/child £10.25/6.20; ⊗9.30am-6pm Apr-Oct, 9.30am-4.30pm Nov-Mar

to experience the graveyard at its scariest – inside a burial vault, in the dark, at night – go on one of Black Hart Storytellers' guided tours (p86).

GREYFRIARS BOBBY STATUE
Monument

The memorials inside Greyfriars Kirkyard are interesting, but the one that draws the biggest crowds is outside, in front of the pub beside the kirkyard gate. It's the tiny statue of Greyfriars Bobby, a Skye terrier who, from 1858 to 1872, maintained a vigil over the grave of his master, an Edinburgh police officer. The story was immortalised (and romanticised) in a novel by Eleanor Atkinson in 1912, and in 1963 was made into a movie by – who else? – Walt Disney. Bobby's own grave, marked by a small, pink granite stone, is just inside the entrance to the kirkyard. You can see his original collar and bowl in the Museum of Edinburgh.

GRASSMARKET
Historic District

The site of a cattle market from the 15th century until the start of the 20th, the **Grassmarket** has always been a focal point of the Old Town. It was also the city's main **place of execution**, and over 100 martyred Covenanters are commemorated by a monument at the eastern end, where the gallows used to stand. The notorious murderers **Burke and Hare** operated from a now-vanished close off the western end. In 1827 they enticed at least 18 victims to their boarding house, suffocated them and sold the bodies to Edinburgh's medical schools. The law finally caught up with Burke and Hare – the latter turned King's evidence and testified against Burke, who was hanged outside St Giles in 1828. In an ironic twist, his corpse was donated to the anatomy school for public dissection, and a pocketbook was made from his flayed skin (now on display in the Surgeons' Hall Museums).

Nowadays the broad, open square, edged by tall tenements and dominated by the looming castle, has many lively pubs and restaurants, including the **White Hart Inn**, which was once patronised by Robert Burns. **Cowgate** – the long, dark ravine leading eastwards from the Grassmarket – was once the road along which cattle were driven from the pastures around Arthur's Seat to the safety of the city walls. Today it is the heart of Edinburgh's nightlife, with around two dozen clubs and bars within five minutes' walk of each other.

SURGEONS' HALL MUSEUMS
Museum

(Map p72; www.museum.rcsed.ac.uk; Nicolson St; adult/child £5/3; ⊘noon-4pm Mon-Fri) These grisly but fascinating museums take a look at surgery in Scotland from the 15th century – when barbers supplemented their income with blood-letting, amputations and other surgical procedures – to the present day. The highlight is the exhibit on Burke and Hare, which includes Burke's death mask and a pocketbook bound in his skin.

New Town

Edinburgh's New Town lies north of the Old Town, on a ridge running parallel to the Royal Mile and separated from it by the valley of Princes Street Gardens. Its regular grid of elegant, Georgian terraces is a complete contrast to the chaotic tangle of tenements and wynds that characterise the Old Town.

Between the end of the 14th century and the start of the 18th, the population of Edinburgh – still confined within the walls of the Old Town – increased from 2000 to 50,000. The tottering tenements were unsafe and occasionally collapsed, fire was an ever-present danger, and the overcrowding and squalor became unbearable.

When the Act of Union in 1707 brought the prospect of long-term stability, the upper classes were keen to find healthier, more spacious living quarters, and in 1766 the lord provost of Edinburgh announced an architectural competition to design an extension to the city. It was won by an unknown 23-year-old, James Craig, a self-taught architect whose simple and elegant plan envisaged the main axis being George St, with grand squares at either end, and with building restricted to one side only of Princes and Queen Sts so that the houses enjoyed views over the Firth of

Forth to the north and to the castle and Old Town to the south.

In the 18th and 19th centuries New Town continued to sprout squares, circuses, parks and terraces, with some of its finest neoclassical architecture designed by Robert Adam. Today Edinburgh's New Town is the world's most complete and unspoilt example of Georgian architecture and town planning. Along with the Old Town, it was declared a Unesco World Heritage site in 1995.

PRINCES STREET

Princes St is one of the world's most spectacular shopping streets. Built up on the north side only, it catches the sun in summer and allows expansive views across Princes Street Gardens to the castle and the crowded skyline of the Old Town.

The western end of Princes St is dominated by the red-sandstone edifice of the Caledonian Hilton Hotel, and the tower of **St John's Church** (Map p72), worth visiting for its fine Gothic Revival interior. It overlooks **St Cuthbert's Parish Church** (Map p72), built in the 1890s on a site of great antiquity – there has been a church here since at least the 12th century, and perhaps since the 7th century. There is a circular **watchtower** in the graveyard – a reminder of the Burke and Hare days when graves had to be guarded against robbers.

At the eastern end is the prominent clock tower – traditionally three minutes fast so that you don't miss your train – of the **Balmoral Hotel** (originally the North British Hotel, built by the railway company of the same name in 1902) and the beautiful 1788 **Register House** (Map p82),

New Town

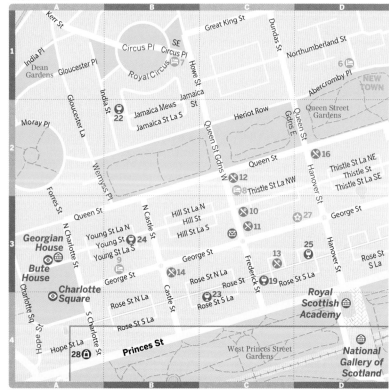

80

designed by Robert Adam, with a statue of the Duke of Wellington on horseback in front. It houses the National Archives of Scotland and the ScotlandsPeople genealogical research centre.

Princes Street Gardens lie in a valley that was once occupied by the Nor' Loch, a boggy depression that was drained in the early 19th century. The gardens are split in the middle by **The Mound**, which was created by around two million cartloads of earth excavated from the foundations of New Town being dumped here to provide a road link across the valley to the Old Town. It was completed in 1830.

SCOTT MONUMENT Monument
(Map p82; East Princes Street Gardens; admission £3; ☺10am-7pm daily Apr-Sep, 9am-4pm Mon-Sat, 10am-4pm Sun Oct-Mar) The eastern half of Princes Street Gardens is dominated by the massive Gothic spire of the Scott Monument, built by public subscription in memory of the novelist Sir Walter Scott after his death in 1832. The exterior is decorated with carvings of characters from his novels; inside you can see an exhibition on Scott's life, and climb the 287 steps to the top for a superb view of the city.

FREE **NATIONAL GALLERY OF SCOTLAND**
Art Gallery
(Map p82; www.nationalgalleries.org; The Mound; fee for special exhibitions; ☺10am-5pm daily, to 7pm Thu; ☎) Designed by William Playfair, this imposing classical building with its Ionic porticoes dates from the 1850s. Its octagonal rooms, lit by skylights, have been restored to their original Victorian decor of deep-green carpets and dark-red walls.

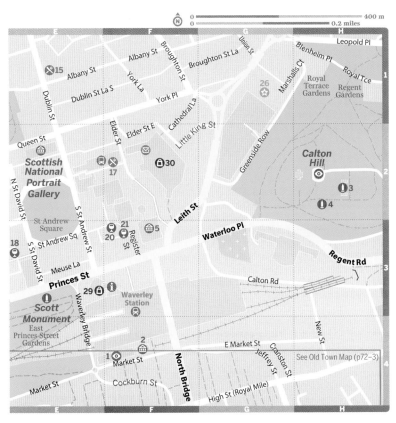

New Town

The gallery houses an important collection of **European art** from the Renaissance to post-Impressionism, with works by Verrocchio (Leonardo da Vinci's teacher), Tintoretto, Titian, Holbein, Rubens, Van Dyck, Vermeer, El Greco, Poussin, Rembrandt, Gainsborough, Turner, Constable, Monet, Pissarro, Gauguin and Cézanne; each year in January the gallery exhibits its collection of **Turner watercolours**, bequeathed by Henry Vaughan in 1900. Room X is graced by Antonio Canova's white marble sculpture, **The Three Graces**; it is owned jointly with London's Victoria & Albert Museum.

The upstairs galleries house portraits by Sir Joshua Reynolds and Sir Henry Raeburn, and a clutch of **Impressionists** including Monet's luminous *Haystacks,* Van Gogh's demonic *Olive Trees* and Gauguin's hallucinatory *Vision After the Sermon*. But the painting that really catches your eye is the gorgeous portrait of *Lady Agnew of Lochnaw* by John Singer Sargent.

The basement galleries dedicated to **Scottish art** include glowing portraits by Allan Ramsay and Sir Henry Raeburn, rural scenes by Sir David Wilkie and impressionistic landscapes by William MacTaggart. Look out for Raeburn's iconic *Reverend Robert Walker Skating on Duddingston Loch,* and Sir George Harvey's hugely entertaining *A Schule Skailin* (A School Emptying) – a stern dominie (teacher) looks on as the boys stampede for the classroom door, one reaching for a spinning top confiscated earlier. Kids will love the fantasy paintings of Sir Joseph Noel Paton in Room B5, incredibly detailed canvases crammed with hundreds of tiny fairies, goblins and elves.

FREE **ROYAL SCOTTISH ACADEMY**
Art Gallery
(Map p82; www.royalscottishacademy.org; The Mound; fee for special exhibitions; ⏰10am-5pm

JONATHAN SMITH

Don't Miss National Museum of Scotland

Broad, elegant Chambers St is dominated by the long facade of the National Museum of Scotland. Its extensive collections are spread between two buildings, one modern, one Victorian.

The golden stone and striking modern architecture of the museum building, opened in 1998, is one of the city's most distinctive landmarks. The five floors of the museum trace the history of Scotland from geological beginnings to the 1990s, with many imaginative and stimulating exhibits – audio guides are available in several languages. Highlights include the **Monymusk Reliquary**, a tiny silver casket dating from AD 750, which is said to have been carried into battle with Robert the Bruce at Bannockburn in 1314, and some of the **Lewis chessmen** (pictured), a set of charming 12th-century chess pieces made from walrus ivory. Don't forget to visit the **roof terrace** for a fantastic view of the castle. The Museum of Scotland connects with the Victorian **Royal Museum** building, dating from 1861, where the stolid, grey exterior gives way to a bright and airy, glass-roofed entrance hall. The museum houses an eclectic collection covering natural history, archaeology, scientific and industrial technology, and the decorative arts of ancient Egypt, Islam, China, Japan, Korea and the West. (The Royal Museum was undergoing a major rebuild at the time of research; it is due to reopen in mid-2011.)

THINGS YOU NEED TO KNOW

Map p72; www.nms.ac.uk; Chambers St; admission free, fee for special exhibitions; ⏰10am-5pm

Mon-Sat, 2-5pm Sun; ☎) The distinguished Greek Doric temple at the corner of The Mound and Princes St, its northern pediment crowned by a seated figure of Queen Victoria, is the home of the Royal Scottish Academy. Designed by William Playfair and built between 1823 and 1836, it was originally called the Royal Institution; the RSA took over the building in 1910. The galleries display a collection of paintings, sculptures and architectural drawings by academy members dating from 1831, and they also host temporary exhibitions throughout the year.

The RSA and the National Gallery of Scotland are linked via an underground mall – the **Weston Link** – which gives them twice the temporary exhibition space of the Prado in Madrid and three times that of London's Royal Academy, as well as housing a lecture theatre and a restaurant. The galleries have become famous in recent years for 'blockbuster' exhibitions such as 'The Age of Titian' and 'Impressionist Gardens'.

GEORGE STREET & CHARLOTTE SQUARE

Until the 1990s George St – the major axis of New Town – was the centre of Edinburgh's financial industry and Scotland's equivalent of Wall St. Today the big financial firms have moved to premises in the Exchange office district west of Lothian Rd, and George St's former banks and offices house upmarket shops, pubs and restaurants.

At the western end of George St is **Charlotte Square**, the architectural jewel of New Town, designed by Robert Adam shortly before his death in 1791. The northern side of the square is Adam's masterpiece and one of the finest examples of Georgian architecture anywhere. **Bute House**, in the centre at No 6, is the official residence of Scotland's first minister.

GEORGIAN HOUSE — Historic House

(Map p82; NTS; 7 Charlotte Sq; adult/child £5.50/4.50; ◷10am-6pm Jul & Aug, 10am-5pm Apr-Jun, Sep & Oct, 11am-4pm Mar, 11am-3pm Nov) Next door to Bute House is the National Trust of Scotland's Georgian House, which has been beautifully restored and furnished to show how Edinburgh's wealthy elite lived at the end of the 18th century. The walls are decorated with paintings by Allan Ramsay, Sir Henry Raeburn and Sir Joshua Reynolds.

FREE ROYAL BOTANIC GARDEN — Garden

(www.rbge.org.uk; 20a Inverleith Row; admission to glasshouses £4.50; ◷10am-7pm Apr-Sep,10am-6pm Mar & Oct, 10am-4pm Nov-Feb) Just north of the New Town is the lovely Royal Botanic Garden. Twenty-eight beautifully landscaped hectares include splendid Victorian **palm houses**, colourful swathes of rhododendron and azalea, and a world-famous **rock garden**. The Terrace Cafe offers good views towards the city centre.

CALTON HILL

Calton Hill (100m), rising dramatically above the eastern end of Princes St, is Edinburgh's acropolis, its summit scattered with grandiose memorials mostly dating from the first half of the 19th century. It is also one of the best viewpoints in Edinburgh, with a panorama that

Glasshouse at the Royal Botanic Garden
PHOTOGRAPHER: KARL BLACKWELL

Underground Edinburgh

As Edinburgh expanded in the late 18th and early 19th centuries, many old tenements were demolished and new bridges were built to link the Old Town to the newly built areas to its north and south. South Bridge (built between 1785 and 1788) and George IV Bridge (built between 1829 and 1834) lead southwards from the Royal Mile over the deep valley of Cowgate, but so many buildings have been built closely around them that you can hardly tell they are bridges – George IV Bridge has a total of nine arches but only two are visible; South Bridge has no less than 18 hidden arches.

These **subterranean vaults** were originally used as storerooms, workshops and drinking dens. But as early-19th-century Edinburgh's population was swelled by an influx of penniless Highlanders cleared from their lands, and Irish refugees from the potato famine, the dark, dripping chambers were given over to slum accommodation and abandoned to poverty, filth and crime.

The vaults were eventually cleared in the late 19th century, then lay forgotten until 1994 when the **South Bridge vaults** were opened to guided tours (see Mercat Tours, p94). Certain chambers are said to be haunted and one particular vault was investigated by paranormal researchers in 2001.

takes in the castle, Holyrood, Arthur's Seat, the Firth of Forth, New Town and the full length of Princes St.

You can reach the summit of Calton Hill via the road beside the Royal High School or by the stairs at the eastern end of Waterloo Pl. The largest structure on the summit is the **National Monument** (Map p82), an over-ambitious attempt to replicate the Parthenon and intended to honour Scotland's dead in the Napoleonic Wars. Construction – paid for by public subscription – began in 1822, but funds ran dry when only 12 columns were complete.

Looking a bit like an upturned telescope – the similarity is intentional – and offering even better views, the **Nelson Monument** (Map p82; Calton Hill; admission £3; ☺1-6pm Mon, 10am-6pm Tue-Sat Apr-Sep, 10am-3pm Mon-Sat Oct-Mar) was built to commemorate Admiral Lord Nelson's victory at Trafalgar in 1805.

Leith

Two miles northeast of the city centre, Leith has been Edinburgh's seaport since the 14th century and remained an independent burgh with its own town council until it was incorporated

by the city in the 1920s. Like many of Britain's dockland areas, it fell into decay in the decades following WWII but has been undergoing a revival since the late 1980s. Old warehouses have been turned into luxury flats, and a lush crop of trendy bars and restaurants has sprouted along the waterfront. The area was given an additional boost in the late 1990s when the Scottish Executive (a government department) moved to a new building on Leith docks.

The city council has formulated a major redevelopment plan for the entire Edinburgh waterfront from Leith to Granton, the first phase of which is **Ocean Terminal**, a shopping and leisure complex that includes the former Royal Yacht *Britannia* and a berth for visiting cruise liners. Parts of Leith are still a bit rough but it's a distinctive corner of the city and well worth exploring.

 Tours

Bus Tours

Open-topped buses leave from Waverley Bridge outside the main train station and

offer hop-on, hop-off tours of the main sights, taking in New Town, the Grassmarket and the Royal Mile. They're a good way to get your bearings, although with a bus map and a Day Saver bus ticket (£3) you could do much the same thing but without the commentary. Tours run daily, year-round, except for 24 and 25 December.

Tickets for the following three tours remain valid for 24 hours.

City Sightseeing   Bus Tours
(www.edinburghtour.com; adult/child £12/5) Lothian Buses' bright red open-top buses depart every 20 minutes from Waverley Bridge.

MacTours   Bus Tours
(www.edinburghtour.com; adult/child £12/5) Offers similar tours to City Sightseeing, but in a vintage bus.

Majestic Tour   Bus Tours
(www.edinburghtour.com; adult/child £12/5) Runs every 30 minutes (every 20 minutes in July and August) from Waverley Bridge to the Royal Yacht *Britannia* at Ocean Terminal via the New Town, Royal Botanic Garden and Newhaven, returning via Leith Walk, Holyrood and the Royal Mile.

Walking Tours

There are plenty of organised walks around Edinburgh, many of them related to ghosts, murders and witches. For starting times of individual walks, check the following websites:

Black Hart Storytellers   Ghost Tours
(www.blackhart.uk.com; adult/concession £9.50/7.50) Not suitable for young children. The 'City of the Dead' tour of Greyfriars Kirkyard is probably the scariest of Edinburgh's 'ghost' tours. Many people have reported encounters with the 'McKenzie Poltergeist'.

Cadies & Witchery Tours   Ghost Tours
(www.witcherytours.com; adult/child £7.50/5) The becloaked and pasty-faced Adam Lyal (deceased) leads a 'Murder & Mystery' tour of the Old Town's darker corners. These tours are famous for their 'jumper-ooters' – costumed actors who 'jump oot' when you least expect it.

Edinburgh Literary Pub Tour   Literary Tours
(www.edinburghliterarypubtour.co.uk; adult/student £10/8) An enlightening two-hour trawl

Left: A ghost walking tour; **Below:** Folk session, White Hart Inn (p79)

through Edinburgh's literary history – and its associated howffs – in the entertaining company of Messrs Clart and McBrain. One of the best of Edinburgh's walking tours.

Mercat Tours   History Tours
(www.mercattours.com; adult/child £9/5)
Mercat offers a wide range of fascinating tours including history walks in the Old Town and Leith, 'Ghosts & Ghouls' tours and visits to haunted underground vaults.

 # Sleeping

A boom in hotel building has seen Edinburgh's tourist capacity swell significantly in the last decade, but you can guarantee that the city will still be packed to the gills during the festival period (August) and over Hogmanay (New Year). If you want a room during these periods, book as far in advance as you can – a year ahead if possible. In general, it's best to book ahead for

accommodation at Easter and from mid-May to mid-September.

Hotels and backpacker hostels are found throughout the Old and New Towns, while midrange B&Bs and guesthouses are mainly concentrated outside the centre in the suburbs of Tollcross, Bruntsfield, Newington and Pilrig.

If you're driving, don't even think about staying in the city centre unless your hotel has its own private car park – parking in the centre is a nightmare. Instead, look for somewhere in a suburb like Newington, where there's a chance of finding free, on-street parking (even then, don't bet on getting a parking space outside the front door). Alternatively, stay outside the city and travel in by bus or train.

Edinburgh accommodation is slightly more expensive than in the rest of Scotland, so the price breakdown in

If You Like...
Art Galleries

If the National Gallery has inspired in you an appreciation for all things artistic, there are several other top-quality galleries in the city.

1 **SCOTTISH NATIONAL PORTRAIT GALLERY**
(Map p82; www.nationalgalleries.org; 1 Queen St; admission free; ⏰10am-5pm daily, to 7pm Thu) Illustrates Scottish history through portraits and sculptures of famous Scottish personalities, from Robert Burns and Bonnie Prince Charlie to Sean Connery and Billy Connolly.

2 **FRUITMARKET GALLERY**
(Map p82; www.fruitmarket.co.uk; 45 Market St; admission free; ⏰11am-6pm Mon-Sat, noon-5pm Sun) Showcases contemporary Scottish and international artists; also has an excellent arts bookshop and cafe.

3 **CITY ART CENTRE**
(Map p72; 2 Market St; admission free, fee for temporary exhibitions; ⏰10am-5pm Mon-Sat, noon-5pm Sun) Comprises six floors of exhibitions with a variety of themes, including an extensive collection of Scottish art.

4 **SCOTTISH NATIONAL GALLERY OF MODERN ART**
(Map p66; www.nationalgalleries.org; 75 Belford Rd; admission free, fee for special exhibitions; ⏰10am-5pm) Concentrates on 20th-century art, with various European movements represented by the likes of Matisse, Picasso, Kirchner, Magritte, Miró, Mondrian and Giacometti.

5 **DEAN GALLERY**
(Map p66; www.nationalgalleries.org; 75 Belford Rd; admission free, fee for special exhibitions; ⏰10am-5pm) Collection of Dada and surrealist art, including works by Dalí, Giacometti, Picasso and the Edinburgh-born sculptor Sir Eduardo Paolozzi.

these listings is different from that described on p49 – budget is less than £60, midrange £60 to £150, and top end is more than £150, based on the cost of a double room with bed and breakfast (B&B).

Accommodation Agencies

If you arrive in Edinburgh without a room, the **Edinburgh & Scotland Information Centre** (p112) booking service will try to find a room to suit you (and will charge a £5 fee if successful). If you have the time, pick up the tourist office's accommodation brochure and ring around yourself.

You can also try VisitScotland's **Booking Hotline** (☎ 0845 859 1006), which has a £3 surcharge; or search for accommodation on the **Edinburgh & Lothians Tourist Board** (www.edinburgh.org/accom) website.

Old Town

Most of the interesting accommodation in the Old Town is either backpacker hostels or expensive hotels. For midrange options you'll have to resort to chain hotels – check the websites of Travelodge, Ibis etc.

HOTEL MISSONI
Boutique Hotel £££
(Map p72; ☎ 0131-220 6666; www.hotelmissoni.com; 1 George IV Bridge; r £180; 🛜) The Italian fashion house has established a style icon in the heart of the medieval Old Town with this bold statement of a hotel – modernistic architecture, black-and-white decor with well-judged splashes of colour, impeccably mannered staff and – most importantly – very comfortable bedrooms and bathrooms with lots of nice little touches, from fresh milk in the minibar to plush bathrobes.

WITCHERY BY THE CASTLE
Boutique B&B £££
(Map p72; ☎ 0131-225 5613; www.thewitchery.com; Castlehill, Royal Mile; ste £295) Set in a 16th-century Old Town house in the shadow of Edinburgh Castle, the Witchery's seven lavish suites are extravagantly furnished with antiques, oak panelling, tapestries, open fires and

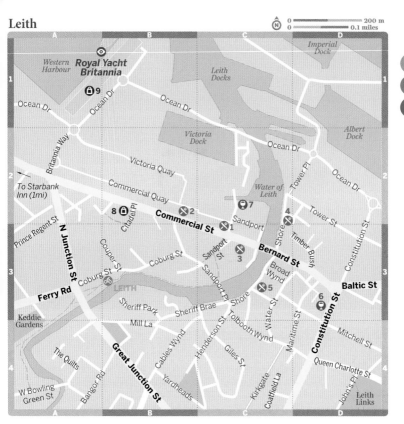

Leith

roll-top baths, and supplied with flowers, chocolates and complimentary champagne. Overwhelmingly popular – you'll have to book several months in advance to be sure of getting a room.

KNIGHT RESIDENCE Apartments **£££** (Map p72; ☎ 0131-622 8120; www.theknight residence.co.uk; 12 Lauriston St; d apt per night £169-199, 2-bedroom apt £249-289; 🛜) Works by contemporary artists adorn these modern one- and two-bedroom apartments (available by the night; the latter sleep up to four adults and one child), each with fully equipped kitchen and comfortable lounge with cable TV, video and stereo. It has a good central location in a quiet street only a few minutes' walk from the Grassmarket.

KARL BLACKWELL

Don't Miss **Royal Yacht** *Britannia*

One of Scotland's biggest tourist attractions is the former Royal Yacht *Britannia*. She was the British royal family's floating home during their foreign travels from the time of her launch in 1953 until her decommissioning in 1997, and is now moored permanently in front of Ocean Terminal.

The tour, which you take at your own pace with an audio guide (available in 20 languages), gives an intriguing insight into the Queen's private tastes – *Britannia* was one of the few places where the royal family could enjoy true privacy. The entire ship is a monument to 1950s decor and technology, and the accommodation reveals Her Majesty's preference for simple, unfussy surroundings – the Queen's own bed is surprisingly tiny and plain.

There was nothing simple or unfussy, however, about the running of the ship. When the Queen travelled, along with her went 45 members of the royal household, five tons of luggage and a Rolls-Royce that was carefully squeezed into a specially built garage on the deck. The ship's company consisted of an admiral, 20 officers and 220 yachtsmen. The decks (of Burmese teak) were scrubbed daily, but all work near the royal accommodation was carried out in complete silence and had to be finished by 8am. A thermometer was kept in the Queen's bathroom to make sure that the water was the correct temperature, and when in harbour one yachtsman was charged with ensuring that the angle of the gangway never exceeded 12 degrees. And note the mahogany windbreak that was added to the balcony deck in front of the bridge. It was put there to stop wayward breezes from blowing up skirts and inadvertently revealing the royal undies.

THINGS YOU NEED TO KNOW

Map p89; www.royalyachtbritannia.co.uk; Ocean Terminal, Leith; adult/child £10.50/6.75; ⊘9.30am-6pm Jul-Sep, 10am-5.30pm Apr-Jun & Oct, 10am-5pm Nov-Mar, last admission 1½hr before closing

SMART CITY HOSTEL   Hostel **£**
(Map p72; ☎ 0870 892 3000; www.smartcity
hostels.com; 50 Blackfriars St; dm £9-22, tw
£80; @ 🛜) A big (620 beds), bright,
modern hostel that feels more like a
hotel, with a convivial cafe where you
can buy breakfast, and mod cons such
as keycard access and secure charging
stations for mobile phones, MP3 players
and laptops. Lockers in every room, bike
parking and a central location just off
the Royal Mile make this the city's new
favourite place to stay.

New Town & Around

SIX MARY'S PLACE   B&B **££**
(Map p66; ☎ 0131-332 8965; www.sixmarysplace
.co.uk; 6 Mary's Pl, Raeburn Pl; s/d/f from
£50/94/150; @ 🛜) Six Mary's Place is an
attractive Georgian town house with a
designer mix of period features, contemporary furniture and modern colours.
Breakfasts are vegetarian-only, served
in an attractive conservatory with a view
of the garden, while the lounge, with its
big, comfy sofas, offers free coffee and
newspapers.

ONE ROYAL CIRCUS   B&B **£££**
(Map p82; ☎ 0131-625 6669; www.oneroyalcircus
.com; 1 Royal Circus; r £180-260; 🛜 🚹) Live
the New Town dream at this incredibly
chic Georgian mansion where genuine
antiques and parquet floors sit comfortably alongside slate bathrooms and
Philippe Starck furniture. Bedrooms are
kitted out with Egyptian cotton sheets,
iPod docks and Arran Aromatics toiletries, and there are babyfoot (foosball)
and pool tables in the drawing room.

GERALD'S PLACE   B&B **££**
(Map p82; ☎ 0131-558 7017; www.geraldsplace
.com; 21b Abercromby Pl; d £119-149; @ 🛜)
Gerald is an unfailingly charming and
helpful host, and his lovely Georgian garden flat (just two guest bedrooms) has
a great location across from a peaceful
park, an easy stroll from the city centre.

TIGERLILY   Boutique Hotel **£££**
(Map p82; ☎ 0131-225 5005; www.tigerlilyedin
burgh.co.uk; 125 George St; r from £195; 🛜)
Georgian meets gorgeous at this glam-
orous, glittering boutique hotel (complete with its own nightclub) decked
out in mirror mosaics, beaded curtains,
swirling Timorous Beasties textiles and
wall coverings, and atmospheric pink up-
lighting. Book the Georgian Suite (£375)
for a truly special romantic getaway.

RICK'S   Boutique Hotel **££**
(Map p82; ☎ 0131-622 7800; www.ricksedin
burgh.co.uk; 55a Frederick St; r £115-175; 🛜)
One of the first boutique hotels to appear in Edinburgh, Rick's offers sharp
styling and a laid-back atmosphere. The
bedrooms boast walnut headboards and
designer fabrics, with fluffy bathrobes,
well-stocked minibars and Molton Brown
toiletries.

DENE GUEST HOUSE   B&B **££**
(Map p66; ☎ 0131-556 2700; www.deneguest
house.com; 7 Eyre Pl; per person £25-50; 🚹)
The Dene is a friendly and informal
place, set in a charming Georgian town
house, with a welcoming owner and spacious bedrooms. The inexpensive single
rooms make it ideal for solo travellers;
children under 10 staying in their parents' room pay half price.

South Edinburgh

There are lots of guesthouses in the
South Edinburgh suburbs of Tollcross,
Morningside, Marchmont and Newington, especially on and around Minto St
and Mayfield Gardens (the continuation
of North Bridge and Nicolson St) in Newington. This is the main traffic artery
from the south and a main bus route into
the city centre.

SOUTHSIDE GUEST HOUSE   B&B **££**
(Map p66; ☎ 0131-668 4422; www.southside
guesthouse.co.uk; 8 Newington Rd; s/d £70/90;
🛜) Though set in a typical Victorian
terrace, the Southside transcends the
traditional guesthouse category and
feels more like a modern boutique hotel.
Its eight stylish rooms just ooze interior
design, standing out from other Newington B&Bs through the clever use of bold
colours and modern furniture.

PRESTONFIELD HOUSE HOTEL
Boutique Hotel £££

(☎ 0131-668 3346; www.prestonfield.com; Priestfield Rd; r £275, ste £350-395; P 🛜) If the blonde wood, brown leather and brushed steel of modern boutique hotels leave you cold, then this is the place for you. A 17th-century mansion set in 20 acres of parkland (complete with peacocks and Highland cattle), Prestonfield House is draped in damask, packed with antiques and decorated in red, black and gold – look out for original tapestries, 17th-century embossed-leather panels, and £500-a-roll hand-painted wallpaper. The hotel's rooms are supplied with all mod cons, including internet access, Bose sound systems, DVD players and plasma-screen TVs. The hotel is southeast of the city centre, east of Dalkeith Rd.

45 GILMOUR RD
B&B £££

(☎ 0131-667 3536; www.edinburghbedbreakfast .com; 45 Gilmour Rd; s/d £60/110) A peaceful setting, large garden and friendly owners contribute to the appeal of this Victorian terraced house, which overlooks the local bowling green. The decor is a blend of 19th- and 20th-century influences, with bold Victorian reds, pine floors and period fireplace in the lounge, a rocking horse and art nouveau lamp in the hallway, and a 1930s vibe in the three spacious bedrooms. Located 1 mile southeast of the city centre.

AONACH MOR GUEST HOUSE
B&B ££

(☎ 0131-667 8694; www.aonachmor.com; 14 Kilmaurs Tce; r per person £30-70; @ 🛜) This elegant Victorian terraced house is located on a quiet back street and has seven bedrooms, beautifully decorated, with many original period features. Our favourite is the four-poster bedroom with polished mahogany furniture and period fireplace. Located 1 mile southeast of the city centre.

TOWN HOUSE
B&B ££

(Map p66; ☎ 0131-229 1985; www.thetownhouse .com; 65 Gilmore Pl; per person £40-58; P 🛜) The five-room Town House is a plush little place, offering the sort of quality and comfort you might expect from a much larger and more expensive hotel. It's an elegant Victorian terraced house with big bay windows, spacious bedrooms (all en suite) and a breakfast menu that includes salmon fishcakes and kippers alongside the more usual offerings.

SHERWOOD GUEST HOUSE
B&B ££

(Map p66; ☎ 0131-667 1200; www.sher wood-edinburgh.com; 42 Minto St; s £30-60, d £40-75; P 🛜) One of the most attractive guesthouses on Minto St's B&B strip, the Sherwood is a refurbished Georgian terraced house decked out with hanging baskets and shrubs. Inside are six en suite rooms that combine Regency-style striped wallpaper with modern fabrics and pine furniture.

Hume statue and St Giles Cathedral (p72)
PHOTOGRAPHER: JONATHAN SMITH

KARL BLACKWELL

Don't Miss **Rosslyn Chapel**

The success of Dan Brown's novel *The Da Vinci Code* and the subsequent Hollywood film has seen a flood of visitors descend on Scotland's most beautiful and enigmatic church: Rosslyn Chapel. The chapel was built in the mid-15th century for William St Clair, third earl of Orkney, and the ornately carved interior – at odds with the architectural fashion of its time – is a monument to the mason's art, rich in symbolic imagery. As well as flowers, vines, angels and biblical figures, the carved stones include many examples of the pagan 'Green Man'; other figures are associated with Freemasonry and the Knights Templar. Intriguingly, there are also carvings of plants from the Americas that predate Columbus' voyage of discovery. The symbolism of these images has led some researchers to conclude that Rosslyn is some kind of secret Templar repository, and it has been claimed that hidden vaults beneath the chapel could conceal anything from the Holy Grail or the head of John the Baptist to the body of Christ himself. The chapel is owned by the Episcopal Church of Scotland and services are still held here on Sunday mornings.

The chapel is on the eastern edge of the village of Roslin, 7 miles south of Edinburgh's centre. Lothian Bus 15 (not 15A) runs from the west end of Princes St in Edinburgh to Roslin (£1.20, 30 minutes, every 30 minutes).

THINGS YOU NEED TO KNOW

off Map p53; Collegiate Church of St Matthew; www.rosslynchapel.com; Roslin; adult/child £7.50/free; 9.30am-6pm Mon-Sat & noon-4.45pm Sun Apr-Sep, 9.30am-5pm Mon-Sat & noon-4.45pm Sun Oct-Mar

---

AMARYLLIS GUEST HOUSE   B&B ££
(Map p66; 0131-229 3293; www.amaryllis guest house.com; 21 Upper Gilmore Pl; per person £25-40; P) The Amaryllis is a cute little Georgian town house on a quiet back street. There are five bedrooms, including a spacious family room that can take two adults and up to four kids. Princes St is only 10 minutes' walk away.

Rosslyn Chapel

Deciphering Rosslyn

Rosslyn Chapel is a small building, but the density of decoration inside can be overwhelming. It's well worth buying the official guidebook by the Earl of Rosslyn first; find a bench in the gardens and have a skim through before going into the chapel – the background information will make your visit all the more interesting. The book also offers a useful self-guided tour of the chapel, and explains the legend of the Master Mason and the Apprentice.

Entrance is through the north door **1**. Take a pew and sit for a while to allow your eyes to adjust to the dim interior; then look up at the ceiling vault, decorated with engraved roses, lilies and stars (can you spot the sun and the moon?). Walk left along the north aisle to reach the Lady Chapel, separated from the rest of the church by the Mason's Pillar **2** and the Apprentice Pillar **3**. Here you'll find carvings of Lucifer **4**, the Fallen Angel, and the Green Man **5**. Nearby are carvings **6** that appear to resemble Indian corn (maize). Finally, go to the western end and look up at the wall – in the left corner is the head of the Apprentice **7**; to the right is the (rather worn) head of the Master Mason **8**.

ROSSLYN CHAPEL & THE DA VINCI CODE

Dan Brown was referencing Rosslyn Chapel's alleged links to the Knights Templar and the Freemasons – unusual symbols found among the carvings, and the fact that a descendant of its founder, William St Clair, was a Grand Master Mason – when he chose it as the setting for his novel's denouement. Rosslyn is indeed a coded work, written in stone, but its meaning depends on your point of view. See *The Rosslyn Hoax?* by Robert LD Cooper (www.rosslynhoax. com) for an alternative interpretation of the chapel's symbolism.

SANDRO VANNINI/CORBIS

Explore Some More

After visiting the chapel, head downhill to see the spectacularly sited ruins of Roslin Castle, then take a walk along leafy Roslin Glen.

Lucifer, the Fallen Angel
At head height, to the left of the second window from left is an upside-down angel bound with rope, a symbol often associated with Freemasonry. The arch above is decorated with the Dance of Death.

The Apprentice
High in the corner, beneath an empty statue niche, is the head of the murdered Apprentice, with a deep wound in his forehead above the right eye. The worn head on the side wall to the left of the Apprentice is that of his mother.

North Door

The Master Mason

8

Baptistery

Practical Tips

Buy your tickets in advance through the chapel's website (except in August, when no bookings are taken). No photography is allowed inside the chapel.

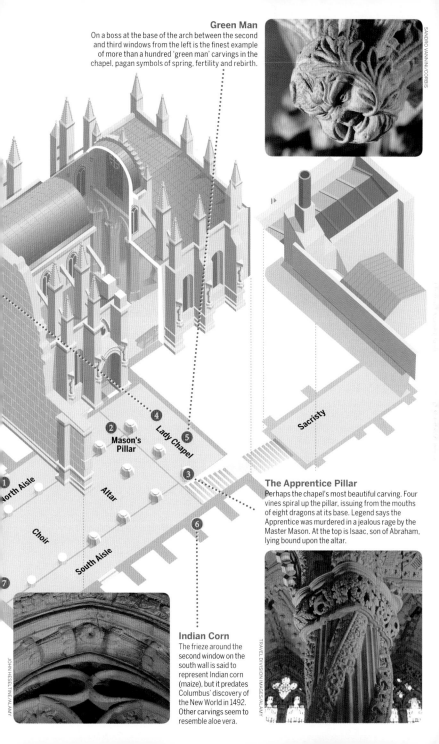

Green Man
On a boss at the base of the arch between the second and third windows from the left is the finest example of more than a hundred 'green man' carvings in the chapel, pagan symbols of spring, fertility and rebirth.

SANDRO VANNINI/CORBIS

The Apprentice Pillar
Perhaps the chapel's most beautiful carving. Four vines spiral up the pillar, issuing from the mouths of eight dragons at its base. Legend says the Apprentice was murdered in a jealous rage by the Master Mason. At the top is Isaac, son of Abraham, lying bound upon the altar.

TRAVEL DIVISION IMAGES/ALAMY

Indian Corn
The frieze around the second window on the south wall is said to represent Indian corn (maize), but it predates Columbus' discovery of the New World in 1492. Other carvings seem to resemble aloe vera.

JOHN HESELTINE/ALAMY

Sacristy

② Mason's Pillar

④

⑤ Lady Chapel

③

① North Aisle

Altar

Choir

South Aisle

⑥

⑦

WILL SALTER

ARGYLE BACKPACKERS Hostel £
(Map p66; ☎ 0131-667 9991; www.argyle-back
packers.co.uk; 14 Argyle Pl; dm £14-20, d & tw £50-
60; 📶) The Argyle, spread across three
adjacent terraced houses, is a quiet and
relaxed hostel offering double and twin
rooms as well as four- to eight-bed dorms
(mixed sex). There is a comfortable TV
lounge, an attractive little conservatory,
and a pleasant walled garden at the back
where you can sit outside in summer.

Leith Walk & Pilrig St

Northeast of the New Town, the area
around Leith Walk and Pilrig St (Map
p66) has lots of guesthouses, all within
about a mile of the centre. To get there,
take bus 11 from Princes St.

MILLERS 64 B&B ££
(off Map p66; ☎ 0131-454 3666; www.millers64
.com; 64 Pilrig St; s from £80, d £80-140; 🅿 📶)
Luxury textiles, colourful cushions, stylish bathrooms and fresh flowers added
to a warm Edinburgh welcome make this
Victorian town house a highly desirable
address. There are just two bedrooms
(and a minimum three-night stay during
festival periods) so book well in advance.

ARDMOR HOUSE B&B ££
(☎ 0131-554 4944; www.ardmorhouse.com; 74
Pilrig St; s £50-75, d £75-145; 📶) The 'gay-
owned, straight-friendly' Ardmor is a
stylishly renovated Victorian house with
five en suite bedrooms, and all those
little touches that make a place special –
an open fire, thick towels, crisp white bed
linen and free newspapers at breakfast.

EDINBURGH CENTRAL YOUTH HOSTEL
Hostel £
(SYHA; Map p66; ☎ 0131-524 2090; www.edin
burghcentral.org; 9 Haddington Pl, Leith Walk;
dm £16-26, s/tw from £34/51; @ 📶) This
modern, purpose-built hostel, about a
half-mile north of Waverley train station,
is a big (300 beds), flashy, five-star
establishment with its own cafe-bistro
as well as self-catering kitchen, smart
and comfortable eight-bed dorms and
private rooms, and mod cons including
keycard entry and plasma-screen TVs.

 Eating

In the last decade there has been a
boom in the number of restaurants
in Edinburgh – the city now has more

DISCOVER EDINBURGH

restaurants per head of population than London. Eating out has become a commonplace event rather than something reserved for special occasions, and the choice of eateries ranges from stylish but inexpensive bistros and cafes to gourmet restaurants.

Old Town

OUTSIDER Bistro ££

(☏ 0131-226 3131; 15 George IV Bridge; mains £8-13; ⏲noon-11pm) This Edinburgh stalwart is known for its rainforest interior (potted ferns in atmospheric dimness) and has a brilliant menu that jumps straight in with mains such as chorizo and chickpea casserole. The Sunday brunch features DJs and hangover-busting breakfasts. Very popular, so best to book ahead.

ONDINE Seafood £££

(☏ 0131-226 1888; www.ondinerestaurant.co.uk; 2 George IV Bridge; mains £14-24; ⏲noon-10pm)

A relative newcomer (part of the Hotel Missoni), Ondine has rapidly become one of Edinburgh's finest seafood restaurants, with a menu based on sustainably sourced fish. Take an octopus-inspired seat at the curved Crustacean Bar and tuck into lobster thermidor or roast shellfish platter. The two-course lunch (noon to 2.30pm) and pre-theatre (5pm to 6.30pm) menu costs £15.

TOWER Scottish £££

(☏ 0131-225 3003; www.tower-restaurant.com; Museum of Scotland, Chambers St; mains £15-25; ⏲noon-11pm) Chic and sleek, with a great view of the castle, Tower is set atop the Museum of Scotland building. A star-studded guest list of celebrities have enjoyed its menu of quality Scottish food, simply prepared – try half a dozen oysters followed by a fillet of Borders beef. A two-course pre-theatre menu (£15) is available from 5pm to 6.30pm.

Edinburgh for Kids

Edinburgh has numerous attractions for children, and most things to see and do are child-friendly. Kids under five travel for free on Edinburgh buses, and five- to 15-year-olds pay a flat fare of 70p.

The Edinburgh & Scotland Information Centre has lots of info on children's events, and the handy guidebook *Edinburgh for Under Fives* can be found in most bookshops. The *List* magazine (www.list.co.uk) has a special kids section listing children's activities and events in and around Edinburgh. The week-long **Imaginate Festival** (www.imaginate.org.uk) of children's theatre, dance and puppetry takes place each year in late May/early June.

There are good, safe **playgrounds** in most Edinburgh parks, including Princes Street Gardens West, Inverleith Park (opposite the Royal Botanic Garden), George V Park (New Town), and the Meadows and Bruntsfield Links.

Some more ideas for outdoor activities include exploring the **Royal Botanic Garden**, going to the **Edinburgh Zoo**, visiting the statue of **Greyfriars Bobby** and playing on the beach at **Cramond**. During the Edinburgh and Fringe Festivals there is also plenty of **street theatre** for kids, especially on the High St and at the foot of The Mound, and in December there's an open-air ice rink and fairground rides in Princes Street Gardens.

If it's raining, you can visit the Discovery Centre, a hands-on activity zone on Level 3 of the **Museum of Scotland**, play on the flumes at the **Royal Commonwealth Pool** (Map p66; www.edinburghleisure.co.uk; 21 Dalkeith Rd), try out the earthquake simulator at **Our Dynamic Earth**, or take a tour of the haunted **Real Mary King's Close**.

Detour:
Abbotsford

Fans of Sir Walter Scott should visit his former residence, **Abbotsford** (www.scottsabbotsford.co.uk; adult/child £7/3.50; ⊙9.30am-5pm Mon-Sat, 11am-4pm Sun late Mar–Oct, 9.30am-5pm Sun Jun-Sep). The inspiration he drew from the surrounding 'wild' countryside influenced many of his most famous works. A collection of Scott memorabilia is on display, including many personal possessions.

The mansion is on the B6360 minor road between Galashiels and Melrose, 38 miles southeast of Edinburgh via the A7.

MUMS   Cafe £
(www.monstermashcafe.co.uk; 4a Forrest Rd; mains £6-8; ⊙8am-10pm Mon-Fri, 9am-10pm Sat, 10am-10pm Sun) After a change of name due to management fall-outs, the original founder of Monster Mash has reopened with a new name. This nostalgia-fuelled cafe continues to serve up classic British comfort food of the 1950s – bangers and mash, shepherd's pie, fish and chips. But there's a twist – the food is all top-quality nosh freshly prepared from local produce, including Crombie's gourmet sausages. And there's even a wine list!

ALWAYS SUNDAY   Cafe £
(www.alwayssunday.co.uk; 170 High St, Royal Mile; mains £4-8; ⊙8am-6pm Mon-Fri, 9am-6pm Sat & Sun) If the thought of a greasy fry-up is enough to put you off your breakfast, head instead for this bright and breezy cafe that dishes up hearty but healthy grub such as fresh fruit smoothies, crisp salads, homemade soups and speciality sandwiches, washed down with fairtrade coffee or herbal tea.

CAFÉ MARLAYNE   French ££
(www.cafemarlayne.com; 7 Old Fishmarket Close, High St; 2-course dinner £15; ⊙lunch & dinner Tue-Sat) The second branch of the New Town French bistro (see p101) is a hidden gem, down a steep cobbled alley off the Royal Mile, with a changed-daily menu of market-fresh produce and a lovely little lunchtime sun-trap of an outdoor terrace.

GRAIN STORE   French/Scottish £££
(☎ 0131-225 7635; www.grainstore-restaurant.co.uk; 30 Victoria St; mains £14-28; ⊙lunch & dinner) An atmospheric upstairs dining room on picturesque Victoria St, the Grain Store has a well-earned reputation for serving the finest Scottish produce, perfectly prepared – from seared scallops with peas and bacon, to tender wild hare cooked in a pastry parcel. Three-course lunch for £15 is good value. Booking recommended.

MAXIE'S BISTRO   Bistro ££
(5b Johnston Tce; mains £8-14; ⊙11am-11pm) Maxie's candlelit bistro, with its cushion-lined nooks set amid stone walls and wooden beams is a pleasant enough setting for a cosy dinner, but at summer lunchtimes people queue for the outdoor tables on the terrace overlooking Victoria St. The food is dependable – Maxie's has been in the food business for more than 20 years – ranging from pastas, steaks and stir-fries to seafood platters and daily specials, and there's an excellent selection of wines.

PANCHO VILLA'S   Mexican ££
(☎ 0131-557 4416; www.panchovillas.co.uk; 240 Canongate; mains £10-15; ⊙noon-10pm Mon-Sat, 5-10pm Sun) With a Mexican-born owner and lots of Latin American and Spanish staff, it's not surprising that this colourful and lively restaurant is one of the most authentic-feeling Mexican places in town. The dinner menu includes delicious steak fajitas and great vegetarian spinach enchiladas. It's often busy, so book ahead.

AMBER   Scottish ££
(☎ 0131-477 8477; www.amber-restaurant.co.uk; 354 Castlehill; mains £12-18; ⊙noon-3.45pm

daily, 7-9pm Tue-Sat) You've got to love a place where the waiter greets you with the words, 'My name is Craig, and I'll be your whisky adviser for this evening'. Located in the Scotch Whisky Experience, this whisky-themed restaurant manages to avoid the tourist clichés and create genuinely interesting and flavoursome dishes such as fillet of pork with black pudding and whisky and apple compote, or vegetarian haggis with a whisky cream sauce.

New Town

OLOROSO   Scottish £££
(Map p82; ☎ 0131-226 7614; www.oloroso.co.uk; 33 Castle St; mains £16-25; ☺restaurant noon-2.30pm & 7-10.30pm, bar 11am-1am) Oloroso is one of Edinburgh's most stylish restaurants, perched on a glass-encased New Town rooftop with views across a Mary Poppins' chimneyscape to the Firth of Forth and Fife hills. Swathed in sophisticated cream linen and charcoal upholstery enlivened with splashes of deep yellow, the dining room serves top-notch Scottish produce with Asian and Mediterranean touches. Two-course lunch £18.50.

CAFÉ MARLAYNE   French ££
(Map p82; ☎ 0131-226 2230; www.cafemarlayne .com; 76 Thistle St; mains £13-15; ☺lunch & dinner) All weathered wood and candlelit tables, little Café Marlayne is a cosy nook offering French farmhouse cooking – *brandade de morue* with green salad, slow roast rack of lamb, *boudin noir* (black pudding) with scallops and sautéed potato – at very reasonable prices. Booking recommended (there's another branch in the Old Town).

VALVONA & CROLLA VINCAFFÈ
Italian ££
(Map p82; ☎ 0131-557 0088; www.valvonacrolla .co.uk; 11 Multrees Walk, St Andrew Sq; mains £10-16; ☺9.30am-late Mon-Sat, noon-5pm Sun; 🛜) Foodie colours dominate the decor at this delightful Italian bistro – bottle-green pillars and banquettes, chocolate-and-cream coloured walls, espresso-black tables – a perfect backdrop for VinCaffè's superb antipasto (£15 for two), washed down with a bottle of pink Pinot Grigio.

MUSSEL INN   Seafood ££
(Map p82; www.mussel-inn.com; 61-65 Rose St; mains £10-22; ☺noon-3pm & 5.30-10pm Mon-Thu,

Sir Walter Scott's library, Abbotsford

99

noon-10pm Fri-Sun) Owned by west-coast shellfish farmers, the Mussel Inn provides a direct outlet for fresh Scottish seafood. The busy restaurant, decorated with bright beechwood indoors, spills out onto the pavement in summer. A kilogram pot of mussels with a choice of sauces – try leek, Dijon mustard and cream – costs £11.50.

CAFE ROYAL OYSTER BAR
Seafood £££

(Map p82; 📞 0131-556 4124; www.caferoyal.org. uk; 17a West Register St; mains £17-24; ⏱noon-2pm & 7-10pm) Pass through the revolving doors on the corner of West Register St and you're transported back to Victorian times – a palace of glinting mahogany, polished brass, marble floors, stained glass, Doulton tiles, gilded cornices and starched table linen so thick that it creaks when you fold it. The menu is mostly classic seafood, from oysters on ice to *coquilles St Jacques Parisienne* and lobster thermidor, augmented by a handful of beef and game dishes.

ETEAKET
Cafe £

(Map p82; www.eteaket.co.uk; 41 Frederick St; mains £4-6; ⏱8am-7pm Mon-Sat, 10am-7pm Sun) A 'tea boutique' serving more than 40 varieties of leaf tea, this cosy cafe also offers a tempting range of breakfasts (bagels, toasted croissants, scrambled eggs) and fresh, wholesome sandwiches (ciabatta with hummus, feta cheese and sunblush tomatoes) and afternoon tea (scones with jam and clotted cream).

STAC POLLY
Scottish £££

(Map p82; 📞 0131-556 2231; www.stacpolly.com; 29-33 Dublin St; mains £18-22; ⏱lunch Mon-Fri, dinner Mon-Sat) Named after a mountain in northwestern Scotland, Stac Polly's kitchen adds sophisticated twists to fresh Highland produce. Dishes such as haggis in filo parcels with sweet plum and red wine sauce, and rump of lamb with chervil cake and puy lentils, keep the punters coming back for more.

BLUE MOON CAFE
Cafe £

(Map p66; www.bluemooncafe.co.uk; 1 Barony St; mains £7-8; ⏱10am-10pm) The Blue Moon is the focus of Broughton St's gay social life, always busy, always friendly, and serving up delicious nachos, salads, sandwiches and baked potatoes. It's famous for its homemade burgers (beef, chicken or falafel), which come with a range of toppings, and delicious daily specials.

Leith

FISHERS BISTRO
Seafood ££

(Map p89; 📞 0131-554 5666; www.fishersbistros.co.uk; 1 The Shore; mains £10-35; ⏱noon-10.30pm) This cosy little restaurant, tucked beneath a 17th-century signal tower, is one of the city's best seafood places. The menu ranges widely in price, from cheaper dishes such as mackerel

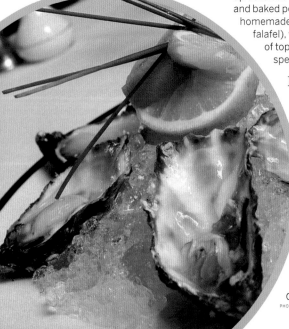

Oysters at the Cafe Royal Oyster Bar
PHOTOGRAPHER: JONATHAN SMITH

Top Three Lunch spots

○ **Urban Angel** (Map p82; ☎ 0131-225 6215; www.urban-angel.co.uk; 121 Hanover St; mains £8-12; ☯9am-10pm Mon-Sat, 10am-5pm Sun) A wholesome deli that puts the emphasis on fair-trade, organic and locally sourced produce, Urban Angel also has a delightfully informal cafe-bistro that serves all-day brunch (porridge with honey, French toast, eggs Benedict), tapas, and a wide range of light, snacky meals.

○ **La P'tite Folie** (Map p82; ☎ 0131-225 7983; 61 Frederick St; mains £16-18; ☯noon-3pm & 6-11pm Mon-Sat, 6-11pm Sun) This is a delightful little restaurant with a Breton owner whose menu includes French classics – onion soup, *moules marinières* – alongside steaks, seafood and a range of *plats du jour*. The two-course lunch is a bargain at £9.

○ **Petit Paris** (Map p72; ☎ 0131-226 2442; www.petitparis-restaurant.co.uk; 38-40 Grassmarket; mains £14-18; ☯noon-3pm & 5.30-11pm, closed Mon Oct-Mar) Like the name says, this is a little piece of Paris, complete with checked tablecloths, friendly waiters and good-value grub – the *moules-frites* (mussels and chips) are excellent. There's a lunch deal offering the *plat du jour* and a coffee for £8; add a starter and it's £11.

with beetroot, chilli and orange dressing, to more expensive delights such as North Berwick lobster served with garlic and herb butter.

DANIEL'S BISTRO　　　　French ££
(Map p89; ☎ 0131-553 5933; www.daniels-bistro.co.uk; 88 Commercial St; mains £8-15; ☯10am-10pm) Daniel comes from Alsace, and his all-French kitchen staff combine top Scottish and French produce with Gallic know-how to create a wide range of delicious dishes. The Provencal fish soup is excellent, and main courses range from boeuf bourguignon to cassoulet. A seriously filling three-course lunch is £9.70.

CHOP CHOP　　　　Chinese £
(Map p89; ☎ 0131-553 1818; 76 Commercial St; mains £7-10; ☯noon-2pm & 5.30-10pm Mon & Wed-Sat, noon-10pm Sun) Chop Chop is a Chinese restaurant with a difference, in that it serves dishes popular in China rather than Britain; as the slogan says, 'Can a billion people be wrong?'. No sweet-and-sour pork here, but a range of delicious dumplings filled with pork and coriander, beef and chilli, or lamb and leek, and unusual vegetarian dishes

such as aubergine fried with garlic and Chinese spices.

DINER 7　　　　Cafe ££
(Map p89; www.diner7.co.uk; 7 Commercial St; mains £8-12; ☯11.30am-11pm Thu-Sun, 4-11pm Mon-Wed) A neat local eatery with rust-coloured leather booths and banquettes, black and copper tables, and local art on the walls, this diner has a menu of succulent Aberdeen Angus steaks and homemade burgers, but also offers more unusual fare such as chicken and chorizo kebabs, or smoked haddock with black-pudding stovies.

MARTIN WISHART　　　　French £££
(Map p89; ☎ 0131-553 3557; www.martin-wishart.co.uk; 54 The Shore; 3-course lunch/dinner £28/60; ☯noon-2pm & 7-10pm Tue-Sat) In 2001 this restaurant became the first in Edinburgh to win a Michelin star. The eponymous chef has worked with Albert Roux, Marco Pierre White and Nick Nairn, and brings a modern French approach to the best Scottish produce, from roast scallop with Bellota ham and black cherry juice to roast loin of lamb in a herb crust with asparagus tortellini.

Drinking

Edinburgh has more than 700 bars, which are as varied as the population – everything from Victorian palaces to rough-and-ready drinking dens, and from real-ale howffs (pubs) to trendy cocktail bars.

Old Town

The pubs in the Grassmarket have outdoor tables on sunny summer afternoons, but in the evenings are favoured by boozed-up lads on the pull, so steer clear if that's not your thing. The Cowgate – the Grassmarket's extension to the east – is Edinburgh's clubland.

BOW BAR   Pub
(Map p72; 80 West Bow) One of the city's best traditional-style pubs (it's not as old as it looks) serving a range of excellent real ales and a vast selection of malt whiskies, the Bow Bar often has standing room only on Friday and Saturday evenings.

JOLLY JUDGE   Pub
(Map p72; www.jollyjudge.co.uk; 7a James Crt; 🛜) A snug little howff tucked away down a close, the Judge exudes a cosy 17th-century atmosphere (low, timber-beamed painted ceilings) and has the added attraction of a cheering open fire in cold weather. No music or gaming machines, just the buzz of conversation.

ECCO VINO   Wine Bar
(Map p72; www.eccovinoedinburgh.com; 19 Cockburn St) With outdoor tables on sunny afternoons, and cosy candlelit intimacy in the evenings, this comfortably cramped Tuscan-style wine bar offers a tempting range of Italian wines, though not all are available by the glass – best to share a bottle.

VILLAGER   Bar
(Map p72; www.villager-e.com; 49-50 George IV Bridge) A cross between a traditional pub and a pre-club bar, Villager has a comfortable, laid-back vibe. It can be standing room only in the main bar in the evenings (the cocktails are excellent), but the

Left: A busy pub in Edinburgh; **Below:** Outdoor dining on the Royal Mile

PHOTOGRAPHER: (LEFT) IZZET KERIBAR; (BELOW) WILL SALTER

side room, with its brown leather sofas and sub-tropical pot plants, comes into its own for a lazy Sunday afternoon with the papers.

ROYAL MILE TAVERN   Pub

(Map p72; www.royalmiletavern.com; 127 High St) An elegant, traditional bar lined with polished wood, mirrors and brass, Royal Mile serves real ale (Deuchars IPA and Caledonian 80/-), good wines and decent pub grub – fish and chips, steak and Guinness pie, sausage and mash etc.

LAST DROP   Pub

(Map p72; 74 Grassmarket) The name commemorates the gallows that used to stand nearby, but the only swingers today are the pub's partying clientele, largely students and backpackers.

BEEHIVE INN   Pub

(Map p72; 18-20 Grassmarket) The historic Beehive – a former coaching inn – is a big, buzzing party-pub, with a range of real ales, but the main attraction is sitting out the back in the Grassmarket's only beer garden, with views up to the castle.

New Town

Rose St (between Princes St and George St) was once a famous pub crawl, where generations of students, sailors and rugby fans would try to visit every pub on the street (around 17 of them) and down a pint of beer in each one.

OXFORD BAR   Pub

(Map p82; www.oxfordbar.com; 8 Young St) The Oxford is that rarest of things these days, a real pub for real people, with no 'theme', no music, no frills and no pretensions. 'The Ox' has been immortalised by Ian Rankin, author of the Inspector Rebus novels, who is a regular here, as is his fictional detective.

CUMBERLAND BAR   Pub

(Map p66; www.cumberlandbar.co.uk; 1-3 Cumberland St) Immortalised as the

103

stereotypical New Town pub in Alexander McCall Smith's serialised novel *44 Scotland Street,* the Cumberland has an authentic, traditional wood-brass-and-mirrors look (despite being relatively new), and serves well-looked-after, cask-conditioned ales and a wide range of malt whiskies. There's also a pleasant little beer garden outside.

GUILDFORD ARMS Pub
(Map p82; www.guildfordarms.com; 1 West Register St) Located next door to the Cafe Royal Circle Bar, the Guildford is another classic Victorian pub full of polished mahogany, brass and ornate cornices. The bar lunches are good – try to get a table in the unusual upstairs gallery, with a view over the sea of drinkers down below.

KENILWORTH Pub
(Map p82; 152-154 Rose St) A gorgeous, Edwardian drinking palace, complete with original fittings – from the tile floors, mahogany circle bar and gantry, to the ornate mirrors and gas lamps – the Kenilworth was Edinburgh's original gay bar back in the 1970s. Today it attracts a mixed crowd of all ages, and serves a good range of real ales and malt whiskies.

ROBERTSONS 37 BAR Pub
(Map p82; 37 Rose St) No 37 is to malt-whisky connoisseurs what the Diggers (now called the Athletic Arms) once was to real-ale fans. Its long gantry sports a choice of more than 100 single malts and the bar provides a quiet and elegant environment in which to sample them.

KAY'S BAR Pub
(Map p82; 39 Jamaica St) Housed in a former wine-merchant's office, tiny Kay's Bar is a cosy haven with a coal fire and a fine range of real ales. Good food is served in the back room at lunchtime, but you'll have to book a table – Kay's is a popular spot.

AMICUS APPLE Cocktail Bar
(Map p82; www.amicusapple.com; 15 Frederick St) This laid-back cocktail lounge is the hippest hang-out in the New Town. The drinks menu ranges from retro classics such as Bloody Mary and mojito, to original and unusual concoctions such as the Cuillin Martini (Tanqueray No 10 gin, Talisker malt whisky and smoked rosemary).

Leith

TEUCHTER'S LANDING Pub
(Map p89; 1 Dock Pl) A cosy warren of timber-lined nooks and crannies housed in a single-storey red-brick building (once a waiting room for ferries across the Firth of Forth), this real-ale and malt-whisky bar also has outdoor tables on a floating terrace in the dock.

PORT O'LEITH Pub
(Map p89; 58 Constitution St) This is a good, old-

Harbourside Leith

Top Five Vegetarian Restaurants

Many Edinburgh restaurants offer vegetarian options on the menu, but the places listed here are all 100% veggie.

○ **David Bann** (Map p72; ✆ 0131-556 5888; www.davidbann.com; 56-58 St Mary's St; mains £9-13; ⏰ noon-10pm Mon-Fri, 11am-10pm Sat & Sun) The food at this stylish restaurant – such as beetroot, apple and Dunsyre blue-cheese pudding, or crepe of Thai-spiced broccoli and smoked tofu – is guaranteed to win carnivore converts.

○ **L'Artichaut** (Map p66; ✆ 0131-558 1608; www.lartichaut.co.uk; 14 Eyre Pl; 2-/3-course meal £15/20; ⏰ lunch & dinner Tue-Sat, 12.30-8pm Sun) Fresh, seasonal produce is used at this inventive restaurant to create dishes such as rosemary and thyme pancake filled with aubergine and mozzarella, or spicy black-bean stew with glazed chicory and spiced cauliflower.

○ **Ann Purna** (Map p66; 45 St Patrick's Sq; mains £5-10; ⏰ noon-2pm & 5.30-11pm Mon-Fri, 5.30-11pm Sat & Sun) This little gem serves exclusively vegetarian dishes from southern India. Try a *thali* – a self-contained platter that has about half a dozen different dishes, including a dessert. You can get a light lunch for £5.

○ **Black Bo's** (Map p72; www.black-bos.com; 57-61 Blackfriars St; mains £10-13; ⏰ 6-10pm) You can't accuse this popular vegetarian and vegan eatery of being unadventurous. The daily specials are always interesting – beetroot and cashew balls stuffed with feta cheese with chilli and garlic yogurt, for example.

○ **Kalpna** (Map p72; www.kalpnarestaurant.com; 2-3 St Patrick Sq; mains £6-11; ⏰ noon-2pm & 5.30-10.30pm Mon-Sat year-round, plus 6-10.30pm Sun May-Sep) One of the best Indian restaurants in the country, vegetarian or otherwise. The lunch buffet (£7) is superb value.

fashioned, friendly local boozer, swathed with flags and cap bands left behind by visiting sailors – the harbour is just down the road. Pop in for a pint and you'll probably stay until closing time.

STARBANK INN Pub
(Map p89; www.starbankinn.co.uk; 64 Laverockbank Rd) The Starbank is an oasis of fine ales and good, homemade food on Edinburgh's windswept waterfront. In summer there's a sunny conservatory, and in winter a blazing fire to toast your toes in front of.

⭐ Entertainment

Edinburgh has a number of fine theatres and concert halls, and there are independent art-house cinemas as well as mainstream movie theatres. Many pubs offer entertainment ranging from live Scottish folk music to pop, rock and jazz as well as karaoke and quiz nights, while a range of stylish modern bars purvey house, dance and hip-hop to the pre-clubbing crowd.

The comprehensive source for what's-on info is *The List* (www.list.co.uk), an excellent listings magazine covering both Edinburgh and Glasgow. It's available from most newsagents, and is published fortnightly on a Thursday.

Live Music

Check out *The List* and the *Gig Guide* (www.gigguide.co.uk), a free email newsletter and listings website, to see who's playing where.

JAZZ, BLUES & ROCK

HENRY'S CELLAR   Rock/Indie
(Map p72; www.theraft.org.uk; 8a Morrison St)
One of Edinburgh's most eclectic live-
music venues, Henry's has something
going on every night of the week, from
rock and indie to 'Balkan-inspired folk',
funk to hip-hop to hardcore, staging
both local bands and acts from around
the world. Open till 3am at weekends.

WHISTLE BINKIE'S   Rock/Blues
(Map p72; www.whistlebinkies.com; 4-6 South
Bridge) This crowded cellar-bar just off
the Royal Mile has live music every night
till 3am, from rock and blues to folk and
jazz. Open-mic night on Monday and
breaking bands on Tuesday are showcases for new talent.

JAZZ BAR   Jazz
(Map p72; www.thejazzbar.co.uk; 1a Chambers
St; 🛜) This atmospheric cellar bar, with
its polished parquet floors, bare stone
walls, candlelit tables and stylish steel-
framed chairs, is owned and operated by
jazz musicians. There's live music every
night from 9pm to 3am, and on Saturday
from 3pm.

LIQUID ROOM   Rock/Indie
(Map p72; www.liquidroom.com; 9c Victoria
St) The Liquid Room (see also Clubs)
stages all kinds of gigs from local rock
bands to tribute bands to the Average
White Band. Check the program on the
website.

TRADITIONAL

The capital is a great place to hear
traditional Scottish (and Irish) folk
music, with a mix of regular spots and
impromptu sessions.

SANDY BELL'S   Folk
(Map p72; 25 Forrest Rd) This unassuming
bar is a stalwart of the traditional-music
scene (the founder's wife sang with The
Corries). There's music almost every
evening at 9pm, and also from 3pm
Saturday and Sunday.

ROYAL OAK   Folk
(Map p72; www.royal-oak-folk.com; 1 Infirmary St)
This popular folk pub is tiny, so get there
early (9pm start weekdays, 2.30pm
Saturday) if you want to be sure of a
place. Sundays from 4pm to 7pm is open

Gentoo Penguin at Edinburgh Zoo

DISCOVER EDINBURGH

session – bring your own instruments (or a good singing voice).

Nightclubs

Edinburgh's club scene has some fine DJ talent and is well worth exploring; there are club-night listings in *The List*. Most of the venues are concentrated in and around the twin sumps of Cowgate and Calton Rd – so it's downhill all the way...

BONGO CLUB   Multi-arts Venue
(Map p66; www.thebongoclub.co.uk; Moray House, Paterson's Land, 37 Holyrood Rd) The weird and wonderful Bongo Club is home to Big N Bashy, a Saturday-night club dedicated to reggae, grime, dubstep and jungle. Also worth checking out is the booming bass of roots and dub reggae night Messenger Sound System (boasting 'a sound system that could knock you out'). The club is open as a cafe and exhibition space during the day.

CABARET VOLTAIRE   Club/Live Music
(Map p72; www.thecabaretvoltaire.com; 36 Blair St) An atmospheric warren of stone-lined vaults houses Edinburgh's most 'alternative' club, which eschews huge dance floors and egotistical DJ-worship in favour of a 'creative crucible' hosting an eclectic mix of DJs, live acts, comedy, theatre, visual arts and the spoken word. Well worth a look.

LIQUID ROOM   Club/Live Music
(Map p72; www.liquidroom.com; 9c Victoria St) Set in a subterranean vault deep beneath Victoria St, the Liquid Room is a superb club venue with a thundering sound system. There are regular club nights Wednesday to Saturday as well as live bands. The long-running and recently relaunched Evol (Friday from 10.30pm) is an Edinburgh institution catering to the indie-kid crowd, and is regularly voted as Scotland's top club night out.

OPAL LOUNGE   Club
(Map p82; www.opallounge.co.uk; 51 George St) The Opal Lounge is jammed at weekends with affluent twenty-somethings who've spent £200 and two hours in front of a mirror to achieve that artlessly scruffy

Detour:
Edinburgh Zoo

Opened in 1913, the **Edinburgh Zoo** (www.edinburghzoo.org.uk; 134 Corstorphine Rd; adult/child £15.50/11; ⏱9am-6pm Apr-Sep, 9am-5pm Oct & Mar, 9am-4.30pm Nov-Feb) is one of the world's leading conservation zoos. Edinburgh's captive breeding program has saved many endangered species, including Siberian tigers, pygmy hippos and red pandas. The main attractions are the **penguin parade** (the zoo's penguins go for a walk every day at 2.15pm), the sea lion training session (daily at 11.15am), the rainbow lorikeet handling session (check the website for details) and the sun bears (newly arrived in 2010).

The zoo is 2.5 miles west of the city centre; take Lothian Bus 12, 26 or 31, First Bus 16, 18, 80 or 86, or the Airlink Bus 100 westbound from Princes St.

look. During the week, when the air-kissing crowds thin out, it's a good place to relax with an expensive but expertly mixed cocktail. Expect to queue on weekend evenings.

LULU   Club
(Map p82; www.luluedinburgh.co.uk; 125 George St) Lush leather sofas, red satin cushions, fetishistic steel mesh curtains and dim red lighting all help to create a decadent atmosphere in this drop-dead-gorgeous club venue beneath the Tigerlily boutique hotel. Resident and guest DJs show a bit more originality than at your average club.

Cinemas

Film buffs will find plenty to keep them happy in Edinburgh's art-house cinemas,

Top Five Traditional Pubs

Edinburgh has many traditional 19th- and early-20th-century pubs with much of their original decorations, serving real ales and a staggering range of whiskies.

○ **Athletic Arms** (Diggers; Map p66; 1-3 Angle Park Tce) Named for workers at the cemetery across the street, the Diggers dates from the 1890s. Staunchly traditional – the decor has barely changed – it's revived its reputation as an ale-drinker's mecca by serving locally brewed Diggers' 80-shilling ale. Packed with football and rugby fans on match days.

○ **Abbotsford** (Map p82; www.theabbotsford.com; 3 Rose St) The Edwardian splendour of the Abbotsford has long attracted writers, actors and journalists. Dating from 1902, the pub's centrepiece is a splendid, mahogany island bar. Good selection of Scottish and English real ales.

○ **Bennet's Bar** (Map p66; 8 Leven St) Situated beside the King's Theatre, Bennet's has managed to hang on to almost all of its beautiful Victorian fittings, from the leaded, stained-glass windows and ornate mirrors to the wooden gantry and the brass taps on the bar. Over 100 malt whiskies to choose from.

○ **Cafe Royal Circle Bar** (Map p82; www.caferoyal.org.uk; 17 West Register St) Perhaps the classic Edinburgh bar, the Cafe Royal's main claims to fame are its magnificent oval bar and the series of Doulton tile portraits of famous Victorian inventors.

○ **Sheep Heid** (www.sheepheid.co.uk; 43-45 The Causeway, Duddingston) Possibly the oldest inn in Edinburgh – the licences dates back to 1360 – the Sheep Heid feels more like a country pub. Near Arthur's Seat, it's famous for its 19th-century skittles alley and the lovely little beer garden.

---

while popcorn munchers can choose from a range of multiplexes.

CAMEO — Cinema
(Map p66; www.picturehouses.co.uk; 38 Home St) The three-screen, independently owned Cameo is a good, old-fashioned cinema showing an imaginative mix of mainstream and art-house movies. There is a good program of midnight movies and Sunday matinees, and the seats in Screen 1 are big enough to get lost in.

FILMHOUSE — Cinema
(Map p72; www.filmhousecinema.com; 88 Lothian Rd; 🛜) The Filmhouse is the main venue for the annual Edinburgh International Film Festival and screens a full program of art-house, classic, foreign and second-run films, with lots of themes, retrospectives and 70mm screenings. It has wheelchair access to all three screens.

Classical Music, Opera & Ballet

The following are the main venues for classical music.

EDINBURGH FESTIVAL THEATRE — Ballet/Opera
(Map p72; www.eft.co.uk; 13-29 Nicolson St; ⏲box office 10am-6pm Mon-Sat, to 8pm show nights, 4pm-showtime Sun) A beautifully restored art deco theatre with a modern frontage, the Festival is the city's main venue for opera, dance and ballet, but also stages musicals, concerts, drama and children's shows.

USHER HALL Classical Music
(Map p72; www.usherhall.co.uk; Lothian Rd; box office 10.30am-5.30pm, to 8pm show nights) The architecturally impressive Usher Hall hosts concerts by the Royal Scottish National Orchestra (RSNO) and performances of popular music.

ST GILES CATHEDRAL Classical Music
(Map p72; www.stgilescathedral.org.uk; High St) The big kirk on the Royal Mile plays host to a regular and varied program of classical music, including popular lunchtime and evening concerts and organ recitals. The cathedral choir sings at the 10am and 11.30am Sunday services.

QUEEN'S HALL Classical Music
(Map p66; www.thequeenshall.net; Clerk St; box office 10am-5.30pm Mon-Sat, or till 15min after show begins) The home of the Scottish Chamber Orchestra also stages jazz, blues, folk, rock and comedy.

Theatre, Musicals & Comedy

ROYAL LYCEUM THEATRE
Drama/Musicals
(Map p72; www.lyceum.org.uk; 30b Grindlay St; box office 10am-6pm Mon-Sat, to 8pm show nights) A grand Victorian theatre located beside the Usher Hall, the Lyceum stages drama, concerts, musicals and ballet.

TRAVERSE THEATRE Drama/Dance
(Map p72; www.traverse.co.uk; 10 Cambridge St; box office 10am-6pm Mon-Sat, till 8pm show nights) The Traverse is the main focus for new Scottish writing and stages an adventurous program of contemporary drama and dance. The box office is only open on Sunday (from 4pm) when there's a show on.

KING'S THEATRE Drama/Musicals
(Map p66; www.eft.co.uk; 2 Leven St, Bruntsfield; box office open 1hr before show) King's is a traditional theatre with a program of musicals, drama, comedy and its famous Christmas pantomime.

EDINBURGH PLAYHOUSE Musicals
(Map p82; www.edinburgh-playhouse.co.uk; 18-22 Greenside Pl; box office 10am-6pm Mon-Sat, to 8pm show nights) This restored theatre at the top of Leith Walk stages Broadway musicals, dance shows, opera and popular-music concerts.

Bennet's Bar

WILL SALTER

🛍 Shopping

Princes St is Edinburgh's principal shopping street, lined with all the big high-street stores, with many smaller shops along pedestrianised Rose St, and more expensive designer boutiques on George St. There are also two big shopping centres in the New Town – **Princes Mall**, at the eastern end of Princes St, and the nearby **St James Centre** at the top of Leith St, plus a designer shopping complex with a flagship Harvey Nichols store on the eastern side of St Andrew Sq. The huge **Ocean Terminal** in Leith is the biggest shopping centre in the city.

For more off-beat shopping – including fashion, music, crafts, gifts and jewellery – head for the cobbled lanes of Cockburn, Victoria and St Mary's Sts, all near the Royal Mile in the Old Town, William St in the western part of New Town, and the Stockbridge district, immediately north of the New Town.

Cashmere & Wool

Woollen textiles and knitwear are one of Scotland's classic exports. Scottish cashmere – a fine, soft wool from young goats and lambs – provides the most luxurious and expensive knitwear and has been seen gracing the torsos of pop star Robbie Williams and England footballer David Beckham.

Kinross Cashmere   Knitwear
(Map p72; www.cashmerestore.com; 2 St Giles St)
Wide range of traditional and modern knitwear.

Joyce Forsyth Designer Knitwear
                                              Knitwear
(Map p72; www.joyceforsyth.co.uk; 42 Candlemaker Row; ☺Tue-Sat) Colourful designs that will drag your ideas about woollens firmly into the 21st century.

Edinburgh Woollen Mill   Knitwear
(Map p82; www.ewm.co.uk; 139 Princes St) An old stalwart of the tourist trade, with a good selection of traditional jerseys, cardigans, scarves, shawls and rugs.

Street performers at the Edinburgh Festival Fringe

Festival City

August in Edinburgh sees a frenzy of festivals, with half a dozen world-class events running at the same time.

EDINBURGH INTERNATIONAL FESTIVAL

First held in 1947 to mark a return to peace after the ordeal of WWII, the **Edinburgh International Festival** (0131-473 2099; www.eif.co.uk) is festooned with superlatives – the oldest, the biggest, the most famous, the best in the world. The original was a modest affair, but today hundreds of the world's top musicians and performers congregate in Edinburgh for three weeks of diverse and inspirational music, opera, theatre and dance.

The festival takes place over the three weeks ending on the first Saturday in September; the program is usually available from April. Tickets for popular events – especially music and opera – sell out quickly, so it's best to book as far in advance as possible. You can buy tickets in person at the **Hub** (Map p72), or by phone or internet.

EDINBURGH FESTIVAL FRINGE

When the first Edinburgh Festival was held in 1947, there were eight theatre companies who didn't make it onto the main program. Undeterred, they grouped together and held their own mini-festival, on the fringe, and an Edinburgh institution was born. Today the **Edinburgh Festival Fringe** (Map p72; 0131-226 0026; www.edfringe.com; Edinburgh Festival Fringe Office, 180 High St) is *the* biggest festival of the performing arts anywhere in the world.

The Fringe take place over 3½ weeks in August, the last two weeks overlapping with the first two of the Edinburgh International Festival.

Tartan & Highland Dress

There are dozens of shops along the Royal Mile and Princes St where you can buy kilts and tartan goods.

Kinloch Anderson Highland Dress
(Map p89; www.kinlochanderson.com; 4 Dock St, Leith) One of the best, this was founded in 1868 and is still family-run. Kinloch Anderson is a supplier of kilts and Highland dress to the royal family.

Geoffrey (Tailor) Inc Highland Dress
(Map p72; www.geoffreykilts.co.uk; 57-59 High St) Can fit you out in traditional Highland dress, or run up a kilt in your own clan tartan. Its offshoot, 21st Century Kilts, offers modern fashion kilts in a variety of fabrics.

ℹ Information

Internet Resources

Edinburgh Architecture (www.edinburgh architecture.co.uk) Informative site dedicated to the city's modern architecture.

Edinburgh & Lothians Tourist Board (www .edinburgh.org) Official tourist-board site, with listings of accommodation, sights, activities and events.

Edinburgh Festival Guide (www.edinburgh festivals.co.uk) Everything you need to know about Edinburgh's many festivals.

Events Edinburgh (www.eventsedinburgh.org .uk) The city council's official events guide.

The List (www.list.co.uk) Listings of restaurants, pubs, clubs and nightlife.

GARETH MCCORMACK

Medical Services

Chemists (pharmacists) can advise you on minor ailments. At least one local chemist remains open round the clock – its location will be displayed in the windows of other chemists. For urgent medical advice you can call the NHS 24 Helpline (☎ 08454 24 24 24; www.nhs24.com).

For urgent dental treatment you can visit the walk-in Chalmers Dental Centre (3 Chalmers St; ⏱ 9am-4.45pm Mon-Thu, 9am-4.15pm Fri). In the case of a dental emergency in the evening or on the weekend, call Lothian Dental Advice Line (☎ 0131-536 4800).

Boots (48 Shandwick Pl; ⏱ 8am-9pm Mon-Fri, 8am-6pm Sat, 10.30am-4.30pm Sun) Chemist open longer hours than most.

Royal Hospital for Sick Children (☎ 0131-536 0000; www.nhslothian.scot.nhs.uk; 9 Sciennes Rd) Casualty department for children aged under 13 years; located in Marchmont.

Royal Infirmary of Edinburgh (☎ 0131-536 1000; www.nhslothian.scot.nhs.uk; 51 Little France Cres, Old Dalkeith Rd) Edinburgh's main general hospital; has 24-hour accident and emergency department.

Western General Hospital (☎ 0131-537 1330; www.nhslothian.scot.nhs.uk; Crewe Rd South; ⏱ 9am-9pm) For non-life-threatening injuries and ailments, you can attend the Minor Injuries Unit without having to make an appointment.

Tourist Information

Edinburgh & Scotland Information Centre (ESIC; Map p82; ☎ 0845 225 5121; www.edinburgh.org; Princes Mall, 3 Princes St; ⏱ 9am-9pm Mon-Sat & 10am-8pm Sun Jul & Aug, 9am-7pm Mon-Sat & 10am-7pm Sun May, Jun & Sep, 9am-5pm Mon-Wed & 9am-6pm Thu-Sun Oct-Apr) Includes an accommodation booking service, currency exchange, gift- and bookshop, internet access, and counters selling tickets for Edinburgh city tours and Scottish Citylink bus services.

ℹ Getting There & Away

Air

Edinburgh Airport (☎ 0131-333 1000; www.edinburghairport.com), 8 miles west of the city, has numerous flights to other parts of Scotland and the UK, Ireland and mainland Europe. See p351 for details of flights to Edinburgh from outside Scotland. FlyBe/Loganair (☎ 0871

700 2000; www.loganair.co.uk) operates daily flights to Inverness, Wick, Orkney, Shetland and Stornoway.

Bus

Edinburgh Bus Station (Map p82) is at the northeast corner of St Andrew Sq, with pedestrian entrances from the square and from Elder St. For timetable information, call **Traveline** (☎0871 200 22 33; www.travelinescotland.com). **Scottish Citylink** (☎0871 266 3333; www.citylink.co.uk) buses connect Edinburgh with all of Scotland's cities and major towns. The following are sample one-way fares departing from Edinburgh.

DESTINATION	FARE (£)	DURATION (HR)	FREQUENCY
Aberdeen	26	3¼	3 daily
Dundee	14	2	hourly
Fort William	30	4-5	8 daily
Glasgow	6	1¼	every 15min
Inverness	26	4	hourly
Portree	46	7	1 daily
Stirling	7	1	hourly

It's also worth checking with **Megabus** (☎0900 160 0900; www.megabus.com) for cheap intercity bus fares (from as little as £3) from Edinburgh to Aberdeen, Dundee, Glasgow, Inverness and Perth.

See the Transport chapter, p349, for details of buses to Edinburgh from London and the rest of the UK.

Car & Motorcycle

Arriving in or leaving Edinburgh by car during the morning and evening rush hours (7.30am to 9.30am and 4.30pm to 6.30pm Monday to Friday) is an experience you can live without. Try to time your journey to avoid these periods.

Edinburgh Military Tattoo

August kicks off with the **Edinburgh Military Tattoo** (Map p82; ☎0131-225 1188; www.edintattoo.co.uk; Tattoo Office, 32 Market St), a spectacular display of military marching bands, massed pipes and drums, acrobats, cheerleaders and motorcycle display teams, all played out in front of the magnificent backdrop of the floodlit castle. Each show traditionally finishes with a lone piper, dramatically lit, playing a lament on the battlements. The Tattoo takes place over the first three weeks of August (from a Friday to a Saturday); there's one show at 9pm Monday to Friday and two (at 7.30pm and 10.30pm) on Saturday, but no performance on Sunday.

Ocean Terminal shopping centre (p110)
PHOTOGRAPHER: JONATHAN SMITH

KARL BLACKWELL

Train

The main terminus in Edinburgh is Waverley train station (Map p82), located in the heart of the city. Trains arriving from, and departing for, the west also stop at Haymarket station (Map p66), which is more convenient for the West End.

You can buy tickets, make reservations and get travel information at the Edinburgh Rail Travel Centre (🕙4.45am-12.30am Mon-Sat, 7am-12.30am Sun) in Waverley station. For fare and timetable information, phone the National Rail Enquiry Service (📞08457 48 49 50; www.nationalrail .co.uk) or use the Journey Planner on the website.

First ScotRail operates a regular shuttle service between Edinburgh and Glasgow (£11, 50 minutes, every 15 minutes), and frequent daily services to all Scottish cities including Aberdeen (£40, 2½ hours), Dundee (£20, 1¼ hours) and Inverness (£55, 3¼ hours).

See the Transport chapter, p350, for details of trains to Edinburgh from London.

🛈 Getting Around

To/From the Airport

The Lothian Buses Airlink (www.flybybus.com) service 100 runs from Waverley Bridge, outside the train station, to the airport (£3/6 one way/ return, 30 minutes, every 10 to 15 minutes) via the West End and Haymarket.

An airport taxi to the city centre costs around £16 and takes about 20 minutes. Both buses and taxis depart from outside the arrivals hall; go out through the main doors and turn left.

Car & Motorcycle

Though useful for day trips beyond the city, a car in central Edinburgh is more of a liability than a convenience. There is restricted access on Princes St, George St and Charlotte Sq, many streets are one way and finding a parking place in the city centre is like striking gold. Queen's Dr around Holyrood Park is closed to motorised traffic on Sunday.

CAR RENTAL

All the big, international car-rental agencies have offices in Edinburgh (see p352).

There are many smaller, local agencies that offer better rates. One of the best is Arnold Clark (📞0131-657 9120; www.arnoldclarkrental.co.uk; 20 Seafield Rd East) near Portobello, which charges from £26 a day, or £128 a week for a small car, including VAT and insurance.

PARKING

There's no parking on main roads into the city from 7.30am to 6.30pm Monday to Saturday. Also,

DISCOVER EDINBURGH

parking in the city centre can be a nightmare. **On-street parking** is controlled by self-service ticket machines from 8.30am to 6.30pm Monday to Saturday, and costs £1 to £2 per hour, with a 30-minute to four-hour maximum. If you break the rules, you'll get a fine, often within minutes of your ticket expiring – Edinburgh's parking wardens are both numerous and notorious. The fine is £60, reduced to £30 if you pay up within 14 days. Cars parked illegally will be towed away. There are large, long-stay car parks at the St James Centre, Greenside Pl, New St, Castle Tce and Morrison St. Motorcycles can be parked free at designated areas in the city centre.

Public Transport

For the moment, Edinburgh's public-transport system consists entirely of buses (a tram network is under construction, due to come into operation in 2012). The main operators are Lothian Buses (www.lothianbuses.co.uk) and First (www.first edinburgh.co.uk); for timetable information contact Traveline (☏ 0871 200 22 33; www .travelinescotland.com).

Bus timetables, route maps and fare guides are posted at all main bus stops, and you can pick up a copy of the free *Lothian Buses Route Map* from **Lothian Buses Travelshops**:

Hanover St (27 Hanover St; ⊘9am-6pm Mon-Fri, 10am-6pm Sat)

Shandwick Pl (7 Shandwick Pl; ⊘9am-6pm Mon-Fri, 10am-6pm Sat)

Waverley Bridge (31 Waverley Bridge; ⊘9am-6pm Mon-Fri, 10am-6pm Sat, 10am-5.15pm Sun)

Adult fares are £1.20 from the driver or £1.10 from automatic ticket machines at bus stops; children aged under five travel free and those aged five to 15 pay a flat fare of 70p. On Lothian Buses you must pay the driver the exact fare, but First buses will give change. Lothian Bus drivers also sell a Daysaver ticket (£3) that gives unlimited travel (on Lothian Buses only, excluding night buses) for a day. **Night-service buses** (www.nightbuses.com), which run hourly between midnight and 5am, charge a flat fare of £3.

You can also buy a **Ridacard** (from Travelshops; not available from bus drivers) that gives unlimited travel for one week for £15.

The Lothian Buses lost property office (☏ 0131-558 8858; lostproperty@lothianbuses .co.uk; Main Depot, Annadale St; ⊘10am-1.30pm Mon-Fri) is north of the city centre.

Taxi

Edinburgh's black taxis can be hailed in the street, ordered by phone (extra 80p charge), or picked up at one of the many central ranks.

Central Taxis (☏ 0131-229 2468)

City Cabs (☏ 0131-228 1211)

ComCab (☏ 0131-272 8000)

Glasgow & Loch Lomond

Regenerating and evolving at a dizzying pace, Glasgow is edgy, modish and downright ballsy. Its Victorian architectural legacy is now swamped with style bars, top-notch restaurants to tickle your taste buds and a hedonistic club culture that will bring out your nocturnal instincts. Glasgow's pounding live-music scene is one of the best in Britain, and accessible through countless venues dedicated to home-grown beats.

Yet nightlife is only the beginning. Top-drawer museums and galleries abound, where the city's proud industrial and artistic heritage is innovatively displayed. Charles Rennie Mackintosh's sublime works dot the town, and the River Clyde, traditionally associated with Glasgow's earthier side, is now a symbol of the city's renaissance.

If that's not enough, one of Glasgow's biggest selling points is that it sits on the doorstep of some of Scotland's finest scenery – Loch Lomond and the Trossachs, the country's first national park, is just 20 miles away.

View of Glasgow from the southern bank of the River Clyde **117**
PHOTOGRAPHER: MARTIN MOOS

Greater Glasgow

Jordanhill

To Loch Lomond (15 mi)

To Milngavie (8mi)

KELVINSIDE

Great Western Rd

A81

Firhill Basin

Hyndland

Hyndland Rd

Botanic Gardens

River Kelvin

Garscube Rd

Victoria Park

BROOMHILL

A814

A82

Clydeside Expressway

Byres Rd

HILLHEAD

❸

Partick

Dumbarton Rd

❶

KELVINGROVE

GARNETHILL

Charing Cross

River Clyde

Exhibition Centre

A814

ANDERSTON

Anderston

Argyle St

GOVAN

West Quay

See West End Map (p136)

To Clydebuilt (2mi); Glasgow International Airport (3mi); Greenock (27mi)

IBROX

Edmiston Dr

M8

Paisley Rd West

KINNING PARK

M8

Eglington St

M8

A737

Scotland St

Paisley Rd West

To Paisley (5mi)

Bellahouston Park

Dumbreck

POLLOKSHIELDS

Mosspark Blvd

M77

Dumbreck Rd

Pollokshields East

Pollokshields West

GOVANHILL

Maxwell Park

Queens Park

M77

Pollok Country Park

Crossmyloof

Pollokshaws Rd

White Cart Water

❷

To Alloway (30mi); Glasgow Prestwick Airport (30mi); (44mi)

❻

Shawlands

A77

Pollokshaws East

Mount Florida

B767

To Holmwood House (0.5mi)

POLLOKSHAWS

Pollokshaws West

POSSILPARK

A879

Saracen St

Springburn Rd

A803

BARMULLOCH

N 0 — 1 km
0 — 0.5 miles

Springburn

To Craigendmuir
Park (1mi)

M80

Barnhill

To Edinburgh (39mi)

M8

A80

COWCADDENS

M8

TOWNHEAD

Buchanan
St

Queen
St

4

RIDDRIE

Cumbernauld Rd

CARNTYNE

Alexandra

Alexandra
Parade

Pde

A80

Edinburgh Rd

DENNISTOUN

Carntyne Rd

Central

Argyle St

Duke St

High St

High
St

Duke Street

St Enoch

London
Rd

A721

Bellgrove

Gallowgate

Shettleston Rd

See Central Glasgow Map (p130–1)

BRIDGETON

Westmuir St A721

Bridgeton

London Rd

PARKHEAD

HUTCHESONTOWN

B767

Dalmarnock Rd

Glasgow
Green

River Clyde

DALMARNOCK

Dalmarnock

Crosshill

Aikenhead Rd

POLMADIE

Rutherglen

Hampden
Park

B766

Main St
RUTHERGLEN

BANKHEAD

1 Kelvingrove Art
   Gallery & Museum

2 Burrell Collection

3 Mackintosh House

4 Glasgow Cathedral

5 Glasgow's Pubs

6 Culzean Castle

Glasgow & Loch Lomond's Highlights

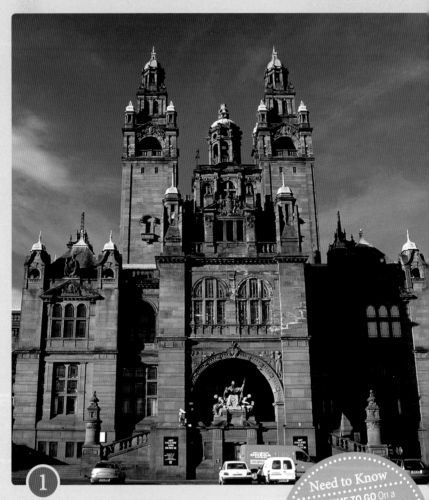

① Kelvingrove Art Gallery & Museum

A grand Victorian cathedral of culture, Kelvingrove is the most visited museum in the UK outside London. Exhibits range from natural history and evolution to arms and armour (as well as a WWII Spitfire fighter aircraft), and from Glasgow history to Charles Rennie Mackintosh design.

Need to Know

BEST TIME TO GO On a weekday, to avoid the weekend crowds. **GOOD NEWS** Admission is free. **TOP TIP** Don't try to see everything – focus on the highlights that interest you most. **For more, see p140.**

Kelvingrove Don't Miss List

DR NEIL BALLANTYNE, MUSEUM MANAGER, KELVINGROVE

1 SALVADOR DALÍ'S *CHRIST OF ST JOHN OF THE CROSS*

One of our most controversial purchases ever, Christ of St John of the Cross has become as iconic as Kelvingrove itself. The painting was proclaimed an outrageous waste of money and in its time has been attacked twice. It is now one of our most valued treasures.

2 CHARLES RENNIE MACKINTOSH AND THE GLASGOW STYLE

The 'Glasgow Style' describes the distinctive form of decorative art produced by Glasgow designers between 1890 and 1920. This gallery contains some fabulous jewellery, stained glass and furniture. My favourite object is the Wassail, a large gesso wall frieze from the Ingram Street Tearooms, designed by Charles Rennie Macintosh.

3 THE PEMBROKE ARMOUR

Dating back to 1557, this is the only complete set of Greenwich armour for man and horse in existence. The rarity of this magnificent exhibit demonstrates the passion of the man behind the collection – RL Scott built up one of the finest collections of European arms and armour in the world; a little-known fact is that he preferred to collect equipment that had actually been used in battle, rather than merely decorative armour or display pieces.

4 THE SARCOPHAGUS OF PA-BA-SA

This granite sarcophagus from around 650 BC holds great mystery and intrigue for visitors of all ages. Perhaps it's a good thing that the occupant is long gone considering the items that visitors have 'posted' through the gap over the years: ticket stubs from past exhibitions and a 1970s Playboy magazine, to name just a few.

5 SCOTTISH IDENTITY IN ART

Paintings of historic heroes such as William Wallace, together with the rugged landscapes and majestic stags beloved by Victorian artists, have all been used to define 'Scottishness'. More controversially, there's an image of Robert Burns as Che Guevara, and a caricature of the modern, kilt-wearing Scotsman with a can of beer and a football for a head.

Burrell Collection

Wealthy industrialist Sir William Burrell bequeathed his magnificent art collection (p148), comprising more than 8000 objects, to the city of Glasgow in 1944. But it wasn't until 1983 that this splendid building was constructed in leafy Pollok Park to display everything from Chinese porcelain and medieval furniture to Islamic art and paintings by Renoir and Cézanne. The most famous piece is Rodin's iconic sculpture, *The Thinker*.

The Age of Bronze by August Rodin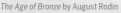

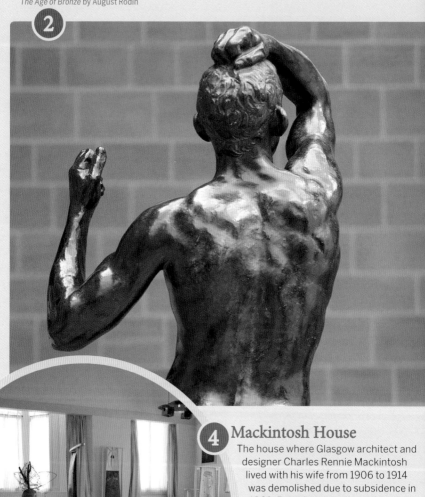

Mackintosh House

The house where Glasgow architect and designer Charles Rennie Mackintosh lived with his wife from 1906 to 1914 was demolished due to subsidence in 1963. But it has risen from the rubble in this faithful reconstruction (p147) by Glasgow University – closely following period drawings and photographs, furnished as much as possible with Mackintosh's original furniture and fittings and decorated as it was when he lived there.

Glasgow Cathedral

The only cathedral on the Scottish mainland to survive the destructive period of the Reformation intact, Glasgow Cathedral (p138) is a superb example of Scottish Gothic architecture, almost all of it dating from the 15th century. The most atmospheric part is the forest of pillars around St Mungo's tomb, but no visit is complete without a stroll through the neighbouring Necropolis, one of the most impressive and picturesque cemeteries in Scotland.

MARTIN MOOS

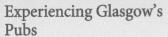

NICHOLAS REUSS

Experiencing Glasgow's Pubs

Some of Scotland's best nightlife is to be found in the din and roar of Glasgow's crowded pubs and bars. There are as many different styles of bar as there are patrons who drink in them, ranging from the classic Victorian polished brass and mirrors of the Horse Shoe (p143) to the hip decadence of baroque Artà (p143). A month of solid drinking wouldn't get you past the halfway mark.

Culzean Castle

This stunning stately home (p155) – considered by many to be Scotland's finest – is the work of the Scottish architect Robert Adam, best known for his show-stopping neoclassical designs. Its famous features include a superb oval staircase leading to an opulent circular drawing room with views of the Isle of Arran and Ailsa Craig. Everywhere you look there are classical friezes and roundels in delicate 18th-century plasterwork.

Glasgow & Loch Lomond's Best…

Wining & Dining

○ **Café Gandolfi** (p139) Classic Glasgow eatery offering everything from breakfast to seafood dinners

○ **The Ubiquitous Chip** (p141) A local institution and the original champion of fresh Scottish produce

○ **Mother India** (p141) The epitome of the famous Glasgow curry restaurant

○ **Stravaigin** (p141) Cool and contemporary, a serious foodie's delight

○ **Oak Tree Inn** (p155) Great lochside lunch spot serving excellent Cullen skink

Pubs & Bars

○ **Horse Shoe** (p143) Legendary Glasgow drinking den with original Victorian decor

○ **Babbity Bowster** (p143) Charming bar in a quiet corner of trendy Merchant City

○ **Corinthian** (p144) Converted bank building with spectacular domed interior

○ **Artà** (p143) Cocktail bar draped in an extravaganza of baroque decadence

○ **Drover's Inn** (p153) Atmospheric Loch Lomond pub with kilted bar staff

Museums & Galleries

○ **Kelvingrove Art Gallery & Museum** (p120) Grand Victorian cathedral of culture, one of Scotland's best

○ **Burrell Collection** (p148) Famous art collection bequeathed to the city, in lovely parkland setting

○ **Hunterian Museum** (p132) Classic old-style museum of natural history in grand Victorian university building

○ **Robert Burns Birthplace Museum** (p153) Brand-new museum dedicated to Scotland's best-known poet, includes his birthplace cottage

Beauty Spots

o **Botanic Gardens** (p133) Perfect summer picnic spot on banks of River Kelvin in Glasgow's West End

o **Culzean Castle & Country Park** (p155) Gorgeous castle grounds with views to the Isle of Arran

o **Loch Lomond Shores** (p153) Top of Drumkinnon tower affords classic view along loch to Ben Lomond

o **Millarochy Bay** (p154) Picnic area with gravel beach and glorious view across loch to Luss Hills

ADVANCE PLANNING

o **One month before** Book accommodation in central Glasgow, and Loch Lomond if visiting in summer

o **Two weeks before** Reserve a table at top Glasgow restaurants, especially for weekend evenings

o **One week before** Make bookings for boat trips on Loch Lomond

RESOURCES

o **Glasgow: Scotland with Style** (www.seeglasgow.com) Official convention-bureau site with accommodation booking, sights, activities and events

o **Glasgow Museums** (www.glasgowmuseums.com) Information on city-owned museums and art galleries

o **Clyde Waterfront** (www.clydewaterfront.com) Latest developments on Glasgow's redeveloped waterfront, including the new Riverside Museum

o **SPT** (www.spt.co.uk) Comprehensive public-transport information for Glasgow and surrounding area

o **Loch Lomond & the Trossachs National Park** (www.lochlomond-trossachs .org) Information on wildlife, activities, things to see and public transport

o **Ayrshire & Arran Tourist Board** (www .ayrshire-arran.com) Tourist information for Culzean Castle and Robert Burns country

GETTING AROUND

o **From the Airport** Bus runs every 10 or so minutes from Glasgow International to Buchanan St bus station

o **Bus** Good city bus network operated by **First Glasgow** (www.firstglasgow .com)

o **Car** Confusing one-way-streets system, and parking in city centre is difficult; best to use public transport

o **On Foot** City centre easily explored on foot; West End, however, will need public transport

o **Subway** Circular underground railway links city centre with the West End; trains run every four to 12 minutes

:: Smoked venison at Café Gandolfi; **Above:** Robert Burns Monument & Gardens (p153)

125

Glasgow Walking Tour

Central Glasgow is famous for its grand Victorian architecture, a legacy of its rich trading history. This stroll takes you to Glasgow Cathedral via trendy Merchant City, once the headquarters for Glasgow industrialists.

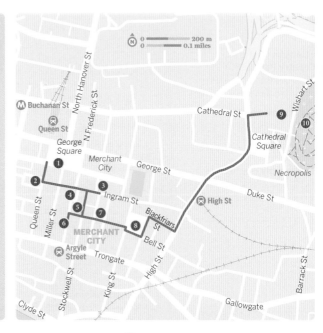

❶ George Square

The square is surrounded by imposing Victorian architecture: the old post office, the Bank of Scotland and the grandiose **City Chambers**. Statues include those of Robert Burns, James Watt and, atop a 24m-high Doric column, Sir Walter Scott.

❷ Gallery of Modern Art

Walk one block south down Queen St to the Gallery of Modern Art. This striking colonnaded building, built in 1827, was once the Royal Exchange and now hosts some of the country's best contemporary art displays.

❸ Hutcheson's Hall

The gallery faces Ingram St, which you should cross and then follow east four blocks to Hutcheson's Hall. Built in 1805, this elegant building is now maintained by the National Trust for Scotland (NTS).

❹ Corinthian Bar

Retrace your steps one block and duck into the former Court House cells that now house the ornate Corinthian Bar for a glimpse of the extravagant interior (and perhaps a pint!).

126

5 Trades Hall

Continue south down Glassford St past Trades Hall, designed by Robert Adam in 1791 to house the trades guild and the only surviving building in Glasgow by this famous Scottish architect. The exterior is best viewed from Garth St.

6 Tobacco Exchange

Turn right into Wilson St and take the first left along Virginia St, which is lined with the old warehouses of the Tobacco Lords (Glasgow merchants who grew rich from the tobacco trade); many of these have been converted into posh flats. The Tobacco Exchange became the Sugar Exchange in 1820.

7 Sheriff Court

Head back to Wilson St, where you'll find the bulky Sheriff Court, which fills a whole block. This arresting building was originally Glasgow's town hall but has been developed as luxury apartments.

8 Merchant Square

Continue east on Wilson St past Ingram Sq, another warehouse development, to Merchant Sq, a covered courtyard that was once the city's fruit market but now bustles with cafes and bars.

9 Glasgow Cathedral

Head up Albion St, then take the first right into Blackfriars St. Emerging onto High St, turn left and follow it up to the cathedral.

10 Necropolis

Behind the cathedral, wind your way up through the noble, crumbling tombs of the Necropolis, which offers great city views.

Glasgow in...

ONE DAY

Glasgow deserves more time than this, but if you're squeezed, hit the East End for **Glasgow Cathedral**, **St Mungo's Museum**, and a wander through the hillside **Necropolis**. In the afternoon take on one of the city's top museums, either the **Burrell Collection** or the **Kelvingrove**. As evening falls, head to trendy **Merchant City** for a stroll and dinner – **Café Gandolfi** perhaps, or the latest trendy newcomer. Head to **Artá** for a pre- or post-meal drink.

TWO DAYS

Visit whichever major museum you missed yesterday, and then it's Mackintosh time: **Glasgow School of Art** (City Centre) is his finest work, or else there's the reproduction **Mackintosh House** (West End) to admire. Later, head for the **River Clyde** and the **Glasgow Science Centre**. Hungry? Thirsty? Down a pint at the **Horse Shoe Bar**, then choose somewhere for dinner – perhaps one of the city's famous curry houses, such as **Mother India**. To round off the evening, check out one of Glasgow's excellent live-music venues.

The Seven Deadly Sins by Felipe Linares and Sons, Gallery of Modern Art

Discover Glasgow & Loch Lomond

Kitchen display at the Tenement House (p142)
PHOTOGRAPHER: HOLMES GARDEN PHOTOS/ALAMY

GLASGOW

 Sights

Glasgow's major sights are fairly evenly
dispersed, with many found along the
Clyde (focus of a long-term regeneration
program), the leafy cathedral precinct
in the East End and the museum-rich
South Side. Many museums are free.
The centre also contains a variety of
attractions, particularly Mackintosha-
nia. The trendy West End swarms with
students during term time.

City Centre

The grid layout and pedestrian streets
of the city centre make it easy to get
around, and there are many cafes
and pubs that make good pit stops
between attractions.

GLASGOW SCHOOL OF ART

Mackintosh Building

(Map p130; ☏ 0141-353 4526; www
.gsa.ac.uk/tours; 167 Renfrew St;
adult/child £8.75/7; ⊙9.30am-
6.30pm Apr-Sep, 10am-5pm Oct-
Mar) Mackintosh's greatest
building, the Glasgow School
of Art, still fulfils its original
function, so just follow the
steady stream of eclecti-
cally dressed students up the
hill to find it. It's hard not to be
impressed by the thoroughness
of the design; the architect's pencil
seems to have shaped everything
inside and outside the building. The
interior design is strikingly austere, with
simple colour combinations (often just
black and cream) and those uncomfort-
able-looking high-
backed chairs for which Mackintosh is
famous. The library, designed as an addition in 1907, is a masterpiece. The

visitor entrance is at the side of the building on Dalhousie St; here you'll find a shop with a small but useful interpretative display. Excellent hour-long guided tours (roughly hourly summer, 11am and 3pm winter) run by architecture students leave from here; this is the only way (apart from enrolling) you can visit the building's interior. They're worth booking by phone at busy times. Multilingual translations are available.

FREE GALLERY OF MODERN ART
Gallery

(Map p130; www.glasgowmuseums.com; Royal Exchange Sq; ⊙10am-5pm Mon-Wed & Sat, to 8pm Thu, 11am-5pm Fri & Sun; 📶) Scotland's most popular contemporary art gallery features modern works from artists worldwide in a graceful neoclassical building. The original interior is used to make a daring, inventive art display. Social issues are a focal point of the museum but it's not all heavy going: there's a big effort made to keep the kids entertained.

FREE CITY CHAMBERS   Town Hall
(Map p130; George Sq) The grand City Chambers, the seat of local government, were built in the 1880s at the high point of the city's wealth. The interior is even more extravagant than the exterior, and the chambers have sometimes been used as a movie location to represent the Kremlin or the Vatican. Free guided tours are held at 10.30am and 2.30pm Monday to Friday.

East End

The oldest part of the city, given a facelift in the 1990s, is concentrated around Glasgow Cathedral (p138), to the east of the modern centre. It takes 15 to 20 minutes to walk from George Sq, but numerous buses pass nearby, including buses 11, 12, 36, 37, 38 and 42.

FREE ST MUNGO'S MUSEUM OF RELIGIOUS LIFE & ART   Museum
(Map p130; www.glasgowmuseums.com; 2 Castle St; ⊙10am-5pm Mon-Thu & Sat, 11am-5pm Fri & Sun) A startling achievement, this museum, set in a reconstruction of the bishop's palace that once stood here in the cathedral forecourt, is an audacious attempt to capture the world's major religions in an artistic nutshell, while presenting the similarities and differences in how they approach common themes such as birth, marriage and death. The result is commendable. The attraction is twofold: firstly, impressive art that blurs the lines between religion and culture; and secondly, the opportunity to delve into different faiths, an experience that can be as deep or shallow as you wish. There are three galleries, representing religion as art, religious life and, on the top floor, religion in Scotland. A Zen garden is outside.

FREE PROVAND'S LORDSHIP
Historic House

(Map p130; www.glasgowmuseums.com; 3 Castle St; ⊙10am-5pm Mon-Thu & Sat, 11am-5pm Fri & Sun) Across the road from St Mungo's Museum is Provand's Lordship, the oldest house in Glasgow. A rare example of 15th-century domestic Scottish architecture, it was built in 1471 as a manse for the chaplain of St Nicholas Hospital. The ceilings and doorways are low, and the rooms are sparsely furnished with period artefacts, except for an upstairs room, which has been furnished to reflect the living space of an early-16th-century chaplain. The building's best feature is its authentic feel – if you ignore the tacky imitation-stone linoleum covering the ground floor.

The Clyde

Once a thriving shipbuilding area, the Clyde sank into dereliction but is being rejuvenated. A major campaign to redevelop Glasgow Harbour, involving the conversion of former docklands into shops and public areas, is underway – to find out more about this project see www.glasgowharbour.com.

GLASGOW SCIENCE CENTRE   Museum
(Map p136; www.glasgowsciencecentre.org; 50 Pacific Quay; Science Mall adult/child £9.95/7.95, extras for IMAX, tower or planetarium £2.50; ⊙10am-5pm) Scotland's flagship millen-

Central Glasgow

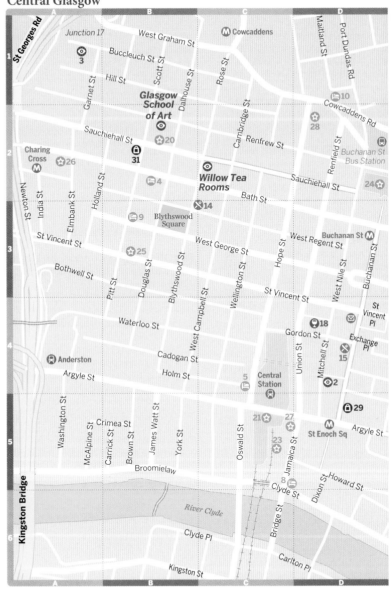

nium project, the superb, ultramodern Glasgow Science Centre will keep the kids entertained for hours (that's middle-aged kids, too!). It brings science and technology alive through hundreds of interactive exhibits on four floors.

Look out for the illusions (like rearranging your features through a 3D head-scan) and the cloud chamber, showing tracks of natural radiation. It consists of an egg-shaped titanium-covered **IMAX** theatre (phone for current screenings)

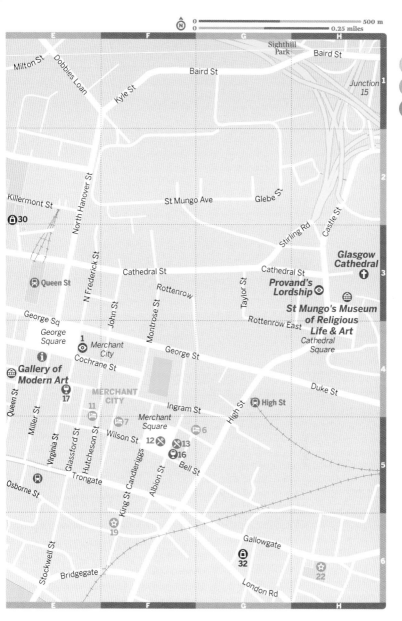

and an interactive **Science Mall** with floor-to-ceiling windows – a bounty of discovery for young, inquisitive minds. There's also a rotating **observation tower**, 127m high. And check out the planetarium, where the **Scottish Power**

Space Theatre brings the night sky to life and a **Virtual Science Theatre** treats visitors to a 3D molecular journey. To get here take Arriva bus 24 from Renfield St or First Glasgow bus 89 or 90 from Union St.

Central Glasgow

West End

With its expectant buzz, trendy bars and cafes and nonchalant swagger, the West End is probably the most engaging area of Glasgow – it's great for people-watching, and is as close as Glasgow gets to bohemian. From the centre, buses 9, 16 and 23 run towards Kelvingrove; 8, 11, and 16 to the university; and 20, 44 and 66 to Byres Rd (among others).

FREE **HUNTERIAN MUSEUM** Museum
(Map p136; www.hunterian.gla.ac.uk; University Ave; ◷9.30am-5pm Mon-Sat) Housed in the glorious sandstone main building of the university, which is in itself reason enough to pay a visit, this quirky museum contains the collection of renowned one-time student of the university, William Hunter (1718–83). Hunter was primarily an anatomist and physician, but as one of those gloriously well-rounded Enlightenment figures, he interested himself in everything the world had to offer. Pickled organs in glass jars take their place alongside geological phenomena, potsherds gleaned from ancient brochs, dinosaur skeletons and a creepy case of deformed animals. The main halls of the exhibition, with their high vaulted roofs, are magnificent in themselves. A highlight is the 1674 'Map of the Whole World' in the World Culture section.

FREE **HUNTERIAN ART GALLERY** Gallery
(Map p136; www.hunterian.gla.ac.uk; 82 Hillhead St; ◷9.30am-5pm Mon-Sat) Across the road from the Hunterian Museum, the bold tones of the Scottish Colourists (Samuel Peploe, Francis Cadell, JD Fergusson) are well represented in this gallery, which also forms part of Hunter's bequest to the university. There are also Sir William MacTaggart's impressionistic Scottish landscapes and a gem by Thomas Millie Dow. There's a special

collection of James McNeill Whistler's limpid prints, drawings and paintings. Upstairs, in a section devoted to late-19th-century Scottish art, you can see works by several of the Glasgow Boys.

BOTANIC GARDENS   Park
(Map p136; 730 Great Western Rd; ☉7am-dusk, glasshouse 10am-4.45pm) The best thing about walking into these beautiful gardens is the noise of Great Western Rd quickly receding into the background. Amazingly, the lush grounds don't seem that popular with locals (except on sunny weekends) and away from the entrance you may just about have the place to yourself. The wooded gardens follow the riverbank of the River Kelvin and there are plenty of tropical species to discover. **Kibble Palace**, an impressive Victorian iron-and-glass structure dating from 1873, is one of the largest glasshouses in Britain; check out the herb garden, too, with its medicinal species. The gorgeous hilly grounds make the perfect place for a picnic lunch. There are also organised walks and concerts in summer – have a look at the noticeboard near the entrance to see what's on.

South Side
The south side is a tangled web of busy roads with a few congestion-relieving oases, but it does contain the excellent Burrell Collection (p148).

Tours

CITY SIGHTSEEING   Bus Tour
(☏ 0141-204 0444; www.citysightseeingglasgow .co.uk; adult/child £11/5) These double-decker tourist buses run along the main sightseeing routes, starting outside the tourist office on George Sq; get on and off as you wish. A ticket (buy from the driver or the tourist office) is valid for two consecutive days. All buses have wheelchair access and multilingual commentary.

GLASGOW TAXIS CITY TOUR   Taxi Tour
(☏ 0141-429 7070; www.glasgowtaxis.co.uk) If you're confident you can understand the driver's accent, a taxi tour is a good way to get a feel of the city and its sights. The 80-minute tour takes you around all the centre's important landmarks, with commentary. The standard tour costs £35 for up to five people.

The Mackintosh Collection at the Hunterian Art Gallery

LOCH LOMOND SEAPLANES

Scenic Flights

(Map p136; ☎ 0870 242 1457; www.lochlomond seaplanes.com; Clyde River, Glasgow Science Centre) This set-up uses the Clyde as its runway and will take you on scenic flights (£139) over Glasgow and Loch Lomond or even run you up to Oban.

WAVERLEY

Boat Trips

(Map p136; www.waverleyexcursions.co.uk; Clyde River near Glasgow Science Centre) The world's last ocean-going paddle steamer (built in 1947) cruises the Firth of Clyde from April to September (tickets £15 to £40); the website lists days of departure. It serves several towns and the islands of Bute, Great Cumbrae and Arran, and departs from Glasgow Science Centre (see p129).

 Sleeping

The city centre gets very rowdy at weekends, and accommodation options fill up fast, mostly with groups who will probably roll in boisterously some time after 3am. If you prefer an earlier appointment with your bed, you'll be better off in a smaller, quieter lodging or in the West End. Booking ahead is essential anywhere at weekends and in July and August.

City Centre

BRUNSWICK HOTEL

Hotel ££

(Map p130; ☎ 0141-552 0001; www.brunswickho tel.co.uk; 106 Brunswick St; d £50-95; 🛜) Some places have dour owners threatening lockouts if you break curfew. Then there's the Brunswick, which every now and then converts the whole hotel into a party venue, with DJs in the lifts and art installations in the rooms. You couldn't ask for a more relaxed and friendly Merchant City base. The rooms are all stylish, with a mixture of minimalism and rich, sexy colours. Compact and standard doubles will do if you're here for a night out, but king-size rooms are well worth the £10 upgrade. There's an excellent restaurant downstairs and an

Left: Interior of Kibble Palace, Botanic Gardens (p133); **Below:** Exterior of the Glasgow Science Centre (p129)

occasional nightclub in the basement.

MALMAISON Hotel £££
(Map p130; ☎ 0141-572 1000; www.malmaison .com; 278 West George St; r Fri-Sun £135, r Mon-Thu £155; ☎) Heavenly Malmaison is the ultimate in seductive urban accommodation. Cutting-edge but decadently stylish living at its best, this sassy sister of hospitality is super slinky and a cornerstone of faith in Glaswegian accommodation. Stylish rooms with their moody lighting have a dark, brooding tone, plush furnishings and a designer touch. It's best to book online, as it's cheaper, and various suite offers can be mighty tempting.

ARTTO Hotel ££
(Map p130; ☎ 0141-248 2480; www.arttohotel .com; 37 Hope St; s/d £70/90; ☎) Right by the train station, this modish but affordable hotel offers soft white, fawn, and burgundy tones in its compact but attractive rooms above a popular bar and eatery. Large windows make staying at the front appealing but, though the double glazing does a good job of subduing the street noise, light sleepers will be happier at the rear. Rates vary widely by the day; the price listed here is a worst-case scenario.

RAB HA'S Inn ££
(Map p130; ☎ 0141-572 0400; www.rabhas.com; 83 Hutcheson St; r £79-89; ☎) This Merchant City favourite is an atmospheric pub-restaurant with four stylish upstairs rooms. Each is a good size with a dark polished-wood theme and a spotless en suite. It's the personal touches, such as fresh flowers in the rooms, and designer photographic prints on the walls, that make you feel special. Breakfast can be delivered to your room and you can come and go as you please, long after the bar downstairs has closed.

135

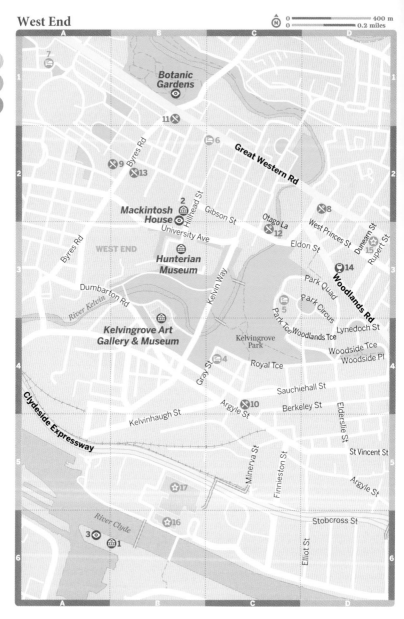

0   400 m
0   0.2 miles

DISCOVER GLASGOW & LOCH LOMOND GLASGOW

PIPERS TRYST HOTEL   Hotel   ££
(Map p130; ☎ 0141-353 5551; www.thepiping
centre.co.uk; 30-34 McPhater St; s/d £50/65;
🛜) The name is no strategy to lure
tartan tourists; this intimate, cosy hotel
is in a noble building actually run by the
adjacent bagpiping centre. Cheery staff,
great value and a prime city-centre location make this a cut above other places.
Of the eight well-appointed rooms, Nos 6
and 7 are our faves; you won't have far to
migrate after a night of Celtic music and

West End

fine single malts in the snug bar-and-restaurant downstairs.

EURO HOSTEL Hostel £
(Map p130; ☎ 0141-222 2828; www.euro-hostels.co.uk; 318 Clyde St; dm £15-25, s £35-50, d £40-70; @ 🛜) With hundreds of beds, this mammoth hostel is handily close to the station and centre. While it feels a bit institutional, it has excellent facilities, though the kitchen is very compact. Dorms range in size, and price varies on a daily basis, so book ahead for the best rates. Private rooms aren't great value. It's very popular with groups and has a rockin' bar on site.

ADELAIDE'S B&B ££
(Map p130; ☎ 0141-248 4970; www.adelaides.co.uk; 209 Bath St; s £35-50, £d/f 60/82; @ 🛉) Quiet and cordial, this is ideal for folk who want location at a reasonable price. It's an unusual place – a simple, friendly guesthouse on prestigious Bath St set in a historic church conversion and still Baptist-run, though there's not a hint of preachiness in the air. Tariffs are room only – various breakfast options are available – and families are very welcome. Aim for the back to minimize weekend noise.

BABBITY BOWSTER Inn ££
(Map p130; ☎ 0141-552 5055; 16-18 Blackfriars St; s/d £45/60) Smack bang in the heart of the trendy Merchant City, this lively bar has simple rooms with sleek furnishings and a minimalist design (No 3 is a good one). Staying here is an excellent Glaswegian experience – the building's design is attributed to Robert Adam. Unusually, room rates do not include breakfast – but that helps keep prices down.

West End

GLASGOW SYHA Hostel £
(Map p136; ☎ 0141-332 3004; www.syha.org.uk; 8 Park Tce; dm/tw £23/62; @ 🛜) Perched on a hill overlooking Kelvingrove Park in a charming town house, this place is simply fabulous and one of Scotland's best official hostels. Dorms are mostly four to six beds with padlock lockers and all have their own en suite – very posh. The common rooms are spacious, plush and good for lounging about. It has no curfew and a good kitchen, and breakfast is available. The prices given here reflect maximums; it's usually cheaper.

ALAMO GUEST HOUSE B&B ££
(Map p136; ☎ 0141-339 2395; www.alamoguesthouse.com; 46 Gray St; s/d/tw with shared bathroom £42/64/68, d with private bathroom £84; 🛜) The Alamo may not sound like a

GLENN BEANLAND

Don't Miss **Glasgow Cathedral**

With a dark imposing interior that conjures up medieval might, Glasgow Cathedral has a rare timelessness. It's a shining example of Gothic architecture, and the only mainland Scottish cathedral to survive the Reformation. Most of the current building dates from the 15th century; only the western towers were destroyed in the turmoil.

Entry is through a side door into the **nave**, which is hung with regimental colours. The wooden roof above has been restored many times since its original construction, but some of the timber dates from the 14th century; note the impressive shields. Many of the cathedral's stunning narrow windows of stained glass are modern; to your left is Francis Spear's 1958 work *The Creation,* which fills the west window.

The cathedral, divided by a late-15th-century stone choir screen, is decorated with seven pairs of figures to represent the Seven Deadly Sins. Beyond is the **choir**. The four stained-glass panels of the east window, depicting the apostles (also by Francis Spear) are particularly effective. At the northeastern corner is the entrance to the 15th-century **upper chapter house**, where Glasgow University was founded. It's now used as a sacristy.

The most interesting part of the cathedral, the **lower church**, is reached by a stairway. Its forest of pillars creates a powerful atmosphere around St Mungo's tomb (St Mungo founded a monastic community here in the 5th century), the focus of a famous medieval pilgrimage that was believed to be as meritorious as a visit to Rome.

Behind the cathedral, the **necropolis** stretches picturesquely up and over a green hill. Its elaborate Victorian tombs of the city's wealthy industrialists make for an intriguing stroll, great views and a vague Gothic thrill.

THINGS YOU NEED TO KNOW

HS; Map p130; www.historic-scotland.gov.uk; Cathedral Sq; ⊙9.30am-5.30pm Mon-Sat & 1-5pm Sun Apr-Sep, 9.30am-4.30pm Mon-Sat & 1-4.30pm Sun Oct-Mar

quiet, peaceful spot, but that's exactly what this great little place is. Opposite Kelvingrove Park, it feels miles from the hustle of the city, but the city centre and West End are within walking distance, and several of the best museums and restaurants in town are close by. The decor is an enchanting mixture of antique furnishings and modern design, and the breezy owners will make you very welcome. All rooms have DVD players and there's an extensive collection to borrow from.

KIRKLEE HOTEL Hotel ££
(Map p136; 0141-334 5555; www.kirkleehotel .co.uk; 11 Kensington Gate; s/d £59/75;) Want to spoil someone special? In a leafy neighbourhood, Kirklee is a quiet little gem that combines the luxury of a classy hotel with the warmth of staying in someone's home. The rooms are simply gorgeous, beautifully furnished and mostly looking onto lush gardens. For families there is an excellent downstairs room with enormous en suite. This could be Glasgow's most beautiful street.

HERITAGE HOTEL Hotel ££
(Map p136; 0141-339 6955; www.theheritage hotel.net; 4 Alfred Tce, Great Western Rd; s/d £40/60; P) A stone's throw from all the action of the West End, this friendly hotel has a very open, airy and bright feel. Generally, the rooms on the 1st and 2nd floors are a bit more spacious (No 21 is best of the doubles) and have a better outlook. Rooms have been recently renovated, and you can smell the newness. This, the staff, and the fair prices, mark it out.

Eating

The West End is the culinary centre of the city; Merchant City also boasts an incredible concentration of quality restaurants and cafes. Many Glasgow restaurants post offers on the internet (changing daily) at **5pm.co.uk** (www.5pm. co.uk). Note also that pubs and bars (see Drinking) are always a good lunchtime option.

City Centre

CAFÉ GANDOLFI Cafe/Bistro ££
(Map p130; 0141-552 6813; 64 Albion St; mains £8-14; 9am-11.30pm Mon-Sat, noon-11.30pm Sun) In the fashionable Merchant City, this cafe was once part of the old cheese market. It's been pulling in the punters for years and packs an interesting clientele: die-hard Gandolfers, the upwardly mobile and tourists. It's an excellent, friendly bistro and upmarket coffee shop – very much the place to be seen. Book a Tim Stead–designed, medieval-looking table in advance for well-prepared Scottish and Continental food. There's an expansion, specialising in fish, next door.

BRUTTI MA BUONI Bistro ££
(Map p130; 0141-552 0001; www.brunswick hotel.co.uk; 106 Brunswick St; mains £8-13; 11am-10pm;) If you like dining in a place that has a sense of fun, Brutti delivers – it's the antithesis of some of the pretentious places around the Merchant City. With dishes such as 'ugly but good' pizza and 'angry or peaceful' prawns, Brutti's menu draws a smile for its quirkiness and its prices. The Italian and Spanish influences give rise to tapas-like servings or full-blown meals, which are imaginative, fresh and frankly delicious.

BAR SOBA Asian Fusion £
(Map p130; 0141-204 2404; www.barsoba.co .uk; 11 Mitchell Lane; mains £8-10) With seating around the edges of the room and candles flickering in windows there's a certain sense of intimacy in stylish and very friendly Bar Soba. You can eat in the plush downstairs restaurant, or in the bar. The food is Asian fusion and the laksas go down a treat – followed up of course with an irresistible chocolate brownie. Background beats are perfect for chilling and it can be a good spot to escape Friday-evening crowds.

WHERE THE MONKEY SLEEPS Cafe £
(Map p130; www.monkeysleeps.com; 182 West Regent St; dishes £5-7; 7am-5pm Mon-Fri, 10am-5pm Sat) This funky little number in the middle of the business district is just what you need to get away from

NEIL SETCHFIELD

Don't Miss **Kelvingrove Art Gallery & Museum**

In a magnificent stone building, this grand Victorian cathedral of culture has been revamped into a fascinating and unusual museum, with a bewildering variety of exhibits, but not too tightly packed to overwhelm. Here you'll find fine art alongside stuffed animals, and Micronesian shark-tooth swords alongside a Spitfire plane, but it's not mix 'n' match: rooms are carefully and thoughtfully themed, and the collection is a manageable size. There's an excellent room of Scottish art, and a room of fine French Impressionist works, alongside quality Renaissance paintings from Italy and Flanders. Salvador Dalí's superb *Christ of St John of the Cross* is also here. Best of all, everything – including every painting – has a easy-reading paragraph of interpretation next to it: what a great idea. You can learn a lot about art and more here and it's excellent for the children, with plenty for them to do and displays aimed at a variety of ages. Bus 17, among many others, runs here from Renfield St.

THINGS YOU NEED TO KNOW

Map p136; www.glasgowmuseums.com; Argyle St; admission free; ⊗10am-5pm Mon-Thu & Sat, 11am-5pm Fri & Sun

the ubiquitous coffee chains. It's laid-back and a little hippie; the bagels and paninis, with names like maverick or renegade, are highlights, as are some very inventive dishes, such as the 'nuclear' beans, dripping with cayenne and Tabasco.

WILLOW TEA ROOMS Cafe £
(www.willowtearooms.co.uk; light meals £4-8; ⊗9am-5pm Mon-Sat, 11am-5pm Sun) Sauchiehall St (Map p130; 217 Sauchiehall St); Buchanan St (Map p130; 97 Buchanan St) These re-creations of tearooms designed by Charles Rennie Mackintosh in 1904 – there are others cropping up around town – back

up the design with excellent bagels, pastries, or, more splendidly, champagne afternoon teas (£17). At busy times the queues for a table can be long.

ARISAIG Scottish ££
(Map p130; ☏ 0141-553 1010; www.arisaigrest aurant.co.uk; 1 Merchant Sq; mains £11-17) Relocated into the Merchant Sq building, a historical location converted into an echoing food court, Arisaig offers a good chance to try well-prepared Scottish cuisine at a fair price, with friendly service to boot. Candlelight and crisp linen makes for atmosphere, with both terrace and indoor seating.

West End

There are numerous excellent restaurants in the West End. They cluster along Byres Rd, and, just off it, on Ashton Lane and Ruthven Lane. Gibson St and Great Western Rd also have plenty to offer.

UBIQUITOUS CHIP Scottish £££
(Map p136; ☏ 0141-334 5007; www.ubiquitous chip.co.uk; 12 Ashton Lane; 2-/3-course dinner £35/40) The original champion of Scottish produce, the Ubiquitous Chip has won lots of awards for its unparalleled Scottish cuisine, and for its lengthy wine list. Named to poke fun at Scotland's

perceived lack of finer cuisine, it offers a French touch but resolutely Scottish ingredients, carefully selected and following sustainable principles. Above, **Upstairs at the Chip** (mains £12 to £20) provides cheaper, bistro-style food with a similarly advanced set of principles. There are also bar meals at the atmospheric upstairs pub, while the cute 'Wee Pub' down the side alley offers plenty of drinking pleasure.

STRAVAIGIN Scottish ££
(Map p136; ☏ 0141-334 2665; www.stravaigin .com; 28 Gibson St; mains £10-19; ⊙dinner Mon-Fri, lunch & dinner Sat & Sun) Stravaigin is a serious foodie's delight, with a menu constantly pushing the boundaries of originality and offering creative culinary excellence. The cool contemporary dining space in the basement has booth seating, and helpful, laid-back waiting-staff to assist in deciphering the audacious menu. Entry level has a buzzing two-level bar that's open 11am to midnight daily; you can also eat here. There are always plenty of menu deals and special culinary nights.

MOTHER INDIA Indian ££
(Map p136; ☏ 0141-221 1663; www.motherindia glasgow.co.uk; 28 Westminster Tce, Sauchiehall

The Glasgow Boys

The great rivalry between Glasgow and Edinburgh has also played out in the art world. In the late 19th century a group of Glaswegian painters challenged the domineering artistic establishment in the capital. Up to this point, paintings were largely confined to historical scenes and sentimental visions of the Highlands. These painters – including Sir James Guthrie, EA Hornel, George Henry and Joseph Crawhall – experimented with colour and themes of rural life, shocking Edinburgh's artistic society. Many of them went to study in Paris studios, and brought back a much-needed breath of European air into the Scottish art scene. Like Charles Rennie Mackintosh, the Glasgow Boys' work met with admiration and artistic recognition on the Continent.

The Glasgow Boys had an enormous influence on the Scottish art world, inspiring the next generation of Scottish painters – the Colourists. The Glasgow Boys' works can be seen in the main Glasgow galleries as well as in Broughton House, Kirkcudbright and the National Gallery of Scotland in Edinburgh.

If You Like…
Museums

Kelvingrove may be the most famous, but Glasgow harbours plenty more distinctively Glaswegian museums.

1 RIVERSIDE MUSEUM
(www.glasgowmuseums.com; Glasgow Harbour; ◷10am-5pm Mon-Thu & Sat, 11am-5pm Fri & Sun) The latest development along the Clyde is this impressive new museum, designed by Iraqi architect Zaha Hadid, due to open in spring 2011 at the time of research. It houses a varied collection, including three re-created Glasgow streets from various points in history, a display of the city's maritime heritage and much of what was formerly in the Museum of Transport.

2 PEOPLE'S PALACE
(www.glasgowmuseums.com; Glasgow Green; ◷10am-5pm Mon-Thu & Sat, 11am-5pm Fri & Sun) Set in the city's oldest park, Glasgow Green, this is an impressive museum of social history telling the story of the city from 1750 to the present.

3 TENEMENT HOUSE
(NTS; Map p130; www.nts.org.uk; 145 Buccleuch St; adult/child/family £5.50/4.50/15; ◷1-5pm Mar-Oct) Gives a vivid insight into middle-class city life in the late 19th century.

4 CLYDEBUILT
(www.scottishmaritimemuseum.com; Kings Inch Rd, Braehead; adult/child £4.25/2.50; ◷10am-5.30pm Mon-Sat, 11am-5.30pm Sun) A superb collection of model ships, industrial displays and narrative, vividly painting the history of the River Clyde, the fate of which has been inextricably linked with Glasgow and its people.

St; mains £9-14; ◷lunch Fri-Sun, dinner daily; 🍴) Glasgow curry buffs are forever debating the merits of the city's numerous excellent south Asian restaurants, and Mother India features in every discussion. It may lack the trendiness of some of the up-and-comers but it's been a stalwart for years and the quality and innovation

on show is superb. They also make a real effort for kids, with a separate menu.

BOTHY Scottish ££
(Map p136; 🕿 0141-334 4040; ww.g1group.co.uk; 11 Ruthven Lane; mains £14-20) A bothy is not normally the most comfortable of abodes but this West End player pays little heed to this tradition, boasting a combo of modern design and comfy retro furnishings. It also blows apart the myth that Scottish food is stodgy and uninteresting. The Bothy dishes out traditional, uniquely Scottish, home-style fare with a modern twist. It's filling, but leave room for dessert. An £11 lunch will get you away cheaper.

ORAN MOR BRASSERIE & CONSERVATORY Scottish ££
(Map p136; 🕿 0141-357 6226; 731 Great Western Rd; mains £10-17) This temple to Scottish dining and drinking is a superb venue in an old church. Giving new meaning to the word 'conversion', the brasserie pumps out high-quality meals in a dark, Mackintosh-inspired space. There are also cheaper bistro-style meals, such as Cullen skink (soup made with smoked haddock, potato, onion and milk) or vegetarian haggis served with Arran mustard sauce, and more relaxed dining in the conservatory, adjoining the main bar (see p144).

BAY TREE CAFÉ Cafe £
(Map p136; 403 Great Western Rd; mains £6-10; ◷9am-10pm Mon-Sat, to 9pm Sun; 🍴) The mostly vegetarian Bay Tree Café is excellent value. It has smiling staff, filling mains (mostly Middle Eastern and Greek), generous salads and a good range of hot drinks. The cafe is famous for its all-day Sunday brunch, including vegetarian burger, tattie scone, mushrooms, beans and tomato. It also serves a vegan breakfast.

🍷 Drinking

Some of Scotland's best nightlife is found in the din and sometimes roar of Glasgow's pubs and bars. There are as many different styles of bar as there are punters to guzzle in them; a month of solid drinking wouldn't get you past the halfway mark.

City Centre

ARTÀ
Bar

(Map p130; www.arta.co.uk; 13-19 Walls St; ⏰until 3am) This extraordinary place is so baroque that when you hear a Mozart concerto over the sound system, it wouldn't surprise you to see the man himself at the other end of the bar. Set in a former cheese market, it really does have to be seen to be believed. As its door slides open, Artà's opulent, cavernous candlelit interior is exposed. There's floor-to-ceiling velvet, with red curtains revealing a staircase to the tapas bar and restaurant above in a show of decadence that the Romans would have appreciated. Despite the luxury, it's got a relaxed, chilled vibe and a mixed crowd. The big cocktails are great.

HORSE SHOE
Pub

(Map p130; www.horseshoebar.co.uk; 17 Drury St) This legendary city pub and popular meeting place dates from the late 19th century and is largely unchanged. It's a picturesque spot, with the longest continuous bar in the UK, but its main attraction is what's served over it – real ale and good food. Upstairs in the lounge is some of the best-value pub food (dishes £3 to £6) in town.

BABBITY BOWSTER
Pub

(Map p130; 16-18 Blackfriars St) In a quiet corner of Merchant City, this handsome spot is perfect for a tranquil daytime drink, particularly in the adjoining beer garden. Service is attentive, and the smell of sausages may tempt you to lunch; there's also accommodation (see p137). This is one of the centre's most charming pubs, in one of its noblest buildings.

The Genius of Charles Rennie Mackintosh

Great cities have great artists, designers and architects contributing to the cultural and historical roots of their urban environment while expressing its soul and individuality. Charles Rennie Mackintosh was all of these. His quirky, linear and geometric designs have had almost as much influence on the city as have Gaudí's on Barcelona. Many of the buildings Mackintosh designed in Glasgow are open to the public, and you'll see his tall, thin, art nouveau typeface repeatedly reproduced.

Born in 1868, Mackintosh studied at the Glasgow School of Art. In 1896, when he was aged only 27, he won a competition for his design of the School of Art's new building. The first section was opened in 1899 and is considered to be the earliest example of art nouveau in Britain, as well as Mackintosh's supreme architectural achievement. This building demonstrates his skill in combining function and style.

Although Mackintosh's genius was quickly recognised on the Continent, he did not receive the same encouragement in Scotland. His architectural career here lasted only until 1914, when he moved to England to concentrate on furniture design. He died in 1928, and it is only since the last decades of the 20th century that Mackintosh's genius has been widely recognised. For more about the man and his work, check out the **Charles Rennie Mackintosh Society** (☎0141-946 6600; www.crmsociety.com; Mackintosh Church, 870 Garscube Rd).

If You Like…
Charles Rennie Mackintosh

If the Glasgow School of Art has fired your enthusiasm for all things Mackintosh, the city has several more delights in store.

1 WILLOW TEA ROOMS
(Map p130; www.willowtearooms.co.uk; 217 Sauchiehall St; ⏱9am-5pm Mon-Sat, 11am-5pm Sun) An authentic reconstruction of tearooms Mackintosh designed and furnished in the early 20th century for restaurateur Kate Cranston.

2 LIGHTHOUSE
(Map p130; www.tlfe.org.uk; 11 Mitchell Lane; ⏱10.30am-5pm Mon-Sat) Mackintosh's first building, designed in 1893, now serves as Scotland's Centre for Architecture & Design.

3 SCOTLAND STREET SCHOOL MUSEUM
(www.glasgowmuseums.com; 225 Scotland St; admission free; ⏱10am-5pm Tue-Thu & Sat, 11am-5pm Fri & Sun) Worth a visit for its superb Mackintosh facade and the interesting museum of education that occupies the interior.

4 HOUSE FOR AN ART LOVER
(www.houseforanartlover.co.uk; Bellahouston Park, Dumbreck Rd; adult/child £4.50/3; ⏱10am-4pm Mon-Wed, to 1pm Thu-Sun) Although designed in 1901, this house was not built until the 1990s. Mackintosh worked closely with his wife on the design and her influence is evident, especially in the rose motif.

5 MACKINTOSH CHURCH
(www.crmsociety.com; 870 Garscube Rd; adult/child £4/2; ⏱10am-5pm Mon-Fri year-round, 2-5pm Sun Mar-Oct) The only one of Mackintosh's church designs to be built.

CORINTHIAN   Bar
(Map p130; www.thecorinthianclub.co.uk; 191 Ingram St) A breathtaking, domed ceiling and majestic chandeliers make Corinthian an awesome venue. Originally a bank and later Glasgow's High Court, this regal building also houses a plush club, downstairs in old court cells, and a piano bar. Closed for renovation at the time of research, it'll be open again by the time you read this.

West End

UISGE BEATHA   Pub
(Map p136; www.uisgebeathabar.co.uk; 232 Woodlands Rd) If you enjoy a drink among dead things, you'll love Uisge Beatha (Gaelic for whisky, literally 'water of life'). This mishmash of church pews, stuffed animal heads and portraits of depressed nobility is patrolled by Andy Capp–like characters during the day and students at night. With 100 whiskies and four quirky rooms to choose from, this unique pub is one of Glasgow's best, and an antidote to style bars.

ORAN MOR   Bar
(www.oran-mor.co.uk; 731 Great Western Rd) Some may be a little uncomfortable with the thought of drinking in a church, but we say the lord *giveth*. Praise be! A converted church – and an almighty one at that – is now a bar, brasserie (see p142) and nightclub. The bar feels like it's been here for years, all wood with thick, exposed stone giving it warmth and a celestial air. There's an excellent array of whiskies. The only thing missing is holy water on your way in.

BREL   Bar
(Map p136; www.brelbarrestaurant.com; 39 Ashton Lane) Perhaps the best on Ashton Lane, this bar can seem tightly packed, but there's a conservatory out the back so you can pretend you're sitting outside when it's raining, and when the sun does peek through there's a beer garden. They've got a huge range of Belgian beers, and they also do mussels and other Lowlands favourites.

⭐ Entertainment

Glasgow is Scotland's entertainment city, from classical music, fine theatres and ballet to cracking nightclubs pumping out state-of-the-art hip-hop, electro, or techno to cheesy chart tunes and contemporary Scottish bands at the cutting edge of modern music.

To tap into your scene, check out *The List* (www.list.co.uk), an invaluable fortnightly events guide available at newsagents and bookshops. The website www.nmbrs.net is good for clubs, while the *Herald* and the *Evening Times* newspapers list events happening around the city.

For theatre tickets book directly with the venue. For concerts, a useful booking centre is **Tickets Scotland** (☎ 0141-204 5151, 0870 220 1116; www.tickets-scotland.com; 239 Argyle St).

Nightclubs

Glasgow has one of Britain's biggest and best clubbing scenes, attracting devotees from afar. Glaswegians usually hit clubs after the pubs have closed, so many clubs offer discounted admission and cheaper drinks if you go before 10.30pm. Entry costs £5 to £10 (up to £25 for big events), although bars often hand out free passes. By law, clubs shut at 3am, so keep your ear to the ground to find out where the after-parties are at.

SUB CLUB   Nightclub
(Map p130; www.subclub.co.uk; 22 Jamaica St) Saturdays at the Sub Club are one of Glasgow's legendary nights, offering serious clubbing with a sound system that aficionados usually rate the city's best. The claustrophobic, last-one-in vibe is not for those faint of heart.

ARCHES   Nightclub
(Map p130; www.thearches.co.uk; 253 Argyle St) R-e-s-p-e-c-t is the mantra with the Arches. The Godfather of Glaswegian clubs, it has a design based around hundreds of arches slammed together, and is a must for funk and hip-hop freaks. It is one of the city's biggest clubs, pulling top DJs, and you'll also hear some of the UK's up-and-coming turntable spinners. It's off Jamaica St.

CLASSIC GRAND   Nightclub
(Map p130; www.classicgrand.com; 18 Jamaica St) Rock, industrial, electronic and power-pop grace the stage and the turntables at this unpretentious central venue. It

The Willow Tea Rooms, designed by Charles Rennie Mackintosh

doesn't take itself too seriously, drinks are cheap and the locals are welcoming.

Live Music

Glasgow is the king of Scotland's live-music scene. Year after year, touring musicians, artists and travellers alike name Glasgow as one of their favourite cities in the world to enjoy live music. As much of Glasgow's character is encapsulated within the soul and humour of its inhabitants, the main reason for the city's musical success lies within its audience and the musical community it has bred and nurtured for years. On any given night you may find your breath taken by a wave of voices as the audience spontaneously harmonises with an artist on a chorus, a song or even, on special nights, an entire show.

There are so many venues it's impossible to keep track of them all. Pick up a copy of the *Gig Guide* (www.gigguide.co.uk), published monthly and available free in most pubs and venues, for the latest on music gigs.

One of the city's premier live-music pub venues, the excellent **King Tut's Wah Wah Hut** (Map p130; www.kingtuts.co.uk; 272a St Vincent St) hosts bands every night of the week. Oasis were signed after playing here.

Other recommendations:

13th Note Cafe   Cafe
(Map p130; www.13thnote.co.uk; 50-60 King St) Also does decent vegetarian food.

ABC   Concert Venue
(O2 ABC; Map p130; www.abcglasgow.com; 300 Sauchiehall St) Former cinema; medium- to large-size acts.

Barrowland   Concert Venue
(Map p130; www.glasgow-barrowland.com; 244 Gallowgate) An exceptional old dancehall catering for some of the larger acts that visit the city.

Captain's Rest   Pub
(Map p136; www.captainsrest.co.uk; 185 Great Western Rd) Variety of indie bands

Clyde Auditorium   Auditorium
(Map p136; ☎0870 040 4000; www.secc.co.uk; Finnieston Quay) Also known as 'the Armadillo'

because of its bizarre shape, adjoins SECC, and caters for big national and international acts.

SECC   Auditorium
(Map p136; ☎0870 040 4000; www.secc.co.uk; Finnieston Quay) Adjoins Clyde Auditorium and hosts major national and international acts. A new venue, Glasgow Arena, is being built alongside.

Theatres & Concert Halls

Theatre Royal   Opera, Ballet
(Map p130; ☎0141-332 3321; www.ambassadortickets.com; 282 Hope St) This is the home of Scottish Opera, and the Scottish Ballet often has performances here. Ask about standby tickets if you'll be in town for a few days.

Glasgow Royal Concert Hall   Concert Hall
(Map p130; ☎0141-353 8080; www.grch.com; 2 Sauchiehall St) A feast of classical music is showcased at this concert hall, the modern home of the Royal Scottish National Orchestra.

King's Theatre   Theatre
(Map p130; ☎0844 871 7648; www.kings-glasgow.co.uk; 297 Bath St) King's Theatre hosts mainly musicals; on rare occasions there are variety shows, pantomimes and comedies.

Citizens' Theatre   Theatre
(☎0141-429 0022; www.citz.co.uk; 119 Gorbals St) This is one of the top theatres in Scotland and it's well worth trying to catch a performance here.

🔒 Shopping

Boasting the UK's largest retail phalanx outside London, Glasgow is a shop-aholic's paradise. The 'Style Mile' around Buchanan St, Argyle St and Merchant City is a fashion hub, while the West End has quirkier, more bohemian shopping options.

BARRAS   Flea Market
(Map p130; btwn Gallowgate & London Rd; ⏱9am-4pm Sat & Sun) Glasgow's flea

NEIL MCALLISTER/ALAMY

Don't Miss **Mackintosh House**

Attached to the Hunterian Art Gallery, this is a reconstruction of the first home that Charles Rennie Mackintosh bought with his wife, noted artist Mary Macdonald. It's fair to say that interior decoration was one of their strong points; the Mackintosh House is startling even today. The quiet elegance of the hall and dining room on the ground floor give way to a stunning drawing room. There's something otherworldly about the very mannered style of the beaten silver panels, the long-backed chairs and the surface decorations echoing Celtic manuscript illuminations. You wouldn't have wanted to be a guest that spilled a glass of red on this carpet.

THINGS YOU NEED TO KNOW

Map p136; www.hunterian.gla.ac.uk; 82 Hillhead St; admission £3, free after 2pm Wed; ⊘9.30am-5pm Mon-Sat

market, the Barras on Gallowgate is the living, breathing heart of this city in many respects. It has almost a thousand stalls and people come here just for a wander as much as for shopping, which gives the place a holiday air. The Barras is notorious for designer frauds, so be cautious. Watch your wallet, too.

Buchanan Galleries   Shopping Centre
(Map p130; www.buchanangalleries.co.uk; Royal Exchange Sq) Huge number of contemporary clothing retailers.

Argyll Arcade   Jewellery
(Map p130; www.argyll-arcade.com; Buchanan St) Splendid, jewellery-laden arcade.

Geoffrey (Tailor) Kiltmaker   Kilts
(Map p130; www.geoffrey kilts.co.uk; 309 Sauchiehall St) The place to head to take some tartan home.

147

MIKE BOOTH/ALAMY

Don't Miss **Burrell Collection**

One of Glasgow's top attractions is the Burrell Collection. Amassed by wealthy industrialist Sir William Burrell before being donated to the city, it is housed in an outstanding museum, 3 miles south of the city centre. This idiosyncratic collection includes everything from Chinese porcelain and medieval furniture to paintings by Renoir and Cézanne, but it's not so big as to be overwhelming.

Visitors will find their own favourite part of this museum, but the exquisite tapestry galleries are outstanding. Intricate stories capturing life in Europe are woven into staggering, wall-size pieces dating from the 13th century. The huge *Triumph of the Virgin* exemplifies the complexity in nature and theme of this medium, while posing the serious question: 'how long must this have taken?'.

Within the spectacular interior, carved-stone Romanesque doorways are incorporated into the structure so you actually walk through them. Floor-to-ceiling windows admit a flood of light, and enable the surrounding landscape outside to enhance the effect of the exhibits. It feels like you're wandering in a huge tranquil greenhouse.

In springtime, it's worth making a full day of your trip here and spending some time wandering in the beautiful park, studded with flowers. Once part of the estates of Pollok House, which can be visited, the grounds have numerous enticing picnic spots; if you're not heading further north, here's the place to see shaggy Highland cattle, as well as heavy horses.

Many buses pass the park gates (including buses 45, 47, 48 and 57 from the city centre), and there's a twice-hourly bus service between the gallery and the gates (a pleasant 10-minute walk). Alternatively catch a train to Pollokshaws West from Central station (four per hour; you want the second station on the line for East Kilbride or Kilmarnock).

THINGS YOU NEED TO KNOW

Map p118; www.glasgowmuseums.com; Pollok Country Park; admission free; ☺10am-5pm Mon-Thu & Sat, 11am-5pm Fri & Sun

Information

Medical Services

To see a doctor, visit the outpatients department at any general hospital. Recommended hospitals:

Glasgow Dental Hospital (0141-211 9600; 378 Sauchiehall St)

Glasgow Royal Infirmary (0141-211 4000; 84 Castle St)

Western Infirmary (0141-211 2000; Dumbarton Rd)

Tourist Information

Tourist Office (Map p130; 0141-204 4400; www.seeglasgow.com; 11 George Sq; 9am-5pm Mon-Sat) Excellent tourist office; makes local and national accommodation bookings (£4). Closes later and opens Sundays in summer.

Tourist office branch (0141-848 4440; Glasgow International Airport; 7.30am-5pm)

 # Getting There & Away

Air

Ten miles west of the city, **Glasgow International Airport** (www.glasgowairport .com) handles domestic traffic and international flights. **Glasgow Prestwick Airport** (www .gpia.co.uk), 30 miles southwest of Glasgow, is used by **Ryanair** (www.ryanair.com) and some other budget airlines, with many connections to the rest of Britain and Europe.

Bus

All long-distance buses arrive and depart from **Buchanan bus station** (Map p130; 0141-333 3708; www.spt.co.uk/bus/bbs; Killermont St), which has pricey lockers, ATMs, and a cafe with wi-fi.

Scottish Citylink (0870 550 5050; www .citylink.co.uk) has buses to most major towns in Scotland, including: Edinburgh (£6.30, 1¼ hours, every 15 minutes), Stirling (£6.60, 45 minutes, at least hourly), Inverness (£25.50, 3½ hours, eight daily), Aberdeen (£26.50, 2¾ to four hours, hourly), Oban (£16.40, three hours, four direct daily), Fort William (£20.50, three hours, seven daily) and Portree on Skye (£38.20, 6¼ to seven hours, three daily).

Car & Motorcyle

There are numerous car-rental companies; the big names have offices at Glasgow and Prestwick airports. Companies include the following:

Arnold Clark (0141-423 9559; www.arnold clarkrental.com; 43 Allison St)

Avis (0141-544 6064; www.avis.co.uk; 70 Lancefield St)

Europcar (0141-249 4106; www.europcar .com; 76 Lancefield Quay)

Train

As a general rule, Glasgow Central station serves southern Scotland, England and Wales, and Queen St station serves the north and east. There are buses every 10 minutes between them. There are direct trains from London's King's Cross and Euston stations; they're much quicker (advance purchase single £60, full fare £144, 4½ hours, more than hourly) and more comfortable than the bus.

First ScotRail (08457 55 00 33; www. scotrail.co.uk) runs Scottish trains. Destinations include: Edinburgh (£11.50, 50 minutes, every 15 minutes), Oban (£19.30, three hours, three to four daily), Fort William (£23.40, 3¾ hours, four to five daily), Dundee (£22.60, 1½ hours, hourly), Aberdeen (£40.30, 2½ hours, hourly) and Inverness (£70.40, 3½ hours, 10 daily, four on Sunday).

 # Getting Around

Public Transport

BUS City bus services, mostly run by **First Glasgow** (0141-423 6600; www.firstglasgow .com), are frequent. You can buy tickets when you board buses but on most you must have the exact change.

TRAIN & UNDERGROUND There's an extensive suburban network of trains in and around Glasgow; tickets should be bought before travel if the station is staffed or from the conductor if it isn't. There's also an underground line that serves 15 stations in the centre, west and south of the city.

Taxi

You can pay by credit card with **Glasgow Taxis** (0141-429 7070; www.glasgowtaxis.co.uk) if you order by phone.

LOCH LOMOND & AROUND

The 'bonnie banks' and 'bonnie braes' of Loch Lomond have long been Glasgow's rural retreat – a scenic region of hills, lochs and healthy fresh air within easy reach of Scotland's largest city (Loch Lomond is within an hour's drive of 70% of Scotland's population). Since the 1930s Glaswegians have made a regular weekend exodus to the hills – by car, by bike and on foot – and today the loch's popularity shows no sign of decreasing.

The region's importance was recognised when it became the heart of **Loch Lomond & the Trossachs National Park** (www.lochlomond-trossachs.org) – Scotland's first national park, created in 2002.

Loch Lomond is the largest lake in mainland Britain and, after Loch Ness, perhaps the most famous of Scotland's lochs. Its proximity to Glasgow (20 miles away) means that the tourist honeypots of Balloch, Loch Lomond Shores and

Luss get pretty crowded in summer. The main tourist focus is along the A82 on the loch's western shore, and at the southern end, around Balloch, which occasionally becomes a nightmare of jet skis and motorboats. The eastern shore, which is followed by the West Highland Way long-distance footpath, is a little quieter.

 Activities

WALKING

The big walk around here is the **West Highland Way** (www.west-highland-way.co.uk), which runs along the eastern shore of the loch. There are shorter lochside walks at Firkin Point on the western shore and at several other places around the loch. You can get further information on local walks from the national park information centres at Loch Lomond Shores and Balmaha.

Rowardennan is the starting point for an ascent of **Ben Lomond** (974m), a

popular and relatively easy five- to six-hour round trip. The route starts at the car park just past the Rowardennan Hotel.

BOAT TRIPS

The main centre for boat trips is Balloch, where **Sweeney's Cruises** (www. sweeney.uk.com; Balloch Rd) offers a range of trips including a one-hour cruise to Inchmurrin and back (adult/child £7/4, departs hourly), and a two-hour cruise (£12.50/6, departs 1pm and 3pm) around the islands. The quay is directly opposite Balloch train station, beside the tourist office. Sweeney's also runs hourly cruises from the Maid of the Loch jetty at Loch Lomond Shores.

Cruise Loch Lomond (www.cruise lochlomondltd.com) is based in Tarbet and offers trips to Inversnaid and Rob Roy MacGregor's Cave. You can also be dropped off at Rowardennan and picked up at Inversnaid after a 9-mile hike along the West Highland Way.

The mail boat, run by **Balmaha Boatyard** (www.balmahaboatyard .co.uk; The Boatyard, Balmaha), cruises from Balmaha to the loch's four inhabited islands, departing at 11.30am and returning at 2pm with a one-hour stop on Inchmurrin (adult/child £9/4.50). Trips depart daily in July and August, and Monday, Thursday and Saturday in May, June and September.

OTHER ACTIVITIES

The mostly traffic-free **Clyde and Loch Lomond Cycle Way** links Glasgow to Balloch (20 miles), where it links with the **West Loch Lomond Cycle Path**, which continues along the loch shore to Tarbet (10 miles).

You can rent **rowing boats** at Balmaha Boatyard for £10/30 per hour/day (or £20/50 for a boat with outboard motor). **Lomond Adventure** (01360-870218), also in Balmaha, rents

151

out Canadian **canoes** (£30 per day) and **sea kayaks** (£25).

At Loch Lomond Shores you can hire canoes (£12/17 per half/full hour) and bicycles (£12/17 per three hours/full day), take a **guided canoe trip** on the loch (£30 for two hours) or try **power kiting** (£30 for 2½ hours).

ℹ Information

Balloch tourist office (☎ 0870 720 0607; Balloch Rd; ⏰ 9.30am-6pm Jun-Aug, 10am-6pm Apr & Sep)

Balmaha National Park Centre (☎ 01389-722100; Balmaha; ⏰ 9.30am-4.15pm Apr-Sep)

National Park Gateway Centre (☎ 01389-751035; www.lochlomondshores.com; Loch Lomond Shores, Balloch; ⏰ 10am-6pm Apr-Sep, 10am-5pm Oct-Mar; @ 🖂)

Tarbet tourist office (☎ 0870-720 0623; ⏰ 10am-6pm Jul & Aug, 10am-5pm Easter-Jun, Sep & Oct) At the junction of the A82 and the A83.

ℹ Getting There & Away

BUS Glasgow company First (www.firstgroup.com) runs buses 204 and 215 from Argyle St in central Glasgow to Balloch and Loch Lomond Shores (1½ hours, at least two per hour).

Citylink (www.citylink.co.uk) coaches from Glasgow to Oban and Fort William stop at Luss (£8, 55 minutes, six daily), Tarbet (£8, 65 minutes) and Ardlui (£14, 1¼ hours).

TRAIN There are frequent trains from Glasgow to Balloch (£4.15, 45 minutes, every 30 minutes) and a less frequent service on the West Highland line from Glasgow to Arrochar & Tarbet station (£10, 1¼ hours, three or four daily), halfway between the two villages, and Ardlui (£13, 1½ hours), continuing to Oban and Fort William.

ℹ Getting Around

Pick up the useful **public transport booklet** (free), which lists timetables for all bus, train and ferry services in Loch Lomond and the Trossachs National Park, available from any tourist office or park information centre.

BUS Bus 309 from McColl's Coaches (www.mccolls.org.uk) runs from Balloch to Balmaha (25 minutes, every two hours). An SPT Daytripper ticket (www.spt.co.uk/tickets) gives a family group unlimited travel for a day on most bus and train services in the Glasgow, Loch Lomond and Helensburgh area. Buy the ticket (£9.80 for one adult and one or two children, £17.50 for two adults and up to four children) from any train station or the main Glasgow bus station.

BOAT There are several passenger ferries on Loch Lomond, with fares ranging from £3 to £7 per person; bicycles are carried free. Except for the ferries out of Loch Lomond Shores, these are mostly small motorboats that operate on demand, rather than to a set timetable.

Western Shore

The town of **Balloch**, which straddles the River Leven where it flows from the southern end of Loch Lomond, is the loch's main population centre and transport

Burns Cottage, Alloway

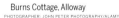

Detour:
Alloway

The pretty town of Alloway (3 miles south of Ayr) should be on the itinerary of every Robert Burns fan – he was born here on 25 January 1759. It's also worth a visit for a good impression of Ayrshire life in the late 18th century.

The brand new **Robert Burns Birthplace Musuem** (NTS; www.nts.org.uk; adult/child £8/5; ⏰10am-5pm Oct-Mar, 10am-5.30pm Apr-Sep) displays a solid collection of Burnsiana, including the poet's manuscripts and possessions (like the pistols he packed for his daily job, as a taxman). A Burns jukebox offers readings of your favourite verses, and there are other entertaining audio and visual performances.

The admission ticket (valid for three days) also covers the atmospheric **Burns Cottage**, connected by a sculpture-lined walkway from the Birthplace Museum. Born in the little box bed in this cramped thatched dwelling, the poet spent the first seven years of his life here. It's an attractive display which gives you a context for reading plenty of his verse, with translations of some of the more obscure Scots farming terms he loved to use.

Near the Birthplace Museum are the ruins of the **Alloway Auld Kirk**, the setting for part of his poem 'Tam o'Shanter'. Burns' father, William Burnes (his son dropped the 'e' from his name), is buried in the kirkyard; read the poem on the back of the gravestone.

The **Burns Monument & Gardens** are nearby. The monument was built in 1823 and affords a view of the 13th-century **Brig o'Doon**.

hub. A Victorian resort once thronged by day-trippers transferring between the train station and the steamer quay, it is now a 'gateway centre' for Loch Lomond and the Trossachs National Park.

Loch Lomond Shores (www.lochlomond shores.com), a major tourism development a half-mile north of Balloch, sports a national park information centre plus various visitor attractions, outdoor activities and boat trips. In keeping with the times, the heart of the development is a large shopping mall. It's also home to the **Loch Lomond Aquarium** (www.sea life.co.uk; adult/child £12/9; ⏰10am-5pm), which has displays on the wildlife of Loch Lomond, an otter enclosure (housing short-clawed Asian otters, not Scottish ones), and a host of sea-life exhibits ranging from sharks to stingrays to sea turtles.

The vintage paddle steamer **Maid of the Loch** (www.maidoftheloch.com; admission free; ⏰11am-4pm daily May-Oct, Sat & Sun only Nov-Apr), built in 1953, is moored here while awaiting full restoration – you can nip aboard for a look around.

Unless it's raining, give Loch Lomond Shores a miss and head for the little picture-postcard village of **Luss**. Stroll among the pretty cottages with roses around their doors (the cottages were built by the local laird in the 19th century for the workers on his estate), then pop into the **Clan Colquhoun tourist office** (adult/child £1/free; ⏰10.30am-6pm Easter-Oct) for some background history before enjoying a cup of tea at the Coach House Coffee Shop.

 Sleeping & Eating

DROVER'S INN   Pub   £
(☎ 01301-704234; www.thedroversinn.co.uk; Inverarnan; bar meals £8-10, steaks £15-17; ⏰lunch & dinner; P) This is one howff (drinking den) you shouldn't miss – a low-ceilinged place with smoke-black-ened stone, bare wooden floors spotted with candle wax, barmen in kilts and walls festooned with moth-eaten stag's heads and stuffed birds. There's even a stuffed bear, and the desiccated husk of a

153

basking shark. The bar serves hearty hill-walking fuel such as steak-and-Guinness pie with mustard mash, and hosts live folk music on Friday and Saturday nights. We recommend this inn more as a place to eat and drink than to stay – accommodation (single/double from £40/78) varies from eccentric, old-fashioned and rather run-down rooms in the old building (including a ghost in room 6), to more comfortable rooms (with en suite bathrooms) in the modern annexe across the road. Ask to see your room before taking it.

LOCH LOMOND YOUTH HOSTEL
Hostel £

(SYHA; ☎ 01389-850226; www.syha.org.uk; Arden; dm £18; ☺Mar-Oct; **P** @ ☎) Forget about roughing it, this is one of the most impressive hostels in the country – an imposing 19th-century country house set in beautiful grounds overlooking the loch. It's 2 miles north of Balloch and very popular, so book in advance in summer. And yes, it *is* haunted.

ARDLUI HOTEL
Hotel ££

(☎ 01301-704243; www.ardlui.co.uk; Ardlui; s/d £60/95; **P**) If the Drover's Inn is a little rough for your bedtime tastes, nip down the road to the plush Ardlui Hotel, a comfy country-house hotel with a great loch-side location and a view of Ben Lomond from the breakfast room.

COACH HOUSE COFFEE SHOP
Cafe £

(Luss; mains £5-11; ☺10am-5pm) With its chunky pine furniture and deep, deep sofa in front of a rustic fireplace, the Coach House is one of the cosiest places to eat on Loch Lomond. The menu includes coffee and tea, home-baked cakes, scones, ciabattas and more substantial offerings such as haggis.

Eastern Shore

The road along the loch's eastern shore passes through the attractive village of **Balmaha**, where you can hire boats or take a cruise on the mail boat. There are several picnic areas along the lochside; the most attractive is at **Millarochy Bay** (1.5 miles north of Balmaha), which has a nice gravel beach and superb views across the loch to the Luss hills.

The road ends at **Rowardennan**, but the West Highland Way continues north along the shore of the loch. It's 7 miles to Inversnaid, which can be reached by

Clyde Auditorium (p146)

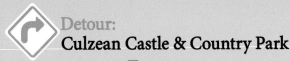

Detour:
Culzean Castle & Country Park

Magnificent **Culzean** (NTS; ☎01655-884400; www.culzeanexperience.org; adult/child/family £13/9/32, park only adult/child £8.50/5.50; ⊙castle 10.30am-5pm Apr-Oct, park 9.30am-sunset year round) is one of Scotland's most impressive stately homes. Designed by Robert Adam, the most influential architect of his time, this 18th-century mansion is perched dramatically on the edge of the cliffs. The entrance to Culzean (kull-*ane*) is a converted viaduct, and on approach the castle appears like a mirage, floating into view.

The beautiful oval staircase here is regarded as one of Adam's finest achievements. On the 1st floor, the opulence of the circular saloon contrasts with the views of the wild sea below. Lord Cassillis' bedroom is said to be haunted by a lady in green, mourning for a lost baby. Even the bathrooms are palatial, and the state bedroom's dressing room has a Victorian state-of-the-art shower.

There are also two ice houses, a swan pond, a pagoda, a re-creation of a Victorian vinery, an orangery, a deer park and an aviary. Wildlife in the area includes otters.

If you really want to experience the magic of this place, it's possible to stay in the **castle** (s/d from £150/225, Eisenhower ste £250/375; P) from April to October.

Culzean is 49 miles south of Glasgow. Maybole is the nearest train station, but since it's 4 miles away it's best to come by bus from Ayr (30 minutes, 11 daily, Monday to Saturday); there are frequent trains from Glasgow to Ayr. Buses pass the park gates, from where it's a 20-minute walk through the grounds to the castle.

road from the Trossachs, and 15 miles to Inverarnan on the main A82 road at the northern end of the loch.

 ## Sleeping & Eating

OAK TREE INN Inn ££
(☎ 01360-870357; www.oak-tree-inn.co.uk; Balmaha; dm/s/d £30/60/75; P🐾) An attractive traditional inn built in slate and timber, the child-friendly Oak Tree offers luxurious guest bedrooms for pampered hikers, and two four-bed bunkrooms for hardier souls. The rustic **restaurant** dishes up hearty lunches and dinners (meals £8 to £15) such as steak-and-mushroom pie, and roast Arctic char with lime and chive butter, and cooks up an excellent bowl of Cullen Skink.

PASSFOOT COTTAGE B&B ££
(☎ 01360-870324; www.passfoot.com; Balmaha; s/d from £55/64; ⊙Apr-Sep) Passfoot is a pretty little whitewashed cottage decked out with colourful flower baskets, with a lovely location overlooking Balmaha Bay. The bright bedrooms have a homely feel, and there's a large lounge with a wood-burning stove and loch view.

ROWARDENNAN HOTEL Hotel, Bar ££
(☎ 01360-870273; www.rowardennanhotel.co.uk; Rowardennan; s/d £65/90; bar meals £7-11; ⊙lunch & dinner; P) Originally an 18th-century drovers' inn, the Rowardennan has two big bars (often crowded with rain-sodden hikers) and a good beer garden (often crowded with midges). It had just been taken over by new owners at the time of research, and much-needed refurbishment has made it a pleasant place to stay, with a choice of traditional but stylish hotel rooms and luxury self-catering lodges.

Stirling & Northeast Scotland

Many visitors pass by this corner of the country in their headlong rush to the tourist honey-pots of Loch Ness and Skye. But they're missing out on a region that's as beautiful and diverse as the more obvious attractions of the western Highlands and islands.

Stirling and the northeast is the historic and cultural heartland of Scotland. Iconic sites that chronicle the country's turbulent history pepper the landscape, from the battlefields of Bannockburn and Killiecrankie to the castles of Stirling and Glamis, and the ancient coronation place of Scottish kings at Scone.

Here too is St Andrews, the home of golf; Balmoral Castle, the holiday retreat of British monarchs since Victorian times; and glorious Speyside, dotted with dozens of whisky distilleries. All set in a landscape that increases in drama from the picturesque lochs and woods of the Trossachs to the full-blown grandeur of the Grampian mountains.

Walker on the summit of Ben A'an (p186) overlooking Loch Katrine, the Trossachs

PHOTOGRAPHER: DAVID ROBERTSON/ALAMY

Bracklinn Falls (p183)

Stirling & the Northeast

1. Stirling Castle
2. Speyside Whisky Trail
3. St Andrews
4. Royal Deeside
5. Scone Palace
6. The Trossachs
7. Blair Castle

Stirling & Northeast Scotland's Highlights

① Stirling Castle

Edinburgh Castle tops the visitor stakes, but in terms of history and heritage its sister fortress at Stirling is arguably more rewarding. This sturdy bastion has played a pivotal role in many key events of Scottish history, and was once a residence of the Stuart monarchs.

Need to Know

BEST TIME TO GO Last two hours before closing (to avoid crowds). **COFFEE STOP** Darnley Coffee House (p176). **BEST PHOTO OP** View across River Forth to Wallace Monument. **For more, see p170.**

Stirling Castle Don't Miss List

PETER YEOMAN, HISTORIC SCOTLAND'S HEAD OF CULTURAL RESOURCES

1 GREAT HALL

The largest medieval banqueting hall ever built in Scotland (pictured left), created by James IV around 1503 as a spectacular setting for great state occasions. Recently restored to its former glory with the only new hammerbeam oak roof built in Britain since medieval times. Now a venue for fabulous evening concerts and dinners.

2 ROYAL PALACE

A sumptuous suite of apartments created by the young James V for his aristocratic French bride, Mary of Guise. Recreated interiors feature period furniture, fittings, textiles and decoration, but the king's lodgings are left bare as they would have been after his untimely death in 1542. These magnificent rooms are enlivened by the carved replicas of oak roundels known as the Stirling Heads, and by a spectacular new tapestry series in the Queen's Lodgings.

3 MUSICAL HEAD

During restoration, John Donaldson, the talented carver who copied all 36 Stirling Heads for the replica ceiling, discovered musical notation secreted in the border of one of the heads. The lady depicted in the portrait even seems to have her lips parted in song. This beautiful harp tune, perhaps created for James V, will be playing in a new permanent exhibition, 'Image-Makers to the King'.

4 PALACE VAULTS

The castle's 'below-stairs' life in the time of James V and Mary of Guise is explored in a series of family-friendly displays on the trades essential to court life. Follow the work of the painters, tailors, musicians, carvers and jesters to explore everyday life at Stirling in the 1540s.

5 BRAVEHEART!

The castle overlooks two great battlefields, Stirling Bridge (1297) and Bannockburn (1314), both fought and won by the Scots against the English over possession of Stirling Castle. William Wallace's decisive victory at Stirling Bridge is powerfully commemorated in the **National Wallace Monument** (p180; pictured left).

Speyside Whisky Trail

No trip to Scotland is complete without visiting a whisky distillery, and the Speyside region is the heartland of Scotch whisky with no fewer than 50 distilleries. Dufftown lies at the middle of it all, within easy reach of seven distilleries, and sporting its own whisky museum.

Need to Know

TOP TIP Distillery tours are popular. Book in advance. **BEST TIME TO GO** May or September, for the Spirit of Speyside festivals. **BEST PHOTO OP** Stacks of casks at Speyside Cooperage. **For more, see p208.**

Speyside Don't Miss List

IAN LOGAN, BRAND AMBASSADOR, CHIVAS BROTHERS

1 THE GLENLIVET DISTILLERY

The home of the most iconic single malt whisky in the world, the Glenlivet (www.theglenlivet.com; at Ballindalloch, 10 miles west of Dufftown), offers a great mix of old and new, and a chance to see how modern technology has been adapted to work alongside traditional techniques. If you are a whisky connoisseur, join me on my weekly tour and discover behind-the-scenes secrets.

2 SPEYSIDE COOPERAGE

The Speyside Cooperage (see the boxed text, p210) gives you a chance to watch a craft that has changed little over the centuries – the quality of the cask is one of the biggest contributing factors to the flavour of a single malt. The team here supply barrels to distilleries all over the world and share with the distillers the passion of creating the finest whiskies in the world.

3 GORDON & MACPHAIL

The most famous whisky shop in the world, Gordon & MacPhail (www.gordonandmacphail.com; 58-60 South St, Elgin) is home to some of the oldest whiskies, including a 70-year-old Mortlach. The Urquhart family (owners) have played an important part in making single malt whisky what it is today, bottling these whiskies long before the distillers ever did.

4 CORGARFF CASTLE

The impressive and remote Corgarff Castle (near Cockbridge, 30 miles south of Dufftown on the road to Ballater) was once home to the redcoats whose job it was to chase down illegal distillers in the early 19th century.

5 GROUSE INN

Set deep in the heart of the old smuggling country, this remote pub at Cabrach, in the hills 10 miles south of Dufftown, has nearly 250 single malts on offer, with many many more on display around the bar – a collection that is home to several rare and unique bottlings.

Bottom left: Clocktower in the centre of Dufftown

163

St Andrews

Scotland is the home of golf, and the Old Course at St Andrews (p188) – the world's oldest golf course – is on every golfer's wish list. But there's more to the place than golf. This was once Scotland's religious capital, and the remains of castle and cathedral are well worth visiting. And don't miss the magnificent West Sands, where scenes from the movie *Chariots of Fire* were filmed.

Royal Deeside

The valley of the River Dee – often called Royal Deeside (p204) because of the royal family's long association with the area – is famed for its salmon fishing, forest walks and grandiose castles, including the Queen's holiday home at Balmoral Castle (p209). Other charms include the pretty village of Ballater, and the remote outpost of Braemar, home to Scotland's most famous Highland games.

SCOTTISH VIEWPOINT/ALAMY

Scone Palace

4

This sumptuous stately home (p188) near Perth exudes history from every corniced nook and cranny. Kenneth MacAilpin, the first king of a united Scotland, was crowned on this site in AD 838, and Scone became the traditional coronation site of Scottish kings. The famous Stone of Destiny was stolen from here by the English King Edward I in 1296; it subsequently became a powerful symbol of Scottish nationhood.

6

The Trossachs

Made famous by Sir Walter Scott's writings in the early 19th century during the first flush of Scottish tourism, the Trossachs is a region of scenic lochs ringed by craggy, wooded hills often described as 'the Highlands in miniature'. At its heart is Loch Katrine, where a classic steamboat cruises the waters among remote hills that were once the territory of the outlaw Rob Roy MacGregor.

7

Blair Castle

The ancient seat of the dukes and earls of Atholl, Blair Castle controls the main route north to Inverness along the valley of the River Tay. Its long and illustrious history is displayed in sumptuous suites and grand drawing rooms, where visitors also learn about the Atholl Highlanders, Europe's only private standing army. Nearby is Killiecrankie, a key battlefield in the Jacobite rebellion of the 18th century.

Stirling & Northeast Scotland's Best…

Castles

○ **Stirling Castle** (p170)
Hilltop fortress that has played a crucial role in Scottish history

○ **Glamis Castle** (p206)
Regal, turreted childhood home of the late Queen Mother

○ **Balmoral Castle** (p209)
The Queen's holiday home, built in classic Scottish Baronial style

○ **St Andrews Castle** (p187)
Historic ruin with coastal views and a warren of former siege tunnels

Museums

○ **British Golf Museum** (p188) The history of golf chronicled in the home of golf

○ **Scottish Fisheries Museum** (p196) Everything you need to know about the fishing industry, including restored wooden boats afloat in the harbour

○ **Angus Folk Museum** (p206) A fascinating insight into rural life in Scotland in the 18th and 19th centuries

○ **Whisky Museum** (p210) Whisky distilling, distilled (as it were)

Cultural Experiences

○ **Braemar Gathering** (p208) The most famous Highland games in the country, favoured by royalty

○ **Spirit of Speyside** (p210) Twice-yearly festival of whisky, complete with tastings, local food stalls and traditional music

○ **St Andrews Festival** (p189) A rip-roaring celebration of all things Scottish, from haggis to Highland dancing

○ **Pitlochry Festival Theatre** (p202) Since its founding in 1951, the 'Theatre in the Hills' has become a national cultural institution

Need to Know

Historic Sites

○ **Bannockburn** (p173) The battlefield where Robert the Bruce won independence for Scotland in 1314

○ **Scone Palace** (p188) Ancient crowning place of Scottish kings, once home to the Stone of Destiny

○ **Balquhidder** (p184) The former stamping ground (and last resting place) of outlaw Rob Roy MacGregor, romanticised in novel and film

○ **Killiecrankie** (p201) Scenic beauty spot and site of pivotal battle in the 18th-century Jacobite rebellion

Clocktower at Balmoral Castle (p211); **Above:** St Andrews Castle (p189)

PHOTOGRAPHER: (BOTH PHOTOS) JONATHAN SMITH

ADVANCE PLANNING

○ **Six months before** Reserve a tee time for playing golf on St Andrews Old Course

○ **Two weeks before** Book accommodation if visiting in summer

○ **One week before** Make bookings for Speyside distillery tours and Trossachs boat trips

RESOURCES

○ **Scottish Heartlands** (www.visitscottishheartlands .com) Tourist information for Stirling and the Trossachs

○ **Aberdeen & Grampian** (www.aberdeen-grampian .com) Tourist information for Royal Deeside

○ **Highlands of Scotland** (www.visithighlands.com) Tourist information for Speyside

○ **Loch Lomond & The Trossachs National Park** (www.lochlomond-trossachs .org) Wildlife, activities, things to see, public transport

○ **Visit Fife** (www.visitfife .com) Tourist information for St Andrews and the East Neuk of Fife

○ **Whisky Trail** (www .maltwhiskytrail.com) Places to visit near Dufftown in Speyside

GETTING AROUND

○ **Bus** Good network of intercity and local buses

○ **Car** The most time-efficient way to get around this region

○ **Train** OK for reaching major centres from Edinburgh or Glasgow, but less useful for day-to-day getting around – the railway lines skirt the region to east and west

BE FOREWARNED

○ **Open Golf Championship** Check to see if it's being staged in St Andrews before you go – if so, accommodation will be impossible to find, and the roads approaching town will be clogged with traffic

Stirling & Northeast Scotland Itineraries

These routes cover the heart-land of Scottish history and nationhood, from Bannockburn battlefield and Stirling Castle to the whisky capital of Speyside.

3 DAYS

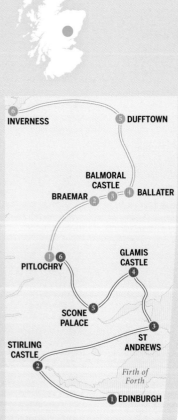

INVERNESS

DUFFTOWN ⑤

BALMORAL CASTLE

BRAEMAR ② ③ ① BALLATER

PITLOCHRY ① ⑥

GLAMIS CASTLE ④

SCONE PALACE ⑤

STIRLING CASTLE ②

ST ANDREWS ③

Firth of Forth

EDINBURGH ①

EDINBURGH TO PITLOCHRY

The History Trail

It's little more than a 30-minute drive along the M9 from **(1) Edinburgh** to the imposing fortress of **(2) Stirling Castle** – approaching this way, along the ancient invasion route from England, it's easy to see how Stirling controls the road to the north. Visiting the castle and the nearby Bannockburn and Wallace Monument will take the best part of the day, before you head east on the A91 to **(3) St Andrews**.

Allow a day for this old ecclesiastical capital, taking in the ruined cathedral, the castle and perhaps even a game of golf on one of several world-famous courses. Cross the Tay Bridge and head for **(4) Glamis Castle**, an imposing turreted pile famous for resident ghosts and royal connections; don't forget the Angus Folk Museum near the castle entrance. The A94 leads back west to **(5) Scone Palace**, the ancient crowning place of Scottish kings and the original resting place of the Stone of Destiny.

A final 35-mile stretch north along the fast A9 road will bring you to **(6) Pitlochry** and nearby Blair Castle, seat of the Duke of Atholl who heads Britain's only private army.

Top Left: Glamis Castle (p208); **Top Right:** The Braemar Gathering Highland Games (p210)

PHOTOGRAPHER: JONATHAN SMITH (BOTH PHOTOS)

5 DAYS

PITLOCHRY TO INVERNESS

Castles & Whisky

If you have a couple more days to play with, you can extend the first itinerary to Inverness via Royal Deeside and Speyside. From **(1) Pitlochry** the day starts with a two-hour scenic drive across the hills on the A924 and B950 to reach the A93. Follow this north over the high pass of Glenshee and down to the classic Highland village of **(2) Braemar**, a good place to stop for lunch.

After a look at Braemar Castle or a walk up Creag Choinnich, a short drive east on the Aberdeen road will bring you to **(3) Balmoral Castle**, the royal family's holiday home (they usually visit in August). Allow at least two hours for exploring this fascinating royal estate before continuing to the pretty village of **(4) Ballater** for an overnight stop.

Another scenic drive awaits on the following morning, on the famous A939 Cockbridge to Tomintoul road, usually the first to be blocked with snow at the onset of winter. From Tomintoul a B-road leads north to Bridge of Avon on the A95, which runs along the Spey valley with whisky distilleries on every side, to reach **(5) Dufftown**, the whisky capital. From here, it's a 90-minute drive via Elgin to **(6) Inverness**.

Discover Stirling & Northeast Scotland

Scottish whisky distillery, Speyside (p212)
PHOTOGRAPHER: ICONPIX/ALAMY

STIRLING

POP 32,673

With an utterly impregnable position atop a mighty wooded crag (the plug of an extinct volcano), Stirling's beautifully preserved Old Town is a treasure-trove of noble buildings and cobbled streets winding up to the ramparts of its dominant castle, which offer views for miles around. Clearly visible is the brooding Wallace Monument, a strange Victorian Gothic creation honouring the legendary freedom fighter of *Braveheart* fame. Nearby is Bannockburn, scene of Robert the Bruce's major triumph over the English.

The castle makes a fascinating visit, but make sure you spend time exploring the Old Town and the picturesque path that encircles it. Near the castle are a couple of snug pubs in which to toast Scotland's hoary heroes. Below the Old Town, retail-minded modern Stirling doesn't offer the same appeal; stick to the high ground as much as possible and you'll love the place.

 Sights

STIRLING CASTLE Castle
(HS; www.historic-scotland.gov.uk;
⊙9.30am-6pm Apr-Sep, to 5pm Oct-Mar) Hold Stirling and you control Scotland. This maxim has ensured that a fortress of some kind has existed here since prehistoric times. With its superb views, you cannot help drawing parallels with Edinburgh castle – but many find Stirling's fortress more atmospheric; the location, architecture and historical significance combine to make it a grand

and memorable visit. This means it draws plenty of visitors, so it's advisable to visit in the afternoon; many tourists come on day trips from Edinburgh or Glasgow, so you may have the castle to yourself by about 4pm.

There has been a fortress of some kind here for several thousand years, but the current building dates from the late 14th to the 16th century, when it was a residence of the Stuart monarchs. The **Great Hall** and **Gatehouse** were built by James IV; observe the hammer-beam roof and huge fireplaces in the largest medieval hall in Scotland – the result of 35 years of restoration.

After a long restoration project, the **Royal Palace** is scheduled to re-open as this book hits the shelves. It'll be a sumptuous recreation of how this luxurious Renaissance palace would have looked when it was constructed by French masons under the orders of James V (in the early 16th century) to impress his (also French) bride and other crowned heads of Europe. Perhaps the most spectacular is the series of **tapestries** that have been painstakingly woven. Based on originals in New York's Metropolitan Museum, they depict the hunting of a unicorn – an event ripe with Christian metaphor – and are utterly beautiful. Until the last one is complete (probably in 2013) you can watch the weavers at work in the **Tapestry Studio**: it's fascinating to see. James VI (r 1567–1625) remodelled the **Chapel Royal** and was the last king of Scots to live at Stirling.

In the King's Old Building is the **Museum of the Argyll & Sutherland Highlanders** (donations encouraged), which traces the history of this famous regiment from 1794 to the present day. It has a great collection of ornately decorated dirks (daggers). In another part of the castle, the **Great Kitchens** are especially interesting, bringing to life the bustle and scale of the enterprise of cooking for the king. Near the entrance, the **Castle Exhibition** gives good background information on the Stuart kings and updates on current archaeological investigations

Admission costs for the castle will rise once the Royal Palace opens. The mooted price at time of research was £14 for adults, which would include an audioguide.

Admission to the castle also includes a guided tour of **Argyll's Lodging**, at the top of Castle Wynd near the bastion itself. Complete with turrets, this spectacular lodge is the most impressive 17th-century town house in Scotland. It's the former home of William Alexander, Earl of Stirling and noted literary figure. It has been tastefully restored and gives an insight into lavish, 17th-century aristocratic life. There are four or five guided tours daily (you can't enter by other means).

By the castle car park, the **Stirling tourist office** (admission free; ⏱ 9.30am-6pm Apr-Sep, to 5pm Oct-Mar) has an audiovisual presentation and exhibition about Stirling, including the history and architecture of the castle.

For more on Stirling Castle, see p178.

OLD TOWN   Historic District

Below the castle, the steep Old Town has a remarkably different feel to modern Stirling, its cobblestone streets packed with 15th- to 17th-century architectural gems. Its growth began when Stirling became a royal burgh (about 1124), and in the 15th and 16th centuries rich merchants built their houses here.

Stirling has the best surviving **town wall** in Scotland. It was built around 1547 when Henry VIII of England began the 'Rough Wooing' – attacking the town in order to force Mary, Queen of Scots to marry his son so that the two kingdoms could be united. The wall can be explored on the **Back Walk**, which follows the line of the wall from Dumbarton Rd (near the tourist office) to the castle. You pass the town cemeteries (check out the Star Pyramid, an outsized affirmation of Reformation values dating from 1863), then the path continues around the back of the castle to Gowan Hill where you can see the **Beheading Stone**, now encased in iron bars to prevent contemporary use.

Stirling

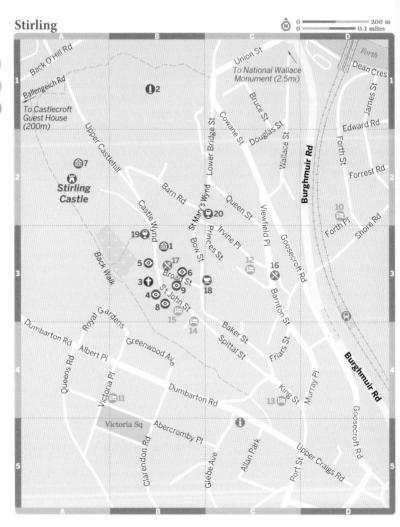

Mar's Wark, on Castle Wynd at the head of the Old Town, is the ornate facade of what was once a Renaissance-style town house commissioned in 1569 by the wealthy Earl of Mar, regent of Scotland during James VI's minority.

The **Church of the Holy Rude** (www .holyrude.org; St John St; admission free; 11am-4pm May-Sep) has been the town's parish church for 600 years and James VI was crowned here in 1567. The nave and tower date from 1456, and the church has one of the few surviving medieval open-timber roofs. Stunning stained-glass windows and huge stone pillars create a powerful effect.

Behind the church is **Cowane's Hospital** (49 St John St; admission free; 9am-5pm Apr-Sep, 10am-4pm Oct-Mar), built as an almshouse in 1637 by the merchant John Cowane. There's a family-tree database here, where you can search for your ancestors if they were born around this area.

The **Mercat Cross**, in Broad St, is topped with a unicorn (known as 'The

Stirling

Puggie'), and was once surrounded by a bustling market. Nearby is the **Tolbooth**, built in 1705 as the town's administrative centre and renovated in 2001 to become the city's premier arts and music venue.

The **Old Town Jail** (www.oldtownjail.com; St John St; adult/child/family £6.50/4/17; ⊙10am-5pm Apr-Oct, 10.30am-4pm Nov-Mar) is a great one for kids, as actors take you through the complex, portraying a cast of characters that illustrate the hardships of Victorian prison life in innovative, entertaining style.

BANNOCKBURN   Battlefield
Though Wallace's heroics were significant, it was Robert the Bruce's defeat of the English on 24 June 1314 at Bannockburn, just outside Stirling, that eventually established lasting Scottish nationhood. Exploiting the marshy ground, Bruce won a great tactical vic-

tory against a much larger and better-equipped force, and sent Edward II 'homeward, tae think again', as *Flower of Scotland* commemorates.

At **Bannockburn Heritage Centre** (NTS; www.nts.org.uk; adult/child £5.50/4.50; ⊙10am-5pm Mar-Oct, to 5.30pm Apr-Sep) the history pre- and post-battle is lucidly explained. The audiovisual could do with a remake, but there's lots to do for kids, and an intriguing recreation of Bruce's face which suggests that he may have suffered from leprosy in later life.

The battlefield itself (which never closes) is harder to appreciate; apart from a statue of the victor astride his horse and a misbegotten flag memorial, there's nothing to see. Bannockburn is 2 miles south of Stirling; you can reach it on bus 51 from Murray Pl in the centre.

 Sleeping

CASTLECROFT GUEST HOUSE B&B ££
(☎ 01786-474933; www.castlecroft-uk.com; Ballengeich Rd; s/d £45/60; P@🖳) Nestling into the hillside under the back of the castle, this great hideaway feels like a rural retreat but is a short, spectacular walk from the heart of historic Stirling. The lounge boasts 180-degree views over green fields to the hills that gird the town, and the compact rooms are appealing and well maintained.

SRUIGHLEA   B&B ££
(☎ 01786-471082; www.sruighlea.com; 27 King St; s/d £40/60; 🖳) This place feels like a secret hideaway – there's no sign – but it's conveniently located smack-bang in the centre of town. You'll feel like a local staying here, and there are eating and drinking places practically on the door-step. It's a B&B that welcomes guests with the kind of warmth that keeps them returning.

STIRLING SYHA   Hostel £
(☎ 01786-473442; www.syha.org.uk; St John St; dm/tw £17.25/45; P@🖳) Right in the Old Town, this hostel has an unbeatable

William Wallace, Scottish Patriot

William Wallace is one of Scotland's greatest heroes: a patriot whose exploits helped revive interest in Scottish history. Born in 1270, he was catapulted into fame and a place in history as a highly successful guerrilla commander who harassed the English invaders for many years.

In the wake of his victory over the English at Stirling Bridge in 1297, Wallace was knighted by Robert the Bruce and proclaimed Guardian of Scotland. However, it was only a short time before English military superiority and the fickle nature of the nobility's loyalties would turn against the defender of Scottish independence.

Disaster struck in July 1298 when King Edward's force defeated the Scots at the Battle of Falkirk. Wallace went into hiding and travelled throughout Europe to drum up support for the Scottish cause. Many of the Scots nobility were prepared to side with Edward, and Wallace was betrayed after his return to Scotland in 1305, tried for treason at Westminster, and hanged, beheaded and disembowelled at Smithfield, London.

location and great facilities. Though its facade is that of a former church, the interior is modern and efficient. The dorms are compact but comfortable with lockers and en suite bathrooms; other highlights include a pool table, bike shed and, at busy times, cheap meals on offer. Lack of atmosphere can be the only problem.

GARFIELD GUESTHOUSE   B&B   ££
(☏ 01786-473730; www.garfieldgh.com; 12 Victoria Sq; d £60-65) Though close to the centre of town, Victoria Sq is a quiet oasis, with noble Victorian buildings surrounding a verdant swathe of lawn. The Garfield's huge rooms, bay windows, ceiling roses and other period features make it a winner. There's a great family room, and some rooms have views to the castle towering above.

FORTH GUEST HOUSE   B&B   ££
(☏ 01786-471020; www.forthguesthouse.co.uk; 23 Forth Pl; s/d £45/55; ☎) Just a couple of minutes' walk from town on the other side of the railway, this noble Georgian terrace offers attractive and stylish accommodation at a fair price. The rooms are very commodious, particularly the cute garret rooms with their coomed

ceilings and good modern bathrooms. Credit cards not accepted.

LINDEN GUEST HOUSE   B&B   ££
(☏ 01786-448850; www.lindenguesthouse.co .uk; 22 Linden Ave; s/d £50/72; P @) Handy if arriving by car from the south, this guesthouse has a warm welcome and easy parking, offering understandable appeal. The rooms, of which two are suitable for families, have fridges, and the gleaming bathrooms could feature in ads for cleaning products. Breakfast features fresh fruit and kippers, among other choices.

STIRLING HIGHLAND HOTEL
        Hotel   £££
(☏ 01786-272727; www.barcelo-hotels.co.uk; Spittal St; s/d £105/134; P @ ☎ ☒) The smartest hotel in town, Stirling Highland Hotel is a sympathetic refurbishment of the old high school. This curious place still feels institutional in parts, but has great facilities that include pool, spa, gym, sauna and squash courts. It's very convenient for the castle and Old Town, and the rooms have been recently refitted, though they vary widely in size. Prices are flexible: those listed here are a guide.

MUNRO GUESTHOUSE — B&B ££

(01786-472685; www.munroguesthouse.co.uk; 14 Princes St; s/d/f £42/65/85;) Cosy and cheery, Munro Guesthouse is right in the centre of town, but on a quiet side street. Things are done with a smile here, and the smallish rooms are most inviting, particularly the cute attic ones. The breakfast is also better than the norm, with fruit salad on hand. There's easy (pay) parking opposite.

Eating & Drinking

Stirling isn't blessed with lots of excellent restaurants. Baker St is the main eating-and-drinking zone.

PORTCULLIS — Pub £

(01786-472290; www.theportcullishotel.com; Castle Wynd; bar meals £8-12; lunch & dinner) Built in stone as solid as the castle that it stands below, this former school is just the spot for a pint and a pub lunch after your visit. With bar meals that would have had even William Wallace loosening his belt a couple of notches, a little beer garden, and a cosy buzz indoors, it's well worth a visit; there are also rooms here (single/double £67/87).

EAST INDIA COMPANY — Indian £

(7 Viewfield Pl; mains £6-11; dinner) This basement Indian restaurant is one of the best spots in Central Scotland for a curry. Sumptuously decorated to resemble a ship's stateroom, with portraits of tea barons on the wall to conjure images of the days of the clippers, it offers exquisite dishes from all parts of India. There's a buffet dinner available Monday to Thursday (£8.95), but go à la carte and savour the toothsome flavours.

HERMANN'S — Restaurant £££

(01786-450632; www.hermanns.co.uk; 58 Broad St; 2-course lunch/3-course dinner £13/20, mains £16-20; lunch & dinner;) Solidly set on a corner above the Mercat Cross and below the castle, this elegant Scottish-Austrian restaurant is a reliable and popular choice. The solid, conservative decor is weirdly offset by magazine-style skiing photos, but the food doesn't miss a beat and ranges from Scottish favourites to gourmet schnitzel and

Stirling Bridge

SIMON GREENWOOD

spätzle noodles. Vegetarian options are good, and quality Austrian wines provide an out-of-the-ordinary accompaniment.

DARNLEY COFFEE HOUSE Cafe £
(www.darnley.connectfree.co.uk; 18 Bow St; snacks £3.50-5; ⊙breakfast & lunch) Just down the hill from the castle, beyond the end of Broad St, Darnley Coffee House is a good pitstop for home baking and speciality coffees during a walk around the Old Town. The building is a historic 16th-century house where Darnley, lover then husband of Mary Queen of Scots, once stayed while visiting her.

SETTLE INN Pub
(91 St Mary's Wynd) A warm welcome is guaranteed at Stirling's oldest pub (1733), a spot redolent with atmosphere, with its log fire, vaulted back room and low-slung ceilings. Guest ales, atmospheric nooks for settling in for the night, and a blend of local characters make it a classic of its kind.

❶ Information

Stirling Royal Infirmary (☎ 01786-434000; Livilands Rd) Hospital; south of the town centre.

Stirling Visitor Centre (☎ 01786-450000; ⊙9.30am-6pm Apr-Sep, to 5pm Oct-Mar) Near the castle entrance.

Tourist office (☎ 01786-475019; www. visitscottishheartlands.com; 41 Dumbarton Rd; ⊙10am-5pm Mon-Sat year-round, plus Sun Jun–mid-Sep; @)

❶ Getting There & Away

BUS The bus station (☎01786-446474) is on Goosecroft Rd. **Citylink** (www.citylink.co.uk) offers a number of services to/from Stirling:

Edinburgh £6.70, one hour, hourly

Glasgow £6.60, 45 minutes, hourly

Some buses continue to Aberdeen, Inverness and Fort William; more frequently a change will be required.

TRAIN Services from **First ScotRail** (www. scotrail.co.uk) run to/from a number of destinations, including:

Left: Loch Katrine, the Trossachs; **Below:** Autumn colours in the Trossachs, Callander (p183)

PHOTOGRAPHER: (LEFT) DAVID HANNAH; (BELOW) DENNIS BARNES/PHOTOLIBRARY

Edinburgh £6.90, 55 minutes, twice hourly Monday to Saturday, hourly Sunday

Glasgow £7.10, 40 minutes, twice hourly Monday to Saturday, hourly Sunday

THE TROSSACHS

The Trossachs region has long been a favourite weekend getaway, offering outstanding natural beauty and excellent walking and cycling routes within easy reach of the southern population centres. With thickly forested hills, romantic lochs and an increasingly interesting selection of places to stay and eat, its popularity is sure to continue, protected by its status as part of Loch Lomond & the Trossachs National Park.

The Trossachs first gained popularity as a tourist destination in the early 19th century, when curious visitors came from all over Britain drawn by the romantic language of Walter Scott's poem *Lady of the Lake*, inspired by Loch Katrine, and *Rob Roy*, about the derring-do of the region's most famous son.

In summer the Trossachs can be overburdened with coach tours, but many of these are day-trippers – peaceful, long evenings gazing at the reflections in the nearest loch are still possible. It's worth timing your visit not to coincide with a weekend.

Aberfoyle & Around
POP 576

Crawling with visitors on most weekends and dominated by a huge car park, little **Aberfoyle** is a fairly uninteresting place, easily overwhelmed by day-trippers. Instead of staying here, we recommend Callander or other Trossachs towns.

Half a mile north of Aberfoyle on the A821 is the **David Marshall Lodge tourist office** (www.forestry.gov.uk/qefp; admission free, car park £2; ☺10am-4pm Nov-

177

Stirling Castle

Planning Your Attack

Stirling's a sizeable fortress, but not so huge that you'll have to decide what to leave out – there's time to see it all. Unless you've got a working knowledge of Scottish monarchs, head to the Castle Exhibition ① first: it'll help you sort one James from another. That done, take on the sights at leisure. First, stop and look around you from the ramparts ②; the views high over this flat valley, a key strategic point in Scotland's history, are magnificent.

Next, head through to the back of the castle to the Tapestry Studio ③, which is open for shorter hours; seeing these skilful weavers at work is a highlight.

Track back towards the citadel's heart, stopping for a quick tour through the Great Kitchens ④; looking at all that fake food might make you seriously hungry, though. Then enter the main courtyard. Around you are the principal castle buildings. During summer there are events (such as Renaissance dancing) in the Great Hall ⑤ – get details at the entrance. The Museum of the Argyll & Sutherland Highlanders ⑥ is a treasure trove if you're interested in regimental history, but missable if you're not. Leave the best for last – crowds thin in the afternoon – and enter the sumptuous Royal Palace ⑦.

The Way Up & Down

If you have time, take the atmospheric Back Walk, a peaceful, shady stroll around the Old Town's fortifications and up to the castle's imposing crag-top position. Afterwards, wander down through the Old Town to admire its facades.

TOP TIPS

Admission Entrance is free for Historic Scotland members. If you'll be visiting several Scottish castles and ruins, a membership will save you plenty.

Vital Statistics First constructed: before 1110. Number of sieges: at least 9. Last besieger: Bonnie Prince Charlie (unsuccessful). Cost of refurbishing the Royal Palace: £12 million.

Museum of the Argyll & Sutherland Highlanders
The history of one of Scotland's legendary regiments – now subsumed into the Royal Regiment of Scotland – is on display here, featuring memorabilia, weapons and uniforms.

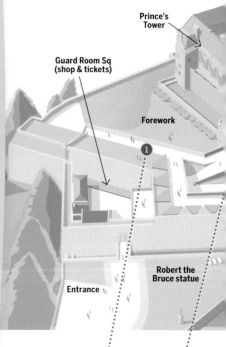

Prince's Tower

Guard Room Sq (shop & tickets)

Forework

Robert the Bruce statue

Entrance

Castle Exhibition
A great overview of the Stewart dynasty here will get your facts straight, and also offers the latest archaeological titbits from the ongoing excavations under the citadel. Analysis of skeletons has revealed surprising amounts of biographical data.

Royal Palace
The impressive new highlight of a visit to the castle is this recreation of the royal lodgings originally built by James V. The finely worked ceiling, ornate furniture and sumptuous unicorn tapestries dazzle.

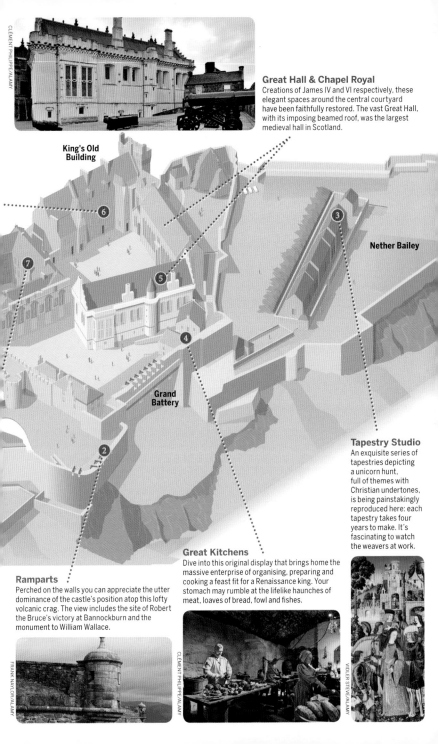

Great Hall & Chapel Royal
Creations of James IV and VI respectively, these elegant spaces around the central courtyard have been faithfully restored. The vast Great Hall, with its imposing beamed roof, was the largest medieval hall in Scotland.

King's Old Building

Nether Bailey

Grand Battery

Tapestry Studio
An exquisite series of tapestries depicting a unicorn hunt, full of themes with Christian undertones, is being painstakingly reproduced here: each tapestry takes four years to make. It's fascinating to watch the weavers at work.

Ramparts
Perched on the walls you can appreciate the utter dominance of the castle's position atop this lofty volcanic crag. The view includes the site of Robert the Bruce's victory at Bannockburn and the monument to William Wallace.

Great Kitchens
Dive into this original display that brings home the massive enterprise of organising, preparing and cooking a feast fit for a Renaissance king. Your stomach may rumble at the lifelike haunches of meat, loaves of bread, fowl and fishes.

CLEMENT PHILIPPE/ALAMY

FRANK NAYLOR/ALAMY

CLEMENT PHILIPPE/ALAMY

VIDLER STEVE/ALAMY

ALABIMAGES/ALAMY

Don't Miss **National Wallace Monument**

Towering over Scotland's narrow waist, this nationalist memorial is so Victorian Gothic it deserves circling bats and ravens. It commemorates the bid for Scottish independence depicted in the film *Braveheart*. From the tourist office, walk or shuttle-bus up the hill to the building itself. Once there, break the climb up the narrow staircase inside to admire Wallace's 66 inches of broadsword and see the man himself recreated in a 3D audiovisual display. More staid is the marble pantheon of lugubrious Scottish heroes, but the view from the top over the flat, green gorgeousness of the Forth Valley, including the site of Wallace's 1297 victory over the English at Stirling Bridge, justifies the steep entry fee.

Buses 62 and 63 run from Murray Place in Stirling to the tourist office, otherwise it's a half-hour walk from central Stirling. There's a cafe here, too.

THINGS YOU NEED TO KNOW

(www.nationalwallacemonument.com; adult/child £7.50/4.50; ⊙10am-5pm Apr-Oct, to 6pm Jul & Aug, 10.30am-4pm Nov-Mar)

Mar, 10am-5pm Apr-Oct, to 6pm Jul & Aug) in the **Queen Elizabeth Forest Park**, which has info about the many walks and cycle routes in and around the park (many departing from the tourist office). The Royal Society for the Protection of Birds (RSPB) has a display here on local bird life, the highlight being a live video link to the resident osprey family. The centre is worth visiting solely for the views.

Three miles east is the **Lake of Menteith** (called lake not loch due to a mistranslation from Gaelic). A ferry takes visitors to the substantial ruins of **Inchmahome Priory** (HS; www.historic-scotland.gov.uk; adult/child incl ferry £4.70/2.80; ⊙9.30am-5.30pm Apr-Sep, last return ferry 4.30pm). Mary, Queen of Scots was kept safe here as a child during Henry VIII's 'Rough Wooing'. Henry attacked Stirling trying to force Mary to marry his son in order to unite the kingdoms.

Activities

Several picturesque but busy way-marked **trails** start from the David Marshall Lodge tourist office centre in the forest park. These range from a light 20-minute stroll to a nearby waterfall to a hilly 4-mile circuit. Also here, **Go Ape!** (www.goape.co.uk; adult/child £30/20; ⊙daily Apr-Oct, Sat & Sun Mar & Nov) will bring out the monkey in you on its exhilarating adventure course of long ziplines, swings and rope bridges through the forest.

An excellent 20-mile circular **cycle route** links with the boat at Loch Katrine. From Aberfoyle, join the Lochs & Glens Cycle Way on the forest trail, or take the A821 over Duke's Pass. Following the southern shore of Loch Achray, you reach the pier on Loch Katrine. The ferry can take you to Stronachlachar (one way with bike £14) on the western shore, from where you can follow the beautiful B829 via Loch Ard back to Aberfoyle.

Sleeping & Eating

LAKE OF MENTEITH HOTEL
Hotel, Restaurant **£££**

(☏01877-385258; www.lake-hotel.com; Port of Menteith; d £130-190; P ⓟ ⓦ) Soothingly situated on a lake (yes, it's the only non-loch in Scotland) 3 miles east of Aberfoyle, this makes a great romantic getaway. Rooms vary substantially in size, and are being upgraded, so it's worth shelling out a little extra for views and modernity. The restaurant serves sumptuous dinners (£40) with excellent service. Check the website for packages.

MAYFIELD GUEST HOUSE
B&B **££**

(☏01877-382962; www.mayfield-aberfoyle.co.uk; Main St; s/d £35/55; P) Nothing is too much trouble for the friendly hosts at this guesthouse. There's a double and two twin rooms, all very well kept, and

a garage at the back for bikes. Pets welcome.

FORTH INN
Pub **£**

(☏01877-382372; www.forthinn.com; Main St; mains £6-9; ⊙breakfast, lunch & dinner; ��) In the middle of the village, the solid Forth Inn seems to be the lifeblood of the town, with locals and visitors alike queuing up for good, honest pub fare. The tasty bar meals are the best in town. It also provides accommodation and beer, with drinkers spilling outside into the sunny courtyard. Single/double rooms are available for £50/80, but they can be noisy at weekends.

ⓘ Information

The **tourist office** (☏01877-382352; aberfoyle@visitscotland.com; Main St; ⊙10am-5pm Apr-Oct, 10am-4pm Sat & Sun Nov-Mar; @) details a history of the Trossachs and provides currency exchange and a soft play area.

ⓘ Getting There & Away

First (www.firstgroup.com) has up to four daily buses from Stirling (40 minutes); you'll have to connect at Balfron on Sundays.

Callander
POP 2754

Callander has been pulling in the tourists for over 150 years, and has a laid-back ambience along its main thoroughfare. It's a far better place than Aberfoyle to spend time in, quickly lulling visitors into lazy pottering. There's also an excellent array of accommodation options here.

◉ Sights & Activities

The **Hamilton Toy Collection** (www.thehamiltontoycollection.co.uk; 111 Main St; adult/child £2/50p; ⊙10am-4.30pm Apr-Oct) is a powerhouse of 20th-century juvenile memorabilia, absolutely bristling with dolls houses, puppets and toy soldiers. It's a guaranteed nostalgia trip.

The impressive **Bracklinn Falls** are reached by track and footpath from Bracklinn Rd (30 minutes each way from the car park). Also off Bracklinn Rd, a woodland trail leads up to **Callander Crags**, with great views over the surroundings; a return trip is about 4 miles from the car park.

The Trossachs is a lovely area to cycle around. On a cycle route and based at Trossachs Tryst hostel, the excellent **Wheels Cycling Centre** (☎ 01877-331100; www.wheelscyclingcentre.com) has a wide range of hire bikes starting from £10/15 per half/full day.

 Sleeping

ROMAN CAMP HOTEL Hotel ££££
(☎ 01877-330003; www.roman-camp-hotel.co
.uk; s £95, d £145-185; P 🖥) Callander's best hotel. It's centrally located but feels rural, set by the river in its own beautiful grounds with birdsong the only sound. Its endearing features include a lounge with blazing fire, and a library with a tiny, secret chapel. There are three grades of room; the standards are certainly luxurious, but the superior ones are even more appealing, with period furniture, armchairs and a fireplace. The upmarket restaurant is open to the public. Reassuringly, the name refers not to toga parties but to a ruin in the adjacent fields.

TROSSACHS TRYST Hostel £
(☎ 01877-331200; www.scottish-hostel.co.uk; Invertrossachs Rd; dm/tw £17.50/45; P @ 🖥) Set up to be the perfect hostel for outdoorsy people, this cracking spot is in fresh-aired surroundings a mile from Callander. Facilities and accommodation are excellent, with dorms offering acres of space and their own bathrooms, and cycle hire with plenty of route advice. Help yourself to a continental breakfast in the morning, and enjoy the great feel that pervades this helpful place. To get there, take Bridge St off Main St, then turn right onto Invertrossachs Rd and continue for a mile.

ABBOTSFORD LODGE B&B ££
(☎ 01877-330066; www.abbotsfordlodge.com; Stirling Rd; s/d £50/75; P @) This friendly Victorian house offers something different to the norm, with tartan and florals consigned to the bonfire, replaced by stylish comfortable contemporary design that enhances the building's original features. Ruffled fabrics and ceramic vases with flower arrangements characterize the renovated rooms. The top-floor ones share a bathroom (doubles £55), but the offbeat under-roof shapes are lovable. It's on the main road on the eastern side of town; look for the monkey puzzle tree.

ARDEN HOUSE B&B ££
(☎ 01877-330235; www.ardenhouse.org.uk; Bracklinn Rd; s/d £35/70; ⊘ Apr-Oct; P 🖥) A redoubt of peaceful good taste, this elegant home features faultlessly welcoming hospitality and a woodsy, hillside location close to the centre but far from the crowds. The commodious rooms have flatscreen TV and plenty of little extras, including a suite (£80) with great views. Homebaked banana bread and a rotating dish-of-the-day keep breakfast well ahead of the competition.

Eating & Drinking

MHOR FISH Bistro, Takeaway ££
(☎ 01877-330213; www.mhor.net; 75 Main St; fish supper £5.50, mains £8-12; ⊘ lunch & dinner Tue-Sun) Both chip shop and fish restaurant, but wholly different, this endearing black-and-white-tiled cafe displays the day's fresh catch. You can choose how you want it cooked, whether pan-seared and accompanied with one of many good wines, or fried and wrapped in paper with chips to take away. The fish and seafood comes from sustainable stock, and includes oysters and other goodies. If they run out of fresh fish, they shut, so opening hours can be a bit variable.

CALLANDER MEADOWS Restaurant ££
(☎ 01877-330181; www.callandermeadows. co.uk; 24 Main St; lunch £7.95, mains £11-17; ⊘ lunch & dinner Thu-Sun) Informal but smart, this well-loved restaurant in the

centre of Callander occupies the two front rooms of a house on the main street. There's a contemporary flair for presentation and unusual flavour combinations, but a solidly British base underpins the cuisine, with things like mackerel, red cabbage, salmon and duck making regular and welcome appearances. They also open on Monday from April to September, and on Wednesday in high summer.

LADE INN Pub £

(www.theladeinn.com; Kilmahog; bar meals £8-11; ☺lunch & dinner; 🚹) Callander's best pub isn't in Callander – it's a mile north of town. They do decent, large and popular bar meals, don't mind kids, and pull a good pint (the real ales here are brewed to a house recipe). Next door, the owners run a shop with a dazzling selection of Scottish beers. There's low-key live music here at weekends too, but they shut early if it's quiet midweek.

ℹ️ Information

Loch Lomond & the Trossachs National Park tourist office (☎ 01389-722600; www.lochlomond-trossachs.org; 52 Main St; ☺9.30am-4.30pm Mon-Fri, 9.30am-12.30pm Sat) This place is a useful centre for specific information on the park.

Rob Roy & Trossachs tourist office (☎ 01877-330342; callander@visitscotland.com; Ancaster Sq; ☺10am-5pm daily Apr-Oct, 10am-4pm Mon-Sat Nov-Mar; @) This centre has heaps of info on the area.

ℹ️ Getting There & Away

First (www.firstgroup.com) operates buses from Stirling (45 minutes, hourly Monday to Saturday), while **Kingshouse** (www.kingshousetravel.co.uk) buses run from Killin (45 minutes, three to six daily Monday to Saturday). There are also daily **Scottish Citylink** (www.citylink.co.uk) buses from Edinburgh to Oban or Fort William via Callander (£15.10, 1¾ hours, daily).

Aberfoyle Coaches (www.aberfoylecoaches .com) runs between Callander and Aberfoyle (30 minutes, four times daily Monday to Saturday).

Lochs Katrine & Achray

This rugged area, 6 miles north of Aberfoyle and 10 miles west of Callander, is the heart of the Trossachs. From April to

Loch Achray and Ben Venue (p186) in autumn

DAVID TOMLINSON

October two **boats** (☎ 01877-332000; www.lochkatrine.com; 1hr cruise adult/child £10/7) run cruises from Trossachs Pier at the eastern tip of Loch Katrine. At 10.30am there's a departure to Stronachlachar at the other end of the loch before returning (single/return adult £12/14, child £8/9). From Stronachlachar (also accessible by car via Aberfoyle), you can reach the eastern shore of Loch Lomond at isolated Inversnaid. A tarmac path links Trossachs Pier with Stronachlachar, so you can also take the boat out and walk/ cycle back (12 miles). At Trossachs Pier, you can hire good bikes from **Katrinewheelz** (www.wheelscyclingcentre.com; hire per half/full day from £10/15; ☉ Apr-Oct). They even have electric buggies for the less mobile or inclined (£40 for two hours).

There are two good **walks** starting from nearby Loch Achray. The path to the rocky cone called **Ben A'an** (460m) begins at a car park near the old Trossachs Hotel. It's easy to follow, and the return trip is just under 4 miles (allow 2½ hours). A tougher walk is up rugged **Ben Venue** (727m) – there is a path all the way to the summit. Start walking from Loch Achray Hotel, follow the Achray Water westwards to Loch Katrine, then turn left and ascend the steep flanks of Ben Venue. There are great views of the Highlands and the Lowlands from the top. The return trip is about 5.5 miles – allow around four to five hours.

Balquhidder & Around

Steeped in clan history, this mountainous and sparsely populated area is the wildest part of the Trossachs; get off the busy A84 for some tranquil lochscapes and great walking. North of Callander, you'll skirt past the shores of gorgeous Loch Lubnaig. Not as famous as some of its cousins, it's still well worth a stop for its sublime views of forested hills. In the small village of **Balquhidder** (ball-whidder), 9 miles north of Callander off the A84, there's a churchyard with **Rob Roy's grave** (the words 'Despite Them' defiantly etched into the headstone). It's an appropriately beautiful spot in a deep, winding glen in big-sky country. Rob Roy's wife and two of his sons are also interred here. In the church is the 8th-century **St Angus' stone**, probably a marker to the original tomb of St Angus, an 8th-century monk who built the first church here.

Four miles on is **Monachyle Mhor** (☎ 01877-384622; www.mhor.net; dinner, bed & breakfast s/d from £166/220; P 🛜 @ ♿), a luxury hideaway with a fantastically peaceful location overlooking two lochs. It's a great fusion of country Scotland and contemporary attitudes to design and food. The rooms and suites are superb, and feature quirkily original decor. The restaurant offers set lunch (£20 for two courses) and

View from above Loch Katrine
PHOTOGRAPHER: DFWALLS/ALAMY

Rob Roy

Nicknamed 'Red' ('ruadh' in Gaelic, anglicised to 'roy') for his ginger locks, Robert MacGregor (1671–1734) was the wild leader of the wildest of Scotland's clans. Although they had rights to the lands the clan occupied, these estates stood between powerful neighbours who had the MacGregors outlawed, hence their sobriquet 'Children of the Mist'. Incognito, Rob became a prosperous livestock trader, before a dodgy deal led to a warrant for his arrest.

A legendary swordsman, the fugitive from justice then became notorious for his daring raids into the Lowlands to carry off cattle and sheep. He was forever hiding from potential captors; he was twice imprisoned, but escaped dramatically on both occasions. He finally turned himself in, and received his liberty and a pardon from the King. He lies buried in the churchyard at Balquhidder (p184); his uncompromising epitaph reads 'MacGregor despite them'. His life has been glorified over the years due to Walter Scott's novel and the 1995 film. Many Scots see his life as a symbol of the struggle of the common folk against the inequable ownership of vast tracts of the country by landed aristocrats.

dinner (£46) menus which are high in quality, sustainably sourced, and deliciously innovative. Enchantment lies in its successful combination of top-class hospitality with a relaxed rural atmosphere; dogs and kids happily romp on the lawns, and no-one looks askance if you come in flushed and muddy after a day's fishing or walking.

At the A84 junction, **Kings House Hotel** (☎ 01877-384646; www.kingshouse-scotland.co.uk; s/d £45/70; 🐾) is a classic inn built in 1779 for £40 at the request of passing drovers. Nowadays it offers B&B in more salubrious surroundings. The upstairs rooms are lovely, with fine views, and there's an ancient, narrow, sloping passageway that reminds visitors they're treading in the 200-year-old-plus footsteps of many a passing traveller. The cosy bar provides food and shelter from the elements.

The minor road at the A84 junction continues along pretty **Loch Voil** to Inverlochlarig, where you can climb **Stob Binnein** (1165m) by its southern ridge. Stob Binnein is one of the highest mountains in the area, and it has a most unusual shape, like a cone with its top chopped off.

Local buses between Callander and Killin stop at the Kings House Hotel, as do daily **Scottish Citylink** (www.citylink.co.uk) buses between Edinburgh and Oban/Fort William.

Killin

POP 666

A fine base for the Trossachs or Perthshire, this lovely village sits at the western end of Loch Tay and has a spread-out, relaxed sort of a feel, particularly around the scenic **Falls of Dochart** which tumble through the centre. On a sunny day people sprawl over the rocks by the bridge, pint or picnic in hand. Killin offers some fine walking around the town, and mighty mountains and glens close at hand.

The helpful, informative **tourist office** (☎ 01567-820254; killin@visitscotland.com) is in the **Breadalbane Folklore Centre** (www.breadalbanefolklorecentre.com; adult/child £2.95/1.95; ⏰ 10am-4pm Wed-Mon Apr-Oct), in an old water mill overlooking the falls. There is an audiovisual presentation about St Fillan, a local saint whose religious teachings are said to have

185

helped unite the ancient kingdoms of the Scots and the Picts in the 8th century. There are displays about local and clan history, including the MacGregors and MacNabs. The **Clan MacNab burial ground** lies on an island in the river by the falls; ask at the tourist office for the gate key.

 ## Activities

Five miles northeast of Killin, **Ben Lawers** (1214m) rises above Loch Tay. Other routes abound; one rewarding **circular walk** heads up into the Acharn forest south of town, emerging above the tree-line to great views of Loch Tay and Ben Lawers. The tourist office has walking leaflets and maps covering the area.

Glen Lochay runs westwards from Killin into the hills of Mamlorn. You can take a **mountain bike** for about 11 miles up the glen to just beyond Batavaime. The scenery is impressive and the hills aren't too difficult to climb. It's possible, on a nice summer day, to climb over the top of **Ben Challum** (1025m) and descend to Crianlarich, but it's hard work. A potholed road also connects this glen with Glen Lyon.

Killin is on the Lochs & Glens cycle route from Glasgow to Inverness. Hire bikes at **Killin Outdoor Centre** (☎ 01567-820652; www.killinoutdoor.co.uk; Main St). They also rent out canoes and kayaks.

 ## Sleeping & Eating

There are numerous good guesthouses strung along the road through town, and a couple of supermarkets for trail supplies.

FALLS OF DOCHART INN　　Pub £ £
(☎ 01567-820270; www.falls-of-dochart-inn.co.uk; s/d from £60/80; P 🛜) In a prime position overlooking the falls, this is an excellent place to stay and eat. Handsome renovated rooms are comfortable, with slate bathrooms; it's worth the investment for one overlooking the falls themselves (double £95), but readers warn

they can be chilly in winter. Downstairs is a very snug, atmospheric space with a roaring fire, personable service and really satisfying pub food, ranging from light meals to tasty, tender steaks and a couple of more advanced creations.

HIGH CREAGAN　　　Campsite £
(☎ 01567-820449; Aberfeldy Rd; campsites per person £6; ◷ Mar-Oct) This place has a well-kept, sheltered campsite with plenty of grass set high on the slopes overlooking sparkling Loch Tay, just outside Killin. Kids under five aren't allowed in the tent area as there's a stream running through it.

🛈 Getting There & Away

Two daily **Citylink** (www.citylink.co.uk) buses between Edinburgh and Oban/Fort William stop here. **Kingshouse Travel** (www.kingshousetravel.co.uk) runs buses to Callander, where you can change to a Stirling service.

ST ANDREWS
POP 14,209

For a small place, St Andrews made a big name for itself, firstly as religious centre, then as Scotland's oldest university town. But its status as the home of golf has propelled it to even greater fame, and today's pilgrims arrive with a set of clubs. It's a lovely place to visit even if you've no interest in the game, with impressive medieval ruins, stately university buildings, idyllic white sands and excellent accommodation and eating options.

The Old Course, the world's most famous, has a striking seaside location at the western end of town. Although it's difficult to get a game (see the boxed text, p194), it's still a thrilling experience to stroll the hallowed turf. Between the students and golfers, St Andrews can feel like the least Scottish of places as, although technically a city, it's not very large.

History

St Andrews is said to have been founded by St Regulus, who arrived from Greece in the 4th century bringing the bones of St Andrew, Scotland's patron saint. The town soon grew into a major pilgrimage centre and St Andrews developed into the ecclesiastical capital of the country. The university was founded in 1410, the first in Scotland.

Golf has been played here for more than 600 years; the Royal & Ancient Golf Club, the game's governing body, was founded in 1754 and the imposing clubhouse was built a hundred years later. The British Open Championship takes place here every few years in July.

Sights

ST ANDREWS CATHEDRAL
Cathedral Ruins
(HS; www.historic-scotland.gov.uk; The Pends; adult/child £4.20/2.50, incl castle £7.20/4.30; ⏱9.30am-5.30pm Apr-Sep, to 4.30pm Oct-Mar) The ruins of this cathedral are all that's left of one of Britain's most magnificent medieval buildings. You can appreciate the scale and majesty of the edifice from the small sections that remain standing.

Although founded in 1160, it was not consecrated until 1318, but stood as the focus of this important pilgrimage centre until 1559 when it was pillaged during the Reformation.

St Andrew's supposed bones lie under the altar; until the cathedral was built, they had been enshrined in the nearby Church of St Regulus (Rule). All that remains of this church is **St Rule's Tower**, worth the climb for the view across St Andrews. The tourist office includes a **museum** with a collection of Celtic crosses and gravestones found on the site. The entrance fee only applies for the tower and museum; you can wander freely around the atmospheric ruins.

ST ANDREWS CASTLE
Castle
(HS; www.historic-scotland.gov.uk; The Scores; adult/child £5.20/3.10, with cathedral £7.20/4.30; ⏱9.30am-5.30pm Apr-Sep, to 4.30pm Oct-Mar) Not far from the cathedral and with dramatic coastline views, the castle is mainly in ruins, but the site itself is evocative. It was founded around 1200 as the bishop's fortified home. After the execution of Protestant

The ruins of St Andrews Cathedral

JONATHAN SMITH

Detour:
Scone Palace

'So thanks to all at once and to each one, whom we invite to see us crowned at Scone.' This line from *Macbeth* indicates the importance of this **palace** (www.scone-palace.co.uk; adult/child/family £9/6/26; ⊙9.30am-5pm Apr-Oct), 2 miles north of Perth. Scone (pronounced 'skoon') Palace itself was built in 1580 on the site where, in 838, Kenneth MacAlpin became the first king of a united Scotland and brought the **Stone of Destiny** (see p75), on which Scottish kings were ceremonially invested, to Moot Hill. In 1296 Edward I of England carted the talisman off to Westminster Abbey, where it remained for 700 years before being returned to Scotland. These days, Scone doesn't really conjure up hoary days of bearded warrior-kings swearing oaths in the mist, however, as the palace, rebuilt in the early 19th century, is a Georgian mansion of extreme elegance and luxury.

The visit takes you through a succession of sumptuous **rooms** filled with fine French furniture and noble artworks. There's an astonishing collection of porcelain and fine portraits, as well as a series of exquisite Vernis Martin papier-mâché. Scone has belonged for centuries to the Murray family, Earls of Mansfield, and many of the objects have a fascinating history (friendly guides are on hand). Each room has comprehensive multilingual information; there are also panels relating histories of some of the Scottish kings crowned at Scone over the centuries.

Outside, peacocks – all named after a monarch – strut around the magnificent **grounds**, which incorporate woods, a butterfly garden, and a maze.

reformers in 1545, other reformers retaliated by murdering Cardinal Beaton and taking over the castle. They spent almost a year holed up, during which they and their attackers dug a complex of **siege tunnels**, said to be the best surviving example of castle-siege engineering in Europe; you can walk (or stoop) along their damp mossy lengths. A tourist office gives a good audiovisual introduction and has a small collection of Pictish stones.

SCORES   Street
From the castle, the Scores follows the coast west down to the first tee at the Old Course. Family-friendly **St Andrews Aquarium** (www.standrewsaquarium.co.uk; adult/child £6.50/4.60; ⊙10am-6pm Mar-Oct, 10am-4.30pm Nov-Feb, last entry 1hr before closing) has a seal pool, rays and sharks from Scottish waters and exotic tropical favourites. Once introduced to our finny friends, you can snack on them with chips in the cafe.

Nearby, the **British Golf Museum** (www.britishgolfmuseum.co.uk; Bruce Embankment; adult/child £6/3; ⊙9.30am-5pm Mon-Sat & 10am-5pm Sun Apr-Oct, 10am-4pm daily Nov-Mar) has an extraordinarily comprehensive overview of the history and development of the game and the role of St Andrews in it. Favourite fact: bad players were formerly known as 'foozlers'. Interactive panels allow you to relive former British Opens (watch Paul Azinger snapping his putter in frustration), and there's a large collection of memorabilia from Open winners both male and female.

Opposite the museum is the **Royal & Ancient Golf Club**, which stands proudly at the head of the **Old Course**, which you can stroll on once play is finished for the day, and all day on Sundays. Beside it stretches magnificent **West Sands** beach, made famous by the film *Chariots of Fire*.

Tours

There is a **Witches Tour** (📞 01334-655057; adult/child £7/5; ⏰7.30pm Thu & Fri) that recounts the history and folklore of St Andrews in an unusual fashion, with tales of ghosts and witches enlivened by theatrical stunts. It starts outside Greyfriars Hotel on North St.

 # Festivals & Events

OPEN CHAMPIONSHIP Golf

(www.opengolf.com) One of international golf's four 'majors', takes place in July. However, the tournament venue changes from year to year, and the Open only comes to St Andrews itself every five years – check the website for future venues.

ST ANDREWS HIGHLAND GAMES
Traditional Sports

(www.albagames.co.uk) Held on the North Haugh on the last Sunday in July.

ST ANDREWS FESTIVAL
Arts, Food & Drink

(www.standrewsfestival.co.uk) Five days of festivities leading up to St Andrews Day (30 November), the feast day of Scotland's patron saint. Celebrations include a festival of Scottish food and drink, and various arts events.

 # Sleeping

St Andrews accommodation is often heavily booked (especially in summer), so you're well advised to book in advance. Almost every house on Murray Park and Murray Pl is a guesthouse: this area couldn't be more convenient, but prices are on the high side.

ABBEY COTTAGE B&B ££

(📞 01334-473727; www.abbeycottage.co.uk; Abbey Walk; s £40, d £59-64; P) You know you've strayed from B&B mainstream when your charming host's hobby is photographing tigers in the wild – don't leave without browsing her albums. This engaging spot sits below the town, surrounded by stone walls which enclose a rambling garden; it feels like you are staying in the

West Sands beach, St Andrews

St Andrews

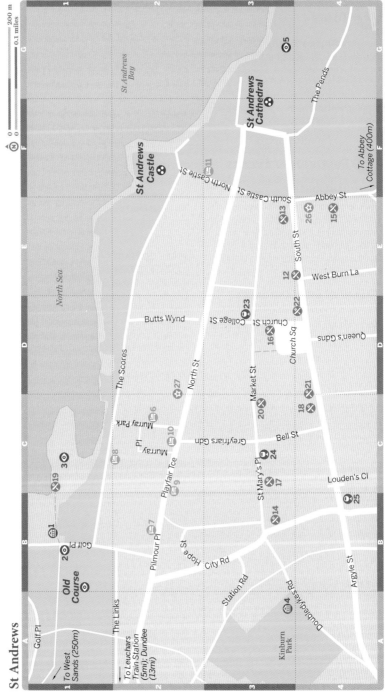

St Andrews

significantly outside the height of summer. There are good portents if you are playing a round – Bobby Locke won the Open in 1957 while staying here.

FIVE PILMOUR PLACE   B&B ££

(☎ 01334-478665; www.5pilmourplace.com; 5 Pilmour Pl; s £75, d £105-130; @ 🛜) Just around the corner from the Old Course, this luxurious and intimate spot offers stylish, compact rooms with an eclectic range of styles as well as modern conveniences such as flatscreen TV and DVD player. The king-size beds are especially comfortable, and the lounge area is a stylish treat.

MEADE B&B   B&B ££

(☎ 01334-477350; annmeade10@hotmail. com; 5 Albany Pl; with shared/private bathroom s £30/55, d £40/60; 🐾) It's always sweet relief to find a B&B unconcerned with VisitScotland's fussy regulations. This economical gem is run by a friendly family and their pets, including a portly marmalade cat and affectionate black lab. The two comfortable rooms are colour-coded and have readable novels, photo albums and films on DVD. They might have moved to a new location by the time you read this, but the phone number will be the same.

OLD FISHERGATE HOUSE   B&B ££

(☎ 01334-470874; www.oldfishergatehouse .uk; North Castle St; s/d £75/100; 🛜) This historic 17th-century townhouse, furnished with period pieces, is in a great location – the oldest part of town, close to the cathedral and castle. The two twin rooms are very spacious and even have their own sitting room and cushioned ledges on their window sills. On a scale of one to 10 for quaintness, we'd rate it about a 9½. Cracking breakfasts feature fresh fish and pancakes.

CAMERON HOUSE   B&B ££

(☎ 01334-472306; www.cameronhouse-sta.co .uk; 11 Murray Park; s/d £45/90; 🛜) Beautifully decorated rooms and warm, cheerful hosts make this guesthouse a real home-away-from-home. The two single rooms share a bathroom. Prices drop £10 per person outside peak season.

country. There are three excellent rooms, all different, with patchwork quilts, sheepskins, and antique furniture.

HAZELBANK HOTEL   Hotel £££

(☎ 01334-472466; www.hazelbank.com; 28 The Scores; s/d £90/151; @ 🛜) Offering a genuine welcome, the family-run Hazelbank is the most likeable of the hotels along the Scores. The front rooms have marvellous views along the beach and out to sea; those at the back are somewhat cheaper and more spacious. Prices drop

OGSTONS ON NORTH STREET
Hotel £££

(☎ 01334-473387; www.ogstonsonnorthst.com; 127 North St; s £100-120, d £120-160; 🛜 👪) If you want to eat, drink and sleep in the same stylish place then this classy inn could be for you. Smartened-up rooms feature elegant contemporary styling and coolly beautiful bathrooms, some with Jacuzzi. There are also DVD players, iPod docks, crisp white linen and large windows that give the rooms an airy feel. The Oak Rooms (serving lunch and dinner) is the place for meals and a read of the paper. The bar is perfect for a snug tipple, and the Lizard Lounge in the basement is a late-night bar that cranks up with live gigs and regular DJs.

🍴 Eating

St Andrews has a great range of eating options. Places compete heavily on price for the student custom, so there are good deals to be had everywhere. Two great options for self-catering or picnic fare are the fine fishmonger **Andrew Keracher** (www.keracher.co.uk; 73 South St), and **IJ Mellis** (www.mellischeese.co.uk; 149 South St), with a wealth of cheeses you can smell halfway down the street.

PEAT INN
Restaurant £££

(☎ 01334-840206; www.thepeatinn.co.uk; 3-course lunch/dinner £16/32; ☺lunch & dinner Tue-Sat) The Peat Inn is one of the best restaurants in Scotland, with an award-winning French-influenced menu that's culinary heaven. It's housed in a rustic country inn about 6 miles west of St Andrews; to get there, head west on the A915 then turn right on the B940.

VINE LEAF
Restaurant ££

(☎ 01334-477497; www.vineleafstandrews.co.uk; 131 South St; 2-course dinner £23.50; ☺dinner Tue-Sat; 🌿) Classy, comfortable and well-established, the friendly Vine Leaf offers a changing menu of sumptuous Scottish seafood, game and vegetarian dishes. It's down a close off South St.

Left: Racers at the ready at the Braemar Gathering (p208); **Below:** The 18th hole and clubhouse at the Old Course (p188), St Andrews

PHOTOGRAPHER: (LEFT) JONATHAN SMITH; (BELOW) JOHN PETER PHOTOGRAPHY/ALAMY

SEAFOOD RESTAURANT

Restaurant £££

(01334-479475; www.theseafoodrestaurant .com; The Scores; lunch/dinner £22/45; lunch & dinner) The Seafood Restaurant occupies a stylish glass-walled room, built out over the sea, with plush navy carpet, crisp white linen, an open kitchen and panoramic views of St Andrews Bay. It offers top seafood and an excellent wine list, and has won a clutch of awards. Look out for its special winter deal – three-course lunch for £15, or dinner for £20.

DOLL'S HOUSE

Restaurant ££

(01334-477422; www.dolls-house.co.uk; 3 Church Sq; mains £10-15; lunch & dinner) With its high-backed chairs, bright colours and creaky wooden floor, the Doll's House blends a Victorian child's bedroom with modern stylings. The result is a surprising warmth and no pretensions. The menu makes the most of local fish and other Scottish produce,

and the two-course lunch for £6.95 is unbeatable value. The early-evening two-course deal for £12.95 isn't bad either.

ZEST

Cafe £

(www.zestjuicing.co.uk; 95 South St; juices £2-4; breakfast & lunch) Serving toasties, paninis and filled rolls along with a good coffee selection, this slick place is popular with students. French doors opening onto the street make it a great spot for people-watching on a breezy summer day. The juices and smoothies here are great, and priced very fairly.

BYRE THEATRE BISTRO

Bistro ££

(www.byretheatre.com; Abbey St; mains £9-15; breakfast, lunch & dinner Tue-Sat;) A happy, buzzy spot with comfy couches, works of art on the wall and a well-developed menu that encompasses some delicious fusion cooking. Lunchtime sandwiches come with interesting

193

Playing the Old Course

Golf has been played at St Andrews since the 15th century. By 1457 it was so popular that James II placed a ban on it because it interfered with his troops' archery practice. Although it lies beside the exclusive, all-male Royal & Ancient Golf Club, the Old Course is public.

Book in advance to play via **St Andrews Links Trust** (☎01334-466666; www .standrews.org.uk). You must reserve on or after the first Wednesday in September the year before you wish to play. No bookings are taken for Saturdays or the month of September.

Unless you've booked months in advance, getting a tee-off time is by lottery; enter the ballot at the **caddie office** (☎01334-466666) before 2pm on the day before you wish to play (there's no Sunday play). Be warned that applications by ballot are normally heavily oversubscribed, and green fees are £130 in summer. Singles are not accepted in the ballot and should start queuing as early as possible – 5.30am is good – in the hope of joining a group. You'll need a handicap certificate (24/36 for men/women).

Guided walks (£2.50; 50min) of the Old Course run at weekends in June and daily in July and August; these will take you to famous landmarks such as the Swilcan Bridge and the Road Hole bunker. They run from outside the shop roughly hourly from 11am to 4pm. On Sundays, a three-hour walk (£5) takes you around the whole course.

---

fillings, such as hummus and red pepper. Dinner gets more sophisticated, featuring dishes such as seared tuna steak on sultana-and-nutmeg couscous with smoked-tomato dressing.

TAILEND   Bistro £
(130 Market St; mains £6-10; ☻breakfast, lunch & dinner) Delicious fresh fish sourced from Arbroath just up the coast put this new St Andrews arrival a class above most chippies. The array of exquisite smoked delicacies at the counter will have you planning a picnic or fighting for a table out the back.

B JANNETTA   Ice Cream £
(www.jannettas.co.uk; 31 South St; 2-dip cone £2.40; ☻breakfast & lunch Mon-Sat) B Jannetta is a St Andrews institution, offering 52 varieties of ice-cream from the weird (Irn-Bru sorbet) to the decadent (strawberries and champagne). There's also a decent cafe next door.

BALAKA   Bangladeshi ££
(www.balaka.com; 3 Alexandra Pl; mains £10-12; ☻lunch & dinner Mon-Sat, dinner Sun) Long-established Bangladeshi restaurant with both standard choices and more inspiring discoveries – all delicious and seasoned with herbs they grow themselves. The £6.95 lunch deal is a bargain.

GRILL HOUSE   Bistro £
(www.grillhouserestaurant.co.uk; St Mary's Pl; mains £6-15; ☻lunch & dinner) This cheerful, sometimes boisterous restaurant offers something for every taste and bank balance, with a big selection ranging from Mexican, pizza and pasta to char-grilled salmon and quality steaks. The upbeat atmosphere and service are pluses, as is the £5 lunchtime deal.

Drinking

CENTRAL BAR   Pub
(77 Market St) Rather staid compared to some of the wilder student-driven drink-

ing options, this likeable pub keeps it real with traditional features, an island bar, lots of Scottish beers, decent service and filling (if uninspiring) pub grub.

WEST PORT   Pub
(www.maclay.com; 170 South St; 🤙) Just by the gateway of the same name, this sleek, modernised pub has several levels, as well as a great beer garden out the back. Cheap cocktails rock the Uni crowd, mixed drinks are above average, and there's some OK bar food.

VICTORIA   Pub
(1 St Mary's Pl) Upstairs at the Victoria is popular with all types of students and serves good bar meals. There's a grungy cafe-bar here with plenty of natural light or a classier lounge bar where you can sink into a sofa. Check out the jazz on Sunday nights.

Entertainment

There's always something on in the pubs around town during term-time.

Byre Theatre   Theatre
(☎01334-475000; www.byretheatre.com; Abbey St) This theatre company started life in a converted cow byre in the 1930s, and now occupies a flashy premises making clever use of light and space.

New Picture House   Cinema
(www.nphcinema.co.uk; North St) Two-screen cinema showing current films.

ℹ Information

St Andrews Memorial Hospital (☎ 01334-472327; Abbey Walk) Located south of Abbey St.

Tourist office (☎ 01334-472021; www.visit-standrews .co.uk; 70 Market St; ⊙9.15am-6.30pm Mon-Sat & 9.30am-5pm

Sun Jul-Sep, 9.15am-5pm Mon-Sat mid-Oct–Jun, plus 11am-4pm Sun Apr-Jun; @) Helpful staff with good knowledge of St Andrews and Fife.

ℹ Getting There & Away

BUS All buses leave from the bus station on Station Rd. There are frequent services to:

Anstruther 40 minutes, regularly

Crail 30 minutes, regularly

Edinburgh £9.40, two hours, hourly

Glasgow £9.40, 2 ½ hours, hourly

Stirling £7.30, two hours, six to seven Monday to Saturday

TRAIN There is no train station in St Andrews itself, but you can take a train from Edinburgh (grab a seat on the right-hand side of the carriage for great firth views) to Leuchars, 5 miles to the northwest (£11.20, one hour, hourly). From here, buses leave regularly for St Andrews.

ℹ Getting Around

To order a cab, call Golf City Taxis (☎01334-477788). A taxi between Leuchars train station and the town centre costs around £10.

St Andrews as seen from the south
PHOTOGRAPHER: JONATHAN SMITH

Spokes (☎ 01334-477835; www.spokescycles
.com; 37 South St; hire per half/full day £8.50/13;
☺ 9am-5.30pm Mon-Sat) hires out mountain bikes.

EAST NEUK OF FIFE

This charming stretch of coast runs
south from St Andrews to the point at
Fife Ness, then west to Leven. Neuk is an
old Scots word for corner, and it's certainly an appealing nook of the country to
investigate, with picturesque fishing villages, some great restaurants and pretty
coastal walks; the Fife Coastal Path's
most scenic stretches are in this area. It's
easily visited from St Andrews, but also
makes a very pleasant place to stay.

Crail

POP 1695

Pretty and peaceful, little Crail has a
much-photographed stone-sheltered
harbour surrounded by wee cottages
with red-tiled roofs. You can buy lobster
and crab from a **kiosk** (☺ lunch Sat &
Sun) there. The benches in the nearby
grassed area are perfectly placed for
munching your alfresco crustaceans
while admiring the view across to the Isle
of May.

The village's history and involvement
with the fishing industry is outlined in
the **Crail Museum** (www.crailmuseum.org.uk;
62 Marketgate; admission free; ☺ 10am-1pm &
2-5pm Mon-Sat, 2-5pm Sun Jun-Sep, 2-5pm Sat
& Sun Apr & May), which also offers tourist
information.

Eighteenth-century **Selcraig House**
(☎ 01333-450697; www.selcraighouse.co.uk;
47 Nethergate; s/d from £50/70; 🛜) is a
character-filled, well-run place with a
variety of rooms. Curiously shaped top-
floor chambers will appeal to the quirky,
while the fantastic four-poster room on
the first floor (£80) will charm those
with a taste for luxury and beautiful
furnishings.

Hazelton Guest House (☎ 01333-
450250; www.thehazelton.co.uk; 29 Marketgate
North; d £70-80; ☺ Mar-Oct; 🛜) is a
welcoming, walker-friendly guest house
across the road from the museum,

while **Caiplie House** (☎ 01333-450564;
www.caipliehouse.co.uk; 53 High St N; s/d
£39/64; ☺ Apr-Nov; 🛜) has large rooms
with lots of lights, and big soft beds
perfect for flopping at the end of the
day. The top room here has views
across to East Lothian. It also does
reader-recommended evening meals.

Crail is 10 miles southeast of St
Andrews. **Stagecoach** (www.stagecoachbus
.com) bus 95 between Leven, Anstruther,
Crail and St Andrews passes through
Crail hourly every day (30 minutes to St
Andrews).

Anstruther

POP 3442

Once among Scotland's busiest ports,
cheery Anstruther has ridden the tribu-
lations of the fishing industry better
than some, and now offers a very pleasant mixture of bobbing boats, historic
streets, and visitors ambling around
the harbour while grazing on fish and
chips or contemplating a trip to the Isle
of May.

 Sights

The displays at the excellent **Scottish
Fisheries Museum** (www.scotfishmuseum
.org; adult/child £6/free; ☺ 10am-5.30pm
Mon-Sat & 11am-5pm Sun Apr-Sep, 10am-4.30pm
Mon-Sat & noon-4.30pm Sun Oct-Mar) include
the **Zulu Gallery**, which houses the
huge, partly restored hull of a traditional
Zulu-class fishing boat, redolent with
the scent of tar and timber. Afloat in the
harbour outside the museum lies the
Reaper, a fully restored Fifie-class fishing
boat built in 1902.

The mile-long **Isle of May**, 6 miles
southeast of Anstruther, is a stunning
nature reserve. Between April and
July the intimidating cliffs are packed
with breeding kittiwakes, razorbills,
guillemots, shags and around 40,000
puffins. Minke whales have also been
spotted around the island in early
summer. Inland are the remains of
the 12th-century **St Adrian's Chapel**,

Boats in the harbour at Crail, East Neuk of Fife

IAIN MASTERTON/ALAMY

dedicated to a monk who was murdered on the island by the Danes in 875.

The five-hour return trip to the island on the **May Princess** (☎ 01333-310054; www.isleofmayferry.com; adult/child £19/9.50), including two to three hours ashore, sails almost daily from May to September. Make reservations and buy tickets at the harbour kiosk near the museum at least an hour before departure. Departure times vary depending on the tide – check upcoming times by phone or via the website. There's also a faster boat, the 12-seater rigid-hull inflatable *Osprey*, which makes non-landing circuits of the island (adult/child £20/12.50) and longer visits (£25/15).

 Sleeping & Eating

SPINDRIFT
B&B ££

(☎ 01333-310573; www.thespindrift.co.uk; Pittenweem Rd; s/d £55/80; P 🛜) Arriving from the west, there's no need to go farther than Anstruther's first house on the left, a redoubt of Scottish cheer and warm hospitality. The rooms are elegant, classy and extremely comfortable –

some have views across to Edinburgh and one is like a ship's cabin, courtesy of the sea-captain who once owned the house. There are DVD players and teddies for company, an honesty-bar with character-filled ales and malts and fine company from your hosts. Breakfast includes porridge once voted the best in the Kingdom. Dinner (from £22) is also available.

CRICHTON HOUSE
B&B ££

(☎ 01333-310219; www.crichtonhouse.com; High St W; d £70; P) You'll spot this B&B on the right as you approach the centre of town from the west. Sparklingly clean rooms with fresh fruit and slate-floored bathrooms are complemented by a cheery host and plenty of breakfast options. The door is a little bit further along the street than you think it'll be.

SHEILING
B&B ££

(☎ 01333-310697; 32 Glenogil Gardens; r per person £25-30; P) Sheiling offers two genteel, elegantly furnished rooms with shared bathroom and a homespun vibe. It also has an excellent breakfast menu. Good for solo travellers.

197

DREEL TAVERN   Pub   £
(16 High St W; mains £8-12; ☺lunch & dinner;
🛉) This charming old pub on the banks
of the Dreel Burn has bucketloads of
character and serves reliably tasty bar
meals, with excellent handwritten daily
specials. Chow down in the outdoor beer
garden in summer. There are also some
top-quality cask ales here.

🍃 WEE CHIPPIE   Takeaway   £
(4 Shore St; fish supper £5; ☺lunch &
dinner) The Anstruther Fish Bar is one
of Britain's best chippies, but we – and
plenty of locals – reckon this one is even
better. The fish is of a very high quality,
portions are larger and there's less of a
queue too. Eat your catch by the water.

CELLAR RESTAURANT Restaurant   £££
(📞 01333-310378; www.cellaranstruther.co.uk;
24 East Green; 2-/3-course set dinner £35/40;
☺lunch Fri & Sat, dinner Tue-Sat) Tucked
away in an alley behind the museum,
the Cellar is famous for its seafood and
fine wines. Try the local crab, lobster or
whatever delicacies they've brought in

that day. Inside it's elegant and upmarket. Advance bookings are essential.

🛈 Information

Tourist office (📞 01333-311073; anstruther@
visitscotland.com; Harbourhead; ☺10am-5pm
Mon-Sat, 11am-4pm Sun Apr-Oct) The best tourist
office in the East Neuk.

🛈 Getting There & Away

Stagecoach (www.stagecoachbus.com) bus 95
runs daily from Leven (more departures from St
Monans) to Anstruther and on to St Andrews (40
minutes, hourly) via Crail.

Around Anstruther

A magnificent example of Lowland
Scottish domestic architecture, **Kellie
Castle** (NTS; www.nts.org.uk; adult/child/
parking £8.50/5.50/3; ☺castle 1-5pm Thu-
Mon Apr-Oct, garden 10am-5pm daily Apr-Oct
& 10am-4pm Mon-Fri Nov-Mar) has creaky
floors, crooked little doorways and some
marvellous works of art, giving it an
air of authenticity. It's set in a beautiful garden, and many rooms contain
superb plasterwork, the Vine room

Kellie Castle

being the most exquisite. The original part of the building dates from 1360; it was enlarged to its present dimensions around 1606.

The castle is 3 miles northwest of Pittenweem on the B9171. Bus 95 from St Andrews gets you closest – about 1.5 miles away.

Three miles north of Anstruther, off the B9131 to St Andrews, is **Scotland's Secret Bunker** (www .secretbunker.co.uk; adult/child/family £9.50/6.50/27; ⏱10am-5pm Apr-Oct; @). This fascinating Cold War relic was to be one of Britain's underground command centres and a home for Scots leaders in the event of nuclear war. Hidden 30m underground and surrounded by nearly 5m of reinforced concrete are the austere operation rooms, communication centre and dormitories. It's very authentic and uses artefacts from the period, which make for an absorbing exploration. The Scottish Campaign for Nuclear Disarmament (CND) has an exhibit, bringing home the realities of Britain's current nuclear Trident policy. The bunker is a gripping experience and highly recommended.

Pittenweem

POP 1747

Just a short stroll from Anstruther, Pittenweem is now the main fishing port on the East Neuk coast, and there are lively fish sales at the harbour from 8am. On a sunny day, buy an ice cream and stroll the short, breezy promenade, admiring the picturesque waterfront. The village name means 'place of the cave', referring to **St Fillan's Cave** (adult/child £1/ free) in Cove Wynd, which was used as a chapel by a 7th-century missionary. The saint reputedly possessed miraculous powers – apparently, when he wrote his sermons in the dark cave, his arm would throw light on his work by emitting a luminous glow. The cave is protected by a

---

If You Like…
Fishing Villages

The fishing villages of the East Neuk of Fife have some competition in the picturesque stakes – if you want to explore more, there are several pretty harbours on the coast of the Moray Firth, north of Speyside.

1 **PENNAN**
The whitewashed houses, tucked beneath red sandstone cliffs, are built gable-end to the sea, and the waves break just a few metres away on the other side of the only street. The village featured in the 1983 film *Local Hero,* and fans of the film still come to make a call from the red telephone box that played a prominent part in the plot.

2 **GARDENSTOWN**
Also known as Gamrie (*game*-rey), Gardenstown was founded by Alexander Garden in 1720, and is built on a series of cramped terraces tumbling down the steep cliffs above the tiny harbour. Drivers should beware of severe gradients and hairpin bends in the village, parts of which can only be reached on foot.

3 **PORTSOY**
Has an atmospheric 17th-century harbour and a maze of narrow streets lined with picturesque cottages. Each year on the last weekend in June or first weekend in July, the harbour is home to the Scottish Traditional Boat Festival, a lively gathering of historic wooden sailing boats.

---

locked gate, but a key is available from a nearby house (see the sign on the gate).

Drop into **Heron Bistro** (www.herongallery .co.uk; 15a High St; mains £5-8; ⏱breakfast & lunch) for a snack or meal. Dressed crab and homemade smoked mackerel pâté feature on the menu, and you dine among local works of art that inject some real colour into this pretty harbour town – good for a browse, and everything is for sale.

Bus details for Pittenweem are as per Anstruther.

St Monans

POP 1450

This ancient fishing village is just over a mile west of Pittenweem and is named after another cave-dwelling saint who was probably killed by pirates. Apart from a picturesque historic windmill overlooking the sea, its main sight is the **parish church**, at the western end of the village. The church was built in 1362 on the orders of a grateful King David II, who was rescued by villagers from a shipwreck in the Firth of Forth. A model of a full-rigged ship, dating from 1800, hangs above the altar. The church commands sweeping views of the firth, and the past echoes inside its cold, whitewashed walls.

St Monans Heritage Collection (5 West Shore; admission free; ⏱11am-1pm & 2-4pm Tue, Thu, Sat & Sun May-Oct), on the harbour, is a wonderful small gallery devoted to the history of St Monans' fishing industry through a collection of 20th-century black-and-white photos and several artefacts. Most of the photos were taken by a local photographer and the collection changes regularly.

There are a couple of B&Bs in St Monans, but more choice in nearby Anstruther.

Harbour Howff Café (6 Station Rd; light meals £3-5; ⏱breakfast & lunch Wed-Sun) is a community-run cafe promoting healthy eating and serving excellent sandwiches and fresh cakes.

Comfortable but classy, the **Seafood Restaurant** (☎01333-730327; www.theseafood restaurant.com; 16 West End; 2-course lunch/ dinner £22/40; ⏱lunch & dinner Wed-Sun Apr-May, daily Jun-Aug) is a fishy stalwart on the harbour. The menu changes – bouillabaisse, Dover sole, scallops – but just swim with the tide. The menu details the provenance of these sustainable morsels.

Stagecoach (www.stagecoachbus.com) bus 95 runs daily from St Monans to St Andrews (50 minutes, at least hourly), via Anstruther.

Elie & Earlsferry

POP 1500

These two attractive villages mark the southwestern end of East Neuk. There are great sandy beaches and good walks along the coast, and there's nothing better than a lazy summer Sunday in Elie, watching the local team play cricket on the strand below.

Elie Watersports (☎01333-330962; www.eliewatersports.com), on the harbour at Elie, hires out windsurfers (per two hours £30), sailing dinghies (Lasers/ Wayfarers per hour £18/22), canoes (per hour £10) and mountain bikes (per day £12), and provides instruction as well.

Ship Inn (www.ship-elie.com; Elie; mains £8-11;

St Monans Parish Church

⊙lunch & dinner; 👫), down by Elie harbour, is a pleasant and popular place for a bar lunch. Seafood and Asian dishes feature on the menu and, on a sunny day, you can tuck in at an outside table overlooking the wide sweep of the bay.

Pitlochry
POP 2564

Pitlochry, with its air already smelling of the Highlands, is a popular stop on the way north and convenient base for exploring northern Central Scotland. On a quiet spring evening it's a pretty place with salmon jumping in the Tummel and good things brewing at the Moulin Hotel. In summer the main street can be a conga-line of tour groups, but get away from that and it'll still charm you.

 Sights

One of Pitlochry's attractions is its beautiful **riverside**; the River Tummel is dammed here, and you can watch salmon swimming (not jumping) up a **fish ladder** to the loch above.

BELL'S BLAIR ATHOL DISTILLERY
Distillery
(☎ 01796-482003; www.discovering-distilleries.com; Atholl Rd; tour £5; ⊙Mon-Fri, plus Sat Apr-Oct, plus Sun Jun-Oct) One of two distilleries around Pitlochry, this is at the southern end of town. Tours focus on whisky making and the blending of this well-known drop. The tour price is discountable off a bottle purchase.

FREE EDRADOUR DISTILLERY
Distillery
(☎ 01796-472095; www.edradour.co.uk) This distillery is – proudly – Scotland's smallest, and it's a great one to visit, as you can have the whole process easily explained in one room. You'll find it located 2.5 miles east of Pitlochry along the Moulin road; it's a pleasant walk to get there.

Detour:
Gleneagles

Deep in rural Perthshire near the town of Auchterarder, one of Scotland's most famous lodgings can be found: the **Gleneagles Hotel** (☎01764-662231; www.gleneagles.com; d from £410; P @ 🤝 ≋ 👫). Not your typical bed-and-breakfast, this is a no-holds-barred luxury spot with three championship golf courses, Andrew Fairlie at Gleneagles – often referred to as Scotland's best restaurant (open dinner Tuesday to Saturday) – and a variety of extravagantly elegant rooms and suites designed to cope with anything from a serious romantic splash-out to a royal family in exile. Despite the imposing building and kilted staff snapping to attention, it's welcoming to non-VIPs, and family-friendly to boot, with lots of activities available. There's Gleneagles train station to arrive sustainably; if not, limousine transfers are available. Check the website for deals.

EXPLORERS GARDEN
Garden
(www.explorersgarden.com; adult/child £3/1; Foss Rd; ⊙10am-5pm Apr-Oct) At the Pitlochry Festival Theatre, this excellent garden commemorates 300 years of plant collecting and those who hunted down 'new' species. The whole collection is based on plants brought back to Scotland by Scottish explorers.

KILLIECRANKIE TOURIST OFFICE
Visitors Centre
(NTS; www.nts.org.uk; ☎ 01796-473233; Killiecrankie; admission free, parking £2; ⊙10am-5.30pm Apr-Oct) Set in a beautiful, rugged gorge 3.5 miles north of Pitlochry, this

centre has great interactive displays on the Jacobite rebellion (in which the Battle of Killiecrankie was pivotal) and local flora and fauna. There's plenty to touch, pull and open – great for kids. There are some stunning walks into the wooded gorge, too; keep an eye out for red squirrels.

 ## Festivals & Events

Pitlochry Festival Theatre Theatre
(☎ 01796-484626; www.pitlochry.org.uk; Foss Rd; tickets £14-25) This well-known theatre stages a different mainstream play for six nights out of seven during its season from May to mid-October.

Étape Cycle Race
(www.etapecaledonia.co.uk) Étape, an 81-mile charity cycling event, brings competitors of all standards onto the beautiful highland roads around Pitlochry in mid-May. It's become a big deal; you'll have to prebook accommodation.

Enchanted Forest Light Show
(www.enchantedforest.org.uk; adults £11-14, children £6) This spectacular sound-and-light show in a forest near Pitlochry is a major family hit in the last week of October and first week of November.

 ## Sleeping

CRAIGATIN HOUSE B&B ££
(☎ 01796-472478; www.craigatinhouse.co.uk; 165 Atholl Rd; d £78-88; P 🖰) Several times more tasteful than the average Pitlochry lodging, this noble house and garden is set back from the main road at the western end of town. Chic contemporary fabrics covering expansive beds offer a standard of comfort above and beyond the reasonable price; the rooms in the converted stable block are particularly inviting. Breakfast choices include whisky-laced porridge, smoked-fish omelettes, and apple pancakes.

PITLOCHRY BACKPACKERS HOTEL
Hostel £
(☎ 01796-470044; www.scotlands-top-hostels.com; 134 Atholl Rd; dm/tw/d £15/38/40; P @ 🖰) Friendly, laid-back and very comfortable, this is a cracking hostel smack-bang in the middle of town, with three- to eight-bed dorms that are in mint condition. There are also good-value en suite twins and doubles, with beds, not bunks. Cheap breakfast and a pool table add to the convivial party atmosphere. No extra charge for linen.

ASHLEIGH B&B £
(☎ 01796-470316; nancy.gray@btinternet.com; 120 Atholl Rd; s/d £25/50; P) Genuine welcomes don't come much better than Nancy's, and her place on the main street makes a top Pitlochry pitstop. Three comfortable rooms share an excellent bathroom, and there's an open kitchen stocked with goodies where you make your own breakfast in the morning. A home-away-from-home and standout budget choice.

KNOCKENDARROCH HOUSE Hotel ££
(☎ 01796-473473; www.knockendarroch.co.uk; Higher Oakfield; dinner, bed & breakfast s/d £120/170; P 🖰) Top of the town and boasting the best views, this genteel, well-run hotel has a range of luxurious rooms with huge windows that take advantage of the highland light. The standard rooms actually have better views than the larger, slightly pricier superior ones. A couple of rooms have great little balconies, perfect for a sundowner. Meals are highly recommended here too.

STRATHGARRY Hotel ££
(☎ 01796-472469; www.strathgarryhotel.co.uk; 113 Atholl Rd; s £40-60, d £60-80; 🖰) With a top main-street location, Strathgarry is a hotel-bar-cafe-restaurant that's all done pretty well. En suite rooms are very snug and have some luxurious touches – we lost a researcher who sunk into one of the beds and was never seen again.

Eating & Drinking

MOULIN HOTEL   Pub/Hotel £

(📞 01796-472196; www.moulinhotel.co.uk; Moulin; bar mains £7-11; ⊙lunch & dinner) A mile away but a world apart, this atmospheric hotel was trading centuries before the tartan tack came to Pitlochry. With its romantic low ceilings, ageing wood and booth seating, the inn is a wonderfully atmospheric spot for a house-brewed ale or a portion of Highland comfort food: try the filling haggis or venison stew. A more formal restaurant (mains £13 to £16) serves equally delicious fare, and the hotel has a variety of rooms (single/double £60/75) as well as a self-catering annexe. The best way to get here from Pitlochry is walking: it's a pretty uphill stroll through green fields, and an easy roll down the slope afterwards.

PORT-NA-CRAIG INN

Restaurant/Pub   ££

(📞 01796-472777; www.portnacraig.com; Port Na Craig; mains £13-17; ⊙lunch & dinner) Right on the river, this top little spot sits in what was once a separate hamlet. Delicious main meals are prepared with confidence and panache – scrumptious scallops or lamb steak bursting with flavour might appeal, but simpler sandwiches, kids' meals and light lunches also tempt. Or you could just sit out by the river with a pint and watch the anglers whisking away their poles.

MCKAY'S HOTEL   Pub

(www.mckayshotel.co.uk; 138 Atholl Rd; mains £9; ⊙lunch & dinner) While the Moulin and the Port-na-Craig are perfect for a quiet beer in the Highland air, this is the place to go to meet locals and have a big night out. Live music at weekends, weekly karaoke and DJs make this Pitlochry's most popular. The action moves from the spacious front bar (which serves food) to the boisterous dancefloor out the back.

 # Information

Tourist office (📞 01796-472215; pitlochry@ visitscotland.com; 22 Atholl Rd; ⊙8.30am-7pm Mon-Sat & 9.30am-5.30pm Sun Easter-Oct, 10am-4pm Mon-Sat Nov-Mar; @) Good information on local walks.

Winter clouds in the forests of Pitlochry

ANDREW MACCOLL

GLF/IMAGEBROKER

Don't Miss **Blair Castle**

One of the most popular tourist attractions in Scotland, magnificent Blair Castle (and the 108 square miles it sits on) is the seat of the Duke of Atholl, head of the Murray clan. It's an impressive white building set beneath forested slopes above the River Garry.

The original tower was built in 1269, but the castle has undergone significant remodelling since. Thirty rooms are open to the public and they present a wonderful picture of upper-class Highland life from the 16th century on. The **dining room** is sumptuous – check out the 9-pint wine glasses – and the **ballroom** is a vaulted chamber that's a virtual stag cemetery.

The current duke visits the castle every May to review the Atholl Highlanders, Britain's only private army.

For a great cycle, walk or drive, take the stunning road to **Glenfender** from Blair Atholl village. It's about 3 miles on a long, windy uphill track to a farmhouse; the views of snowcapped peaks along the way are spectacular.

Blair Atholl is 6 miles northwest of Pitlochry, and the castle a further mile beyond it. Local buses run a service between Pitlochry and Blair Atholl (25 minutes, three to seven daily). Four buses a day (Monday to Saturday) go directly to the castle. There's a train station in the village, but not all trains stop here.

THINGS YOU NEED TO KNOW

www.blair-castle.co.uk; Blair Atholl; adult/child/family £8.75/5.25/24; ☻9.30am-5.30pm Apr-Oct

ROYAL DEESIDE

The valley of the **River Dee** – often called **Royal Deeside** because of the royal family's long association with the area –

stretches west from Aberdeen to Braemar, closely paralleled by the A93 road. From Deeside north to Strathdon is serious castle country – there are more examples of fanciful Scottish Baronial architecture here than anywhere else in Scotland.

The Dee, world-famous for its **salmon fishing**, has its source in the Cairngorm Mountains west of Braemar, the starting point for long walks into the hills. The **FishDee website** (www.fishdee.co.uk) has all you need to know about fishing on the river.

Ballater

POP 1450

The attractive little village of Ballater owes its 18th-century origins to the curative waters of nearby Pannanich Springs (now bottled commercially as Deeside Natural Mineral Water) and its prosperity to nearby Balmoral Castle.

The **tourist office** (☑ 01339-755306; Station Sq; ⊙9am-6pm Jul & Aug, 10am-5pm Sep-Jun) is in the Old Royal Station.

 Sights & Activities

When Queen Victoria travelled to Balmoral Castle she would alight from the royal train at Ballater's **Old Royal Station** (Station Sq; admission £2; ⊙9am-6pm Jul & Aug, 10am-5pm Sep-Jun). The station has been beautifully restored and now houses the tourist office, a cafe and a museum with a replica of Victoria's royal coach. Note the crests on the shop fronts along the main street proclaiming 'By Royal Appointment' – the village is a major supplier of provisions to Balmoral.

Also on Station Sq is **Dee Valley Confectioners** (www.dee-valley.co.uk; Station Sq; admission free; ⊙9am-noon & 2-4.30pm Mon-Thu Apr-Oct), where you can drool over the manufacture of traditional Scottish sweeties.

As you approach Ballater from the east the hills start to close in, and there are many pleasant **walks** in the surrounding area. The steep woodland walk up **Craigendarroch** (400m) takes just over one hour. **Morven** (871m) is a more serious prospect, taking about six hours, but offers good views from the top; ask at the tourist office for more info.

You can hire bicycles from **CycleHighlands** (www.cyclehighlands.com; The Pavilion, Victoria Rd; per day £16; ⊙9am-6pm), which also offers guided bike rides and advice on local trails, and **Cabin Fever** (Station Sq; per 2hrs £8; ⊙9am-6pm), which can also arrange pony-trekking, quad-biking, clay-pigeon shooting or canoeing.

 Sleeping & Eating

Accommodation here is fairly expensive and budget travellers usually continue to Braemar.

AULD KIRK Restaurant with Rooms ££
(☑ 01339-755762; www.theauldkirk.com; Braemar Rd; s/d from £73/110; 🛜) Here's something a little out of the ordinary – a six-bedroom 'restaurant with rooms' housed in a converted 19th-century church. The interior blends original features with sleek modern decor, and the stylish Scottish restaurant (two-/three-course dinner £29/35) serves local lamb, venison and seafood.

GREEN INN Restaurant with Rooms ££
(☑ 01339-755701; www.green-inn.com; s/d from £58/76; P) A lovely old house dotted with plush armchairs and sofas, this is another 'restaurant with rooms' – three comfortable en suite bedrooms, with the accent on fine dining. The menu includes French-influenced dishes such as roast quail with crayfish, truffle and wild mushrooms. A two-/three-course dinner costs £34/41 and meals are served from 7pm till 9pm Tuesday to Saturday.

CELICALL B&B ££
(☑ 01339-755699; www.celicallguesthouse.co.uk; 3 Braemar Rd; d from £54; P) Celicall is a friendly, family-run B&B in a modern cottage right across the street from Station Sq, within easy walking distance of all attractions.

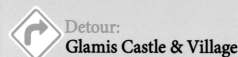

Detour:
Glamis Castle & Village

Looking every inch the Scottish Baronial castle, with its roofline a forest of turrets and battlements, **Glamis Castle** (www.glamis-castle.co.uk; adult/child £8.75/6; ⏰10am-6pm mid-Mar–Oct, 10.30am-4.30pm Nov & Dec, closed Jan–mid-Mar) claims to be the legendary setting for Shakespeare's *Macbeth*. A royal residence since 1372, it's the family home of the earls of Strathmore and Kinghorne. The Queen Mother (born Elizabeth Bowes-Lyon; 1900–2002) spent her childhood at Glamis (pronounced 'glams') and Princess Margaret (the Queen's sister; 1930–2002) was born here.

The five-storey, L-shaped castle was given to the Lyon family in 1372, but significantly altered in the 17th century. The most impressive room is the **drawing room**, with a vaulted plasterwork ceiling. There's a display of armour and weaponry in the haunted crypt and frescoes in the chapel. Duncan's Hall is named for the murdered king in *Macbeth*, though the real Macbeth had nothing to do with the castle, having died long before it was built.

You can also look around the royal apartments, including the Queen Mother's bedroom. The one-hour guided tours depart every 15 minutes (last tour at 4.30pm, or 3.30pm in winter).

The **Angus Folk Museum** (NTS; Kirkwynd, Glamis; adult/child £5.50/4.50; ⏰noon-5pm daily Jul & Aug, noon-5pm Sat & Sun only Easter-Jun, Sep & Oct), in a row of 18th-century cottages just off the flower-bedecked square in Glamis village, houses a fine collection of domestic and agricultural relics.

Glamis Castle is 12 miles north of Dundee. There are two to four buses a day from Dundee (35 minutes) to Glamis.

OLD STATION CAFE   Cafe   ££

(Station Sq; mains £9-15; ⏰10am-5pm daily, 6.30-8.30pm Thu-Sat) The former waiting room at Queen Victoria's train station is now an attractive dining area with black-and-white floor tiles, basketwork chairs, and marble fireplace and table tops. Daily specials make good use of local produce, from salmon to venison, and good coffee and home-baked goods are available all day.

ℹ Getting There & Away

Bus 201 runs from Aberdeen to Ballater (£9, 1¾ hours, hourly Monday to Saturday, six on Sunday) via Crathes Castle, and continues to Braemar (30 minutes) every two hours.

Braemar
POP 400

Braemar is a pretty little village with a grand location on a broad plain ringed by mountains where the Dee valley and Glen Clunie meet. In winter this is one of the coldest places in the country – temperatures as low as minus 29°C have been recorded – and during spells of severe cold, hungry deer wander the streets looking for a bite to eat. Braemar is an excellent base for hill walking, and there's skiing at nearby Glenshee.

The **tourist office** (📞 01399-741600; The Mews, Mar Rd; ⏰9am-6pm Aug, 9am-5pm Jun, Jul, Sep & Oct, 10am-1.30pm & 2-5pm Mon-Sat & 2-5pm Sun Nov-May), opposite the Fife Arms Hotel, has lots of useful info on walks in the area. There's a bank with an **ATM** in the village centre, a couple of **outdoor equipment shops** and an **Alldays** (⏰7.30am-9pm Mon-Sat, 9am-6pm Sun) grocery store.

Sights & Activities

The **Braemar Highland Heritage Centre** (Mar Rd; admission free; ⏱9am-6.30pm Jul & Aug, 10am-6pm Jun & Sep, 10am-5.30pm Mon-Sat, noon-5pm Sun Mar-May, shorter hrs winter), beside the tourist office, tells the story of the area with displays and videos.

Just north of the village, turreted **Braemar Castle** (www.braemarcastle.co.uk; adult/child £5/3; ⏱11am-6pm Sat & Sun, plus Wed Jul & Aug) dates from 1628 and served as a government garrison after the 1745 Jacobite rebellion. It was taken over by the local community in 2007, and now offers guided tours of the historic castle apartments.

An easy walk from Braemar is up **Creag Choinnich** (538m), a hill to the east of the village above the A93. The route is waymarked and takes about 1½ hours. For a longer walk (three hours) and superb views of the Cairngorms, head for the summit of **Morrone** (859m), southwest of Braemar. Ask at the tourist office for details of these and other walks.

Sleeping

RUCKSACKS BUNKHOUSE
Bunkhouse **£**
(📞 01339-741517; 15 Mar Rd; bothy £7, dm £12-15, tw £36; P @)
An appealing cottage bunkhouse, with comfy dorm and cheaper beds in an alpine-style bothy (shared sleeping platform for 10 people; bring your own sleeping bag). Extras including a drying room (for wet-weather gear), laundry and even a sauna (£10 an hour). Nonguests are

welcome to use the internet (£3 per hour, 10.30am to 4.30pm), laundry and even the showers (£2), and the friendly owner is a fount of knowledge about the local area.

CRAIGLEA
B&B **££**
(📞 01339-741641; www.craigleabraemar.com; Hillside Dr; r £70; P)
Craiglea is a homely B&B set in a pretty stone-built cottage with three en suite bedrooms. Vegetarian breakfasts are available and the owners can give advice on local walks.

CLUNIE LODGE GUESTHOUSE
B&B **££**
(📞 01339-741330; www.clunielodge.com; Cluniebank Rd; r per person from £30; P) A spacious Victorian villa set in beautiful gardens, the Clunie is a great place to relax after a hard day's hiking, with its comfortable residents lounge, bedrooms with views of the hills, and red squirrels scampering through the neighbouring woods. There's a drying room and secure storage for cycles.

Drummer at the Braemar Gathering (p210)
PHOTOGRAPHER: JONATHAN SMITH

BRAEMAR LODGE HOTEL
Hotel/Bunkhouse ££

(☎ 01339-741627; www.braemarlodge.co.uk; Glenshee Rd; dm from £12, s/d £75/120; P) This Victorian shooting lodge on the southern outskirts of the village has bags of character, not least in the wood-panelled Malt Room bar, which is as well stocked with mounted deer heads as it is with single malt whiskies. There's a good restaurant with views of the hills, plus a 12-berth hikers' bunkhouse in the hotel grounds.

BRAEMAR YOUTH HOSTEL
Hostel £

(SYHA; ☎ 01339-741659; 21 Glenshee Rd; dm £16-17; ⊙ Jan-Oct; @) This hostel is housed in a grand former shooting lodge just south of the village centre on the A93 to Perth; it has a comfy lounge with pool table, and a barbecue in the garden.

 Eating

GATHERING PLACE
Bistro ££

(☎ 01339-741234; www.the-gathering-place.co.uk; 9 Invercauld Rd; mains £15-18; ⊙ dinner Tue-Sun) This bright and breezy bistro is an unexpected corner of culinary excellence, with a welcoming dining room and sunny conservatory, tucked below the main road junction at the entrance to the village.

Taste
Cafe £

(www.taste-braemar.co.uk; Airlie House, Mar Rd; mains £3-5; ⊙ 10am-5pm Thu-Mon; 🖒) Taste is a relaxed little cafe with armchairs in the window, serving soups, snacks, coffee and cakes.

Hungry Highlander
Fish & Chips £

(14 Invercauld Rd; mains £3-7; ⊙ 10am-9pm Mon, Wed & Thu & Sun, 10am-10pm Fri & Sat, 10am-8pm Sun) Serves a range of takeaway meals and hot drinks.

❶ Getting There & Away

Bus 201 runs from Aberdeen to Braemar (£9, 2¼ hours, eight daily Monday to Saturday, five on Sunday). The 50-mile drive from Perth to Braemar is beautiful, but there's no public transport on this route.

SPEYSIDE
Dufftown

POP 1450

Rome may be built on seven hills, but Dufftown's built on seven stills, say the locals. Founded in 1817 by James Duff, 4th earl of Fife, Dufftown is 17 miles south of Elgin and lies at the heart of the Speyside whisky-distilling region.

The **tourist office** (☎ 01340-820501; ⊙ 10am-1pm & 2-5.30pm Mon-Sat, 11am-3pm Sun Easter-Oct) is in the clock tower in the main square; the adjoining museum contains some interesting local items.

Braemar Gathering

There are Highland games in many towns and villages throughout the summer, but the best known is the **Braemar Gathering** (www.braemargathering.org), which takes place on the first Saturday in September. It's a major occasion, organised every year since 1817 by the Braemar Royal Highland Society. Events include highland dancing, pipers, tug-of-war, a hill race up Morrone, tossing the caber, hammer- and stone-throwing and the long jump. International athletes are among those who take part.

These kinds of events took place informally in the Highlands for many centuries as tests of skill and strength, but they were formalised around 1820 as part of the rise of Highland romanticism initiated by Sir Walter Scott and King George IV. Queen Victoria attended the Braemar Gathering in 1848, starting a tradition of royal patronage that continues to this day.

ANN CECIL

Don't Miss **Balmoral Castle**

Eight miles west of Ballater lies Balmoral Castle, the Queen's Highland holiday home, screened from the road by a thick curtain of trees. Built for Queen Victoria in 1855 as a private residence for the royal family, it kicked off the revival of the Scottish Baronial style of architecture that characterises so many of Scotland's 19th-century country houses.

The admission fee includes an interesting and well-thought-out audio guide, but the tour is very much an outdoor one through garden and grounds; as for the castle itself, only the ballroom, which displays a collection of Landseer paintings and royal silver, is open to the public. Don't expect to see the Queen's private quarters! The main attraction is learning about Highland estate management, rather than royal revelations. Guided tours are available on Saturdays from October to December – check the website for details.

The massive, pointy-topped mountain that looms to the south of Balmoral is **Lochnagar** (1155m), immortalised in verse by Lord Byron, who spent his childhood years in Aberdeenshire:

England, thy beauties are tame and domestic
To one who has roamed o'er the mountains afar.
O! for the crags that are wild and majestic:
The steep frowning glories of dark Lochnagar.

Balmoral is beside the A93 at Crathie and can be reached on the Aberdeen to Braemar bus.

THINGS YOU NEED TO KNOW

www.balmoralcastle.com; adult/child £8.70/4.60; ☉10am-5pm Apr-Jul, last admission 4pm

Blaze Your Own Whisky Trail

Visiting a distillery can be memorable, but only hardcore malthounds will want to go to more than two or three. The following are some recommendations.

○ **Aberlour** (www.aberlour.com; tours £10; ⏰10.30am & 2pm daily Easter-Oct, Mon-Fri by appointment Nov-Mar) Has an excellent, detailed tour with a proper tasting session. It's on the main street in Aberlour.

○ **Glenfarclas** (www.glenfarclas.co.uk; admission £3.50; ⏰10am-4pm Mon-Fri Oct-Mar, 10am-5pm Mon-Fri Apr-Sep, plus 10am-4pm Sat Jul-Sep) Small, friendly and independent, Glenfarclas is 5 miles south of Aberlour on the Grantown road. The last tour leaves 90 minutes before closing.

○ **Glenfiddich** (www.glenfiddich.com; admission free; ⏰9.30am-4.30pm Mon-Fri year-round, 9.30am-4.30pm Sat & noon-4.30pm Sun Easter-mid-Oct) Big and busy, but handiest for Dufftown and foreign languages are available. The standard tour starts with an overblown video, but it's fun, informative and free. An in-depth Connoisseur's Tour (£20) must be prebooked.

○ **Macallan** (www.themacallan.com; standard tours £5; ⏰9.30am-4.30pm Mon-Sat Apr-Oct, ring for winter hours) Excellent sherry-casked malt. Several small-group tours are available (last tour at 3.30pm), including an expert one (£15); all should be prebooked. Lovely location 2 miles northwest of Craigellachie.

○ **Speyside Cooperage** (www.speysidecooperage.co.uk; admission £3.30; ⏰9am-4pm Mon-Fri) A place where you can see the fascinating art of barrel-making in action. It's a mile from Craigellachie on the Dufftown road.

○ **Spirit of Speyside** (www.spiritofspeyside.com) A biannual whisky festival in Dufftown with a number of great events. It takes place in early May and late September; both accommodation and events should be booked well ahead.

◉ Sights & Activities

With seven working distilleries nearby, Dufftown has been dubbed Scotland's malt whisky capital. Ask at the tourist office for a **Malt Whisky Trail** (www.maltwhiskytrail.com) booklet, a self-guided tour around the seven stills plus the Speyside Cooperage.

KEITH & DUFFTOWN RAILWAY
Heritage Railway

(www.keith-dufftown-railway.co.uk; Dufftown Station) A heritage railway line running for 11 miles from Dufftown to Keith. Trains hauled by 1950s diesel motor units run on Saturday and Sunday from June to September, plus Friday in July and August; a return ticket costs £9.50/4.50 for an adult/child. There are also two 1930s 'Brighton Belle' Pullman coaches on display, and a cafe housed in a 1957 British Rail cafeteria car.

WHISKY MUSEUM
Museum

(www.dufftown.co.uk; The Hub, 12 Conval St; ⏰1-4pm Mon-Fri May-Sep) As well as housing a selection of distillery memorabilia (try saying that after a few drams), the Whisky Museum (recently moved to new premises in Conval St) holds 'nosing and tasting evenings' where you can learn what to look for in a fine single malt (£8 per person; 8pm Wednesday in July and August). You can then test your newfound skills at the nearby **Whisky Shop** (www.whiskyshopdufftown.co.uk; 1 Fife St), which stocks hundreds of single malts.

Sleeping & Eating

DAVAAR B&B   B&B ££
(☎ 01340-820464; www.davaardufftown
.co.uk; 17 Church St; s/d from £40/60) Just
along the street opposite the tourist
office, Davaar is a sturdy Victorian
villa with three smallish but comfy
rooms; the breakfast menu is superb,
offering the option of Portsoy kippers instead of the traditional fry-up
(which uses eggs from the owners'
own chickens).

FIFE ARMS HOTEL   Hotel ££
(☎ 01340-820220; www.fifearmsdufftown
.co.uk; 2 The Square; s/d from £35/60; P)
This welcoming hotel offers slightly
cramped but comfortable accommodation in a modern block around
the back; its bar is stocked with a
wide range of single malts, and the
restaurant (mains £9 to £16) dishes
up sizzling steaks, homemade steak
pies and locally farmed ostrich
steaks.

🍴 LA FAISANDERIE
     French/Scottish £££
(☎ 01340-821273; The Square; mains
£18-21; ⊙noon-1.30pm & 5.30-8.30pm)
This is a great place to eat, run by a
local chef who shoots much of his
own game, guaranteeing freshness.
The interior is decorated in French
auberge style with a cheerful mural
and pheasants hiding in every corner.
The set menus (three-course lunch
£18.50, four-course dinner £32) won't
disappoint, but you can order à la carte
as well.

🍴 A TASTE OF SPEYSIDE Scottish ££
(☎ 01340-820860; 10 Balvenie St; mains
£16-20; ⊙noon-9pm Tue-Sun Easter-Sep,
noon-2pm & 6-9pm Tue-Sun Oct-Easter) This
upmarket restaurant prepares traditional Scottish dishes using fresh local
produce, including a challenging platter
of smoked salmon, smoked venison,
brandied chicken liver pâté, cured herring, a selection of Scottish cheeses and

homemade bread (phew!). A two-course
lunch costs £13.50.

♥ If You Like...
Castles

The royal connection means that Balmoral
is the name that everyone knows, but there
are many other castles in and around Royal
Deeside.

1 CASTLE FRASER
(NTS; adult/child £8.50/5.50; ⊙11am-5pm Jul &
Aug, noon-5pm Thu-Sun Apr-Jun, noon-5pm Thu-Sun
Sep & Oct) The 16th-century ancestral home of the
Fraser family. The largely Victorian interior includes the
great hall (with a hidden opening where the laird could
eavesdrop on his guests); 16 miles west of Aberdeen.

2 FYVIE CASTLE
(NTS; adult/child £10.50/7.50; ⊙11am-5pm
Jul & Aug, noon-5pm Sat-Tue Apr-Jun, Sep & Oct) A
magnificent example of Scottish Baronial architecture,
probably more famous for its ghosts which include a
phantom trumpeter and the mysterious Green Lady;
25 miles north of Aberdeen.

3 CRATHES CASTLE
(NTS; adult/child £10.50/7.50; ⊙10.30am-5pm
Jun-Aug, 10.30am-4.30pm Sat-Thu Apr, May, Sep &
Oct, 10.30am-3.45pm Sat & Sun Nov-Mar) Famous for
its Jacobean painted ceilings, magnificently carved
canopied beds, and the 'Horn of Leys', presented to
the Burnett family by Robert the Bruce in the 14th
century; 16 miles west of Aberdeen.

4 CRAIGEIVAR CASTLE
(NTS; adult/child £10/7; ⊙noon-5.30pm Jul
& Aug, noon-5.30pm Fri-Tue Easter-Jun & Sep) A
superb example of the original Scottish Baronial
style, Craigievar has managed to survive pretty
much unchanged since its completion in the 17th
century; 15 miles north of Ballater.

❶ Getting There & Away

Buses link Dufftown to Inverness. On summer
weekends, you can take a train from Inverness
to Keith, and then ride the Keith and Dufftown
Railway to Dufftown.

Skye & the Islands

Skye epitomises the romantic image of Scotland. The jagged peaks of the Cuillin tear through the mist, and the ghosts of Bonnie Prince Charlie and Flora MacDonald haunt the hallways of Dunvegan Castle. Weather permitting, Skye is also a paradise for walkers and wildlife enthusiasts; its rugged hills, lonely lochs and scenic coastlines are home to golden eagles, red deer, otters and seals.

To the south, the bustling port of Oban is the 'gateway to the isles', with regular ferries to the peaceful backwaters of Kerrera and Lismore, the dramatic landscapes of Mull and the wild, windswept beaches of Coll and Tiree.

Mull can lay claim to some of the finest and most varied scenery in the Scottish islands. Add in two impressive castles, a narrow-gauge railway and the sacred island of Iona and you can see why it's sometimes impossible to find a spare bed on the island.

Eilean Donan Castle (p229), Loch Duich
PHOTOGRAPHER: MICAH WRIGHT

Grave of Flora MacDonald (p238), Isle of Skye

Skye & the Islands

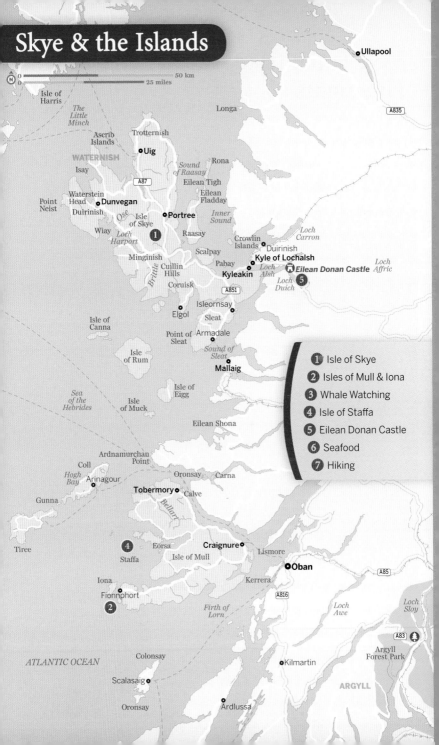

Ullapool

Isle of Harris

The Little Minch

Longa

A835

Ascrib Islands

Trotternish

●Uig

WATERNISH

Isay

Sound of Raasay

Rona

A87

Eilean Tigh

Waterstein Head

Point Neist

Duirinish

Dunvegan

Ose

Isle of Skye

Eilean Fladday

Inner Sound

●**Portree**

Wiay

Loch Harport

Raasay

Loch Carron

Minginish

Scalpay

Crowlin Islands ● **Duirinish**

Cuillin Hills

Pabay

Kyle of Lochalsh

Loch Alsh

🏰 *Eilean Donan Castle*

Loch Affric

Brittle

Kyleakin

Loch Duich

Coruisk

A851

⑤

Isle of Canna

Isleornsay

Elgol

Sleat

Point of Sleat

Armadale

Isle of Rum

Sound of Sleat

Mallaig

Sea of the Hebrides

Isle of Muck

Isle of Eigg

Eilean Shona

① Isle of Skye

② Isles of Mull & Iona

③ Whale Watching

④ Isle of Staffa

⑤ Eilean Donan Castle

⑥ Seafood

⑦ Hiking

Ardnamurchan Point

Coll

Hogh Bay

Arinagour

Oronsay

Carna

Gunna

Tobermory●

Calve

Bellart

Tiree

Eorsa

Craignure●

Lismore

④

Staffa

Isle of Mull

●**Oban**

A85

Iona

Kerrera

Fionnphort

A816

Loch Awe

Loch Sloy

②

Firth of Lorn

A83 🌲

Argyll Forest Park

ATLANTIC OCEAN

Colonsay

●Kilmartin

Scalasaig●

ARGYLL

Oronsay

●Ardlussa

0 — 50 km

0 — 25 miles

Skye & the Islands' Highlights

1 Isle of Skye

Travellers and tourists have been going 'over the sea to Skye' for centuries, although these days the journey is rather more straightforward thanks to a controversial modern road bridge. But Skye remains as alluring as ever, boasting some of the most beautiful and dramatic landscapes in Europe.

Need to Know

BEST TIME TO GO May and September (best chance of dry weather). **BEST PHOTO OP** In fine weather, almost anywhere! **TOP TIP** Don't forget the midge repellent. **For more, see p226.**

Isle of Skye Don't Miss List

SUU RAMSAY, DRIVER AND GUIDE

1 CUILLIN HILLS
Rising from the ground in a dramatic skyline of black volcanic gabbro, these serrated pinnacles (p234; pictured facing page) will test hikers and climbers alike; the aptly named Inaccessible Pinnacle is the pièce de résistance. For those looking for a more leisurely option, superb boat trips operate from **Elgol** (p230) to Coruisk, where the Cuillin rise spectacularly from the sea.

2 DUNVEGAN CASTLE
Home of Clan MacLeod, Dunvegan (p236; pictured bottom left) claims to be the longest occupied castle in Britain, having had someone in residence since the 13th century. The castle's array of interesting artefacts, such as the Fairy Flag and Rory Mor's Drinking Horn, are enough to whet the interest of any clan aficionado. The castle sits on the shores of Loch Dunvegan, where you'll find seals frequenting the surrounding waters.

3 QUIRAING
This impressive rock formation (p238; pictured top left) affords superb views across a landscape where time appears to have stood still. The jurassic scene offers careful walking out to the pillared columns of the 'Prison', which eerily protrude from the slopes. For the more agile, there's a scramble up to the 'Table' where, in days of old, the final of the annual shinty match used to take place.

4 FAIRY GLEN
A plethora of fairy knolls sit quietly in this peaceful and little-known glen (p239). Locals believe that the 'wee people' (*sith*, in Gaelic) live here deep inside these dark caverns of the earth. Rowan trees planted to keep away evil spirits keep a close vigil. Also look out for the fairy tower and the fairy circle. This place will have you believing before you leave. Go with care!

5 SKYE MUSEUM OF ISLAND LIFE
Run by local Gaelic speakers, this recreation of an island township (p238) provides an educational and informative look at Skye history and a nostalgic glimpse of daily life during the 19th century. Thatched cottages include the original croft house, the barn, the weaver's cottage, the old smithy and the ceilidh house.

Isles of Mull & Iona

One of the most accessible of Scotland's islands (45 minutes by ferry from Oban), Mull is also one of the most beautiful. From Duart Castle perched on its dramatic headland to the holy island of Iona, there are miles and miles of scenic single-track roads to explore.

Need to Know

BEST TIME TO GO June to August (for whale spotting). **BEST PHOTO OP** Summit of Dun I (Iona). **WILDLIFE SPOTTING** You can cheat by viewing sea eagles on CCTV at the Aros Centre. For more, see p244 & p251.

Isles of Mull & Iona Don't Miss List

DAVID SEXTON, RSPB MULL OFFICER & BIRDWATCHING GUIDEBOOK AUTHOR

1 EAGLE HIDE

Loch Frisa (p250) is the only place on the planet with a public viewing hide overlooking the nesting area of rare white-tailed sea eagles. The hide offers a unique and privileged view of the UK's largest bird of prey, and income goes to help local good causes.

2 SPIRIT OF IONA

Too many visitors race through Mull. Slow down and try to spend a night on Iona (p251). On a warm, sunny day in summer you can't beat it. In the evening take a stroll or cycle along the quiet lanes and listen to the amazing call of the endangered corncrake, which the local farmers and crofters have helped recover from the brink of extinction in the UK.

3 STAFFA & THE TRESHNISH ISLES

A bit of puffin spotting on these magical islands (p253; pictured top left) is a must. Other seabirds such as guillemots, razorbills and kittiwakes cram onto the narrow cliff ledges and their 'aroma' will stay in your nostrils for a long time. The geology of the islands, especially Staffa, is remarkable.

4 TOBERMORY

The colourful waterfront houses of Tobermory (p247; pictured facing page) will be familiar to many around the world as the home of the popular BBC children's TV show *Balamory*. In real life it's a thriving town with a lively atmosphere, great pubs and seafood cafes. Several whale-watch boats depart from here in search of minke whales, dolphins and basking sharks. If the weather is good, get your fresh fish and chips from the van on the pier (like Prince Charles did on his last visit).

5 BEACHES

You can't come to Mull and Iona and not sample some of the beautiful white-sand beaches. Iona has many to choose from; on your way, visit Ardalanish or Uisken on the Ross of Mull for an idyllic beach experience, or head north to the stunning Calgary Bay (p250; pictured bottom left).

Whale Watching

The waters off the west coast of Scotland attract large numbers of marine mammals, from harbour porpoises and dolphins to minke whales and even – though sightings are rare – humpback and killer whales. Whale-watching boat trips (p250) tend to run from April to September because of the weather (whales are easier to spot in calm conditions). Basking sharks can also often be spotted on these trips.

3

Isle of Staffa

5

The impressive rock architecture of Fingal's Cave on the Isle of Staffa (p253) provided the inspiration for Felix Mendelsson's famous *Hebrides Overture*, and is a don't-miss experience for anyone ticking off Scotland's west-coast sights. Weather permitting, the boat trip lands you at some rocky steps from which a walkway and natural ledge allow you to go all the way to the back of the cave.

BALL MIWAKO/ALAMY

Eilean Donan Castle

SEAN CAFFREY

Perched on a tiny island linked to the shore by a picturesque arched bridge, Eilean Donan (p229) is the most iconic of Scottish castles. Its image has graced everything from postcards to shortbread tins and has appeared in many movies including *Highlander* and *The World Is Not Enough*. Despite its venerable appearance, it is actually a relatively modern restoration, built in the early 20th century.

Savouring Scottish Seafood

The waters of the west coast of Scotland are some of the most productive in Europe, yielding rich harvests of seafood. Scottish specialities to look out for in quayside restaurants such as Waterfront (p242) and Café Fish (p248) include juicy langoustines (also known as Dublin Bay prawns), scallops (often hand-picked by divers), razor clams (gathered on sandy beaches at low tide) and squat lobster (a smaller cousin of the common lobster).

FEARGUS COONEY

Hiking the Hills

The Scottish islands boast some of the finest landscapes in Europe; the best way to appreciate the view is to pull on your hiking boots and climb a hill. Skye and Mull have some truly challenging hikes, but there are many routes that can be tackled by mortals, such as the trail up to the Old Man of Storr (p237), and Dun I (p252), the highest point on Iona. The Old Man of Storr, Isle of Skye

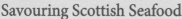

Skye & the Islands' Best…

Restaurants

○ **Three Chimneys** (p237)
Fine dining in a remote and beautiful corner of Skye

○ **Lochbay Seafood Restaurant** (p237) One of Skye's most romantic restaurants

○ **Waterfront** (p242)
Converted seamen's mission that serves superb seafood freshly landed at the quay

○ **Café Fish** (p248)
Welcoming little restaurant overlooking Tobermory harbour, serving fresh shellfish straight from the boat

Classic Views

○ **Elgol** (p230) Classic panorama of the Cuillin Hills.

○ **Sligachan Hotel** (p234)
Postcard view of the Cuillin's jagged skyline

○ **Eilean Donan Castle** (p229) Set against a backdrop of sea and mountains, this castle has graced a million shortbread tins

○ **McCaig's Tower** (p239)
Panorama over Oban Bay to the Isles of Kerrera and Mull

○ **Dun I** (p252) A 360-degree panorama of sea and islands

Walks

○ **Coire Lagan** (p234) Hike into the heart of the Cuillin Hills

○ **Coral Beaches** (p236)
Easy walk to unusual white-gravel beaches with views to Outer Hebrides

○ **Old Man of Storr** (p237)
A short uphill hike to an amazing pinnacle giving great views of mainland hills

○ **Quiraing** (p238) Another easy option, mostly level, amid strange and impressive rock scenery

Boat Trips

○ **Loch Coruisk** (p231) Sail from Elgol to the mountain-ringed fastness of Coruisk

○ **Whale-watching, Isle of Skye** (p229) High-speed RIB (rigid inflatable boat) takes you wildlife spotting in the waters off Skye

○ **Whale-watching, Isle of Mull** (p250) Quality whale-watching cruises out of Tobermory harbour

○ **Isle of Staffa** (p252) Cruise from Iona to visit Fingal's Cave on the Isle of Staffa

Need to Know

ADVANCE PLANNING

○ **One month before** Reserve a table at the Three Chimneys (p237) on Skye, to avoid disappointment; book accommodation on Mull and Skye

○ **Two weeks before** If travelling by car, make reservations for any ferry crossings, especially in summer

○ **One week before** Make bookings for wildlife-spotting boat trips

RESOURCES

○ **Skye & Lochalsh** (www.skye.co.uk) Tourist information for the Isle of Skye

○ **Oban** (www.oban.org.uk) Tourist information for Oban and area

○ **Isle of Mull** (www.explore -isle-of-mull.co.uk) Lots of useful information, from accommodation to wildlife

○ **Isle of Iona** (www.isle -of-iona.com) Official island website

○ **Scottish Heartlands** (www.visitscottishheartlands .com) Official tourist-board website for Oban and Mull

○ **Caledonian Macbrayne** (www.calmac.co.uk) Timetables and fares for ferries to the islands

GETTING AROUND

○ **Bus** Reasonable network of local buses on islands

○ **Car** The most time-efficient way to get around the islands

○ **Ferry** Frequent services from Oban to Mull year-round

○ **Train** From Edinburgh or Glasgow to Oban, Mallaig or Kyle of Lochalsh

BE FOREWARNED

○ **Midges** Tiny biting flies are a pest from June to September, especially in still weather around dawn and dusk; bring insect repellent and wear long-sleeved clothing

○ **Weather** Always unpredictable on the west coast; be prepared for wet and windy days, even in the middle of summer

eft: Oban (p239) as seen from McCaig's Tower; **Above:** The Cuillin Hills (p234)

Skye & the Islands Itineraries

These itineraries take in the best of Skye and Mull. Both start and finish at a town with a railway station; you can pick up a rental car at Kyle of Lochalsh and drop it at Armadale.

3 DAYS

KYLE OF LOCHALSH TO MALLAIG
Over the Sea to Skye

From **(1) Kyle of Lochalsh** the Skye Bridge carries you over the water to the legendary Isle of Skye; pray for clear weather! Follow signs toward Portree, and at the far end of Broadford village detour southwest on the narrow road to **(2) Elgol** where a boat trip to **(3) Coruisk** awaits. It'll be afternoon by the time you return; continue north to the island capital of **(4) Portree**.

Spend your second day on a slow circuit of the **(5) Trotternish Peninsula** to visit the Old Man of Storr, Kilt Rock, the Quiraing and the Skye Museum of Island Life, returning to Portree for the night. On day three head west to **(6) Dunvegan Castle**, and afterwards take a stroll to the Coral Beaches.

Return south on the A863 via Bracadale, perhaps stopping to tour the **(7) Talisker Distillery**. Back at Broadford, you have the choice of returning to Kyle of Lochalsh, or heading south on the A851. If you're still hungry for dramatic scenery, be sure to detour west on the minor road via **(8) Tarskavaig** for stunning views of the Cuillin Hills and the Isle of Rum. Be sure to arrive at **(9) Armadale** in time for the ferry to **(10) Mallaig**.

Top Left: Portree (p231);
Top Right: Houses along the harbour in Tobermory (p247)
PHOTOGRAPHER: (TOP LEFT) DAVID TOMLINSON; (TOP RIGHT) MARTIN MOOS

6 DAYS

MALLAIG TO OBAN
Island-Hopping to Mull

This itinerary continues from the previous one. From Mallaig a very scenic 67-mile drive (allow two hours) leads south via the A861 and A884 to **(1) Lochaline**, from where you take the ferry to Fishnish on Mull. Head north to **(2) Tobermory**, the colourful capital of the island and, after a seafood lunch, make a circuit of northern Mull, perhaps pausing for a picnic on the sandy beach at **(3) Calgary Bay**. Return to Tobermory to stay overnight.

The following day head south then west on a narrow, twisting road around the spectacular shores of Loch na Keal. Turn right on the road to **(4) Fionnphort**. It doesn't look far on the map, but Tobermory to Fionnphort will take you two to three hours, especially if you stop to soak up the magnificent scenery. Take advantage of an overnight stay in Fionnphort by exploring the holy isle of **(5) Iona** until the last ferry leaves (or you could even stay the night here), enjoying the peace after the day-trippers have departed.

In the morning, make the long drive towards Craignure (35 miles, mostly on single-track road; allow an hour and a half), stopping to visit **(6) Duart Castle**, the seat of Clan MacLean, before catching a ferry from **(7) Craignure** to Oban.

Discover Skye & the Islands

Pillars and arches at Iona Abbey (p252)
PHOTOGRAPHER: MARTIN MOOS

ISLE OF SKYE

POP 9900

The Isle of Skye (an t-Eilean Sgiathanach in Gaelic) takes its name from the old Norse *sky-a*, meaning 'cloud island', a Viking reference to the often mist-enshrouded Cuillin Hills. It's the biggest of Scotland's islands, a 50-mile-long smorgasbord of velvet moors, jagged mountains, sparkling lochs and towering sea cliffs. The stunning scenery is the main attraction, but when the mist closes in there are plenty of castles, crofting museums and cosy pubs and restaurants to retire to.

Along with Edinburgh and Loch Ness, Skye is one of Scotland's top three tourist destinations. However, the hordes tend to stick to Portree, Dunvegan and Trotternish, and it's almost always possible to find peace and quiet in the island's farther-flung corners. Come prepared for changeable weather: when it's fine it's very fine indeed, but all too often it isn't.

 Activities

WALKING

Skye offers some of the finest – and in places the roughest and most difficult – walking in Scotland. There are many detailed guidebooks available, including a series of four walking guides by Charles Rhodes, available from the Aros Centre and the tourist office in Portree. You'll need Ordnance Survey (OS) 1:50,000 maps 23 and 32. Don't attempt the longer walks in bad weather or in winter.

Easy, low-level routes include: through Strath Mor from Luib (on the Broadford–Sligachan road) to Torrin (on the

Broadford–Elgol road, allow 1½ hours, 4 miles); from Sligachan to Kilmarie via Camasunary (four hours, 11 miles); and from Elgol to Kilmarie via Camasunary (2½ hours, 6.5 miles). The walk from Kilmarie to Coruisk via Camasunary and the 'Bad Step' (allow five hours, 11 miles round trip) is superb but slightly harder (the Bad Step is a rocky slab poised above the sea that you have to scramble across; it's easy in fine, dry weather, but some walkers find it intimidating).

SEA KAYAKING

The sheltered coves and sea lochs around the coast of Skye provide magnificent sea-kayaking opportunities. The following centres provide kayaking instruction, guiding and equipment hire for beginners and experts. It costs around £35 for a half-day kayak hire with instruction.

Skyak Adventures (☎ 01471-820002; www .skyakadventures.com; 29 Lower Breakish, Breakish)

Whitewave Outdoor Centre (☎ 01470-542414; www.white-wave.co.uk; 19 Linicro, Kilmuir; ☼ Mar-Oct)

 Tours

There are several operators who offer guided tours of Skye, covering history, culture and wildlife. Rates are from £140 for a six-hour tour for up to six people.

Red Deer Travel (☎ 01478-612142) Historical and cultural tours by minibus.

Isle of Skye Tour Guide Co (☎ 01471-844440; www.isle-of-skye-tour-guide.co.uk) Geology, history and wildlife by car.

ℹ Information

Portree and Broadford are the main population centres on Skye.

MEDICAL SERVICES

Portree Community Hospital (☎ 01478-613200; Fancyhill, Portree) There's a casualty department and dental surgery here.

MONEY

Only Portree and Broadford have banks with ATMs. Portree's tourist office has a currency exchange desk.

TOURIST INFORMATION

Broadford tourist office (☎ 01471-822361; The Car Park, Broadford; ☼ 9.30am-5pm Mon-Sat, 10am-4pm Sun Apr-Oct)

Dunvegan tourist office (☎ 01470-521581; 2 Lochside, Dunvegan; ☼ 10am-5pm Mon-Sat Jun-Oct plus 10am-4pm Sun Jul & Aug, 10am-5pm Mon-Fri Apr & May, limited opening Nov-Mar)

Portree tourist office (☎ 01478-612137; Bayfield Rd, Portree; ☼ 9am-6pm Mon-Sat & 10am-4pm Sun Jun-Aug, 9am-5pm Mon-Fri & 10am-4pm Sat Apr, May & Sep, limited opening Oct-Mar)

ℹ Getting There & Away

BOAT

Despite there being a bridge, there are still a couple of ferry links between Skye and the mainland.

MALLAIG–ARMADALE CalMac (www.calmac .co.uk) operates the Mallaig to Armadale ferry (driver or passenger £3.85, car £20.30, 30 minutes, eight daily Monday to Saturday, five to seven on Sunday). It's very popular in July and August, so book ahead if you're travelling by car.

GLENELG–KYLERHEA Skye Ferry (www.skye ferry.co.uk) runs a tiny vessel (six cars only) on the short Glenelg to Kylerhea crossing (car and up to four passengers £12, five minutes, every 20 minutes). The ferry operates from 10am to 6pm daily from Easter to October only, till 7pm June to August.

BUS

Scottish Citylink runs buses from Glasgow to Portree (£38, seven hours, four daily) and Uig via Crianlarich, Fort William and Kyle of Lochalsh. Buses also run from Inverness to Portree (£17, 3½ hours, five daily).

CAR & MOTORCYCLE

The Isle of Skye became permanently tethered to the Scottish mainland when the Skye Bridge opened in 1995. The controversial bridge tolls were abolished in 2004 and the crossing is now free.

There are **petrol stations** at Broadford (open 24 hours), Armadale, Portree, Dunvegan and Uig.

ℹ Getting Around

Getting around the island by public transport can be a pain, especially if you want to explore away from the main Kyleakin–Portree–Uig road. Here, as in much of the Highlands, there are only a few buses on Saturdays, and only one Sunday service (between Kyle of Lochalsh and Portree).

BUS Stagecoach (www.stagecoachbus.com) operates the main bus routes on the island, linking all the main villages and towns. Its Skye Dayrider ticket gives unlimited bus travel for one day for £6.70. For timetable info, call Traveline (☎0871 200 22 33).

TAXI You can order a taxi or rent a car from Kyle Taxi Company (☎01599-534323). Rentals cost from around £38 a day, and you can arrange for the car to be waiting at Kyle of Lochalsh train station.

Kyleakin (Caol Acain)

POP 100

Poor wee Kyleakin had the carpet pulled from under it when the Skye Bridge opened – it went from being the gateway to the island to a backwater bypassed by the main road. It's now a pleasant, peaceful little place, with a harbour used by yachts and fishing boats.

A **shuttle bus** runs half-hourly between Kyle of Lochalsh and Kyleakin (five minutes), and there are eight to 10 buses daily (except Sunday) to Broadford and Portree.

Eilean Ban – the island used as a stepping stone by the Skye Bridge – was where **Gavin Maxwell** (author of *Ring of Bright Water*) spent the last years of his life in the 1960s, living in the lighthouse keeper's cottage. The island is now a nature reserve and the community-run **Brightwater Visitor Centre** (☎01599-530040; www.eileanban.org; Kyleakin) serves as a base for tours of the island (11am and 2pm daily in summer), and also houses an exhibition on Maxwell, the lighthouse and the island's wildlife. Opening times were uncertain at the time of research – best call ahead to check.

Sleat

If you cross over the sea to Skye on the ferry from Mallaig you arrive in Arma-dale, at the southern end of the long, low-lying peninsula known as Sleat (pro-nounced 'slate'). The landscape of Sleat itself is not exceptional, but it provides a grandstand for ogling the magnificent scenery on either side – take the steep and twisting minor road that loops through **Tarskavaig** and **Tokavaig** for

A country lane near Tarskavaig offers views of the Cuillin Hills (p234)

DAVID TOMLINSON

stunning views of the Isle of Rum, the Cuillin Hills and Bla Bheinn.

Armadale
POP 150

Armadale, where the ferry from Mallaig arrives, is little more than a store, a post office and a couple of houses. There are six or seven buses a day (Monday to Saturday) from Armadale to Broadford and Portree.

 Sights & Activities

MUSEUM OF THE ISLES   Museum, Castle
(www.clandonald.com; adult/child £6.95/4.95; ⊙9.30am-5.30pm Easter-Oct) Just along the road from the ferry is the partly ruined **Armadale Castle**, former seat of Lord Macdonald of Sleat. The neighbouring museum will tell you all you ever wanted to know about Clan Donald, as well as providing an easily digested history of the Lordship of the Isles. Prize exhibits include rare portraits of clan chiefs, and a wine glass that was once used by Bonnie Prince Charlie. The ticket also gives admission to the lovely castle gardens.

FREE **AIRD OLD CHURCH GALLERY**
     Art Gallery
(www.skyewatercolours.co.uk; ⊙10am-5pm Mon-Sat Easter-Sep) At the end of the narrow road that leads southwest from Armadale through Ardvasar village, this small gallery exhibits the powerful landscape paintings of Peter McDermott. The track beyond the gallery provides a good walk to the lighthouse and pretty little beach at **Point of Sleat** (5 miles round trip).

SEA.FARI   Boat Trips
(☎ 01471-844787, 01471-833316; www.seafari .co.uk) Runs one- to three-hour boat trips (adults £27 to £37) in high-speed RIBs. These trips have a high success rate for spotting minke whales in summer (an average of 180 sightings a year), with rarer sightings of bottlenose dolphins and basking sharks – even a humpback whale was spotted in August 2004, and two killer whales in 2007.

Detour:
Eilean Donan Castle

Photogenically sited at the entrance to Loch Duich, near Dornie village, **Eilean Donan Castle** (www. eileandonancastle.com; Dornie; adult/ child £5.50/4.50; ⊙9.30am-6pm mid-Mar–mid-Nov) is one of Scotland's most evocative castles, and must be represented in millions of photo albums. It's on an offshore islet, magically linked to the mainland by an elegant, stone-arched bridge. It's very much a re-creation inside, with an excellent introductory exhibition. Keep an eye out for the photos of castle scenes from the movie *Highlander*. There's also a sword used at the battle of Culloden in 1746. The castle was ruined in 1719 after Spanish Jacobite forces were defeated at the Battle of Glenshiel, and it was rebuilt between 1912 and 1932.

The castle is 8 miles east of Kyle of Lochalsh and the Skye Bridge. Citylink buses from Fort William and Inverness to Portree stop opposite the castle.

Isleornsay

This pretty harbour, 8 miles north of Armadale, is opposite Sandaig Bay on the mainland, where Gavin Maxwell lived and wrote his much-loved memoir *Ring of Bright Water*. **Gallery An Talla Dearg** (www. eilean-iarmain.co.uk/art-gallery; admission free; ⊙10am-6pm Mon-Fri, 10am-4pm Sat & Sun Apr-Oct) exhibits the works of artists inspired by Scottish landscape and culture.

Sleeping & Eating

TORAVAIG HOUSE HOTEL   Hotel   £££
(☎ 01471-820200; www.skyehotel.co.uk; Sleat; r from £169; P ☎) This hotel, 3 miles south

of Isleornsay, is one of those places where the owners know a thing or two about hospitality – as soon as you arrive you'll feel right at home, whether relaxing on the plump sofas by the log fire in the lounge or admiring the view across the Sound of Sleat from the lawn chairs in the garden. The spacious bedrooms – ask for room No 1 (Eriskay), with its enormous sleigh bed – are luxuriously equipped, from the rich and heavy bed linen to the huge, high-pressure shower heads. The elegant Iona restaurant (four-course dinner £43) serves the best of local fish, game and lamb. After dinner, you can retire to the lounge with a single malt and flick through the yachting magazines – you can even arrange a day trip aboard the owners' 42ft sailing yacht.

HOTEL EILEAN IARMAIN   Hotel £££
(☎ 01471-833266; www.eilean-iarmain.co.uk; s/d from £100/160; 🅿) A charming old Victorian hotel with log fires, an excellent restaurant and 12 luxurious rooms, many with sea views. The hotel's cosy, wood-panelled An Praban bar serves

delicious, gourmet-style bar meals (£7 to £10) – try the haddock in beer batter, venison burger or vegetarian lasagne.

Elgol (Ealaghol)

On a clear day, the journey along the road from Broadford to Elgol is one of the most scenic on Skye. It takes in two classic postcard panoramas – the view of **Bla Bheinn** across Loch Slapin (near Torrin), and the superb view of the entire **Cuillin range** from Elgol pier.

Bus 49 runs from Broadford to Elgol (40 minutes, three daily Monday to Friday, two Saturday).

 **Activities**

BELLA JANE   Boat Trips
(☎ 0800 731 3089; www.bellajane.co.uk; ☉Easter–mid-Oct) *Bella Jane* offers a three-hour cruise (adult/child £20/8) from Elgol harbour to the remote **Loch na Cuilce**, an impressive inlet surrounded by soaring peaks and acres of bare rock slabs. On a calm day, you can clamber ashore here to make the short

A hiker looking towards the Old Man of Storr (p237), Trotternish Peninsula

DAVID TOMLINSON

walk to **Loch Coruisk** in the heart of the Cuillin Hills. You get 1½ hours ashore and visit a seal colony en route.

AQUAXPLORE Boat Trips
(☎ 0800 731 3089; www.aquaxplore.co.uk; ☉Easter–mid-Oct) Runs 1½-hour high-speed boat trips from Elgol to an abandoned shark-hunting station on the island of Soay (adult/child £20/15), once owned by *Ring of Bright Water* author Gavin Maxwell. There are longer trips (£45/32, four hours) to Rum, Canna and Sanday to visit breeding colonies of puffins, with the chance of seeing minke whales on the way.

Misty Isle Boat Trips
(☎ 01471-866288; www.mistyisleboattrips.co.uk; ☉Apr-Oct) The prettier and more traditional wooden launch *Misty Isle* offers cruises to Coruisk with 1½ hours ashore for adult/child £18/7.50 (no Sunday service).

Minginish

Loch Harport, to the north of the Cuillin, divides the Minginish Peninsula from the rest of Skye. On its southern shore lies the village of Carbost, home to the smooth, sweet and smoky Talisker malt whisky, produced at **Talisker Distillery** (www.discovering-distilleries.com; Carbost; guided tour £5; ☉9.30am-5pm Mon-Sat Easter-Oct, noon-5pm sun Jul & Aug, 10-5pm Mon-Fri Nov-Easter). This is the only distillery on Skye; the guided tour includes a free dram. Magnificent **Talisker Bay**, 5 miles west of Carbost, has a sandy beach, sea stack and waterfall.

The **Old Inn** (☎ 01478-640205; www.carbost.f9.co.uk; Carbost; s/d £42/74; P) is an atmospheric wee pub, offering accommodation in bright B&B bedrooms and an appealing chalet-style **bunkhouse** (from £14 per person). The bar is a favourite with walkers and climbers from Glenbrittle – there's an outdoor patio at the back with great views over Loch Harport – and between noon and 10pm it serves excellent **pub grub** (£8 to £12), from fresh oysters to haddock and chips.

There are five buses a day on weekdays (one on Saturday) from Portree to Carbost via Sligachan.

Portree (Port Righ)
POP 1920

Portree is Skye's largest and liveliest town. It has a pretty harbour lined with brightly painted houses, and there are great views of the surrounding hills. Its name (from the Gaelic for King's Harbour) commemorates James V, who came here in 1540 to pacify the local clans.

 Sights & Activities

AROS EXPERIENCE Visitor Centre
(www.aros.co.uk; Viewfield Rd; ☉9am-5.30pm; 🚻) On the southern edge of Portree, the Aros Experience is a combined visitor centre, book and gift shop, restaurant, theatre and cinema. The visitor centre (adult/child £3/2) offers a look at some fascinating, live CCTV images from local sea eagle and heron nests, and a viewing of a strangely commentary-free wide-screen video of Skye's impressive scenery (it's worth waiting for the aerial shots of the Cuillin). The centre is a useful rainy-day retreat, with an indoor, soft play area for children.

MV STARDUST Boat Trips
(☎ 07798-743858; www.skyeboat-trips.co.uk; Portree Harbour) MV *Stardust* offers one- to two-hour boat excursions to the Sound of Raasay (£12 to £15 per person), with the chance to see seals, porpoises and – if you're lucky – white-tailed sea eagles. On Saturday there are longer cruises to the Isle of Rona (£25). You can also arrange to be dropped off for a hike on the Isle of Raasay and picked up again later.

 Festivals & Events

The annual **Isle of Skye Highland Games** (www.skye-highland-games.co.uk) are held in Portree in early August.

 Sleeping

Portree is well supplied with B&Bs but many of them are in bland, modern bungalows that, though comfortable, often lack character. Accommodation fills up fast in July and August so be sure to book ahead.

BEN TIANAVAIG B&B B&B ££
(☎ 01478-612152; www.ben-tianavaig.co.uk; 5 Bosville Tce; r £65-75; P 🛜) A warm welcome awaits from the Aussie/Brit couple who run this appealing B&B bang in the centre of town. All four bedrooms have a view across the harbour to the hill that gives the house its name, and breakfasts include free-range eggs and vegetables grown in the garden.

BOSVILLE HOTEL Hotel ££
(☎ 01478-612846; www.bosvillehotel.co.uk; 9-11 Bosville Tce; s/d from £120/128; 🛜) The Bosville brings a little bit of metropolitan style to Portree with its designer fabrics and furniture, flatscreen TVs, fluffy bathrobes and bright, spacious bathrooms. It's worth splashing out a bit for the 'premier' rooms, with leather recliner chairs from which you can lap up the view over the town and harbour.

PEINMORE HOUSE B&B ££
(☎ 01478-612574; www.peinmorehouse.co.uk; r per person £55; P) Located around 2 miles south of Portree, this former manse has recently been cleverly converted into a stylish and comfortable guesthouse with a spectacular, oak-floored lounge, enormous bedrooms, excellent breakfasts and panoramic views.

ROSEDALE HOTEL Hotel ££
(☎ 01478-613131; www.rosedalehotelskye.co.uk; Beaumont Cres; s/d from £60/90; ⏰ Mar-Nov) The Rosedale is a cosy, old-fashioned hotel – you'll be welcomed with a glass of whisky or sherry when you check in – delightfully situated down by the waterfront. Its three converted fishermen's cottages are linked by a maze of narrow

Left: The peak of Bla Bheinn rises over Loch Slapin (p230);
Below: The colourful town of Portree

PHOTOGRAPHER: (LEFT) DAVID TOMLINSON; (BELOW) ANDREW MARSHALL & LEANNE WALK

stairs and corridors, and the excellent restaurant has a view of the harbour.

WOODLANDS
B&B £

(☎ 01478-612980; www.woodlands-portree.co.uk; Viewfield Rd; r per person £32-34; **P**) A great location, with views across the bay, and unstinting hospitality make this modern B&B, a half-mile south of the town centre, a good choice.

 Eating & Drinking

CAFÉ ARRIBA
Cafe £

(www.cafearriba.co.uk; Quay Brae; light meals £5-8, dinner mains £10-13; ⏲7am-10pm May-Sep, 8am-5.30pm Oct-Apr; 🖋) Arriba is a funky little cafe, brightly decked out in primary colours and offering the best choice of vegetarian grub on the island, ranging from a veggie breakfast fry-up to Indian-spiced bean cakes with mint yoghurt, as well as carnivorous treats such as slow-cooked haunch of venison

with red wine and beetroot gravy. Also serves excellent coffee.

BISTRO AT THE BOSVILLE
Bistro ££

(☎ 01478-612846; www.bosvillehotel.co.uk; 7 Bosville Tce; mains £9-20; ⏲noon-2.30pm & 5.30-10pm) This hotel bistro sports a relaxed atmosphere, an award-winning chef and a menu that makes the most of Skye-sourced produce including lamb, game, seafood, cheese, organic vegetables and berries, and adds an original twist to traditional dishes.

HARBOUR VIEW SEAFOOD RESTAURANT
Seafood ££

(☎ 01478-612069; www.harbourviewskye.co.uk; 7 Bosville Tce; mains £10-19; ⏲noon-2.30pm & 5.30-10pm) The Harbour View is Portree's most congenial place to eat. It has a homely dining room with a log fire in winter, books on the mantelpiece and bric-a-brac on the shelves. And on the table, superb Scottish seafood,

233

EOIN CLARKE

Don't Miss Cuillin Hills

The Cuillin Hills are Britain's most spectacular mountain range. Though small in stature (**Sgurr Alasdair**, the highest summit, is only 993m), the peaks are near-alpine in character, with knife-edge ridges, jagged pinnacles, scree-filled gullies and acres of naked rock. While they are a paradise for experienced mountaineers, the higher reaches of the Cuillin are off limits to the majority of walkers.

The good news is that there are also plenty of good, low-level hikes within the ability of most walkers. One of the best (on a fine day) is the steep climb from Glenbrittle camping ground to **Coire Lagan** (6 miles round trip; allow at least three hours). The impressive upper corrie contains a lochan for bathing (for the hardy!), and the surrounding cliffs are a playground for rock climbers – bring along your binoculars.

The **Sligachan Hotel**, or The Slig, as it as it has been known to generations of climbers, is a near village in itself, encompassing a luxurious hotel, a microbrewery, self-catering cottages, a bunkhouse, a campsite and an adventure playground. Its big barn of a pub, **Seamus's Bar**, dishes up decent bar meals, including haggis, neeps and tatties, steak and ale pie, and fish pie, and serves real ales from its own microbrewery plus a range of 200 malt whiskies in serried ranks above the bar. As well as the adventure playground outside, there are games, toys and a play area indoors.

Sligachan, on the main Kyle–Portree road, is easily accessible by bus. Bus 53 runs five times a day Monday to Friday (once on Saturday) from Portree to Carbost via Sligachan (50 minutes).

THINGS YOU NEED TO KNOW

Sligachan Hotel (01478-650204; www.sligachan.co.uk; Sligachan; per person from £59; P @);
Seamus's Bar (Sligachan Hotel, Sligachan; mains £8-10; food served 11am-11pm; @)

such as fresh Skye oysters, seafood chowder, king scallops, langoustines and lobster.

SEA BREEZES   Seafood £production

(☎ 01478-612016; 2 Marine Buildings, Quay St; mains £10-20; ⏰noon-2.30pm & 5.30-10pm Tue-Sun, closed Nov, Jan & Feb) A good choice for seafood, Sea Breezes is an informal, no-frills restaurant specialising in local fish and shellfish fresh from the boat – try the impressive seafood platter, a small mountain of langoustines, crab, oysters and lobster. Book early, as it's often hard to get a table.

Shopping

SKYE BATIKS   Crafts/Gifts

(www.skyebatiks.com; The Green; ⏰9am-6pm May, Jun & Sep, 9am-9pm Jul & Aug, 9am-5pm Mon-Sat Oct-Apr) Skye Batiks is a cut above your average gift shop, selling a range of interesting crafts such as carved wood, jewellery and batik fabrics with Celtic designs.

OVER THE RAINBOW   Crafts/Gifts

(www.skyeknitwear.com; Quay Brae) Crammed with colourful knitwear, tweeds and country and casual clothing, as well as glassware, crafts and all kinds of interesting gifts.

ISLE OF SKYE SOAP CO   Cosmetics

(www.skye-soap.co.uk; Somerled Sq; ⏰9am-5.30pm Mon-Fri, 9am-5pm Sat) A sweet-smelling gift shop that specialises in handmade soaps and cosmetics made using natural ingredients and aromatherapy oils.

Carmina Gadelica   Music

(Bank St; ⏰9am-5.30pm Mon-Sat, 9am-9pm Jul & Aug) Browse the shelves here for CDs of Gaelic music and books on local subjects.

Getting There & Around

BUS The main bus stop is in Somerled Sq. There are seven Scottish Citylink buses a day, including Sundays, from Kyle of Lochalsh to Portree (£13, one hour) and on to Uig.

Stagecoach services (Monday to Saturday only) run from Portree to Broadford (40 minutes, at least hourly) via Sligachan (15 minutes); to Armadale (1¼ hours, connecting with the ferries to Mallaig); to Carbost (40 minutes, four daily); to Uig (30 minutes, six daily) and to Dunvegan Castle (40 minutes, five daily Monday to Friday, three on Saturday). There are also five or six buses a day on a circular route around Trotternish (in both directions) taking in Flodigarry (20 minutes), Kilmuir (1¼ hours) and Uig (30 minutes).

BIKE You can hire bikes at Island Cycles (☎01478-613121; The Green; ⏰9am-5pm Mon-Sat) for £10/15 per half/full day.

Duirinish & Waternish

The **Duirinish Peninsula** to the west of Dunvegan, and **Waternish** to the north, boasts some of Skye's most atmospheric hotels and restaurants, plus an eclectic range of artists' studios and crafts workshops. Portree tourist office provides a free booklet listing them all.

It's worth making the long drive beyond Dunvegan to the west side of the Duirinish Peninsula to see the spectacular sea cliffs of **Waterstein Head**, and to walk down to **Neist Point lighthouse** with its views to the Outer Hebrides.

At Stein on the Waternish Peninsula is **Dandelion Designs** (www.dandelion-designs.co.uk; Captain's House, Stein; ⏰11am-5pm Easter-Oct), an interesting little gallery with a good range of colour and monochrome landscape photography, lino prints by Liz Myhill, and a range of handmade arts and crafts.

A few miles north of Stein you'll find **Shilasdair Yarns** (www.shilasdair-yarns.co.uk; Carnach; ⏰10am-6pm Apr-Oct). The couple who run this place moved to Skye in 1971 and now raise sheep, hand-spin woollen yarn, and hand-dye a range of wools and silks using natural dyes. You can see the dyeing process in the workshop behind the studio, which sells finished knitwear as well as yarns.

JMC/IMAGEBROKER

Don't Miss **Dunvegan Castle**

Skye's most famous historic building, and one of its most popular tourist attractions, is **Dunvegan Castle**, seat of the chief of Clan MacLeod. It has played host to Samuel Johnson, Sir Walter Scott and, most famously, Flora MacDonald. The oldest parts are the 14th-century keep and dungeon but most of it dates from the 17th to 19th centuries.

In addition to the usual castle stuff – swords, silver and family portraits – there are some interesting artefacts, most famous being the **Fairy Flag**, a diaphanous silk banner that dates from some time between the 4th and 7th centuries. Bonnie Prince Charlie's waistcoat and a lock of his hair, donated by Flora MacDonald's granddaughter, share a room with **Rory Mor's Drinking Horn**, a beautiful 16th-century vessel of Celtic design that could hold half a gallon of claret. Upholding the family tradition in 1956, John Macleod – the 29th chief, who died in 2007 – downed the contents in one minute and 57 seconds 'without setting down or falling down'.

From the end of the minor road beyond Dunvegan Castle entrance, an easy walk of 1 mile leads to the **Coral Beaches** – a pair of blindingly white beaches composed of the bleached exo-skeletons of coralline algae known as maerl.

On the way to Dunvegan from Portree you'll pass **Edinbane Pottery**, one of the island's original craft workshops, established in 1971, where you can watch potters at work creating beautiful and colourful stoneware.

THINGS YOU NEED TO KNOW

Dunvegan Castle (www.dunvegancastle.com; Dunvegan; adult/child £8/4; ⊙10am-5pm Easter-Oct, 11am-4pm Nov-Easter); **Edinbane Pottery** (www.edinbane-pottery.co.uk; Edinbane; ⊙9am-6pm, closed Sat & Sun Nov-Easter)

Sleeping & Eating

THREE CHIMNEYS
Restaurant with Rooms **£££**
(📞 01470-511258; www.threechimneys.co.uk; Colbost, Dunvegan; 3-course lunch/dinner £35/55; ⏰12.30-2pm Mon-Sat Mar-Oct, 6.30-9pm daily year-round; 🅿) In Colbost, half-way between Dunvegan and Waterstein, Three Chimneys is a superb romantic retreat combining a gourmet restaurant in a candlelit crofter's cottage with sumptuous five-star rooms (double £285, dinner B&B per couple £405) in the modern house next door. Book well in advance, and note that children are not welcome in the restaurant in the evenings.

STEIN INN
Inn **££**
(📞 01470-592362; www.steininn.co.uk; Stein, Waternish; bar meals £7-10; ⏰food served noon-4pm & 6-9.30pm Mon-Sat, 12.30-4pm & 6.30-9pm Sun Easter-Oct; 🅿) This old country inn dates from 1790 and has a handful of bedrooms (per person £34 to £50) all with sea views, a lively little bar and a delightful beer garden – a real suntrap on summer afternoons – beside the loch. The bar serves real ales from the Isle of Skye Brewery and does an excellent crab sandwich for lunch.

LOCHBAY SEAFOOD RESTAURANT
Seafood **£££**
(📞 01470-592235; www.lochbay-seafood-restaurant.co.uk; Stein, Waternish; mains £13-22, lobster £28-40; ⏰lunch & dinner Tue-Fri) Just along the road from the Stein Inn is one of Skye's most romantic restaurants, a cosy farmhouse kitchen with terracotta tiles and a wood-burning stove, and a menu that includes most things that either swim in the sea or live in a shell. Best to book ahead.

Trotternish

The Trotternish Peninsula to the north of Portree has some of Skye's most beautiful – and bizarre – scenery.

East Coast

First up is the 50m-high, potbellied pinnacle of crumbling basalt known as the **Old Man of Storr**, prominent above the road 6 miles north of Portree. Walk up to its foot from the car park in the woods

Flora MacDonald

Flora MacDonald, who became famous for helping Bonnie Prince Charlie escape after his defeat at the Battle of Culloden, was born in 1722 at Milton in South Uist, in the Outer Hebrides.

In 1746, she helped Bonnie Prince Charlie make his way from Benbecula to Skye disguised as her Irish maidservant. With a price on the prince's head their little boat was fired on, but they managed to land safely and Flora escorted the prince to Portree where he gave her a gold locket containing his portrait before setting sail for Raasay.

Waylaid on the way home, the boatmen admitted everything. Flora was arrested and imprisoned in the Tower of London. She never saw or heard from the prince again.

In 1747, she returned to Skye, marrying Allan MacDonald and having nine children. Dr Samuel Johnson stayed with her in 1773 during his trip to the Western Isles, but later poverty forced her family to emigrate to North Carolina. There her husband was captured by rebels. Flora returned to Kingsburgh on Skye, where she died in 1790. She was buried in Kilmuir churchyard, wrapped in the sheet on which both Bonnie Prince Charlie and Dr Johnson had slept.

at the northern end of Loch Leathan (round trip 2 miles). This seemingly unclimbable pinnacle was first scaled in 1955 by English mountaineer Don Whillans, a feat that has been repeated only a handful of times since. North again, near Staffin (Stamhain), is spectacular **Kilt Rock**, a stupendous cliff of columnar basalt whose vertical ribbing is fancifully compared to the pleats of a kilt.

Staffin Bay is dominated by the dramatic basalt escarpment of the **Quiraing**, whose impressive land-slipped cliffs and pinnacles constitute one of Skye's most remarkable landscapes. From a parking area at the highest point of the minor road between Staffin and Uig you can walk north to the Quiraing in half an hour. The adventurous (and energetic) can scramble up to the left of the slim pinnacle called the **Needle** to find a hidden, grass-topped plateau known as the **Table**.

 Sleeping & Eating

FLODIGARRY COUNTRY HOUSE HOTEL
Hotel **££**

(01470-552203; www.flodigarry.co.uk; Flodigarry; s/d from £90/120; P) Flora MacDonald lived in a farmhouse cottage at Flodigarry in northeast Trotternish from 1751 to 1759. The cottage and its pretty garden are now part of this delightful hotel – you can stay in the cottage itself (there are seven bedrooms), or in the more spacious rooms in the hotel. The bright, modern bistro (mains £10 to £25) has great views over the Inner Sound, and serves lunch and dinner featuring local produce such as langoustines, lobster, lamb and venison.

West Coast

The peat-reek of crofting (smallholding farming) life in the 18th and 19th centuries is preserved in thatched cottages at **Skye Museum of Island Life** (www.skyemuseum.co.uk; Kilmuir; adult/child £2.50/50p; 9.30am-5pm Mon-Sat Easter-Oct). Behind is Kilmuir Cemetery, where a tall Celtic cross marks the **grave of Flora MacDon-**

Harbourside at Oban, with McCaig's Tower in the background

DAVID ELSE

ald; the cross was erected in 1955 to replace the original, which was ruined by tourists picking at it for souvenirs.

Whichever way you arrive at **Uig** (*oo*-ig), the picture-perfect bay, ringed by steep hills, rarely fails to impress. If you've time to kill while waiting for a ferry to the Outer Hebrides, visit the **Isle of Skye Brewery** (www.skyebrewery.co.uk; The Pier, Uig; ⏰9am-5pm Mon-Fri), which sells locally brewed cask ales and bottled beers.

Just south of Uig, a minor road (signposted 'Sheader and Balnaknock') leads in a mile or so to the **Fairy Glen**, a strange and enchanting natural landscape of miniature conical hills, rocky towers, ruined cottages and a tiny roadside lochan.

OBAN
POP 8120

Oban is a peaceful waterfront town on a delightful bay, with sweeping views to Kerrera and Mull. OK, that first bit about peaceful is true only in winter; in summer the town centre is a heaving mass of humanity, its streets jammed with traffic and crowded with holidaymakers, daytrippers and travellers headed for the islands. But the setting is still lovely.

There's not a huge amount to see in the town itself, but it's an appealingly busy place with some excellent restaurants and lively pubs, and it's the main gateway to the islands of Mull, Iona, Colonsay, Barra, Coll and Tiree.

 Sights

MCCAIG'S TOWER Historic Building
(admission free; ⏰24hr) Crowning the hill above the town centre is the Victorian folly known as McCaig's Tower. Its construction was commissioned in 1890 by local worthy John Stuart McCaig, an art critic, philosophical essayist and banker, with the philanthropic intention of providing work for unemployed stonemasons. To reach it on foot, make the steep climb up **Jacob's Ladder** (a flight of stairs) from Argyll St and then follow the signs. The views over the bay are worth the effort.

OBAN DISTILLERY Distillery
(www.discovering-distilleries.com; Stafford St; tour £7; ⏰9.30am-5pm Mon-Sat Easter-Oct, plus noon-5pm Sun Jul-Sep, closed Sat & Sun Nov-Dec & Feb-Easter, closed Jan) This distillery has been producing Oban single-malt whisky since 1794. There are guided tours available (last tour begins one hour before closing time), but even without a tour, it's still worth a look at the small exhibition in the foyer.

FREE **WAR & PEACE MUSEUM** Museum
(www.obanmuseum.org.uk; Corran Esplanade; ⏰10am-6pm Mon-Sat & 10am-4pm Sun May-Sep, 10am-4pm daily Mar, Apr, Oct & Nov) Military buffs will enjoy the little War & Peace Museum, which chronicles Oban's role in WWII as a base for Catalina seaplanes and as a marshalling area for Atlantic convoys.

 Activities

A tourist-office leaflet lists local **bike rides**, which include a 7-mile Gallanach circular tour, a 16-mile route to the Isle of Seil and routes to Connel, Glenlonan and Kilmore. You can hire mountain bikes from **Evo Bikes** (www.evobikes.co.uk; 29 Lochside St; ⏰9am-5.30pm Mon-Sat), opposite Tesco supermarket, from £15 to £30 per day.

Various operators offer **boat trips** to spot seals and other marine wildlife, departing from the North Pier slipway (adult/child £8/5.50); ask for details at the tourist office.

 Tours

From April to October, **Bowman's Tours** (☎ 01631-563221/566809; www.bowmanstours .co.uk; 3 Stafford St & 1 Queens Park Pl) offers a **Three Isles day trip** (adult/child £49/24.50, 10 hours, daily) from Oban

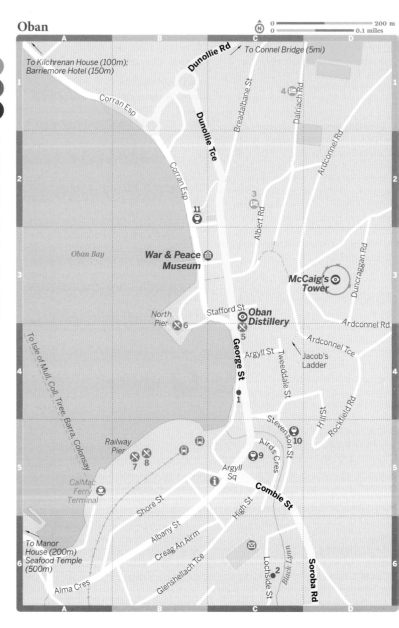

Oban

that visits Mull, Iona and Staffa. Note that the crossing to Staffa is weather dependent.

Bowman's also runs a **wildlife tour** (adult/child £49/24.50) departing from Oban at 9.50am Sunday to Friday from May to July, and returning to Oban at 8pm. The trip takes in a ferry crossing to Craignure on Mull, travel by coach to Fionnphort, and a cruise around Staffa and the Treshnish Isles, plus two hours ashore on Lunga to visit a puffin colony.

Oban

 Festivals & Events

Argyllshire Gathering Highland Games
(www.obangames.com; adult/child £8/4) Held
over two days in late August, this is one of
the most important events on the Scottish
highland-games calendar and includes a
prestigious pipe-band competition. The main
games are held at Mossfield Park on the eastern
edge of town.

West Highland Yachting Week Sailing
(www.whyw.co.uk) At the end of July/beginning
of August, Oban becomes the focus of one of
Scotland's biggest yachting events. Hundreds
of yachts cram into the harbour and the town's
bars are jammed with thirsty sailors.

 Sleeping

Despite having lots of B&B accommodation, Oban's beds can still fill up quickly
in July and August so try to book ahead.
If you can't find a bed in Oban, consider
staying at Connel, 4 miles to the north.

BARRIEMORE HOTEL B&B ££
(☎ 01631-566356; www.barriemore-hotel.co.uk;
Corran Esplanade; s/d from £65/92; P) The
Barriemore enjoys a grand location,
overlooking the entrance to Oban Bay.
There are 13 spacious rooms here (ask
for one with a sea view), plus a guest
lounge with magazines and newspapers,
and plump Loch Fyne kippers on the
breakfast menu.

HEATHERFIELD HOUSE B&B ££
(☎ 01631-562681; www.heatherfieldhouse.co.uk;
Albert Rd; s/d from £35/70; P @ 🛜) The welcoming Heatherfield House occupies a
converted 1870s rectory set in extensive
grounds and has six spacious rooms.
If possible, ask for room 1, complete
with fireplace, sofa and a view over the
garden to the harbour.

KILCHRENAN HOUSE B&B ££
(☎ 01631-562663; www.kilchrenanhouse.co.uk;
Corran Esplanade; s/d £50/90; P) You'll get
a warm welcome at the Kilchrenan, an
elegant Victorian villa built for a textile
magnate in 1883. Most of the rooms
have views across Oban Bay, but rooms
5 and 9 are the best: room 5 has a huge
freestanding bath tub, perfect for soaking weary bones.

OLD MANSE GUEST HOUSE B&B ££
(☎ 01631-564886; www.obanguesthouse.co.uk;
Dalriach Rd; s/d from £62/74; P 🛜 👪) Set on
a hillside above the town, the Old Manse
commands great views over to Kerrera
and Mull. The sunny, brightly decorated
bedrooms have some nice touches (a
couple of wine glasses and a cork-
screw), and kids are made welcome with
Balamory books, toys and DVDs.

MANOR HOUSE Hotel £££
(☎ 01631-562087; www.manorhouseoban.
com; Gallanach Rd; r £154-199; P) Built in
1780 for the Duke of Argyll as part of his
Oban estates, the Manor House is now
one of Oban's finest hotels. It has small
but elegant rooms in Georgian style, a
posh bar frequented by local and visiting
yachties, and a fine restaurant serving
Scottish and French cuisine. Children
under 12 are not welcome.

Eating

WATERFRONT RESTAURANT
Seafood ££

(☎ 01631-563110; www.waterfrontoban.co.uk; Waterfront Centre, Railway Pier; mains £10-18; ⏾lunch & dinner) Housed on the top floor of a converted seamen's mission, the Waterfront has stylish, unfussy decor – dusky pink and carmine with pine tables and local art on the walls – that does little to distract from the superb seafood freshly landed at the quay just a few metres away. The menu ranges from crispy-battered haddock and chips to pan-fried scallops with lime, chilli and coriander pickle. There's an early-evening menu (5.30pm to 6.45pm) offering two courses for £11.50, or soup followed by fish and chips for £9.75. Best to book for dinner.

SHELLFISH BAR
Seafood £

(Railway Pier; mains £2-7; ⏾breakfast & lunch) If you want to savour superb Scottish seafood without the expense of an upmarket restaurant, head for Oban's famous seafood stall – it's the green shack on the quayside near the ferry terminal. Here you can buy fresh and cooked seafood to take away – excellent prawn sandwiches (£2.75), dressed crab (£4.75), and fresh oysters for only 65p each.

SEAFOOD TEMPLE
Seafood £££

(☎ 01631-566000; Gallanach Rd; mains £15-25; ⏾dinner Thu-Sun) Locally sourced seafood is the god that's worshipped at this tiny temple – a former park pavilion with glorious views over the bay. Owned by a former fisherman who smokes his own salmon, what must be Oban's smallest restaurant serves up whole lobster cooked to order, scallops in garlic butter, plump langoustines, and the 'platter magnifique' (£60 for two persons), which offers a taste of everything. Booking essential.

CUAN MOR
Bistro ££

(www.cuanmor.co.uk; 60 George St; mains £8-16; ⏾lunch & dinner) This always-busy bar and bistro sports a no-nonsense menu of old

The hill fort of Dunadd

ROBERT JUDGES/ALAMY

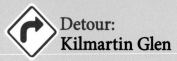

Detour:
Kilmartin Glen

This magical glen is the focus of one of the biggest concentrations of prehistoric sites in Scotland. Burial cairns, standing stones, stone circles, hill forts and cup-and-ring-marked rocks litter the countryside. Within a 6-mile radius of Kilmartin village (28 miles south of Oban) there are 25 sites with standing stones and over 100 rock carvings.

The oldest monuments at Kilmartin date from 5000 years ago and comprise a linear cemetery of **burial cairns** that runs south from Kilmartin village for 1.5 miles. There are also ritual monuments (two stone circles) at **Temple Wood**, three-quarters of a mile southwest of Kilmartin. The museum bookshop sells maps and guides.

The hill fort of **Dunadd**, 3.5 miles south of Kilmartin village, was the seat of power of the first kings of Dalriada, and may have been where the **Stone of Destiny** (p75) was originally located. The faint rock carvings of a wild boar and two footprints with an Ogham inscription may have been used in some kind of inauguration ceremony. A slippery path leads to the summit where you can gaze out on much the same view that the kings of Dalriada enjoyed 1300 years ago.

favourites – from haddock and chips to sausage and mash with onion gravy – spiced with a few more sophisticated dishes such as scallops with black pudding, and a decent range of vegetarian dishes. And the sticky toffee pudding is not to be missed!

EE'USK — Seafood ££
(01631-565666; www.eeusk.com; North Pier; mains £12-20; lunch & dinner) Bright and modern Ee'usk (it's how you pronounce *iasg*, the Gaelic word for fish) occupies Oban's prime location on the North Pier. Floor-to-ceiling windows allow diners on two levels to enjoy views over the harbour to Kerrera and Mull, while sampling a seafood menu ranging from fragrant Thai fish cakes to langoustines with chilli and ginger. A little pricey, perhaps, but both food and location are first class.

 **Drinking**

OBAN CHOCOLATE COMPANY — Cafe
(www.obanchocolate.co.uk; 34 Corran Esplanade; 10am-5pm Mon-Sat & 12.30-4pm Sun Easter-Sep, shorter hours in winter, closed Jan)

This shop specialising in hand-crafted chocolates (you can watch them being made) also has a cafe serving excellent coffee and hot chocolate (try the chilli chocolate for a kick in the tastebuds), with big leather sofas in a window with a view of the bay.

LORNE BAR — Pub
(www.thelornebar.co.uk; Stevenson St;) A traditional pub with a lovely old island bar, the Lorne serves Deuchars IPA and local Oban Brewery real ales, as well as above-average pub grub. Food is served from noon to 9pm, and there's a trad music session every Wednesday from 10pm.

AULAY'S BAR — Pub
(8 Airds Cres) An authentic Scottish pub, Aulay's is cosy and low-ceilinged, its walls covered with old photographs of Oban ferries and other ships. It pulls in a mixed crowd of locals and visitors with its warm atmosphere and wide range of malt whiskies.

If You Like...
Folk Museums

The history of rural communities in Scotland is preserved in a wide range of fascinating museums, often located in original farm buildings and historic houses.

1 EASDALE ISLAND FOLK MUSEUM
(Easdale Island; www.easdalemuseum.org; adult/child £2.25/50p; ⊙11am-4.30pm Apr-Oct, to 5pm Jul & Aug) Displays about the local slate industry and life on the islands in the 18th and 19th centuries; 10 miles southwest of Oban.

2 ISLAND LIFE MUSEUM
(Hynish, Isle of Tiree; admission free; ⊙2-4pm Mon-Fri Easter-Sep) A row of quaint thatched cottages on the west coast of Tiree, each restored as a 19th-century crofter's home. Four-hour ferry crossing from Oban.

3 KILMARTIN HOUSE MUSEUM
(Kilmartin; www.kilmartin.org; adult/child £5/2; ⊙10am-5.30pm Mar-Oct, 11am-4pm Nov-23 Dec) Exhibits of artefacts recovered from important sites in Kilmartin Glen, illustrating prehistoric life here; 28 miles south of Oban.

ℹ Information

Lorn & Islands District General Hospital (☏ 01631-567500; Glengallan Rd) Southern end of town.

Tourist office (☏ 01631-563122; www.oban.org.uk; Argyll Sq; ⊙9am-7pm daily Jul & Aug, 9am-5.30pm Mon-Sat & 10am-5pm Sun May, Jun & Sep, 9am-5.30pm Mon-Sat Oct-Apr; @) Internet access available (£1 per 20 minutes).

ℹ Getting There & Away

The bus, train and ferry terminals are all grouped conveniently together next to the harbour on the southern edge of the bay.
BOAT CalMac (www.calmac.co.uk) ferries link Oban with the islands of Kerrera, Mull, Coll, Tiree, Lismore, Colonsay, Barra and Lochboisdale. Information and reservations for all CalMac ferry services are available at the ferry terminal on

Oban's West Pier. Ferries to the Isle of Kerrera depart from a separate jetty, about 2 miles southwest of Oban town centre.
BUS Scottish Citylink (www.citylink.co.uk) buses run to Oban from Glasgow (£17, three hours, four daily).
   West Coast Motors (www.westcoastmotors.co.uk) bus 918 goes to Fort William via Appin and Ballachulish (£9, 1½ hours, three daily Monday to Saturday).
TRAIN Oban is at the terminus of a scenic route that branches off the West Highland line at Crianlarich. There are up to three trains daily from Glasgow to Oban (£19, three hours).
   The train isn't much use for travelling north from Oban – to reach Fort William requires a detour via Crianlarich (3¾ hours). Take the bus instead.

ℹ Getting Around

CAR HIRE Hazelbank Motors (☏ 01631-566476; www.obancarhire.co.uk; Lynn Rd; ⊙8.30am-5.30pm Mon-Sat) rents small cars per day/week from £40/225 including VAT, insurance and CDW (Collision Damage Waiver).
TAXI There's a taxi rank outside the train station. Otherwise, call Oban Taxis (☏ 01631-564666).

ISLE OF MULL
POP 2600

From the rugged ridges of Ben More and the black basalt crags of Burg to the blinding white sand, rose-pink granite and emerald waters that fringe the Ross, Mull can lay claim to some of the finest and most varied scenery in the Inner Hebrides. Add in two impressive castles, a narrow-gauge railway, the sacred island of Iona and easy access from Oban and you can see why it's sometimes impossible to find a spare bed on the island.

Despite the number of visitors who flock to the island, it seems to be large enough to absorb them all; many stick to the well-worn routes from Craignure to Iona or Tobermory, returning to Oban in the evening. Besides, there are plenty of hidden corners where you can get away from the crowds.

The waters to the west of Mull provide some of the best whale-spotting opportunities in Scotland, with several operators offering **whale-watching cruises**.

About two-thirds of Mull's population lives in and around Tobermory, the island's capital, in the north. Craignure, at the southeastern corner, has the main ferry terminal and is where most people arrive. Fionnphort is at the far western end of the long Ross of Mull peninsula, and is where the ferry to Iona departs.

 Tours

See Bowman's Tours, p239 for details of day trips from Oban to Mull, Staffa and Iona by ferry and bus.

Gordon Grant Marine　　　　Boat Tour
(☎ 01681-700388; www.staffatours.com) Runs boat trips from Fionnphort to Staffa (adult/child £25/10, 2½ hours, daily April to October), and to Staffa and the Treshnish Isles (£45/20, five hours, Sunday to Friday May to July).

Mull Magic　　　　Walking Tour
(☎ 01688-301213; www.mullmagic.com) Offers guided wildlife walking tours in the Mull countryside (£35-45 per person including packed lunch), as well as customised tours and four-day walking holidays.

Duart Castle (p247)

 **Festivals & Events**

Mishnish Music Festival　　　　Music
(www.mishnish.co.uk) Last weekend of April; three days of foot-stomping traditional Scottish and Irish folk music at Tobermory's favourite pub.

Mendelssohn on Mull　　　　Music
(www.mullfest.org.uk) A week-long festival of classical music in early July.

Mull Highland Games　　　　Highland Games
(www.mishnish.co.uk) Third Thursday in July; piping, highland dancing etc.

Mull & Iona Food Festival　　　　Food & Drink
(www.mict.co.uk) Five days of food and drink tastings in early September, with chef demonstrations, farm tours, produce markets, restaurant visits and a host of other events.

ℹ Information

MEDICAL Dunaros Hospital (☎ 01680-300392; Salen) Has a minor-injuries unit; the nearest casualty department is in Oban.

MONEY Clydesdale Bank (Main St, Tobermory; ⏰ 9.15am-4.45pm Mon-Fri) The island's only bank and 24-hour ATM. You can get cash using a

PATRICK HORTON

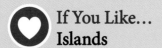

If You Like… Islands

If you like exploring islands, Oban is the perfect jumping-off point for more than just Mull and Iona.

1 KERRERA
(ferry adult/child return £5/2.50, bicycle free)
Kerrera faces Oban across the bay and offers the chance to spot wildlife such as Soay sheep, wild goats, otters, golden eagles, peregrine falcons, seals and porpoises. Boat trip takes 10 minutes, departing half-hourly.

2 COLONSAY
(ferry passenger/car return £23/114) Colonsay is a jewel box of varied delights – an ancient priory, a woodland garden, a golden beach – set amid a Highland landscape in miniature. Trips take 2¼ hours, daily except Saturday.

3 COLL
(ferry passenger/car return £16.70/85.50)
Rugged and low lying, Coll's main attraction is the peace and quiet – empty beaches, bird-haunted coastlines and long walks along the shore.Boats run daily from Oban, taking 2¾ hours.

4 TIREE
(ferry passenger/car return £16.70/85.50)
Tiree's white-sand beaches are hugely popular with windsurfers. Most visitors, however, come for the birdwatching, beachcombing and lonely coastal walks. Boats leave daily and take four hours.

debit card from the post offices in Salen and Craignure, or get cash back with a purchase from Co-op food stores.

TOURIST INFORMATION Craignure tourist office (☏01680-812377; Craignure; ◷8.30am-5pm Mon-Sat, 10.30am-5pm Sun)

Tobermory tourist office (☏01688-302182; The Pier, Tobermory; ◷9am-6pm Mon-Sat & 10am-5pm Sun Jul & Aug, 9am-5pm Mon-Sat & 11am-5pm Sun May & Jun, shorter hours rest of year)

❶ Getting There & Away

There are frequent **CalMac** (www.calmac.co.uk) car ferries from Oban to Craignure (passenger/car £4.65/41.50, 40 minutes, every two hours). There's another car-ferry link from Lochaline to Fishnish, on the east coast of Mull (£2.80/12.55, 15 minutes, at least hourly).

A third CalMac car ferry links Tobermory to Kilchoan on the Ardnamurchan peninsula (£4.45/23, 35 minutes, seven daily Monday to Saturday). From June to August there are also five sailings on Sunday.

❶ Getting Around

BICYCLE You can hire bikes for around £10 to £15 per day from the following places.

Brown's Hardware Shop (☏01688-302020; www.brownstobermory.co.uk; Main St, Tobermory)

On Yer Bike (☏01680-300501; Inverinate, Salen) Easter to October only. Also has an outlet by the ferry terminal at Craignure.

BUS Public transport on Mull is fairly limited. Bowman's Tours (☏01680-812313; www.bowmanstours.co.uk) is the main operator, connecting the ferry ports and the island's main villages. Bus 495 goes from Craignure to Tobermory (£7 return, one hour, six daily Monday to Friday, four or five Saturday and Sunday), and bus 496 links Craignure to Fionnphort (£11 return, 1¼ hours, three or four daily Monday to Saturday, one Sunday). Bus 494 goes from Tobermory to Dervaig and Calgary (three daily Monday to Friday, two on Saturday).

CAR Almost all of Mull's road network consists of single-track roads. There are petrol stations at Craignure, Fionnphort, Salen and Tobermory.

TAXI Mull Taxi (☏07760 426351; www.mulltaxi.co.uk) is based in Tobermory, and has a vehicle that is wheelchair accessible.

Craignure & Around

There's not much to see at Craignure other than the ferry terminal and the hotel, so turn left, walk 200m and hop onto the **Mull Railway** (www.mullrail.co.uk; Old Pier Station; adult/child return £5/3.50; ◷Apr-Oct), a miniature steam train that will take you 1.5 miles south to Torosay Castle.

Torosay Castle & Gardens (www.torosay.com; adult/child £7/4; ◷house 10.30am-5pm

Apr-Oct, gardens 9am-sunset year-round) is a rambling Victorian mansion in the Scottish Baronial style, stuffed with antique furniture, family portraits and hunting trophies. You're left to wander at will: a sign advises, 'Take your time but not our spoons.'

Two miles beyond Torosay is **Duart Castle** (www.duartcastle.com; adult/child £5.30/2.65; ☉10.30am-5.30pm daily May–mid-Oct, 11am-4pm Sun-Thu Apr), a formidable fortress dominating the Sound of Mull. The seat of the Clan Maclean, this is one of the oldest inhabited castles in Scotland – the central keep was built in 1360. It was bought and restored in 1911 by Sir Fitzroy Maclean and has damp dungeons, vast halls and bathrooms equipped with ancient fittings. A bus to the castle meets the 9.50am, 11.55am and 2pm ferries from Oban to Craignure.

Tobermory
POP 750

Tobermory, the island's main town, is a picturesque little fishing port and yachting centre with brightly painted houses arranged around a sheltered harbour, with a grid-patterned 'upper town'. The village was the setting for the children's TV program *Balamory*, and while the series stopped filming in 2005 regular repeats mean that the town still swarms in summer with toddlers towing parents around looking for their favourite TV characters (frazzled parents can get a *Balamory* booklet from the tourist offices in Oban and Tobermory).

◉ Sights & Activities

Places to go on a rainy day include **Mull Museum** (www.mullmuseum .org.uk; Main St; admission by donation; ☉10am-4pm Mon-

Fri Easter-Oct), which records the history of the island. There are also interesting exhibits on crofting, and on the **Tobermory Galleon**, a ship from the Spanish Armada that sank in Tobermory Bay in 1588 and has been the object of treasure seekers ever since.

There's also **An Tobar Arts Centre** (www.antobar.co.uk; Argyll Tce; admission free; ☉10am-5pm Mon-Sat May-Sep, plus 1-4pm Sun Jul & Aug, 10am-4pm Tue-Sat Oct-Apr), an art gallery and exhibition space with a good vegetarian-friendly cafe; and the tiny **Tobermory Distillery** (www.tobermorymalt .com; tour £3; ☉10am-5pm Mon-Fri Easter-Oct), established in 1798.

The Hebridean Whale & Dolphin Trust's **Marine Discovery Centre** (www .whaledolphintrust.co.uk; 28 Main St; admission free; ☉10am-5pm Mon-Fri & 11am-4pm Sun Apr-Oct, 11am-5pm Mon-Fri Nov-Mar) has displays, videos and interactive exhibits on whale and dolphin biology and ecology, and is a great place for kids to learn about sea mammals. It also provides information about volunteering and reporting sightings of whales and dolphins.

Torosay Castle
PHOTOGRAPHER: IMAGEBROKER/ALAMY

 ## Sleeping

Tobermory has dozens of B&Bs, but the place can still be booked solid in July and August, especially at weekends.

HIGHLAND COTTAGE HOTEL
Boutique Hotel £££

(☎ 01688-302030; www.highlandcottage.co.uk; Breadalbane St; d £155-190; ☺mid-Mar–Oct; P ⓢ) Antique furniture, four-poster beds, embroidered bedspreads and fresh flowers and candlelight lend this small hotel (only six rooms) an appealing old-fashioned cottage atmosphere, but with all mod cons including cable TV, full-size baths and room service. There's also an excellent fine-dining restaurant here.

SONAS HOUSE
B&B £££

(☎ 01688-302304; www.sonashouse.co.uk; The Fairways, Erray Rd; s/d £80/125; P ⓢ ⓢ) Sonas is a large, modern house that offers luxury B&B (a heated indoor swimming pool!) in a beautiful setting with superb views over Tobermory Bay; ask for the 'Blue Poppy' bedroom, which has its own balcony.

CUIDHE LEATHAIN
B&B ££

(☎ 01688-302504; www.cuidhe-leathain.co.uk; Salen Rd; r per person £35; ⓢ) A handsome 19th-century house in the upper town, Cuidhe Leathain (coo-lane), which means Maclean's Corner, exudes a co-sily cluttered Victorian atmosphere. The breakfasts will set you up for the rest of the day, and the owners are a fount of knowledge about Mull and its wildlife.

2 Victoria St
B&B £

(☎ 01688-302263; 2 Victoria St; s/d £25/40; ☺Easter-Oct) Traditional, old-school B&B with simple, homely bedrooms (with shared bathroom) and a friendly and hospitable landlady.

Eating & Drinking

CAFÉ FISH
Seafood ££

(☎ 01688-301253; www.thecafefish.com; The Pier; mains £10-16; ☺lunch & dinner) Sea-

Left: Tobermory's colourful waterfront; **Below:** Duart Castle (p247)
PHOTOGRAPHER: (LEFT) DAVID GOWANS/ALAMY; (BELOW) DEREK CROUCHER/ALAMY

food doesn't come much fresher than the stuff served at this warm and welcoming little restaurant overlooking Tobermory harbour – as their motto says, 'The only thing frozen here is the fisherman'! Langoustines and squat lobsters go straight from boat to kitchen to join rich shellfish bisque, fat scallops, seafood pie and catch of the day on the daily-changing menu. Freshly-baked bread, homemade desserts and a range of Scottish cheeses also available.

FISH & CHIP VAN — Seafood £
(Main St; mains £4-7; ⏱12.30-9pm Mon-Sat Apr-Dec) If it's a takeaway you're after, you can tuck into some of Scotland's best gourmet fish and chips down on the waterfront. And where else will you find a chip van selling freshly cooked prawns and scallops?

MACGOCHAN'S — Pub ££
(Ledaig; mains £9-15; ⏱lunch & dinner) A lively pub beside the car park at the southern end of the waterfront, MacGochan's does good bar meals (haddock and chips, steak pie, vegetable lasagne), and often has outdoor barbecues on summer evenings. There's a more formal restaurant upstairs, and live music in the bar on weekends.

MISHNISH HOTEL — Pub ££
(www.mishnish.co.uk; Main St; mains £11-20; ⏱lunch & dinner; 📶) 'The Mish' is a favourite hang-out for visiting yachties and a good place for a bar meal, or dinner at the more formal restaurant upstairs. Wood-panelled and flag-draped, this is a good old traditional pub where you can listen to live folk music, toast your toes by the open fire, or challenge the locals to a game of pool.

North Mull

The road from Tobermory west to Calgary cuts inland, leaving most of the north coast of Mull wild and inacces-

Watching Wildlife on Mull

Mull's varied landscapes and habitats, from high mountains and wild moorland to wave-lashed sea cliffs, sandy beaches and seaweed-fringed skerries, offer the chance to spot some of Scotland's rarest and most dramatic wildlife, including eagles, otters, dolphins and whales.

Mull Wildlife Expeditions (01688-500121; www.torrbuan.com; Ulva Ferry) offers full-day Land Rover tours of the island with the chance of spotting red deer, golden eagles, peregrine falcons, white-tailed sea eagles, hen harriers, otters and perhaps dolphins and porpoises. The cost (adult/child £43/40) includes pick-up from your accommodation or from any of the ferry terminals, a picnic lunch and use of binoculars. The timing of this tour makes it possible as a day trip from Oban, with pick-up and drop-off at the Craignure ferry.

Sea Life Surveys (01688-302916; www.sealifesurveys.com) runs whale-watching trips from Tobermory harbour to the waters north and west of Mull. An all-day whale watch (£60 per person) gives up to seven hours at sea (not recommended for kids under 14), and has a 95% success rate for sightings. The four-hour family whale-watch is geared more towards children (£39/35 per adult/child).

Loch Frisa Sea Eagle Hide (01680-812556; www.forestry.gov.uk/mullseaeagles) runs escorted trips to a viewing hide on Loch Frisa where you can watch white-tailed sea eagles. Tours (£5/2 per adult/child) leave twice a day, Monday to Friday, from the Aros end of the Loch Frisa access trail (book in advance at the Craignure tourist office).

sible. Just outside Tobermory a long, single-track road leads north for 4 miles to majestic **Glengorm Castle** (www.glen gorm.com; Glengorm; admission free; 10am-5pm Easter–mid-Oct) with views across the sea to Ardnamurchan, Rum and the Outer Hebrides. The castle outbuildings house an art gallery featuring the work of local artists, a farm shop selling local produce, and an excellent coffee shop. The castle itself is not open to the public, but you're free to explore the beautiful castle grounds.

The **Old Byre Heritage Centre** (www.old -byre.co.uk; Dervaig; adult/child £4/2; 10.30am-6.30pm Wed-Sun Easter-Oct) brings Mull's heritage and natural history to life through a series of tableaux and half-hour film shows. The prize for most bizarre exhibit goes to the 40cm-long model of a midge. The centre's tearoom serves good, inexpensive snacks, including homemade soup and clootie dumpling, and there's a kids' outdoor play area.

Mull's best (and busiest) silver-sand **beach**, flanked by cliffs and with views out to Coll and Tiree, is at **Calgary**, about 12 miles west of Tobermory. And yes – this is the place from which the more famous Calgary in Alberta, Canada, takes its name.

South Mull

The road from Craignure to Fionnphort climbs through some wild and desolate scenery before reaching the southwest-ern part of the island, which consists of a long peninsula called the **Ross of Mull**. The Ross has a spectacular south coast lined with black basalt cliffs that give way further west to white-sand beaches and pink granite crags. The cliffs are highest at Malcolm's Point, near the superb **Carsaig Arches**.

The little village of **Bunessan** has a hotel, tearoom, pub and some shops, and is home to the **Ross of Mull Historical Centre** (www.romhc.org.uk; admission £2; 10am-4pm Mon-Fri Apr-Oct), a cottage museum that houses displays on local history, geology, archaeology, genealogy and wildlife.

At the western end of the Ross, 38 miles from Craignure, is **Fionnphort** (*finn*-a-fort) and the ferry to **Iona**. The coast here is a beautiful blend of pink granite rocks, white sandy beaches and vivid turquoise sea.

Sleeping & Eating

SEAVIEW B&B ££
(☎ 01681-700235; www.iona-bed-breakfast-mull.com; Fionnphort; s/d £55/75; P 🛜)
Barely a minute's walk from the Iona ferry, the Seaview has five beautifully decorated bedrooms and a breakfast conservatory with grand views across to Iona. The owners – a semiretired fisherman and his wife – offer tasty three-course dinners (£22 per person, September to April only), often prepared using locally caught seafood. Bike hire available for guests only.

STAFFA HOUSE B&B ££
(☎ 01681-700677; www.staffahouse.co.uk; Fionnphort; s/d from £48/66; P) This is a charming and hospitable B&B, packed with antiques and period features, and like the Seaview it offers breakfast in a conservatory with a view of Iona. Solar panels top up the hot-water supply, and the hearty breakfasts, packed lunches (£5.50 to £7) and evening meals (£25 per person) are made using local and organic produce where possible.

ISLE OF IONA
POP 130

There are few more uplifting sights on Scotland's west coast than the view of Iona from Mull on a sunny day – an emerald island set in a sparkling turquoise sea. From the moment you step off the ferry you begin to appreciate the hushed, spiritual atmosphere that pervades this sacred island. Not surprisingly, Iona attracts a lot of day-trippers, so if you want to experience the island's peace and quiet, the solution is to spend a night here. Once the crowds have gone for the day, you can wander in peace around the ancient graveyard where the early kings of Scotland are buried, at-

Thar She Blows!

The North Atlantic Drift – a swirling tendril of the Gulf Stream – carries warm water into the cold, nutrient-rich seas off the Scottish coast, resulting in huge blooms of plankton. Small fish feed on the plankton, and bigger fish feed on the smaller fish...This huge seafood smorgasbord attracts large numbers of marine mammals, from harbour porpoises and dolphins to minke whales and even – though sightings are rare – humpback and sperm whales.

In contrast to Iceland and Norway, Scotland has cashed in on the abundance of minke whales off its coast by embracing whale-watching rather than whaling. There are now dozens of operators around the coast offering whale-watching boat trips lasting from a couple of hours to all day; some have whale-sighting success rates of 95% in summer.

While seals, porpoises and dolphins can be seen year-round, minke whales are migratory. The best time to see them is from June to August, with August being the peak month for sightings. The website of the **Hebridean Whale & Dolphin Trust** (www.whaledolphintrust.co.uk) has lots of information on the species you are likely to see, and how to identify them.

A booklet titled *Is It a Whale?* is available from tourist offices and bookshops, and provides tips on identifying the various species of marine mammal that you're likely to see.

tend an evening service at the abbey, or walk to the top of Dun I and gaze south towards Ireland, as St Columba must have done so many centuries ago.

History

St Columba sailed from Ireland and landed on Iona in 563 before setting out to spread Christianity throughout Scotland. He established a monastery on the island and it was here that the *Book of Kells* – the prize attraction of Dublin's Trinity College – is believed to have been transcribed. It was taken to Kells in Ireland when Viking raids drove the monks from Iona.

The monks returned and the monastery prospered until its destruction during the Reformation. The ruins were given to the Church of Scotland in 1899, and by 1910 a group of enthusiasts called the **Iona Community** (www.iona.org.uk) had reconstructed the abbey. It's still a flourishing spiritual community that holds regular courses and retreats.

Sights & Activities

Head uphill from the ferry pier and turn right through the grounds of a ruined 13th-century **nunnery** with fine cloistered gardens, and exit at the far end. Across the road is the **Iona Heritage Centre** (adult/child £2/free; ⏰10.30am-4.30pm Mon-Fri Apr-Oct), which covers the history of Iona, crofting and lighthouses; the centre's **coffee shop** serves delicious home baking.

Turn right here and continue along the road to **Reilig Oran**, an ancient cemetery that holds the graves of 48 of Scotland's early kings, including Macbeth, and a tiny Romanesque chapel. Beyond rises the spiritual heart of the island – **Iona Abbey** (HS; www.iona.org.uk; adult/child £4.70/2.80; ⏰9.30am-5.30pm Apr-Sep, 9.30am-4.30pm Oct-Mar). The spectacular nave, dominated by Romanesque and early Gothic vaults and columns, contains the elaborate, white marble tombs of the 8th duke of Argyll and his wife. A door on the left leads to the beautiful Gothic cloister, where medieval grave slabs sit alongside

modern religious sculptures. A replica of the intricately carved **St John's Cross** stands just outside the abbey – the massive 8th-century original is in the **Infirmary Museum** (around the far side of the abbey) along with many other fine examples of early Christian and medieval **carved stones**.

Continue past the abbey and look for a footpath on the left signposted **Dun I** (dun-ee). An easy walk of about 15 to 20 minutes leads to the highest point on Iona, with fantastic views in all directions.

Boat Trips

Alternative Boat Hire　　　　Boat Tour
(☎01681-700537; www.boattripsiona.com) Offers cruises in a traditional wooden sailing boat for fishing, bird-watching, picnicking or just drifting along admiring the scenery. One-/three-hour trips cost £9.50/18.50 per adult (child £5/8.50).

MV Iolaire　　　　Boat Tour
(☎01681-700358; www.staffatrips.co.uk) Three-hour boat trips to Staffa (adult/child £25/10), departing Iona pier at 9.45am and 1.45pm, and from Fionnphort at 10am and 2pm, with one hour ashore on Staffa.

MV Volante　　　　Boat Tour
(☎01681-700362; www.volanteiona.com) Four-hour sea-angling trips (£35 per person including tackle and bait), as well as 1½-hour round-the-island wildlife cruises (adult/child £15/8) and 3½-hour whale-watching trips (£35 per person).

Sleeping & Eating

ARGYLL HOTEL　　　　Hotel　£££
(☎01681-700334; www.argyllhoteliona .co.uk; Baile Mor; s/d from £61/97; ⏰Mar-Oct) The terrace of cottages above the ferry slip houses this cute little hotel, which has 16 snug rooms (a sea view costs more: £131 for a double) and a country-house restaurant (mains £8 to £15, open for lunch and dinner) with a fireplace and antique tables and chairs. The kitchen is supplied by a huge organic garden out back, and the menu includes Cullen skink (soup made with smoked haddock,

MARTIN MOOS

Don't Miss **Isle of Staffa**

Felix Mendelssohn, who visited the uninhabited island of Staffa in 1829, was inspired to compose his *Hebrides Overture* after hearing waves echoing in the impressive and cathedral-like **Fingal's Cave** (pictured). The cave walls and surrounding cliffs are composed of vertical, hexagonal basalt columns that look like pillars (Staffa is Norse for 'Pillar Island'). You can land on the island and walk into the cave via a causeway. Nearby **Boat Cave** can be seen from the causeway, but you can't reach it on foot. Staffa also has a sizable puffin colony, north of the landing place.

Northwest of Staffa lies a chain of uninhabited islands called the **Treshnish Isles**. The two main islands are the curiously shaped **Dutchman's Cap** and **Lunga**. You can land on Lunga, walk to the top of the hill and visit the shag, puffin and guillemot colonies on the west coast at **Harp Rock**.

Unless you have your own boat, the only way to reach Staffa and the Treshnish Isles is on an organised boat trip – see p239 and p252 for details.

potato, onion and milk), home-grown salads, and venison-and-rabbit hotpot.

IONA HOSTEL Hostel **£**
(01681-700781; www.ionahostel.co.uk; Lagandorain; dm £18.50; check-in 4-7pm) This hostel is set in an attractive, modern timber building on a working croft, with stunning views out to Staffa and the Treshnish Isles. Rooms are clean and functional, and the well-equipped lounge/kitchen area has an open fire. It's at the northern end of the island – to get here, continue along the road past the abbey for 1.5 miles (a 20- to 30-minute walk).

ℹ **Getting There & Away**

The **passenger ferry** from Fionnphort to Iona (£4.30 return, five minutes, hourly) runs daily. There are also various day trips available from Oban to Iona (see p239).

Inverness
& the
Highlands

From the high, subarctic plateau of the Cairngorms to the rugged, rocky peaks of Glen Coe and Ben Nevis, the mountains of the Highlands are testimony to the sculpting power of ice and weather. Here the Scottish landscape is at its grandest, with soaring hills of rock and heather bounded by wooded glens and rushing waterfalls.

Unsurprisingly, this part of the country is an adventure playground for outdoor-sports enthusiasts. Aviemore, Glen Coe and Fort William draw hordes of hill walkers and rock climbers in summer, and skiers, snowboarders and ice climbers in winter. The Highland capital Inverness provides urban relaxation, while nearby Loch Ness and its elusive monster add a hint of mystery.

From Fort William, base camp for climbing Ben Nevis, the Road to the Isles leads past the gorgeous beaches of Arisaig and Morar to Mallaig, the jumping-off point for the Isle of Skye.

A model Nessie at the Loch Ness Exhibition Centre
PHOTOGRAPHER: DENNIS JOHNSON

Inverness & the Highlands

North Sea

Butt of Lewis

Tarbet

Scourie

Point of Stoer

Clachtoll

Achmelvich

Lochinve

Knocka

Stornoway

The Minch

North Harris

Achiltibuie

Summer Isles

Ullapool

Drumchork

Dundonnell

Tarbert

Melvaig

Midtown

Gairloch

The Little Minch

Kinlochewe

Uig

Torridon

Achnasheen

Trotternish

Shieldaig

Loch Damh

Carro

Lochmaddy

Inner Sound

Applecross

Farrar

Dunvegan

Portree

Kishorn

Lochcarron

Plockton

Loch Carron

Lin e

Isle of Skye

Loch Alsh

Kyleakin

ATLANTIC OCEAN

Loch Duich

Glenelg

Loch Chuanie

Lochboisdale

Arnisdale

Sleat

Loch Hourn

Loyne

Knoydart Peninsula

Inverie

Loch Nevis

Strathan

Mallaig

Morar

Pea

Achnacar

Isle of Rum

Arisaig

Glenfinnan

Isle of Eigg

Con

❼

Loch Shiel

Sea of the Hebrides

Ardmolich

Fort William

Achosnich

Ardnamurchan Point

Salen

Strontian

Glencoe

Kilchoan

Bonnavoulin

Ardgou

Tobermory

❸

Loch Linnhe

Isle of Mull

Lochaline

Inverness & the Highlands' Highlights

① Loch Ness

Stretching along the glacier-gouged trench of the Great Glen, 23-mile-long Loch Ness contains more water than all the lakes in England and Wales combined. Its peaty depths conceal the long-standing mystery of its legendary monster, and thousands flock to its shores each year in hope of catching a glimpse.

Need to Know

BEST TIME TO GO A calm day with no wind, for monster-spotting. **TOP TIP** Avoid crowds by driving the minor road on the loch's east side. **BEST PHOTO OP** View from Urquhart Castle. **For more, see p276.**

Loch Ness Don't Miss List

ADRIAN SHINE, LEADER OF THE
LOCH NESS PROJECT

1 LOCH NESS EXHIBITION CENTRE

I designed this exhibition (p277) myself, presenting the results of eight decades of research. The collection has everything from one-man submarines to the Rosetta apparatus that opened the 10,000-year-old time capsule concealed within the loch's sediment layers. The exhibition does not have all the answers and it will certainly not try to sell you a monster. Instead, it places the mystery in its proper context, which is the environment of Loch Ness.

2 URQUHART CASTLE

If, having learned some of the inner secrets of the loch, you want to see it through new eyes, you cannot do better than visiting Urquhart Castle (p280; pictured facing page). Perched on a rocky promontory jutting into Loch Ness, its exhibits recount the castle's history, from a vitrified Pictish fort to its role in the Scottish Wars of Independence. The view from the Grant Tower is truly breathtaking.

3 FORT AUGUSTUS LOCKS

At the southern end of the loch is a flight of locks on the **Caledonian Canal** (p279; pictured bottom left), built by the great engineer Thomas Telford. It is always interesting to watch vessels being worked up this 'staircase' of water. British Waterways has a fascinating exhibition halfway up.

4 CRUISING THE LOCH

Venturing onto the water puts the seemingly tiny trunk road and Urquhart Castle into a new perspective. The Deepscan cruise boat runs from the Loch Ness Centre; I use this boat for my research and the skipper will tell you about his experiences. There are other cruise boats operating from Drumnadrochit, and the larger Jacobite vessels (p269) depart from Inverness.

5 WATERFALL WALKS

Starting from the car park at Invermoriston, cross the road to find the magnificent waterfall, then go back to take the path down the river through a mature beech wood to the shores of the loch. There is another famous waterfall at Foyers, on the southeastern shore of Loch Ness, as well as Divach Falls (pictured top left) up Balmacaan Rd at Drumnadrochit.

Cairngorms National Park

The rounded, snow-patched mountains of the Cairngorms form the largest area of high ground in Britain, with five of Scotland's six highest summits. The national park spreads out around their shoulders, encompassing pine forests, lochs, rivers and waterfalls, home to red deer, eagles, ospreys and wildcats. Ben Avon

Need to Know

BEST TIME TO GO Spring for snow-patched mountains, August for purple heather. **TOP TIP** Bring waterproofs in case of bad weather. **BEST PHOTO OP** View from top of Cairngorm. **For more info, see p281.**

Cairngorms National Park Don't Miss List

ERIC BAIRD, HEAD RANGER, GLEN TANAR, CAIRNGORMS NATIONAL PARK

1 LOCH MORLICH

Not far from Aviemore, this is a perfect loch (p286; pictured left), set in a perfect forest, surrounded by perfect mountains. Go early in the morning, or out of season: you'll want to feel like the first person to discover it, and you still can.

2 LOCHNAGAR

Rising above Balmoral Castle, Lochnagar mountain (see p209) is a serious – and massive – piece of rock, with terrific climbing on the north-facing corrie walls (summer and winter – different tools, techniques and temperatures!). But any fit person can walk up it: just be careful, stay on the path and check the weather forecast.

3 GLAS-ALLT WATERFALL

This comes tumbling, sometimes roaring, off Lochnagar into Loch Muick. It's the setting that makes it – you can go up from Loch Muick, past the Glas-allt Sheil house. (The building itself has a story: Queen Victoria had the place locked and unused after the death of Prince Albert. Last time I looked in the window, I saw ancient dried roses in a vase.) The path by the stream is steep, and narrow in places, but safe enough if you pay attention.

4 CRAIGENDARROCH

Craigendarroch (p205) – the 'rock of the oaks' – is on the edge of Ballater. You can go up after breakfast and be down for morning coffee, but you'll probably take longer. There are anthills in the spring sunshine, blueberries in late summer, turning leaves of oak and larch in autumn and terrific views up and down the River Dee all year.

5 FOREST OF GLEN TANAR

You can wander – for a day or a week, on foot or on a mountain bike – through the native forest of Scots pine, alongside the Water of Tanar. If it's quiet, you will see crossbills, birds of prey, red and roe deer and red squirrels. You can stay in the forest or head up onto the hill – Mount Keen, at the head of the Glen, is a possibility.

Glen Coe

One of Scotland's wildest, most scenic and most famous glens, Glen Coe's (p288) peacefulness and beauty today belies the fact that it was the scene of a ruthless 17th-century massacre, in which the local MacDonalds were murdered by soldiers of the Campbell clan. Besides the history, there are many fine walks both easy and difficult, and enough photo opportunities to keep keen snappers happy.

5 Climbing Ben Nevis

The highest summit in all of Britain and Ireland, Ben Nevis (p300) is within reach of anyone who's reasonably fit. Don't take it lightly – it's a long, strenuous hike, and the weather can deteriorate rapidly. But treat Britain's tallest peak with respect and your reward (weather permitting) is a truly magnificent view, a great sense of achievement and a well-earned drink in the Ben Nevis Inn.

EOIN CLARKE

Watching Wildlife

The Highlands are home to some of Scotland's most spectacular wildlife, including the country's largest land mammal, the red deer, and its largest native bird, the capercaillie. There are countless opportunities for spotting wildlife, from nature reserves such as Loch Garten (p287), where you can see nesting ospreys, to places like the Highland Wildlife Park (p287), which provides your best chance of seeing Scotland's most elusive creature, the wildcat.

TERRY WHITTAKER/ALAMY

GARETH MCCORMACK

Glen Affric

Gorgeous Glen Affric (p283) is a walkers' wonderland, a scenic extravaganza of shimmering lochs, rugged mountains, roaring waterfalls and native-pine woods. Often described as the most beautiful glen in Scotland, Affric is home to pine martens, wildcats, otters, red squirrels and golden eagles. Easily reached by car from Inverness or Loch Ness, it offers walks for all abilities, from a half-hour stroll to challenging cross-country hikes.

The Great Outdoors

Between them, the Cairngorms and the West Highlands have the highest concentration of challenging outdoor activities in the country: Fort William (p291) calls itself the 'Outdoor Capital of the UK'. Hiking, hill walking, rock climbing, mountain biking, skiing, snowboarding, sailing, sea kayaking and canoeing, for everyone from beginners to experts – all combine to create the finest outdoor playground in Britain.

Inverness & the Highlands' Best...

Historic Sites

○ **Culloden** (p275) The battlefield where Jacobite dreams were crushed

○ **Glen Coe** (p288) Site of one of Scottish history's most tragic episodes, the Glencoe Massacre

○ **Ruthven Barracks** (p287) A poignant relic of the Jacobite rebellion

○ **Fort George** (p276) One of Europe's most impressive 18th-century artillery fortresses

○ **Urquhart Castle** (p280) Impressive medieval castle, blown up to prevent Jacobite use

Scenery

○ **Loch Ness** (p276) Classic loch views from Fort Augustus and Urquhart Castle

○ **Glen Affric** (p283) Mountains, lochs, Caledonian pine forests – sublime

○ **Glen Coe** (p288) Brooding mountain scenery looms over narrow glen

○ **Arisaig** (p302) White-sand beaches with glorious sunset views over islands

Wildlife Experiences

○ **Loch Garten** (p287) Watch ospreys feeding and nesting in the wild.

○ **Cairngorm Reindeer Centre** (p287) Britain's only herd of reindeer will eat out of your hand

○ **Rothiemurchus Estate** (p282) Red squirrel, capercaillie and crossbill in remnant of Caledonian pine forest

○ **Moray Firth** (p269) Boat trips to see Scotland's only resident pod of bottlenose dolphins

Need to Know

Highland Pubs

○ Lock Inn (p281) Cosy nook close to Loch Ness, serving real ale and fish & chips.

○ Kings House Hotel (p289) Remote former military outpost guarding the eastern entrance to Glen Coe

○ Ben Nevis Inn (p298) Welcoming hill-walkers' retreat at the foot of Ben Nevis

○ Clachnaharry Inn (p273) Wonderful old real ale pub near Caledonian Canal

Left: Crofter's cottage at Culloden battlefield;
Above: Cannon at Fort George.

PHOTOGRAPHERS: (LEFT) ARTERRA PICTURE LIBRARY/ALAMY; (ABOVE) ROCCO FASANO

Inverness & the Highlands Itineraries

These two circular routes – one from Inverness (the 'Highland capital') and one from Fort William (the UK's 'outdoor capital') – showcase the superb scenery and landscapes of the Scottish Highlands.

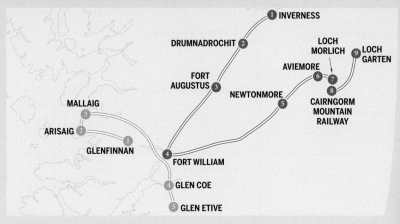

INVERNESS TO INVERNESS
Monsters, Mountains and Wildlife

3 DAYS

Head south from **(1) Inverness** on the A82 to legendary Loch Ness, and stop at **(2) Drumnadrochit** to visit the Loch Ness monster exhibitions and Urquhart Castle, and perhaps take a cruise on the loch. In the afternoon, continue south to **(3) Fort Augustus** for a stroll beside the Caledonian Canal, then on to **(4) Fort William** – detour right on the B8004 before Spean Bridge for superb views of Ben Nevis.

Begin day two with a short side trip along beautiful Glen Nevis, which curls around the foot of Britain's highest mountain, then head east on the A86 past Loch Laggan to reach **(5) Newtonmore**.

After a visit to the Highland Folk Museum, take the quiet B9152 from Kingussie past the Highland Wildlife Park at Kincraig to reach the resort town of **(6) Aviemore**.

Spend your third day exploring the Cairngorms National Park. You can drive to **(7) Loch Morlich** for pleasant woodland walks, and continue up to the **(8) Cairngorm Mountain Railway** for a trip to the subarctic summit plateau. Stick to the B-roads as you continue north from Aviemore, stopping to see the ospreys at the **(9) Loch Garten** nature reserve. From here, the A9 leads easily back to Inverness.

FORT WILLIAM TO FORT WILLIAM

Scenery Galore

This second itinerary tacks onto the first, adding two day trips from Fort William. On day one, head west along the A830 towards Mallaig: the famous 'Road to the Isles'. First stop is **(1) Glenfinnan**, where you can visit the monument to Bonnie Prince Charlie before taking a walk along the glen to view the railway viaduct that features in the Harry Potter films.

Continue west through delightful scenery and leave the main road at **(2) Arisaig** for the B8008 (signposted 'Alternative Coastal Route'). This winding road leads past a series of gorgeous white-sand beaches, with stunning views to the islands of Eigg and Rum.

The road ends at **(3) Mallaig**, a less-than-pretty fishing harbour, where the ferry departs to Skye; time your trip to sample some local seafood before travelling back to Fort William.

The following day drive south to **(4) Glen Coe**, and make the most of any good weather by hiking into the hills. If a peaceful roadside picnic is more to your taste, continue through the glen and turn south along gorgeous **(5) Glen Etive**. Return to Fort William for the night, then continue towards the Cairngorms.

Dawn breaks over Buachaille Etive Mor (p288), Glen Coe.
PHOTOGRAPHER: GARETH MCCORMACK

Discover Inverness & the Highlands

INVERNESS

POP 55,000

Inverness, the primary city and shopping centre of the Highlands, has a great location astride the River Ness at the northern end of the Great Glen. In summer it overflows with visitors intent on monster hunting at nearby Loch Ness, but it's worth a visit in its own right for a stroll along the picturesque River Ness and a cruise on the Moray Firth in search of its famous bottlenose dolphins.

The city was probably founded by King David in the 12th century, but thanks to its often violent history few buildings of real age or historical significance have survived – much of the older part of the city dates from the period following the completion of the Caledonian Canal in 1822. The broad and shallow River Ness, which flows a short 6 miles from Loch Ness into the Moray Firth, runs through the heart of the city.

◎ Sights & Activities

NESS ISLANDS   Park

Save the indoor sights for a rainy day – the main attraction in Inverness is a leisurely stroll along the river to the Ness Islands. Planted with mature Scots pine, fir, beech and sycamore, and linked to the river banks and each other by elegant Victorian footbridges, the islands make an appealing picnic spot. They're a 20-minute walk south of the castle – head upstream on either side of the river (the start of the Great Glen Way), and return on the opposite bank. On the way you'll pass the red sand-

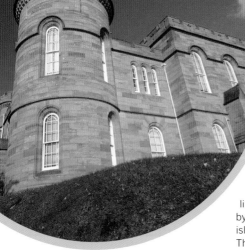

Inverness Castle
PHOTOGRAPHER: ROCCO FASANO

stone towers of **St Andrew's Cathedral (11 Ardross St)**, dating from 1869, and the modern Eden Court Theatre (p273), which hosts regular art exhibits, both on the west bank.

FREE INVERNESS MUSEUM & ART GALLERY
Museum

(www.inverness.highland.museum; Castle Wynd; admission free; ⏲10am-5pm Mon-Sat) Between the castle and the tourist office is Inverness Museum & Art Gallery, with wildlife dioramas, geological displays, period rooms with historic weapons, Pictish stones and contemporary Highland arts and crafts.

VICTORIAN MARKET
Market

If the rain does come down, you could opt for a spot of retail therapy in the Victorian Market, a shopping mall that dates from the 1890s and has rather more charm than its modern equivalents.

INVERNESS CASTLE
Castle

The hill above the city centre is topped by the picturesque Baronial turrets of Inverness Castle, a pink-sandstone confection dating from 1847 that replaced a medieval castle blown up by the Jacobites in 1746; it serves today as the Sheriff's Court. It's not open to the public, but there are good views from the surrounding gardens.

 Tours

MORAY FIRTH CRUISES
Boat

(☎ 01463-717900; www.inverness-dolphin-cruises.co.uk; Shore St Quay, Shore St; ⏲10.30am-4.30pm Mar-Oct) Offers 1½-hour wildlife cruises (adult/child £14/10) to look for dolphins, seals and bird life. Sightings aren't guaranteed, but the commentaries are excellent, and on a fine day it's good just being out on the water. Follow the signs to Shore St Quay from the far end of Chapel St or catch the free shuttle bus that leaves from the tourist office 15 minutes before sailings (which depart every 1½ hours). In July and August there are also departures at 6pm.

JACOBITE CRUISES
Boat

(☎ 01463-233999; www.jacobite.co.uk; Glenurquhart Rd) Cruise boats depart at 10.35am and 1.35pm from Tomnahurich Bridge for a 3½-hour trip along Loch Ness, including visits to Urquhart Castle and Loch Ness 2000 Monster Exhibition (adult/child £26/20 including admission fees). You can buy tickets at the tourist office and catch a free minibus to the boat. Other cruises, from one to 6½ hours, are available.

Happy Tours
Walking

(www.happy-tours.biz; adult/child £10/free) Offers 1¼-hour guided walks exploring the town's history and legends. Tours begin outside the tourist office at 11am, 1pm and 3pm daily.

Inverness Taxis
Taxi

(☎ 01463-222900; www.inverness-taxis.co.uk) Wide range of day tours to Urquhart Castle, Loch Ness and Culloden, and even Skye. Fares per car (up to four people) range from £50 (two hours) to £200 (all day).

 Sleeping

There are lots of guesthouses and B&Bs along Old Edinburgh Rd and Ardconnel St on the east side of the river, and on Kenneth St and Fairfield Rd on the west bank; all are within 10 minutes' walk of the city centre.

The city fills up quickly in July and August, so either prebook your accommodation or get an early start looking for somewhere to stay.

TRAFFORD BANK
B&B ££

(☎ 01463-241414; www.traffordbankguesthouse.co.uk; 96 Fairfield Rd; s/d from £85/110; P 🛜) Lots of word-of-mouth rave reviews for Trafford Bank, an elegant Victorian villa that was once home to a bishop, just a mitre-toss from the Caledonian Canal and only 10 minutes' walk west from the city centre. The luxurious rooms include fresh flowers and fruit, bathrobes and fluffy towels – ask for the Tartan Room, with its wrought-iron king-size bed and Victorian roll-top bath.

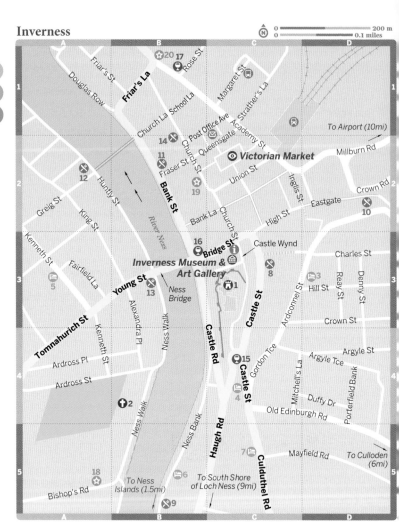

ROCPOOL RESERVE

Boutique Hotel **£££**

(☏ 01463-240089; www.rocpool.com; Culduthel Rd; s/d from £160/195; **P** 🛜) Boutique chic meets the Highlands in this slick and sophisticated little hotel, where an elegant Georgian exterior conceals an oasis of contemporary cool. A gleaming white entrance hall lined with contemporary art leads to designer rooms in shades of chocolate, cream and coffee; expect lots of high-tech gadgetry in the more expensive rooms, ranging from iPod docks to balcony hot tubs with aquavision TV. A new restaurant by Albert Roux completes the package.

ARDCONNEL HOUSE

B&B **££**

(☏ 01463-240455; www.ardconnel-inverness. co.uk; 21 Ardconnel St; per person from £35; 🛜) The six-room Ardconnel is another of our favourites – a terraced Victorian house with comfortable en suite rooms, a dining room with crisp white table linen, and a breakfast menu that includes Vegemite for homesick Antipodeans. Kids under 10 not allowed.

Inverness

ACH ALUINN   B&B ££

(☎ 01463-230127; www.achaluinn.com; 27 Fairfield Rd; per person £25-35; P) This large, detached Victorian house is bright and homely, and offers all you might want from a guesthouse – private bathroom, TV, reading lights, comfy beds with two pillows each, and an excellent breakfast. Five minutes' walk west from city centre.

LOCH NESS COUNTRY HOUSE HOTEL
                        Hotel £££

(☎ 01463-230512; www.lochnesscountryhouse hotel.co.uk; Dunain Park; d from £165; P 🛜) This sumptuous country house hotel offers more traditional decor, with its Vic-

torian four-poster beds, Georgian-style furniture and Italian marble bathrooms, all set in beautiful wooded grounds just five minutes' stroll from the Caledonian Canal and River Ness. The hotel is a mile southwest of Inverness on the A82 to Fort William.

CROWN HOTEL GUEST HOUSE
                        B&B ££

(☎ 01463-231135; www.inverness-guesthouse .info; 19 Ardconnel St; s/d from £36/56; P 🚻) Similar in layout to the ever-popular Ardconnel next door, but child-friendly, the Crown has kind and helpful owners. Two of the six bedrooms are family rooms (with a double, single and folding bed in each), and there's a spacious lounge equipped with games consoles, DVDs and board games.

MACRAE GUEST HOUSE   B&B ££

(☎ 01463-243658; joycemacrae@hotmail.com; 24 Ness Bank; s/d from £45/64; P) This pretty, flower-bedecked Victorian house on the eastern bank of the river has smart, tastefully decorated bedrooms – one is wheelchair accessible – and vegetarian breakfasts are available. Minimum two-night bookings in July and August.

BAZPACKERS BACKPACKERS HOTEL
                        Hostel £

(☎ 01463-717663; 4 Culduthel Rd; dm/tw £14/38; @) This may be Inverness's smallest hostel (30 beds), but it's hugely popular – it's a friendly, quiet place with a convivial lounge centred on a wood-burning stove, a small garden and great views. Though the dorms can be a bit cramped, the showers are great.

Glenmoriston Town House Hotel
                        Boutique Hotel £££

(☎ 01463-223777; www.glenmoristontownhouse .com; 20 Ness Bank; s/d from £105/150; P 🛜) Luxurious boutique hotel on the banks of the River Ness. Can organise golfing and fishing for guests.

Mardon Guest House   B&B ££

(☎ 01463-231005; www.mardonguesthouse.co .uk; 37 Kenneth St; r per person £30-38; P 🛜) Friendly B&B, with six cosy rooms (all en suite), just five minutes' walk west from the city centre.

Moyness House Hotel
B&B ££

(☏ 01463-233836; www.moyness.co.uk; 6 Bruce Gardens; r per person £40-50; P 🛜) Elegant Victorian villa with a beautiful garden and peaceful setting, 10 minutes' walk southwest of the city centre.

Bluebell House
B&B ££

(☏ 01463-238201; www.bluebell-house.com; 31 Kenneth St; r per person £30-45; P 🛜) Warm and welcoming hosts, top breakfasts, close to city centre.

Amulree
B&B ££

(☏ 01463-224822; amulree@btinternet.com; 40 Fairfield Rd; per person £30; P 🛜) Comfortable, four-bedroom Victorian B&B less than 10 minutes' walk west of the city centre.

Eating

CONTRAST BRASSERIE Brasserie ££

(☏ 01463-227889; www.glenmoristontownhouse.com/contrast; 22 Ness Bank; mains £10-19; ◷noon-2.30pm & 5-10pm) Book early for what we think is the best restaurant in Inverness – a dining room that drips designer style, smiling professional staff, a jug of water brought to your table without asking, and truly delicious food. Try mussels with Thai red curry, wild mushroom risotto, or pork belly with glazed walnuts and watercress; 10 out of 10. And at £10 for a two-course lunch, the value is incredible.

CAFÉ 1 Bistro ££

(☏ 01463-226200; www.cafe1.net; 75 Castle St; mains £10-20; ◷noon-2pm & 5.30-9.30pm Mon-Sat) Café 1 is a friendly and appealing little bistro with candlelit tables amid elegant blonde-wood and wrought-iron decor. There is an international menu based on quality Scottish produce, from succulent Aberdeen Angus steaks to crisp sea bass with chilli, lime and soy sauce. Lunch and early-bird menu (two courses for £9.50) is served noon to 6.45pm weekdays, and noon to 3pm Saturday.

ROCPOOL Mediterranean ££

(☏ 01463-717274; www.rocpoolrestaurant.com; 1 Ness Walk; mains £13-18; ◷noon-2.30pm & 5.45-10pm) Lots of polished wood, navy-blue leather and crisp white linen lend a nautical air to this relaxing bistro, which

Inverness in autumn

FERGUS MACKAY/ALAMY

offers a Mediterranean-influenced menu that makes the most of quality Scottish produce, especially seafood. The two-course lunch (noon to 2.30pm Monday to Saturday) is £12.

MUSTARD SEED
Modern Scottish **££**

(☏ 01463-220220; www.mustardseedrestaurant.co.uk; 16 Fraser St; mains £12-16; ☾noon-10pm) This bright and bustling bistro brings a dash of big-city style to Inverness. The menu changes weekly, but focuses on Scottish and French cuisine with a modern twist. Grab a table on the upstairs balcony if you can – it's the best outdoor lunch spot in Inverness, with a great view across the river. And a two-course lunch for £6 – yes, that's right – is hard to beat.

SAM'S INDIAN CUISINE
Indian **££**

(77-79 Church St; mains £8-13; ☾noon-2.30pm & 6-11pm) The stylish decor in Sam's is a cut above your average curry shop, and so is the food – lots of fresh and flavoursome spices and herbs make dishes such as jeera chicken (cooked with cumin seed) really zing. Wash it down with Indian Cobra beer.

River House
Modern Scottish **£££**

(☏ 01463-222033; www.riverhouseinverness.co.uk; 1 Greig St; mains £16-22; ☾noon-2pm & 5.30-9.30pm Tue-Sat, 6-9.30pm Sun) The River House is an elegant restaurant of the polished wood and crisp white linen variety, serving the best of British venison, beef, lamb, duck and seafood.

Délices de Bretagne
French **£**

(6 Stephen's Brae; mains £3-7; ☾9am-5pm Mon-Sat, 10am-5pm Sun) This cafe brings a little taste of France to the Highlands, with its art nouveau decor and a menu of tasty *galettes* (savoury pancakes), crepes, Breton cider and excellent coffee.

🍷 Drinking

CLACHNAHARRY INN
Pub

(www.clachnaharryinn.co.uk; 17-19 High St; Clachnaharry) Just over a mile northwest of the city centre, on the bank of the Caledonian Canal just off the A862, this is a delightful old coaching inn (with beer garden out back) serving an excellent range of real ales and good pub grub.

CASTLE TAVERN
Pub

(www.castletavern.net; 1-2 View Pl) Under the same management as the Clachnaharry Inn and with a tasty selection of real ales, this pub has a wee suntrap of a terrace out the front, a great place for a pint on a summer afternoon.

PHOENIX
Pub

(108 Academy St) This is the best of the traditional pubs in the city centre, with a mahogany horseshoe bar, a comfortable, family-friendly lounge, and good food at both lunchtime and in the evening. Real ales on tap include the rich and fruity Orkney Dark Island.

JOHNNY FOXES
Bar

(www.johnnyfoxes.co.uk; 26 Bank St) Stuck beneath the ugliest building on the riverfront, Johnny Foxes is a big and boisterous Irish bar, with a wide range of food served all day and live music nightly. Part of the premises, The Den, is now a smart cocktail bar.

⭐ Entertainment

HOOTANANNY
Live Music

(www.hootananny.com; 67 Church St) Hootananny is the city's best live-music venue, with traditional folk and/or rock music sessions nightly, including big-name bands from all over Scotland (and, indeed, the world). The bar is well stocked with a range of beers from the local Black Isle Brewery.

EDEN COURT THEATRE
Theatre

(www.eden-court.co.uk; Bishop's Rd) The Highlands' main cultural venue, with theatre, art-house cinema and conference centre, Eden Court stages a busy program of drama, dance, comedy, music, film and children's events, and has a good bar and restaurant. Pick up a program from the foyer or check the website.

IRONWORKS   Live Music/Comedy
(www.ironworksvenue.com; 122 Academy St)
With live bands (rock, pop, tribute) and
comedy shows two or three times a
week, the Ironworks is the town's main
venue for big-name acts.

ℹ Information

Tourist office (📞 01436-234353; www.visit
highlands.com; Castle Wynd; ⏱9am-6pm Mon-
Sat & 9.30am-5pm Sun Jul & Aug, 9am-5pm Mon-
Sat & 10am-4pm Sun Jun, Sep & Oct, 9am-5pm
Mon-Sat Apr & May; @) Bureau de change and
accommodation booking service; also sells
tickets for tours and cruises. Internet access
£1 per 20 minutes. Openings hours limited
November to March.

ℹ Getting There & Away

Air

Inverness airport (www.hial.co.uk/inverness
-airport) At Dalcross, 10 miles east of the
city on the A96 towards Aberdeen. There
are scheduled flights to London, Bristol,
Manchester, Belfast, Stornoway, Benbecula,
Orkney, Shetland and several other British
airports. For more information, see p350.

Stagecoach Jet (www.stagecoachbus.com)
Buses run from the airport to Inverness bus
station (£3, 20 minutes, every 30 minutes). A
taxi costs around £15.

Bus

Scottish Citylink (www.citylink.co.uk) has
connections to Glasgow (£26, 3½ to 4½ hours,
hourly), Edinburgh (£26, 3½ to 4½ hours, hourly),
Fort William (£11, two hours, five daily) and Portree
(£17, 3½ hours, five daily) on the Isle of Skye.

If you book far enough in advance, **Megabus**
(www.megabus.com) offers fares from as little
as £5 for buses from Inverness to Glasgow and
Edinburgh.

Train

There are several direct trains a day from Glasgow
(£55, 3½ hours), Edinburgh (£55, 3¼ hours) and
Aberdeen (£25, 2¼ hours).

The line from Inverness to Kyle of Lochalsh
(£18, 2½ hours, four daily Monday to Saturday,

Left: Memorial cairn at Culloden battlefield;
Below: Gravestone at Culloden battlefield
PHOTOGRAPHER: (LEFT) ARTERRA PICTURE LIBRARY/ALAMY; (BELOW) GRAEME CORNWALLIS

two Sunday) provides one of Britain's great scenic train journeys.

Getting Around

Bicycle

Great Glen Cycle Hire (☎ 07752 102700; www.greatglencyclehire.com; 18 Harbour Rd) Rent mountain bikes for £20 a day. Will deliver bikes to local hotels and B&Bs.

Bus

City services and buses to places around Inverness, including the Culloden battlefield, are operated by **Stagecoach** (www.stagecoachbus .com). An Inverness City Dayrider ticket costs £3.20 and gives unlimited travel for a day on buses throughout the city.

Car

Sharp's Vehicle Rental (☎ 01436-236694; www.sharpsreliablewrecks.co.uk; Inverness train station) Has rates starting at £30 per day.

Taxi

Highland Taxis (☎ 01436-222222)

Around Inverness

Culloden Battlefield

The Battle of Culloden in 1746, the last pitched battle ever fought on British soil, saw the defeat of Bonnie Prince Charlie and the end of the Jacobite dream when 1200 Highlanders were slaughtered by government forces in a 68-minute rout. The duke of Cumberland, son of the reigning King George II and leader of the Hanoverian army, earned the nickname 'Butcher' for his brutal treatment of the defeated Scottish forces. The battle sounded the death knell for the old clan system, and the horrors of the Clearances soon followed. The sombre moor where the conflict took place has scarcely changed in the ensuing 260 years.

The impressive new **visitor centre** (NTS; www.nts.org.uk/culloden; adult/child £10/7.50 ⏰9am-6pm Apr-Oct, 10am-4pm Nov-Mar) presents detailed information about the battle, including the lead-up and the aftermath, with perspectives from both sides. An innovative film puts you on the battlefield in the middle of the mayhem, and a wealth of other audio presentations must have kept Inverness' entire acting community in business for weeks. The admission fee includes an audioguide for a self-guided tour of the battlefield itself.

Culloden is 6 miles east of Inverness. Bus No 1 runs from Queensgate in Inverness to Culloden battlefield (30 minutes, hourly).

Fort George

The headland guarding the narrows in the Moray Firth opposite Fortrose is occupied by the magnificent and virtually unaltered 18th-century artillery fortification of **Fort George** (HS; adult/child £6.70/4; ⏰9.30am-5.30pm Apr-Sep, 9.30am-4.30pm Oct-Mar). One of the finest examples of its kind in Europe, it was established in 1748 as a base for George II's army of occupation in the Highlands – by the time of its completion in 1769 it had cost the equivalent of around £1 billion in today's money. The mile-plus walk around the ramparts offers fine views out to sea and back to the Great Glen. Given its size, you'll need at least two hours to do the place justice. The fort is off the A96 about 11 miles northeast of Inverness.

Cawdor

Cawdor Castle (www.cawdorcastle.com; adult/child £8.30/5.20; ⏰10am-5.30pm May–mid-Oct) was the 14th-century home of the Thanes of Cawdor, one of the titles prophesied by the three witches for the eponymous character of Shakespeare's *Macbeth*. Macbeth couldn't have moved in, though, since the central tower dates from the 14th century (the wings were 17th-century additions) and he died in 1057. The castle is 5 miles southwest of Nairn.

Cawdor Tavern (www.cawdortavern.co.uk; bar meals £8-15; ⏰lunch & dinner) in the nearby village is worth a visit, though it can be difficult deciding what to drink as it stocks over 100 varieties of whisky. There's also good pub food, with tempting daily specials.

LOCH NESS

Deep, dark and narrow, Loch Ness stretches for 23 miles between Inverness and Fort Augustus. Its bitterly cold waters have been extensively explored in search of Nessie, the elusive Loch Ness monster, but most visitors see her only in cardboard-cutout form at the monster exhibitions. The busy A82 road runs along the north-western shore, while the more tranquil and picturesque B862 follows

Cawdor Castle and its gardens
PHOTOGRAPHER: HAN/IMAGEBROKER

Detour:
John O'Groats

A car park surrounded by tourist shops, John O'Groats offers little to the visitor beyond a means to get across to Orkney; even the pub has been shut for a while now (there are a couple of cafes). Though it's not the northernmost point of the British mainland (that's Dunnet Head), it still serves as the endpoint of the 874-mile trek from Land's End in Cornwall, a popular if arduous route for cyclists and walkers, many of whom raise money for charitable causes.

Two miles east, **Duncansby Head** provides a more solemn end-of-Britain moment with a small lighthouse and 60m cliffs sheltering nesting fulmars. From here a 15-minute walk through a sheep paddock yields spectacular views of the sea-surrounded monoliths known as **Duncansby Stacks**.

From May to September, **John O'Groats Ferries** (☎ 01955-611353; www.jogferry .co.uk; ⏱ departs 7.30am) runs daily tours (lasting 13½ hours; adult/child £57/28.50) by bus and passenger ferry from Inverness bus station to Orkney via John O'Groats.

the southeastern shore. A complete circuit of the loch is about 70 miles – travel anticlockwise for the best views.

Drumnadrochit
POP 800

Seized by monster madness, its gift shops bulging with Nessie cuddly toys, Drumnadrochit is a hotbed of beastie fever, with two monster exhibitions battling it out for the tourist dollar.

 ## Sights & Activities

LOCH NESS EXHIBITION CENTRE
Monster Exhibition

(www.loch-ness-scotland.com; adult/child £6.50/4.50; ⏱ 9am-6.30pm Jul & Aug, to 6pm Jun & Sep, 9.30am-5pm Feb-May & Oct, 10am-3.30pm Nov-Jan) This is the better of the two Nessie-themed attractions, with a scientific approach that allows you to weigh the evidence for yourself, and featuring original footage of monster sightings plus exhibits of equipment used in the various underwater monster hunts.

NESSIELAND CASTLE MONSTER CENTRE
Monster Exhibition

(www.lochness-hotel.com; adult/child £5.50/4; ⏱ 9am-8pm Jul & Aug, 10am-5.30pm Apr-Jun, Sep & Oct, 10am-4pm Nov-Mar) This more homely option is more of a miniature theme park aimed squarely at the kids, but its main function is to sell you Loch Ness monster souvenirs.

Nessie Hunter
Cruise

(☎ 01456-450395; www.lochness-cruises.com; adult/child £10/8) One-hour monster-hunting cruises, complete with sonar and underwater cameras, Cruises depart from Drumnadrochit hourly from 9am to 6pm daily from Easter to December.

 ## Sleeping & Eating

LOCH NESS INN
Inn ££

(☎ 01456-450991; www.staylochness.co.uk; Lewiston; s/d/f £69/99/140; P 🛜) Conveniently located in the quiet hamlet of Lewiston, between Drumnadrochit and Urquhart Castle, the Loch Ness Inn ticks all the weary traveller's boxes with comfortable bedrooms (the family suite sleeps two adults and two children), a cosy bar pouring real ales from the Cairngorm and Isle of Skye breweries, and a rustic restaurant (mains £8 to £16) serving hearty, wholesome fare such as smoked haddock chowder, and venison sausages with mash and onion gravy.

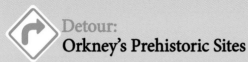

Detour:
Orkney's Prehistoric Sites

There's a magic to the Orkneys that you'll begin to feel as soon as the Scottish mainland slips away astern. It's an archipelago of old-style hospitality and Viking heritage, whose ports tell of lives led with the blessings and rough moods of the sea. Above all, it's famous for a series of magnificent prehistoric monuments.

Skara Brae (HS; www.historic-scotland.gov.uk; Bay of Skaill; adult/child £6.70/4; ⏱9.30am-5.30pm Apr-Sep, 9.30am-4.30pm Oct-Mar) is one of the world's most evocative ancient sites, offering an authentic glimpse of Stone Age life. Idyllically situated by a sandy bay 8 miles north of Stromness, and predating Stonehenge and the pyramids of Giza, Skara Brae is northern Europe's best-preserved prehistoric village.

Egypt has the pyramids, Scotland has **Maes Howe** (HS; ☎01856-761606; www.historic-scotland.gov.uk; adult/child £5.20/3.10; ⏱tours hourly 10am-3pm Oct-Mar, also 4pm Apr-Sep). Constructed about 5000 years ago, it's an extraordinary place, a Stone Age tomb built from enormous sandstone blocks. Creeping down the long stone passageway to the central chamber, you feel the indescribable gulf of years that separate us from the architects of this mysterious place. Though nothing is known about who and what was interred here, the scope of the project suggests it was a structure of great significance.

Across the loch from Maes Howe is the atmospheric **Ring of Brodgar** (www.historic-scotland.gov.uk; ⏱24hr), a circle of standing stones build around 2500–2000 BC. Twenty-one of the original 60 stones still stand among the heather, their curious shapes mutilated by years of climatic onslaught.

DRUMBUIE FARM B&B ££
(☎01456-450634; www.loch-ness-farm.co.uk; Drumnadrochit; per person from £30; ⏱Mar-Oct; P) A B&B in a modern house on a working farm – the surrounding fields are full of sheep and highland cattle – with views over Urquhart Castle and Loch Ness. Walkers and cyclists are welcome.

LOCH NESS BACKPACKERS LODGE
Hostel £
(☎01456-450807; www.lochness-backpackers.com; Coiltie Farmhouse, East Lewiston; dm/d/f £12.50/30/45; P) This snug, friendly hostel housed in a cottage and barn has six-bed dorms, one double and a large barbecue area. It's about 0.75 miles from Drumnadrochit, along the A82 towards Fort William; turn left where you see the sign for Loch Ness Inn, just before the bridge.

LOCH NESS YOUTH HOSTEL Hostel £
(SYHA; ☎01320-351274; near Invermoriston; dm £18; ⏱Apr-Sep; @) This hostel is housed in a big lodge overlooking Loch Ness, and many dorms have loch views. It's located on the A82 road, 13 miles southwest of Drumnadrochit, and 4 miles northeast of Invermoriston. Buses from Inverness to Fort William stop nearby.

FIDDLER'S COFFEE SHOP & RESTAURANT Cafe/Restaurant ££
(www.fiddredrum.co.uk; Drumnadrochit; mains £8-16; ⏱11am-11pm) The coffee shop does cappuccino and croissants, while the restaurant serves traditional Highland fare, such as venison casserole, and a wide range of bottled Scottish beers. There's also a whisky bar with a huge range of single malts.

❶ Getting There & Away

Scottish Citylink and Stagecoach buses from Inverness to Fort William run along the shores of Loch Ness (six to eight daily, five on Sunday); those headed for Skye turn off at Invermoriston.

There are bus stops at Drumnadrochit (£6.20, 30 minutes), Urquhart Castle car park (£6.60, 35 minutes) and Loch Ness Youth Hostel (£10, 45 minutes).

Fort Augustus

POP 510

Fort Augustus, at the junction of four old military roads, was originally a government garrison and the headquarters of General George Wade's road-building operations in the early 18th century. Today it's a neat and picturesque little place, often overrun by tourists in summer.

 **Sights & Activities**

CALEDONIAN CANAL   Canal

At Fort Augustus, boats using the Caledonian Canal are raised and lowered 13m by a 'ladder' of five consecutive locks. It's fun to watch, and the neatly landscaped canal banks are a great place to soak up the sun or compare accents with fellow tourists. The **Caledonian Canal Heritage Centre** (admission free; ⏱10am-5pm Apr-Oct), beside the lowest lock, showcases the history of the canal.

CLANSMAN CENTRE   Museum

(www.scottish-swords.com; admission free; ⏱10am-6pm Apr-Oct) An exhibition on 17th-century Highland life, with live demonstrations of how to put on a plaid (the forerunner of the kilt) and how the claymore (Highland sword) was made and used. There is also a workshop where you can purchase handcrafted reproduction swords, dirks and shields.

Royal Scot   Cruise

(www.cruiselochness.com; ⏱10am-4pm Mar-Oct, 2pm Sat & Sun only Nov & Dec) One-hour cruises (adult/child £11/6.50) on Loch Ness accompanied by the latest high-tech sonar equipment so you can keep an underwater eye open for Nessie.

Strange Spectacle on Loch Ness

Highland folklore is filled with tales of strange creatures living in lochs and rivers. The term 'monster', however, dates from a May 1933 article in the *Inverness Courier*. Entitled 'Strange Spectacle on Loch Ness', it recounted the sighting of a disturbance in the loch by a local couple. A rash of sightings followed, including a notorious on-land encounter with London tourists in July 1933, again reported in the *Courier*.

The London newspapers couldn't resist. In December 1933 the *Daily Mail* sent Marmaduke Wetherall, a film director and big-game hunter, to Loch Ness to track down the beast. Within days he found 'reptilian' footprints in the shoreline mud (soon revealed to have been made with a stuffed hippopotamus foot, possibly an umbrella stand). Then in April 1934 came the famous 'long-necked monster' photograph taken by a seemingly reputable surgeon, Colonel Kenneth Wilson. The press went mad and the rest, as they say, is history.

In 1994, however, Christian Spurling – Wetherall's stepson, by then 90 years old – revealed that the most famous photo of Nessie ever taken was in fact a hoax, perpetrated by his stepfather with Wilson's help. Today, of course, there are those who claim that Spurling's confession is itself a hoax. Ironically, the researcher who exposed the surgeon's photo as a fake still believes wholeheartedly in the monster's existence.

Hoax or not, the bizarre mini-industry that has grown up around Loch Ness and its mysterious monster since that eventful summer 75 years ago is the strangest spectacle of all.

CREDIT

Don't Miss **Urquhart Castle**

Commanding a brilliant location with outstanding views (on a clear day), Urquhart Castle is a popular Nessie-watching hot spot. A huge visitor centre (most of which is beneath ground level) includes a video theatre (with a dramatic 'unveiling' of the castle at the end of the film), displays of medieval items discovered in the castle, a huge gift shop and a restaurant. The site is often very crowded in summer.

The castle was repeatedly sacked and rebuilt over the centuries, but was finally blown up in 1692 to prevent the Jacobites from using it. The five-storey tower house at the northern point is the most impressive remaining fragment and offers wonderful views across the water.

THINGS YOU NEED TO KNOW

HS; adult/child £7/4.20; ⊙9.30am-6pm Apr-Sep, to 5pm Oct, to 4.30pm Nov-Mar

---

Sleeping & Eating

 LOVAT ARMS HOTEL   Hotel **££**
(☏ 01456-459250; www.thelovat.com; Main Rd; d from £110; P ⬚ ⬚) Recently given a luxurious but eco-conscious boutique-style makeover in shades of pink and grey, this former huntin'n'shootin' hotel is set apart from the tourist crush around the canal. The bedrooms are spacious and stylishly furnished, while the lounge is equipped with a log fire, comfy arm-chairs and grand piano. The restaurant (mains £10 to £17, separate kids' menu) serves top-quality cuisine, from posh fish and chips to roast venison, seared sea bass and wild mushroom risotto.

MORAG'S LODGE   Hostel **£**
(☏ 01320-366289; www.moragslodge.com; Bun-noich Brae; dm/tw/f from £18/46/59; P @ ⬚) This large and well-run hostel is based in a big Victorian house with great views of Fort Augustus' hilly surrounds, and has a convivial bar with open fire. It's hidden

away in the trees up the steep side road just north of the tourist-office car park.

LORIEN HOUSE
B&B ££

(☎ 01320-366736; www.lorien-house.co.uk; Station Rd; s/d £45/70) Lorien is a cut above your usual B&B: the bathrooms come with bidets, the breakfasts with smoked salmon. There's a library of walking, cycling and climbing guides in the lounge.

LOCK INN
Pub ££

(Canal Side; mains £9-14) A superb little pub right on the canal bank, the Lock Inn has a vast range of malt whiskies and a tempting menu of bar meals (served noon to 8pm) that includes Orkney salmon, Highland venison and daily seafood specials; the house speciality is beer-battered haddock and chips.

 Information

There's an ATM and bureau de change (in the post office) beside the canal.

Tourist office (☎ 01320-366367; ⊗ 9am-6pm Mon-Sat, to 5pm Sun Easter-Oct) In the central car park.

 Getting There & Away

Scottish Citylink and Stagecoach buses from Inverness to Fort William stop at Fort Augustus (£10, one hour, six to eight daily Monday to Saturday, five on Sunday).

THE CAIRNGORMS

The **Cairngorms National Park** (www.cairngorms.co.uk) encompasses the highest landmass in Britain – a broad mountain plateau, riven only by the deep valleys of the Lairig Ghru and Loch Avon, with an average altitude of over 1000m and including five of the six highest summits in the UK. This wild mountain landscape of granite and heather has a sub-Arctic climate and supports rare alpine tundra vegetation and high-altitude bird species, such as snow bunting, ptarmigan and dotterel.

The harsh mountain environment gives way lower down to scenic glens softened by beautiful open forests of native Caledonian pine, home to rare

animals and birds such as pine marten, wildcat, red squirrel, osprey, capercaillie and crossbill.

This is prime hill-walking territory, but even couch potatoes can enjoy a taste of the high life by taking the Cairngorm Mountain Railway up to the edge of the Cairngorm plateau.

Aviemore
POP 2400

Aviemore is the gateway to the Cairngorms, the region's main centre for transport, accommodation, restaurants and shopping. It's not the prettiest town in Scotland by a long stretch – the main attractions are in the surrounding area – but when bad weather puts the hills off limits, Aviemore fills up with hikers, cyclists and climbers (plus skiers and

Orkney Tours

Discover Orkney

(☎ 01856-872865; www.discoverorkney .com; 44 Clay Loan, Kirkwall, Mainland) Offers guided tours and walks throughout the islands in the company of a qualified guide. Specific tours are tailored to your interests.

Orkney Archaeology Tours

(☎ 01856-721217; www.orkneyarchaeology tours.co.uk) Runs private half- (£160 for up to four) and full-day (£240) tours with an archaeologist guide.

John O'Groats Ferries

(☎ 01955-611353; www.jogferry.co.uk; John O'Groats) If you're in a hurry, these guys run a one-day tour of the main sites for £46, including the ferry from John O'Groats. You can do the whole thing as a long day trip from Inverness.

Wildabout Orkney

(☎ 01856-851011; www.wildaboutorkney .com) Operates tours covering Orkney's history, ecology, folklore and wildlife. Day trips operate year-round and cost £49, with pick-ups in Stromness and Kirkwall.

snowboarders in winter) cruising the outdoor-equipment shops or recounting their latest adventures in the cafes and bars. Add in tourists and locals and the eclectic mix makes for a lively little town.

Aviemore is on a loop off the A9 Perth–Inverness road; almost everything of note is to be found along the main drag, Grampian Rd. The train station and bus stop are towards the southern end.

The Cairngorm skiing area and mountain railway lie 9 miles east of Aviemore along the B970 (Ski Rd) and its continuation through Coylumbridge and Glenmore.

Sights

STRATHSPEY STEAM RAILWAY
Heritage Railway

(www.strathspeyrailway.co.uk; Station Sq) Aviemore's mainline train station is also home to the Strathspey Steam Railway, which runs steam trains on a section of restored line between Aviemore and Broomhill, 10 miles to the northeast, via Boat of Garten. There are four or five trains daily from June to September, and a more limited service in April, May, October and December; a return ticket from Aviemore to Broomhill is £10.50/5.25 per adult/child. An extension to Grantown-on-Spey is planned; in the meantime, you can continue from Broomhill to Grantown-on-Spey by bus.

ROTHIEMURCHUS ESTATE
Forest Reserve

(www.rothiemurchus.net) The Rothiemurchus Estate, which extends from the River Spey at Aviemore to the Cairngorm summit plateau, is famous for having Scotland's largest remnant of **Caledonian forest**, the ancient forest of Scots pine that once covered most of the country. The forest is home to a large population of red squirrel, and is one of the last bastions of the Scottish wildcat.

The estate **visitor centre** (Inverdruie; admission free; ⏰9am-5.30pm), a mile southeast of Aviemore along the B970, sells an *Explorer Map* detailing more than 50 miles of footpaths and cycling trails, including the wheelchair-accessible 4-mile trail around **Loch an Eilein**, with its ruined castle and peaceful pine woods.

CRAIGELLACHIE NATURE RESERVE
Nature Reserve

(www.snh.org.uk/nnr-scotland) A trail leads west from Aviemore Youth Hostel and passes under the A9 into the Craigellachie Nature Reserve, a great place for short hikes across steep hill sides covered in natural birch forest. Look out for birds and other wildlife, including the peregrine falcons that nest on the crags from April to July. If you're very lucky, you may even spot a capercaillie.

Woodlands, Rothiemurchus Estate
PHOTOGRAPHER: JOHN MACPHERSON/ALAMY

Detour:
Glen Affric

Glen Affric (www.glenaffric.org), one of the most beautiful glens in Scotland, extends deep into the hills west of Loch Ness. The upper reaches of the glen, now designated as **Glen Affric National Nature Reserve**, is a scenic wonderland of shimmering lochs, rugged mountains and native Scots pine, home to pine marten, wildcat, otter, red squirrel and golden eagle.

About 4 miles southwest of the village of Cannich is **Dog Falls**, a scenic spot where the River Affric squeezes through a narrow, rocky gorge. A waymarked walking trail leads there easily from Dog Falls car park.

The road continues beyond Dog Falls to a parking area and picnic site at the eastern end of **Loch Affric** where there are several short walks along the river and the loch shore. The circuit of Loch Affric (10 miles, allow five hours) follows good paths right around the loch and takes you deep into the heart of some very wild scenery.

Activities

AVIEMORE HIGHLAND RESORT
Leisure Complex

(www.aviemorehighlandresort.com) This complex of hotels, chalets and restaurants to the west of Grampian Rd includes a swimming pool, gym, spa, videogame arcade and a huge, shiny shopping mall. The **swimming pool** (adult/child £10/5; ⊙8am-8pm) and other leisure facilities are open to nonresidents.

BOTHY BIKES
Mountain Biking

(www.bothybikes.co.uk; Inverdruie; ⊙9am-5.30pm) Located just outside Aviemore on the way to Cairngorm, this place rents out mountain bikes for £15/20 per half/full day. It can also advise on routes and trails; a good choice for beginners is the **Old Logging Way** which runs from the hire centre to Glenmore, where you can make a circuit of Loch Morlich before returning. For experienced bikers, the whole of the Cairngorms is your playground.

CAIRNGORM MOUNTAIN
Winter Sports

(www.cairngormmountain.co.uk) Aspen or Val d'Isere it ain't, but with 19 runs and 23 miles of piste Cairngorm is Scotland's biggest ski area. When the snow is at its best and the sun is shining you can close your eyes and imagine you're in the Alps; sadly, low cloud, high winds and horizontal sleet are more common. The season usually runs from December until the snow melts, which may be as late as the end of April, but snowfall here is unpredictable – in some years the slopes can be open in November, but closed for lack of snow in February.

A ski pass for one day is £30/18 for adults/under-16s. Ski or snowboard rental is around £20/14.50 per adult/child a day; there are lots of rental outlets at Coire Cas, Glenmore and Aviemore.

During the season the tourist office displays snow conditions and avalanche warnings. You can check the latest snow conditions on the **Ski Hotline** (☏ 0900 165 4655) and at http://ski.visitscotland.com, or tune into Cairngorm Radio Ski FM on 96.6MHz.

ROTHIEMURCHUS FISHERY
Angling

(www.rothiemurchus.net; Rothiemurchus Estate, Inverdruie) Cast for rainbow trout at this loch at the southern end of the village; buy permits (from £10 to £30 a day, plus £3.50 for tackle hire) at the Fish Farm Shop in Inverdruie. If you're a fly-fishing virgin, there's a beginner's package,

FEARGUS COONEY

including tackle hire, one hour's instruction and one hour's fishing, for £35. For experienced anglers, there's also salmon and sea-trout fishing on the River Spey – a day permit costs around £20; numbers are limited, so it's best to book in advance.

CAIRNGORM SLEDDOG CENTRE

Dog Sledding

(☏ 07767 270526; www.sled-dogs.co.uk; Ski Rd) If you prefer the smell of wet dog to the whiff of petrol, you can be taken on a two- to three-hour sled tour of local forest trails in the wake of a team of huskies (adult/child £60/40). The sleds have wheels, so snow's not necessary. There are also one-hour guided tours of the kennels (adult/child £8/4).

Alvie & Dalraddy Estate　Quad Biking

(☏ 01479-810330; www.alvie-estate.co.uk; Dalraddy Holiday Park; per person £39) Join a cross-country quad-bike trek at this estate, 3 miles south of Aviemore on the B9152 (call first).

 Sleeping

OLD MINISTER'S HOUSE

B&B　££

(☏ 01479-812181; www.theoldministershouse .co.uk; Rothiemurchus; s/d £65/96; P ඹ) This former manse dates from 1906 and has four rooms with a homely, country farmhouse feel. It's in a lovely setting amid Scots pines on the banks of the River Druie, just 0.75 miles southeast of Aviemore.

ARDLOGIE GUEST HOUSE

B&B　£

(☏ 01479-810747; www.ardlogie.co.uk; Dalfaber Rd; s/d from £40/60; P ඹ) Handy for the train station, the five-room Ardlogie has great views over the River Spey towards the Cairngorms, there's a boules pitch in the garden, and guests get free use of the local country club's pool, spa and sauna.

AVIEMORE BUNKHOUSE

Hostel　£

(☏ 01479-811181; www.aviemore-bunkhouse .com; Dalfaber Rd; dm/tw/f £15/50/60; P @ ඹ) This independent hostel, next door to the Old Bridge Inn, provides accommodation in bright, modern six- or eight-bed dorms, each with private bathroom, and one twin/family room. There's a drying room, secure bike storage and wheelchair-accessible dorms. From the train station, cross the pedestrian bridge over the tracks, turn right and walk south on Dalfaber Rd.

RAVENSCRAIG GUEST HOUSE B&B ££
(01479-810278; www.aviemoreonline.com; Grampian Rd; r per person £30-40; P) Ravenscraig is a large, flower-bedecked Victorian villa with six spacious en suite rooms, plus another six in a modern annexe at the back (one wheelchair accessible). It serves traditional and veggie breakfasts in an attractive conservatory dining room.

CAIRNGORM HOTEL Hotel ££
(01479-810233; www.cairngorm.com; Grampian Rd; s/d £55/88; P) Better known as the Cairn, this long-established hotel is set in the fine old granite building opposite the train station. It's a welcoming place with comfortable rooms and a determinedly Scottish atmosphere, all tartan carpets and stags' antlers. There's live music on weekends, so it can get a bit noisy – not for early-to-bedders.

HILTON COYLUMBRIDGE Hotel ££
(01479-810661; www.coylumbridge.hilton.com; Coylumbridge; d from £98; P) This modern, low-rise Hilton, set amid the pine woods just outside Aviemore, is a wonderfully child-friendly hotel, with bedrooms for up to two adults and two children, indoor and outdoor play areas, a crèche and a baby-sitting service.

Kinapol Guest House B&B ££
(01479-810513; www.kinapol.co.uk; Dalfaber Rd; s/d from £30/40; P) The Kinapol is a modern bungalow offering basic but comfortable B&B accommodation, across the tracks from the train station. All three rooms have shared bathrooms.

Aviemore Youth Hostel Hostel £
(SYHA; 01479-810345; 25 Grampian Rd; dm £17; P @) Upmarket hostelling in a spacious, well-equipped building, five minutes' walk from the village centre. There are four- and six-bed rooms, and the doors stay open until 2am.

 Eating & Drinking

OLD BRIDGE INN Pub ££
(www.oldbridgeinn.co.uk; 23 Dalfaber Rd; mains £10-16;) The Old Bridge has a snug bar, complete with roaring log fire in winter, and a cheerful, chalet-style restaurant (food served noon to 3pm and 6pm to 9pm Sunday to Thursday, and to 10pm on Friday and Saturday) at the back serving quality Scottish cuisine.

MOUNTAIN CAFE Cafe £
(www.mountaincafe-aviemore.co.uk; 111 Grampian Rd; mains £4-9; 8.30am-5pm Tue-Thu, to 5.30pm Fri-Mon;) Fresh, healthy breakfasts of muesli, porridge and fresh fruit (till 11.30am), hearty lunches of seafood chowder, salads or burgers, and home-baked breads, cakes and biscuits. Vegan, coeliac and nut-allergic diets catered for.

SKI-ING DOO Bistro ££
(9 Grampian Rd; mains £7-11, steaks £14-16; noon-2.30pm & 5-11pm;) A long-standing Aviemore institution, the child-friendly Ski-ing Doo (it's a pun...oh, ask the waiter!) is a favourite with family skiers and hikers. An informal place offering a range of hearty, homemade burgers, chilli dishes and juicy steaks; the Doo Below cafe bar is open all day from noon.

CAFÉ MAMBO Cafe-Bar £
(The Mall, Grampian Rd; mains £5-10; food noon-8.30pm Mon-Thu, noon-7.30pm Fri & Sat, 12.30-8.30pm Sun;) The Mambo is a popular chill-out cafe in the afternoon, serving burgers, steaks and Tex-Mex grub, and turns into a clubbing and live-band venue in the evenings.

Coffee Corner Tearoom £
(85 Grampian Rd; snacks £3-5; 9am-5pm) This cosy cafe is a good place to relax with newspapers and a steaming mug of coffee on a rainy day. It does good breakfasts, scones and ice-cream sundaes.

Information

There are ATMs outside the Tesco supermarket, and currency exchange at the post office and the tourist office, all located on Grampian Rd.

ⓘ Getting There & Away

BUS Buses stop on Grampian Rd opposite the
train station; buy tickets at the tourist office.
Services include:
Inverness (£9, 45 minutes) Scottish Citylink
Perth (£18, 21/4 hours) Scottish Citylink
Glasgow (£23, 3¾ hours) Scottish Citylink
Edinburgh (£23, 3¾ hours) Scottish Citylink
TRAIN There are direct train services to Glasgow/
Edinburgh (£40, three hours, three daily) and
Inverness (£10, 40 minutes, nine daily).

ⓘ Getting Around

BIKE Several places in Aviemore, Rothiemurchus
Estate and Glenmore have mountain bikes for hire.
Bothy Bikes (www.bothybikes.co.uk; Ski Rd,
Rothiemurchus) Charges £20 a day for a quality
bike with front suspension and disc brakes.
BUS Bus 34 links Aviemore to Cairngorm car park
(20 to 30 minutes, hourly, no Sunday service late
October to late December) via Coylumbridge and

Glenmore. A Strathspey Dayrider/Megarider ticket
(£6/20) gives one/seven days unlimited bus travel
from Aviemore as far as Cairngorm, Carrbridge
and Kingussie (buy from the bus driver).

Around Aviemore

Loch Morlich

Six miles east of Aviemore, Loch Morlich
is surrounded by some 8 sq miles of pine
and spruce forest that make up the **Glenmore Forest Park**. Its attractions include
a sandy beach (at the east end).

⦿ Sights & Activities

The park's visitor centre has a small
exhibition on the Caledonian forest and
sells the *Glen More Forest Park Map*,
detailing local walks. The circuit of Loch
Morlich (one hour) makes a pleasant
outing; the trail is pram- and wheelchair-
friendly.

**LOCH MORLICH WATERSPORTS
CENTRE**   Watersports
(www.lochmorlich.com; Glenmore; ☺9am-5pm
May-Oct) Popular outfit which rents out
Canadian canoes (£18 an hour), kayaks

Horse outside the ruins of Ruthven Barracks

CODY DUNCAN/ALAMY ©

(£8.50), windsurfers (£16.50), sailing dinghies (£20) and rowing boats (£18).

CAIRNGORM REINDEER CENTRE
Wildlife Park

(www.cairngormreindeer.co.uk; Glenmore; adult/child £9.50/5) The warden here will take you on a tour to see and feed Britain's only herd of reindeer, who are very tame and will even eat out of your hand. Walks take place at 11am, plus another at 2.30pm from May to September, and 3.30pm Monday to Friday in July and August.

GLENMORE LODGE   Adventure Sports

(www.glenmorelodge.org.uk; Glenmore;; P) One of Britain's leading adventure-sports training centres, offers courses in hill walking, rock climbing, ice climbing, canoeing, mountain biking and mountaineering. The centre's comfortable **B&B accommodation** (£25 to £33 per person) is available to all, even if you're not taking a course, as is the indoor-climbing wall, gym and sauna.

Kincraig

The **Highland Wildlife Park** (www.highland wildlifepark.org; adult/child £13.50/10; ☺10am-5pm Apr-Oct, to 6pm Jul & Aug, to 4pm Nov-Mar) near Kincraig, 6 miles southwest of Aviemore, features a drive-through safari park and animal enclosures that offer the chance to get close to rarely seen native wildlife, such as wildcat, capercaillie, pine marten, white-tailed sea eagle and red squirrel, as well as species that once roamed the Scottish hills but have long since disappeared, including wolf, lynx, wild boar, beaver and European bison. Visitors without cars get driven around by staff (at no extra cost). Last entry is two hours before closing.

At Kincraig the Spey widens into Loch Insh, home of the **Loch Insh Watersports Centre** (www.lochinsh.com), which offers canoeing, windsurfing, sailing, bike hire and fishing, as well as B&B accommodation from £27 per person. The food here is good, especially after 6.30pm when the loch-side cafe metamorphoses into a cosy restaurant.

Boat of Garten

Boat of Garten is known as the Osprey Village because these rare and beautiful birds of prey nest nearby at the **RSPB Loch Garten Osprey Centre** (www.rspb.org .uk; Tulloch, Nethybridge; adult/child £3/50p; ☺10am-6pm Apr-Aug). The ospreys migrate here each spring from Africa and nest in a tall pine tree – you can watch from a hide as the birds feed their young. The centre is signposted about 2 miles east of the village.

Boat of Garten is 6 miles northeast of Aviemore. The most interesting way to get here is on the Strathspey Steam Railway.

Kingussie & Newtonmore

The gracious old Speyside towns of Kingussie (kin-*yew*-see) and Newtonmore sit at the foot of the great heather-clad humps known as the Monadhliath Mountains. The towns are best known as the home of the excellent Highland Folk Museum.

◉ Sights & Activities

FREE **HIGHLAND FOLK MUSEUM**
Open-Air Museum

(www.highlandfolk.museum; Kingussie Rd, Newtonmore; ☺10.30am-5.30pm Apr-Aug, 11am-4.30pm Sep & Oct) The open-air Highland Folk Museum comprises a collection of historical buildings and relics revealing many aspects of Highland culture and lifestyle. The museum is laid out like a farming township and has a community of traditional thatch-roofed cottages, a sawmill, a schoolhouse, a shepherd's bothy and a rural post office. Actors in period costume give demonstrations of woodcarving, spinning and peat-fire baking. You'll need two to three hours to make the most of a visit here.

RUTHVEN BARRACKS   Historic Building

(admission free; ☺24hr) Perched dramatically on a river terrace and clearly visible from the main A9 road near Kingussie, the roofless Ruthven Barracks was one of four garrisons built by the British government after the first Jacobite rebellion of 1715 as part of a Hanoverian scheme to take control of the Highlands. Ironically, the barracks were last occupied by Jacobite troops awaiting the return of Bonnie Prince Charlie after the Battle of Culloden. Learning of his defeat and subsequent flight, they destroyed the barracks before taking to the glens. The ruins are spectacularly floodlit at night.

WEST HIGHLANDS

This area extends from the bleak blanket-bog of the Moor of Rannoch to the west coast beyond the valley of Glen Coe and Fort William, and includes the southern reaches of the Great Glen. The scenery is grand throughout, with high and wild mountains dominating the glens. Great expanses of moor alternate with lochs and patches of commercial forest. Fort William, at the inner end of Loch Linnhe, is the only sizable town in the area.

Since 2007 the region has been promoted as **Lochaber Geopark** (www .lochabergeopark.org.uk), an area of outstanding geology and scenery.

Glen Coe

Scotland's most famous glen is also one of the grandest and, in bad weather, the grimmest. The approach to the glen from the east, watched over by the rocky pyramid of **Buachaille Etive Mor** – the Great Shepherd of Etive – leads over the Pass of Glencoe and into the narrow upper valley. The southern side is dominated by three massive, brooding spurs, known as the **Three Sisters**, while the northern side is enclosed by the continuous steep wall of the knife-edged Aonach Eagach ridge. The main road threads its lonely way through the middle of all this mountain grandeur, past deep gorges and crashing waterfalls, to the more pastoral lower reaches of the glen around Loch Achtriochtan and Glencoe village.

Glen Coe was written into the history books in 1692 when the resident MacDonalds were murdered by Campbell soldiers in what became known as the Glencoe Massacre (see the boxed text, p293).

 Activities

There are several short, pleasant walks around **Glencoe Lochan**, near the village. To get there, turn left off the minor road to the youth hostel, just beyond the bridge over the River Coe. There are three walks (40 minutes to an hour), all detailed on a signboard at the car park. The artificial lochan was created by Lord Strathcona in 1895 for his homesick Canadian wife Isabella

Sunset over Glencoe Lochan
PHOTOGRAPHER: GARETH MCCORMACK

Mountain Walks in the Cairngorms

The climb from the car park at the Coire Cas ski area to the summit of **Cairn Gorm** (1245m) takes about two hours (one way). From there, you can continue south across the high-level plateau to **Ben Macdui** (1309m), Britain's second-highest peak. This takes eight to 10 hours return from the car park and is a serious undertaking; for experienced and well-equipped walkers only.

The **Lairig Ghru trail**, which can take eight to 10 hours, is a demanding 24-mile walk from Aviemore through the Lairig Ghru pass (840m) to Braemar. An alternative to doing the full route is to make the six-hour return hike up to the summit of the pass and back to Aviemore. The path starts from Ski Rd, a mile east of Coylumbridge, and involves some very rough going.

Warning – the Cairngorm plateau is a sub-Arctic environment where navigation is difficult and weather conditions can be severe, even in midsummer. Hikers must have proper hill-walking equipment, and know how to use a map and compass. In winter it is a place for experienced mountaineers only.

and is surrounded by a North American-style forest.

A more strenuous hike, but well worth the effort on a fine day, is the climb to the **Lost Valley**, a magical mountain sanctuary still haunted by the ghosts of the murdered MacDonalds (only 2.5 miles round trip, but allow three hours). A rough path from the car park at Allt na Reigh (on the A82, 6 miles east of Glencoe village) bears left down to a footbridge over the river, then climbs up the wooded valley between Beinn Fhada and Gearr Aonach (the first and second of the Three Sisters). The route leads steeply up through a maze of giant, jumbled, moss-coated boulders before emerging – quite unexpectedly – into a broad, open valley with an 800m-long meadow as flat as a football pitch. Back in the days of clan warfare, the valley – invisible from below – was used for hiding stolen cattle; its Gaelic name, Coire Gabhail, means 'corrie of capture'.

The summits of Glen Coe's mountains are for experienced mountaineers only. Details of hill-walking routes can be found in the Scottish Mountaineering Club's guidebook *Central Highlands* by Peter Hodgkiss.

ⓘ Getting There & Away

Scottish Citylink buses run between Fort William and Glencoe (£7, 30 minutes, eight daily) and from Glencoe to Glasgow (£19, 2½ hours, eight daily). Buses stop at Glencoe village, Glencoe Visitor Centre, and Glencoe Mountain Resort.

Stagecoach bus 44 links Glencoe village with Fort William (35 minutes, hourly Monday to Saturday, three on Sunday) and Kinlochleven (25 minutes).

East of the Glen

A few miles east of Glencoe proper, on the south side of the A82, is the car park and base station for the **Glencoe Mountain Resort** (www.glencoemountain.com), where commercial skiing in Scotland first began back in 1956. The Lodge Café-Bar has comfy sofas where you can soak up the view through the floor-to-ceiling windows.

The **chairlift** (adult/child £10/5; ⊘9.30am-4.30pm Thu-Mon May-Sep) continues to operate in summer – there's a grand view over the Moor of Rannoch from the top station – and provides access to a downhill mountain-biking track. In winter a lift pass costs £30 a day and equipment hire is £25 a day.

The remote **Kings House Hotel** (☎ 01855-851259; www.kingy.com; Glencoe; s/d £30/65; ⓟ) claims to be one of Scotland's

oldest licensed inns, dating from the 17th century. It lies on the old military road from Stirling to Fort William (now followed by the West Highland Way), and after the Battle of Culloden it was used as a Hanoverian garrison – hence the name. The hotel serves good pub grub (mains £8 to £12) and has long been a meeting place for climbers, skiers and hill walkers – the rustic **Climbers Bar** (⏰11am-11pm) is round the back.

Glencoe Village
POP 360

The little village of Glencoe stands on the south shore of Loch Leven at the western end of the glen, 16 miles south of Fort William.

◉ Sights & Activities

GLENCOE FOLK MUSEUM   Museum
(Glencoe; adult/child £2/free; ⏰10am-5.30pm Mon-Sat Apr-Oct) The small, thatched museum houses a varied collection of military memorabilia, farm equipment, and tools of the woodworking, blacksmithing and slate-quarrying trades.

GLENCOE VISITOR CENTRE
Visitor Centre
(NTS; ☎ 01855-811307; www.glencoe-nts.org.uk; Inverigan; adult/child £5.50/4.50; ⏰9.30am-5.30pm Apr-Aug, 10am-5pm Sep & Oct, 10am-4pm Thu-Sun Nov-Mar) About 1.5 miles east of the village, towards the glen, is this modern facility with an ecotourism angle. The centre provides comprehensive information on the geological, environmental and cultural history of Glencoe via high-tech interactive and audiovisual displays, and tells the story of the Glencoe Massacre in all its gory detail.

LOCHABER WATERSPORTS
Watersports
(www.lochaberwatersports.co.uk; West Laroch; ⏰9.30am-5pm Apr-Oct) You can hire kayaks (£12 an hour), rowing boats (£15), sailing dinghies (£12), and even a 10m sailing yacht complete with skipper (£150 for three hours, up to five people) here.

Left: Boats in the Caledonian Canal, Fort William;
Below: Celtic cross in churchyard, Fort William

PHOTOGRAPHER: (LEFT) D.G.FARQUHAR/ALAMY; (BELOW) ROCCO FASANO

Fort William

POP 9910

Basking on the shores of Loch Linnhe amid magnificent mountain scenery, Fort William has one of the most enviable settings in the whole of Scotland. If it wasn't for the busy dual carriageway crammed between the town centre and the loch, and one of the highest rainfall records in the country, it would be almost idyllic. Even so, the Fort has carved out a reputation as 'Outdoor Capital of the UK' (www.outdoorcapital.co.uk), and its easy access by rail and bus makes it a good place to base yourself for exploring the surrounding mountains and glens.

Magical Glen Nevis begins near the northern end of the town and wraps itself around the southern flanks of **Ben Nevis** (1344m) – Britain's highest mountain and a magnet for hikers and climbers. The glen is also popular with movie makers – parts of *Braveheart, Rob Roy* and the Harry Potter movies were filmed there.

History

There is little left of the original fort from which the town derives its name – it was pulled down in the 19th century to make way for the railway. The first castle here was constructed by General Monk in 1654 and called Inverlochy, but the meagre ruins by the loch are those of the fort built in the 1690s by General Mackay and named after King William II/III. In the 18th century it became part of a chain of garrisons (along with Fort Augustus and Fort George) that controlled the Great Glen in the wake of the Jacobite rebellions.

Originally a tiny fishing village called Gordonsburgh, the town took its present name with the opening of the railway in 1901, which, along with the building of the Caledonian Canal, helped it grow into a tourist centre. This has been consolidated in the last

291

JOHN PETER PHOTOGRAPHY/ALAMY

Don't Miss **Cairngorm Mountain Railway**

Aviemore's most popular attraction is the Cairngorm Mountain Railway, a funicular train that will whisk you to the edge of Cairngorm plateau (1085m) in just eight minutes. The bottom station is at the Coire Cas car park at the end of Ski Rd; at the top is an exhibition, a shop (of course) and a restaurant. Unfortunately, for environmental and safety reasons, you're not allowed out of the top station in summer, not even to walk down – you must return to the car park on the funicular. However, a trial project launched in 2010 offers 90-minute guided walks to the summit (adult/child £13/10) four times a day from mid-July to October. Check the website for details.

THINGS YOU NEED TO KNOW

☎ 01479-861261; www.cairngormmountain.co.uk; adult/child return £9.75/6.15; ⏰ 10am-5pm May-Nov, 9am-4.30pm Dec-Apr

three decades by the huge increase in popularity of climbing, skiing, mountain biking and other outdoor sports.

 Sights

WEST HIGHLAND MUSEUM   Museum
(www.westhighlandmuseum.org.uk; Cameron Sq; adult/child £4/1; ⏰ 10am-5pm Mon-Sat Jun-Sep, plus 2-5pm Sun Jul & Aug, 10am-4pm Mon-Sat Oct-May) The small but fascinating West Highland Museum is packed with all

manner of Highland memorabilia. Look out for the secret portrait of Bonnie Prince Charlie – after the Jacobite rebellions all things Highland were banned, including pictures of the exiled leader, and this tiny painting looks like nothing more than a smear of paint until viewed in a cylindrical mirror, which reflects a credible likeness of the prince.

Ben Nevis Distillery   Distillery
(www.bennevisdistillery.com; Lochy Bridge; ⏰ 9am-5pm Mon-Fri year-round, plus 10am-4pm Sat Easter-Sep & noon-4pm Sun Jul & Aug) A tour

of the distillery makes for a warming rainy-day alternative to exploring the hills; the guided tour costs £4/2 per adult/child.

Events

UCI MOUNTAIN BIKE WORLD CUP
Mountain Biking
(www.fortwilliamworldcup.co.uk) In June, Fort William pulls in crowds of more than 18,000 spectators for this World Cup downhill mountain-biking event. The gruelling downhill course is at nearby Nevis Range ski area.

Tours

Al's Tours
Taxi
(01397-700700; www.alstours.com) Taxi tours with driver-guide around Lochaber and Glencoe cost £80/195 for a half/full day.

Crannog Cruises
Boat
(01397-700714; www.crannog.net/cruises; Town Pier) Operates 1½-hour wildlife cruises (adult/child £10/5, four daily) on Loch Linnhe, visiting a seal colony and a salmon farm.

Sleeping

It's best to book well ahead in summer, especially for hostels. You can also book a room in Glen Nevis (see p298).

LIME TREE
Hotel **££**
(01397-701806; www.limetreefortwilliam .co.uk; Achintore Rd; s/d from £70/100; P) Much more interesting than your average guesthouse, this former Victorian manse overlooking Loch Linnhe is an 'art gallery with rooms', decorated throughout with the artist-owner's atmospheric Highland landscapes. Foodies rave about the restaurant (see p295) and the gallery space – a triumph of sensitive design – stages everything from serious exhibitions (David Hockney in summer 2010) to folk concerts.

DISCOVER INVERNESS & THE HIGHLANDS **FORT WILLIAM**

The Glencoe Massacre

Glen Coe is sometimes said to mean 'the glen of weeping', a romantic mistranslation that stems from the brutal murders that took place here in 1692.

Following the Glorious Revolution of 1688, supporters of the exiled Roman Catholic King James – known as Jacobites – rose up against the Protestant King William. William offered the Highland clans (most of them Catholic and Jacobite) an amnesty on condition that all clan chiefs take an oath of loyalty to him before 1 January 1692.

MacIain, the elderly chief of the MacDonalds of Glencoe, was three days late in taking the oath, and William's government decided to use that fact to punish the troublesome MacDonalds and set an example to other Highland clans.

A company of 120 soldiers, mainly from Campbell territory, were sent to the glen under cover of collecting taxes. It was traditional for clans to provide hospitality to travellers and so the troops were billeted in MacDonald homes.

After 12 days, the government order came for the soldiers to 'fall upon the rebels the MacDonalds of Glencoe and put all to the sword under 70'. The soldiers turned on their hosts at 5am on 13 February, killing MacIain and 37 other men, women and children. Some of the soldiers alerted the MacDonalds to their intended fate, allowing them to escape; many fled into the snow-covered hills, where another 40 people died of exposure. A monument in Glencoe village commemorates the massacre.

The Ben Nevis Distillery (p292)

JOHN MCKENNA/ALAMY

GRANGE
B&B ££

(☑ 01397-705516; www.grangefortwilliam
.com; Grange Rd; r per person £56-59; P) An
exceptional 19th-century villa set in its
own landscaped grounds, the Grange is
crammed with antiques and fitted with
log fires, chaise longues and Victorian
roll-top baths. The Turret Room, with its
window seat in the turret overlooking
Loch Linnhe, is our favourite. It's 500m
southwest of the town centre.

CROLINNHE
B&B ££

(☑ 01397-702709; www.crolinnhe.co.uk; Grange
Rd; r per person £56-64; P) If you can't get
into the Grange try the neighbouring
Crolinnhe, another grand 19th-century
villa, with loch-side location, beautiful
gardens and sumptuous accommodation. A vegetarian breakfast is provided
on request.

CALLUNA
Apartment £

(☑ 01397-700451; www.fortwilliamholiday.co.uk;
Heathercroft, Connochie Rd; dm/tw £15/34;
P) Run by well-known mountain
guide Alan Kimber and wife, Sue, the
Calluna offers self-catering apartments
geared to groups of hikers and climbers,
but also takes individual travellers prepared to share; there's a fully equipped
kitchen and an excellent drying room for
your soggy hiking gear.

ST ANDREW'S GUEST HOUSE
B&B ££

(☑ 01397-703038; www.standrewsguesthouse
.co.uk; Fassifern Rd; r per person £22-28; P ☎)
Set in a lovely 19th-century building that
was once a rectory and choir school, St
Andrew's retains period features, such
as carved masonry, wood panelling and
stained-glass windows. It has six spacious
bedrooms, some with stunning views.

GLENLOCHY GUEST HOUSE
B&B ££

(☑ 01397-702909; www.glenlochyguesthouse
.co.uk; Nevisbridge; r per person £35-38; P)
Convenient for Glen Nevis, Ben Nevis and
the end of the West Highland Way, the
Glenlochy is a sprawling modern place,
with 12 en-suite rooms set in a huge
garden beside the River Nevis; a pleasant
place to sit on summer evenings.

Fort William Backpackers
Hostel £

(☑ 01397-700711; www.scotlands-top
-hostels.com; Alma Rd; dm/tw from £14/38;
@) A 10-minute walk from the bus and train
stations, this lively and welcoming hostel is set
in a grand Victorian villa, perched on a hillside
with great views over Loch Linnhe.

Fort William

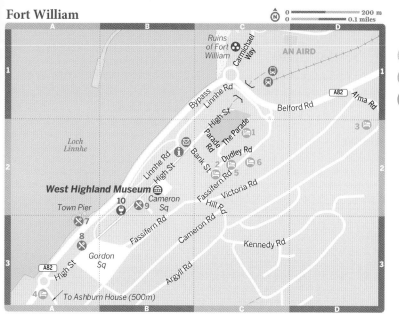

Fort William

Bank Street Lodge   Hostel £

(📞01397-700070; www.bankstreetlodge
.co.uk; Bank St; dm/tw £14.50/48) Part of a
modern hotel and restaurant complex, the Bank
Street Lodge offers the most central budget
beds in town, only 250m from the train station.
It has kitchen facilities and a drying room.

No 6 Caberfeidh   B&B ££

(📞01397-703756; www.6caberfeidh.com; 6
Caberfeidh, Fassifern Rd; r per person £22-35;
🛜) Friendly B&B; vegetarian breakfast on
request.

Ashburn House   B&B ££

(📞01397-706000; www.highland5star.co.uk;
Achintore Rd; r per person £45-55; P🛜) Grand
Victorian villa south of the centre; children
under 12 not welcome.

Alexandra Hotel   Hotel ££

(📞01397-702241; www.strathmorehotels.com;
The Parade; s/d from £69/109; P🛜) Large,
traditional, family-oriented hotel bang in the
middle of town.

 Eating & Drinking

LIME TREE   Modern Scottish £££

(📞 01397-701806; www.limetreefortwilliam
.co.uk; Achintore Rd; mains £19-25; ⏱dinner daily,
noon-3pm Sun) Fort William is not over-
endowed with great places to eat, but the
restaurant at this small hotel-cum-art
gallery (see p293) has certainly put the
UK's Outdoor Capital on the gastronomic

If You Like...
Scenic Glens

If it's Scotland's moody lochs and epic beauty that steals your heart, you may want to set some time aside to explore these scenic glens.

1 GLEN ETIVE
At the eastern end of Glen Coe a minor road leads south along this peaceful and beautiful glen. On a hot summer's day the River Etive contains many tempting pools for swimming, and there are lots of good picnic sites.

2 GLEN ROY
Near Spean Bridge, 10 miles north of Fort William, this glen is noted for its intriguing, so-called 'parallel roads'. These prominent horizontal terraces are actually ancient shorelines formed during the last ice age by the waters of an ice-dammed glacial lake.

3 GLEN FESHIE
Tranquil Glen Feshie extends south from Kincraig, deep into the Cairngorms, with Scots pine woods in its upper reaches surrounded by big, heathery hills. The 4WD track to the head of the glen makes a great mountain-bike excursion (25 miles round trip).

4 GLEN LYON
This remote and stunningly beautiful glen runs for some 34 unforgettable miles of rickety stone bridges, Caledonian pine forest and sheer, heather-splashed peaks poking through swirling clouds. It's reached from the A9 via Aberfeldy.

map. The chef won a Michelin star in his previous restaurant, and turns out technically accomplished dishes such as beer-braised beef with shallot mousse, and slow-roast pork belly with truffled honey. The two-course Sunday lunch costs £13.

CRANNOG SEAFOOD RESTAURANT
Seafood ££
(☎ 01397-705589; www.crannog.net; Town Pier; mains £14-20; ⏰lunch & dinner) The Crannog easily wins the prize for the best location in town – it's perched on the Town Pier,

giving window-table diners an uninterrupted view down Loch Linnhe. Informal and unfussy, it specialises in fresh local seafood – there are three or four daily fish specials plus the main menu – though there are beef, poultry and vegetarian dishes too. Two-course lunch £10.

GROG & GRUEL
Pub ££
(www.grogandgruel.co.uk; 66 High St; mains £9-12; ⏰bar meals noon-9pm) The Grog & Gruel is a traditional-style, wood-panelled pub with an excellent range of cask ales from regional Scottish and English microbreweries. Upstairs is a lively Tex-Mex **restaurant** (⏰5-9pm), with a crowd-pleasing menu of tasty enchiladas, burritos, fajitas, burgers, steaks and pizza.

FIRED ART CAFE
Cafe £
(www.fired-art.co.uk; mains £3-4; ⏰10am-5pm Mon-Sat; 📶 👶) Enjoy what is probably the best coffee in town at this colourful cafe, or go for a hot chocolate, milkshake or smoothie; the kids can be kept busy painting their own coffee mugs in the pottery studio at the back.

BEN NEVIS BAR
Pub
(105 High St) The Ben Nevis, whose lounge bar enjoys a good view over the loch, exudes a relaxed, jovial atmosphere where climbers and tourists can work off leftover energy jigging to live music (Thursday and Friday nights).

ℹ Information

Belford Hospital (☎ 01397-702481; Belford Rd) Opposite the train station.

Post office (☎ 0845 722 3344; 5 High St)

Tourist office (☎ 01397-703781; www.visithighlands.com; 15 High St; ⏰9am-6pm Mon-Sat, 10am-5pm Sun Apr-Sep, limited hours Oct-Mar) Internet access (£1 per 20 minutes).

ℹ Getting There & Away

Bus
Scottish Citylink buses link Fort William with Glasgow (£21, three hours, eight daily) and

Edinburgh (£30, 4½ hours, one daily direct, seven with a change at Glasgow) via Glencoe and Crianlarich, as well as Oban (£9, 1½ hours, three daily), Inverness (£11, two hours, five daily) and Portree (£28, three hours, four daily) on Skye.

Shiel Buses service 500 runs to Mallaig (1½ hours, three daily Monday to Friday only) via Glenfinnan (30 minutes) and Arisaig (one hour).

Car

Fort William is 146 miles from Edinburgh, 104 miles from Glasgow and 66 miles from Inverness. The tourist office has a leaflet listing car-hire companies.

Easydrive Car Hire (☎ 01397-701616; www .easydrivescotland.co.uk; Unit 36a, Ben Nevis Industrial Estate, Ben Nevis Dr) Rents small cars from £32/185 a day/week, including tax and unlimited mileage, but not CDW.

Train

The spectacular West Highland line runs from Glasgow to Mallaig via Fort William. There are three trains daily (two on Sunday) from Glasgow to Fort William (£24, 3¾ hours), and four daily (three on Sunday) between Fort William and Mallaig (£10, 1½ hours). Travelling from Edinburgh (£40, five hours), you have to change at Glasgow's Queen St station.

There's no direct rail connection between Oban and Fort William – you have to change at Crianlarich, so it's faster to use the bus.

ℹ Getting Around

Bike

Off-Beat Bikes (☎ 01436-704008; www .offbeatbikes.co.uk; 117 High St; ☻9am-5.30pm) Rents mountain bikes for £17/12 a day/half-day.

Bus

The Fort Dayrider ticket (£2.60) gives unlimited travel for one day on Stagecoach bus services in the Fort William area. Buy from the bus driver.

Taxi

There's a taxi rank on the corner of High St and The Parade.

Around Fort William

Glen Nevis

You can walk the 3 miles from Fort William to scenic Glen Nevis in about an hour or so. The **Glen Nevis Visitor Centre**

Waterfall in Steall Meadows (p298), Glen Nevis.

(☎ 01397-705922; www.bennevisweather.co.uk; ⏰9am-5pm Apr-Oct) is situated 1.5 miles up the glen, and provides information on walking as well as specific advice on climbing Ben Nevis.

From the car park at the far end of the road along Glen Nevis, there is an excellent 1.5-mile walk through the spectacular Nevis Gorge to **Steall Meadows**, a verdant valley dominated by a 100m-high bridal-veil waterfall. You can reach the foot of the falls by crossing the river on a wobbly, three-cable wire bridge – one cable for your feet and one for each hand – a real test of balance!

 ## Sleeping & Eating

BEN NEVIS INN　　　　　Hostel　£
(☎ 01397-701227; www.ben-nevis-inn.co.uk; Achintee; dm £14; P @) A good alternative to the youth hostel is this great barn of a pub (real ale and tasty bar meals available; mains £9 to £12), with a comfy 24-bed hostel downstairs. It's at the Achintee start of the path up Ben Nevis,

and only a mile from the end of the West Highland Way. Food served noon to 9pm; closed Monday to Wednesday in winter.

ACHINTEE FARM　　　　Hostel/B&B　£
(☎ 01397-702240; www.achinteefarm.com; Achintee; dm £15, tw £34) This attractive farmhouse offers excellent B&B accommodation and also has a small bunkhouse attached. It's just 100m from the Ben Nevis Inn, and ideally positioned for climbing Ben Nevis.

Glen Nevis Youth Hostel　　　Hostel　£
(SYHA; ☎ 01397-702336; www.glennevishostel .co.uk; Glen Nevis; dm £19; @ 🛜) Large, impersonal and reminiscent of a school camp, this hostel is 3 miles from Fort William, right beside one of the starting points for the tourist track up Ben Nevis.

🛈 Getting There & Away

Bus 41 runs from Fort William bus station up Glen Nevis to the youth hostel (10 minutes, five daily Monday to Saturday, three on Sunday, limited service October to April) and on to the Lower Falls 3 miles beyond the hostel (20 minutes). Check at the tourist office for the latest timetable, which is liable to alteration.

Ardgour & Ardnamurchan

The drive from Corran Ferry, 8 miles south of Fort William, to **Ardnamurchan Point** (www .ardnamurchan.com), the most westerly point on the British mainland, is one of the most beautiful in the western Highlands, especially in late spring and early summer when much of the narrow, twisting road is lined with the bright pink and purple blooms of rhododendrons. A **car ferry** (car £6.20, passenger free, 10 minutes, two

Lighthouse at Ardnamurchan Point
PHOTOGRAPHER: JOHN PETER PHOTOGRAPHY/ALAMY

CREDIT

Don't Miss **Jacobite Steam Train**

From late May to early October, the Jacobite Steam Train makes the scenic two-hour run from Fort William to Mallaig, departing from Fort William train station at 10.20am Monday to Friday (plus weekends in July and August), returning from Mallaig at 2.10pm (adult/child £31/17.50 day return). There's a brief stop at Glenfinnan station, and you get 1½ hours in Mallaig. Classed as one of the great railway journeys of the world, the route crosses the historic **Glenfinnan Viaduct**, made famous in the Harry Potter films – the train's owners supplied the steam locomotive and rolling stock used in the film.

THINGS YOU NEED TO KNOW

📞 01463-239026; www.steamtrain.info

an hour) crosses from the Fort William–Glencoe road to Ardgour at Corran Ferry.

The road clings to the northern shore of Loch Sunart, going through the pretty villages of **Strontian** – which gave its name to the element strontium, first discovered in ore from nearby lead mines in 1790 – and **Salen**.

The mostly single-track road from Salen to Ardnamurchan Point is only 25 miles long, but it'll take you 1½ hours each way. It's a dipping, twisting, low-speed rollercoaster of a ride through sun-dappled native woodlands draped with lichen and fern. Just when you're

getting used to the views of Morvern and Mull to the south, it makes a quick detour to the north for a panorama over the islands of Rum and Eigg.

 Sights

KILCHOAN   Village

The scattered crofting (smallhold farming) village of Kilchoan, the only village of any size west of Salen, is best known for the scenic ruins of 13th-century **Mingary Castle**. The village has a **tourist office** (📞 01972-510222; Pier Rd; ⏰ Easter-Oct), a

Climbing Ben Nevis

As the highest peak in the British Isles, Ben Nevis (1344m) attracts many would-be ascensionists who wouldn't normally think of climbing a Scottish mountain – a staggering 100,000 people reach the summit each year.

Although anyone who is reasonably fit should have no problem climbing Ben Nevis on a fine summer's day, an ascent should not be undertaken lightly; every year people have to be rescued from the mountain. You will need proper walking boots (the path is rough and stony, and there may be soft, wet snowfields on the summit), warm clothing, waterproofs, a map and compass, and plenty of food and water. And don't forget to check the weather forecast (see www.bennevisweather.co.uk).

The tourist track (the easiest route to the top) was originally called the Pony Track. It was built in the 19th century for the pack ponies that carried supplies to a meteorological observatory on the summit (now in ruins), which was manned continuously from 1883 to 1904.

The path climbs gradually to the shoulder at the Halfway Lochan, then zigzags steeply up beside the Red Burn to the summit plateau. The highest point is marked by a trig point on top of a huge cairn beside the ruins of the old observatory.

The total distance to the summit and back is 8 miles; allow at least four or five hours to reach the top, and another 2½ to three hours for the descent.

---

shop and a hotel, and there's a ferry to Tobermory on the Isle of Mull.

ARDNAMURCHAN NATURAL HISTORY CENTRE Wildlife Centre
(www.ardnamurchannaturalhistorycentre.co.uk; Glenmore; adult/child £4/2; ⊙10.30am-5.30pm Mon-Sat, noon-5.30pm Sun Easter-Oct) Midway between Salen and Kilchoan is this fascinating centre, devised by local photographer Michael MacGregor, that tries to bring you face to face with the flora and fauna of the Ardnamurchan peninsula. The Living Building exhibit is designed to attract local wildlife, with a mammal den that is occasionally occupied by hedgehogs or pine martens, an owl nest-box, a mouse nest and a pond. If the beasties are not in residence, you can watch recorded video footage of the animals. There's also live CCTV coverage of a golden eagle feeding site.

ARDNAMURCHAN LIGHTHOUSE
Historic Lighthouse
(www.nlb.org.uk; adult/child £3/1.70; ⊙10am-5pm Apr-Oct) The final 6 miles of road from Kilchoan ends at the 36m-high, grey granite tower of Ardnamurchan Lighthouse, built in 1849 by the Stevensons to guard the westernmost point of the British mainland. There's a good **tearoom**, and the **visitor centre** will tell you more than you'll ever need to know about lighthouses, with lots of hands-on stuff for kids; the **guided tour** (£6) includes a trip to the top of the lighthouse. But the main attraction here is the expansive view over the ocean – this is a superb sunset viewpoint, provided you don't mind driving back in the dark.

Road to the Isles

The 46-mile A830 from Fort William to Mallaig is traditionally known as the Road to the Isles, as it leads to the jumping-off point for ferries to the Small Isles and Skye, itself a stepping stone to the Outer Hebrides. This is a region steeped in Jacobite history, having witnessed both the beginning and the end of Bonnie Prince Charlie's doomed attempt to regain the British throne.

The final section of this scenic route, between Arisaig and Mallaig, has recently been upgraded to a fast straight road. Unless you're in a hurry, opt for the old coastal road (signposted 'Alternative Coastal Route').

Between the A830 and the A87 far to the north lies Scotland's 'Empty Quarter', a rugged landscape of wild mountains and lonely sea lochs roughly 20 miles by 30 miles in size, mostly uninhabited and penetrated only by two minor roads (along Lochs Arkaig and Quoich). If you want to get away from it all, this is the place to go.

ⓘ Getting Around

BUS Shiel Buses bus 500 runs to Mallaig (1½ hours, three daily Monday to Friday only) via Glenfinnan (30 minutes) and Arisaig (one hour).

TRAIN The Fort William–Mallaig railway line has four trains a day (three on Sunday), with stops at many points along the way, including Corpach, Glenfinnan, Lochailort, Arisaig and Morar.

Glenfinnan

POP 100

Glenfinnan is hallowed ground for fans of Bonnie Prince Charlie; its monument to him is its central shrine.

◎ Sights & Activities

GLENFINNAN MONUMENT Monument
This tall column, topped by a statue of a kilted Highlander, was erected in 1815 on the spot where the Young Pretender first raised his standard and rallied the clans on 19 August 1745, marking the start of the ill-fated campaign that would end in disaster 14 months later. The setting, at the north end of Loch Shiel, is hauntingly beautiful.

GLENFINNAN VISITOR CENTRE
Visitor Centre
(NTS; adult/child £3/2; ⊗9.30am-5.30pm Jul & Aug, 10am-5pm Easter-Jun, Sep & Oct) The story of the '45, as the Jacobite rebellion of 1745 is known – when the prince's loyal clansmen marched and fought

Glenfinnan Monument, Loch Shiel

DAVID TOMLINSON

If You Like…
Outdoor Activities

If climbing Ben Nevis has given you a taste for the great outdoors, here's a selection of activities that may whet your appetite.

1 WALKING
The final leg of the **West Highland Way** long-distance footpath from Kinlochleven to Fort William makes a satisfying one-day hike – 16 miles in total, including views of the Glen Coe hills and a final stretch through lovely Glen Nevis.

2 MOUNTAIN BIKING
Laggan Wolftrax (www.basecampmtb.com; Strathmashie Forest, Laggan; admission free; ⊙10am-6pm Mon, 9.30am-5pm Tue, Thu & Fri, 9.30am-6pm Sat & Sun), one of Scotland's top mountain-biking centres, offers daily cycle hire from £25 for a hardtail mountain bike to £40 for a full-suspension downhill rig.

3 ICE CLIMBING
If you fancy trying your hand at ice climbing, even in the middle of summer, **Ice Factor** (www.ice-factor.co.uk; Leven Rd, Kinlochleven; ⊙9am-10pm Tue & Thu, to 7pm Mon, Wed & Fri) has the world's biggest indoor ice-climbing wall; a one-hour beginner's 'taster' session costs £30.

4 SEA KAYAKING
Rockhopper Sea Kayaking (www.rockhopperscotland.co.uk; 2 Montrose Mansions, Corpach, Fort William) can take you on a guided full-/half-day sea-kayaking tour (£70/40) along the wild and beautiful West Highland coastline.

from Glenfinnan south to Derby, then back north to final defeat at Culloden – is recounted here.

GLENFINNAN STATION MUSEUM   Museum
(www.glenfinnanstationmuseum.co.uk; adult/child £1/50p; ⊙9am-5pm Jun–mid-Oct) A half-mile west of the visitor centre, this museum is a shrine of a different kind whose object of veneration is the great days of steam on the West Highland line. The famous 21-arch **Glenfinnan Viaduct**,

just east of the station, was built in 1901, and featured in the movie *Harry Potter & the Chamber of Secrets*. A pleasant walk of around 0.75 miles leads to a viewpoint for the viaduct and the loch.

LOCH SHIEL CRUISES   Boat Trip
(07801 537617; www.highlandcruises.co.uk; ⊙Apr-Sep) Offers boat trips along Loch Shiel, departing from a jetty near Glenfinnan House Hotel. There are one- to 2½-hour cruises (£8 to £16 per person) daily except Saturday and Wednesday. On Wednesday the boat goes the full length of the loch to **Acharacle** (£15/22 one way/return), calling at Polloch and Dalilea, allowing for a range of walks and bike rides using the forestry track on the eastern shore.

Arisaig & Morar

The 5 miles of coast between Arisaig and Morar is a fretwork of rocky islets, inlets and gorgeous silver-sand beaches backed by dunes and machair, with stunning sunset views across the sea to the silhouetted peaks of Eigg and Rum. The **Silver Sands of Morar**, as they are known, draw crowds of bucket-and-spade holidaymakers in July and August, when the many camping grounds scattered along the coast are filled to overflowing.

⊙ Sights

CAMUSDARACH BEACH   Beach
Fans of the movie *Local Hero* still make pilgrimages to Camusdarach Beach, just south of Morar, which starred in the film as Ben's beach. To find it, look for the car park 800m north of Camusdarach campsite; from here, a wooden footbridge and a 400m walk through the dunes lead to the beach. (The village that featured in the film is on the other side of the country, at Pennan.)

LAND, SEA & ISLANDS VISITOR CENTRE
Visitor Centre

(www.arisaigcentre.co.uk; Arisaig; adult/child £2/free; ⏰10am-4pm Mon-Fri, 1-4pm Sun)This centre in Arisaig village houses a small but fascinating exhibition on the part played by the local area as a base for training spies for the SOE (Special Operations Executive, forerunner of MI6) during WWII.

LOCH NAN UAMH
Historic Site

The waters of Loch nan Uamh (loch nan oo-ah; 'the loch of the caves') lap at the southern shores of Arisaig; this was where Bonnie Prince Charlie first set foot on the Scottish mainland on 11 August 1745, on the shingle beach at the mouth of the Borrodale burn. Just 2 miles to the east of this bay, on a rocky point near a parking area, the **Prince's Cairn** marks the spot where he finally departed Scottish soil, never to return, on 19 September 1746.

 Sleeping & Eating

There are at least a half-dozen **camping grounds** between Arisaig and Morar; all are open in summer only, and are often full in July and August, so book ahead. Some are listed on www.road-to-the-isles.org.uk.

GARRAMORE HOUSE
B&B ££

(☎ 01687-450268; South Morar; r per person £25-35; P👪) Built as a hunting lodge in 1840, this house served as a Special Operations Executive HQ during WWII. Today it's a wonderfully atmospheric, child- and pet-friendly guesthouse set in lovely woodland gardens with great views to the Small Isles and Skye.

OLD LIBRARY LODGE & RESTAURANT
Restaurant ££

(☎ 01687-450651; www.oldlibrary.co.uk; Arisaig; mains £10-15; ⏰food served noon-2.30pm & 6.30-9.30pm) The Old Library is a charming restaurant with rooms (B&B per person £45 to £55) set in converted 200-year-old stables overlooking the waterfront in Arisaig village. The lunch menu concentrates on soups and freshly made sandwiches, while dinner is a more sophisticated affair offering local seafood, game and lamb.

View from the Jacobite Steam Train (p299)

SANDY YOUNG/ALAMY

Mallaig

POP 800

If you're travelling between Fort William and Skye, you may find yourself overnighting in the bustling fishing and ferry port of Mallaig. Indeed, it makes a good base for a series of day trips by ferry to the Small Isles and Knoydart.

 Sights

MALLAIG HERITAGE CENTRE

Heritage Centre

(www.mallaigheritage.org.uk; Station Rd; adult/child £2/free; ⏰ 9.30am-4.30pm Mon-Sat, noon-4pm Sun) The village's rainy-day attractions are limited to this centre, which covers the archaeology and history of the region, including the heart-rending tale of the Highland Clearances in Knoydart.

MV Grimsay Isle Tours

(📞 07780 815158) Provides entertaining, customised sea-fishing trips and seal-watching tours (book at the tourist office).

 Sleeping & Eating

SEAVIEW GUEST HOUSE B&B ££

(📞 01687-462059; www.seaviewguesthouse mallaig.com; Main St; r per person £28-35; ⏰ Mar-Nov; P) Just beyond the tourist office, this comfortable three-bedroom B&B has grand views over the harbour, not only from the upstairs bedrooms but also from the breakfast room. There's also a cute little cottage next door that offers self-catering accommodation (www.selfcateringmallaig.com; one double and one twin room) for £350 to £450 a week.

SPRINGBANK GUEST HOUSE B&B £

(📞 01687-462459; www.springbank-mallaig .co.uk; East Bay; r per person £25; P 🛜) A little further around the bay than the Seaview, the Springbank is a traditional West Highland house with seven homely guest bedrooms, again with superb views across the harbour to the Cuillin of Skye.

MALLAIG BACKPACKER'S LODGE

Hostel £

(📞 01687-462764; www.mallaigbackpackers .co.uk; Harbour View; dm £14.50) Sheena's is a friendly, 12-bed hostel in a lovely old house overlooking the harbour. On a sunny day the hostel's Tea Garden terrace cafe (mains £5 to £10), with its flowers, greenery and cosmopolitan backpacker staff, feels more like the Med than Mallaig. The speciality of the house is a pint-glass full of Mallaig prawns with dipping sauce (£10). From late May to September the cafe opens in the evening with a bistro menu.

FISH MARKET

Seafood ££

(📞 01687-462299; Station Rd; mains £9-20; ⏰ lunch & dinner) There are at least half-a-dozen signs in Mal-

Fishing boats in Mallaig's harbour
PHOTOGRAPHER: MANFRED GOTTSCHALK

laig advertising 'seafood restaurant', but this bright, modern, bistro-style place next to the harbour is our favourite, serving simply prepared scallops with smoked salmon and savoy cabbage, grilled langoustines with garlic butter, and fresh Mallaig haddock fried in breadcrumbs, as well as the tastiest Cullen skink (soup made with smoked haddock, potato, onion and milk) on the west coast. Upstairs is a **coffee shop** (mains £4-5; ⊙11am-5pm) that serves delicious hot roast-beef rolls with horseradish sauce, and scones with clotted cream and jam.

Information

There's a tourist office (☎01687-462170; ⊙10am-5.30pm Mon-Fri, 10.15am-3.45pm Sat, noon-3.30pm Sun), a post office, a bank with ATM and a Co-op supermarket (⊙8am-10pm Mon-Sat, 9am-9pm Sun).

🛈 Getting There & Away

BOAT Ferries run from Mallaig to the Small Isles, the Isle of Skye and Knoydart; see the transport information for these areas for more details.

BUS Shiel Buses bus 500 runs from Fort William to Mallaig (1½ hours, three daily Monday to Friday only) via Glenfinnan (30 minutes) and Arisaig (one hour).

TRAIN The West Highland line runs between Fort William and Mallaig (£10, 1½ hours) four times a day (three on Sunday).

Scotland
in Focus

Bagpipe player on the Royal Mile, Edinburgh
PHOTOGRAPHER: WILL SALTER

Scotland Today

Rural cottage on the Isle of Lewis

Though part of Great Britain, Scotland has maintained a separate identity for the last 300 years

belief systems
(% of population)

43 Church of Scotland
28 Non-Religious
16 Roman Catholic
6.8 Other Christian
6.2 Other

if Scotland were 100 people

98 would be white
1 would be South Asian
1 would be other

population per sq mile

≈ 80 people

Scotland   USA   England

Scottish Politics

Although an integral part of Great Britain since 1707, Scotland has maintained a separate and distinct identity through-out the last 300 years. The return of a devolved Scottish parliament to Edinburgh in 1999 marked a growing confidence and pride in the nation's achievements.

The first decade of devolution has seen Scottish politics diverge significantly from the Westminster way, with Holyrood led by a minority Scottish National Party (SNP) administration since 2007. Distinctive policies that have been applied in Scotland but not in the rest of the UK include free long-term care for the elderly, the abolition of tuition fees for university students and higher pay for teachers. The SNP has committed itself to a referendum on whether Scotland should have full independence, but opinion polls show that most Scots are happy with the status quo.

The election of a Conservative/Lib Dem coalition government in Westminster in

GRAEME CORNWALLIS

driver what they think about the trams – if you have an hour or two to spare!).

In 2008 the Scottish government introduced a scheme called the Road Equivalent Tariff (RET) on certain ferry crossings. This reduced the price of ferry transport to what it would cost to drive the same distance by road, in the hope of attracting more tourists and reducing business costs in the islands. The routes in the pilot scheme, which runs till 2012, are Ullapool to Stornoway, Uig (Skye) to Tarbert (Harris) and Lochmaddy (North Uist), Oban to Castlebay (Barra) and Lochboisdale (South Uist), and Oban to Coll and Tiree. Fares on these crossings have been cut by around 40%, and initial signs are that the scheme has been successful.

2010 only served to heighten the political difference between Scotland and the rest of the UK – only one of Scotland's 59 constituencies returned a Conservative MP, while the Labour Party (which was defeated in Westminster) increased its share of the Scottish vote.

Transport

If you're unfortunate enough to find yourself driving into one of Scotland's cities during the weekday rush hour, you'll soon find that traffic congestion is one of the country's curses. Edinburgh has led the way in trying to discourage car use with popular measures like cycle routes, dedicated bus lanes and Park & Ride schemes, and unpopular ones like increased parking charges and fines. Construction work is well under way on a scheme to reintroduce trams to the city by 2011 (try asking an Edinburgh taxi

Highlands Development

Crofting (smallhold farming) and land ownership are important issues in the Gaelic-speaking areas of northwest Scotland, especially since a headline-grabbing clause in the Land Reform (Scotland) Act (2003) allowed crofting communities to buy out the land that they live on with the aid of taxpayers' money, in the hope of reversing the gradual depopulation of the Highlands.

Several estates have followed Eigg, Gigha, Knoydart and North Harris into community ownership. In 2006 South Uist saw the biggest community buy-out yet. The latest case to make the headlines is the Pairc estate on Lewis, where a Warwickshire-based accountant, whose family has owned the estate since 1920, has leased the land to a power company that plans to erect a £200 million wind farm. The locals voted in favour of a community buy-out, but the landowner is challenging the legality of the Land Reform Act.

309

History

Scottish Parliament Building (p77), Edinburgh

WILL

From the decline of the Vikings onwards, Scottish history has been predictably and often violently bound to that of its southern neighbour, England. Battles and border raids were commonplace until the shared monarchy of the Stuart dynasty, then political union, drew the two together. Even then, 18th-century Jacobite risings asserted a widely held desire for freedom, finally realised with the devolution of the late 20th century.

Romans & Picts

The Roman invasion of Britain by Emperor Claudius began in AD 43, almost a century after Julius Caesar first invaded. However, the Roman onslaught ground to a halt in the north, not far beyond the present-day Scottish border. Between AD 78 and 84, the Roman governor Agricola marched northwards and spent several years trying to subdue the wild tribes the Romans called the Picts (from the Latin *pictus*, meaning painted).

4000 BC

Neolithic farmers mov
Scotland from mainla
Europe.

Little is known about these people, who inhabited northern and eastern Scotland. The Roman presence had probably helped to forge disparate Celtic tribes into a unified group; we can assume they were fierce fighters given the trouble the hardy Roman army had with them. The main material evidence of their culture is their fabulous carved symbol stones, found in many parts of eastern Scotland.

By the 2nd century, Emperor Hadrian, tired of fighting the tribes in the north, decided to cut his losses and built the wall (AD 122–28) that bears his name across northern England. Two decades later Hadrian's successor, Antoninus Pius, invaded Scotland again and built a turf rampart, the Antonine Wall, between the Firth of Forth and the River Clyde. In northern Britain, the Romans found they had met their match.

Christianity & St Columba

Eventually the Romans left Britain and at this time there were at least two indigenous peoples in the northern region of the British Isles: the Picts in the north and east, and the Britons in the southwest. The Scots probably arrived around AD 500, crossing to Argyll from northern Ireland and establishing a kingdom called Dalriada.

St Ninian was the earliest recorded bringer of Christianity to the region, establishing a mission in Whithorn in Scotland's southwest. He remains a mysterious figure shrouded in myth, but there is little doubt that his influence was profound.

In the 6th century, St Columba, Scotland's most famous missionary, resumed St Ninian's work. According to legend, Columba was a scholar and a soldier-priest who went into exile after involvement in a bloody battle. After fleeing Ireland in AD 563 he established a monastery on Iona, and also travelled to the northeast to take his message to the Picts. After his death he was credited with miraculous feats such as defeating what is today known as the Loch Ness monster.

Kingdom of the Scots

The Picts and Scots were drawn together by the threat of a Norse invasion and by the combination of political and spiritual power from their common Christianity. Kenneth MacAlpin, first king of a united Scotland, achieved power using a mixture of blood ties and diplomacy. He set his capital in Pictland at Scone, and brought to it the sacred Stone of Destiny (see the boxed text, p75), used in the coronation of Scottish kings.

Nearly two centuries later, Kenneth MacAlpin's great-great-great-grandson, Malcolm II (r 1005–18), defeated the Northumbrian Angles led by King Canute.

AD 43

Claudius begins the Roman conquest of Britain, almost a century after Julius Caesar first invaded.

AD 142

Antonine Wall built across central Scotland marks northern limit of Roman Empire.

Early 6th century

A Celtic tribe, the Scots, cross from northern Ireland and establish kingdom called Dalriada.

This victory brought Edinburgh and Lothian under Scottish control and extended Scottish territory as far south as the Tweed.

With his Saxon queen, Margaret, Malcolm III Canmore (r 1058–93) – whose father Duncan was murdered by Macbeth (as described in Shakespeare's eponymous play) – founded a dynasty of able Scottish rulers. They introduced new Anglo-Norman systems of government and religious foundations.

But the Highland clans, inaccessible in their glens, remained a law unto themselves for another 600 years. The exploits of Rob Roy (p185), especially his daring raids into the Lowlands and reputation as a champion of the poor, typified the romantic notion of these wild clans. A cultural and linguistic divide grew between the Gaelic-speaking Highlanders and Lowlanders who spoke the Scots tongue (a variant of English).

Robert the Bruce & William Wallace

When Alexander III fell to his death over a coastal cliff in Fife in 1286, there followed a dispute over the succession to the throne. There were no less than 13 claimants, but in the end it came down to a choice of two: Robert de Brus, lord of Annandale, and John Balliol, lord of Galloway. Edward I of England, as the greatest feudal lord in Britain, was asked to arbitrate. He chose Balliol, whom he thought he could manipulate more easily.

Seeking to tighten his feudal grip on Scotland, Edward – known as the 'Hammer of the Scots' – treated the Scots king as his vassal rather than his equal. The humiliated Balliol finally turned against him and allied Scotland with France in 1295, thus beginning the enduring 'Auld Alliance' and ushering in the Wars of Independence.

Edward's response was bloody. In 1296 he invaded Scotland and Balliol was incarcerated in the Tower of London; in a final blow to Scots pride, Edward I removed the Stone of Destiny from Scone and took it back to London.

Enter arguably Scotland's most tragic hero, William Wallace (see p174). Bands of rebels were attacking the English occupiers and one such band, led by Wallace, defeated the English army at the Battle of Stirling Bridge in 1297. A wanted man from that time on, Wallace was eventually captured and executed. Robert the Bruce, grandson of the lord of Annandale, saw his chance, defied Edward (whom he had previously aligned himself with), murdered his rival John Comyn and had himself crowned king of Scotland at Scone in 1306. Bruce mounted a campaign to drive the English out of Scotland but suffered repeated defeats.

According to legend, while Bruce was on the run he was inspired to renew his efforts by a spider's persistence in spinning its web. And the inspiration was not in vain – he went on to secure an illustrious victory over the English at Bannockburn in 1314, enshrined in Scottish legend as one of the finest moments in the country's history.

563
St Columba establishes Christian mission on Iona. By 8th century most of Scotland is converted.

BLICKWINKEL/ALAMY

780
Norsemen in longboats from Scandinavia begin to pillage the Scottish coast and islands.

The Declaration of Arbroath

During the Wars of Independence, Scottish nobles sent a letter to Pope John XXII requesting his support. Written by the abbot of Arbroath in 1320, it is the earliest document that seeks to place limits on royal power.

After railing against the tyranny of Edward I of England, the declaration famously states: 'For so long as a hundred of us remain alive, we will yield in no least way to English dominion. For we fight, not for glory nor for riches nor for honours, but only and alone for freedom, which no good man surrenders but with his life.'

The Stewarts & the Renaissance

After the death of Robert the Bruce in 1329, the country was ravaged by civil disputes and continuing wars with England. Edinburgh was occupied several times by English armies and in 1385 the Kirk of St Giles was burned to the ground.

James IV (r 1488–1513) married the daughter of Henry VII of England, the first of the Tudor monarchs, thereby linking the two royal families through 'the Marriage of the Thistle and the Rose'. This didn't prevent the French from persuading James to go to war with his in-laws, and he was killed at the Battle of Flodden in 1513, along with 10,000 of his subjects.

Renaissance ideas flourished during James IV's reign. Scottish poetry thrived, created by *makars* (makers of verses) such as William Dunbar, the court poet of James IV, and Gavin Douglas. Much graceful Scottish architecture is from this period, and examples of Renaissance style can be seen in alterations to palaces at Holyroodhouse and Stirling Castle.

Mary, Queen of Scots

In 1542, King James V, childless, lay on his deathbed broken-hearted after his defeat by the English at Solway Moss. On 8 December a messenger brought word that his wife had given birth to a baby girl at the Palace of Linlithgow. Fearing the end of the Stewart dynasty, and recalling its origin through Robert the Bruce's daughter, James sighed, 'It cam' wi' a lass, and it will gang wi' a lass'. He died a few days later, leaving his week-old daughter, Mary, to inherit the throne as Queen of Scots.

She was sent to France at an early age and Scotland was ruled by regents, who rejected overtures from Henry VIII of England urging them to wed the infant queen to his son. Henry was furious, and sent his armies to take vengeance on the Scots. The 'Rough Wooing', as it was called, failed to persuade the Scots of the error of

848

Kenneth MacAlpin unites Scottish and Pictish thrones, forging a single kingdom.

1018

King Malcolm II defeats Northumbrians at battle of Carham, gains Lothian region for Scotland.

1296

King Edward I marches on Scotland with army of 30,000, butchering citizens and capturing castles.

their ways. In 1558 Mary was married to the French dauphin and became queen of France as well as Scotland.

Following the death of her sickly husband, the 18-year-old Mary returned to Scotland in 1561. She was formally welcomed to her capital city and held a famous audience at Holyrood Palace with John Knox. The great reformer harangued the young queen and she later agreed to protect the budding Protestant Church in Scotland while continuing to hear Mass in private.

She married Henry Stewart, Lord Darnley, in the Chapel Royal at Holyrood and gave birth to a son (later James VI) in Edinburgh Castle in 1565. Any domestic bliss was short-lived and, in a scarcely believable train of events, Darnley was involved in the murder of Mary's Italian secretary David Rizzio (rumoured to be her lover), before he himself was murdered, probably by Mary's new lover and third-husband-to-be, the earl of Bothwell!

The Scots had had enough – Mary's enemies finally confronted her and Mary was forced to abdicate in 1567 and thrown into prison at Castle Leven. She managed to escape, and fled to England where she was imprisoned for 19 years by Queen Elizabeth I before finally being executed in 1587.

Union of the Crowns

Mary's son, the infant James VI (r 1567–1625) had meanwhile been crowned at Stirling, and a series of regents ruled in his place. In England, Elizabeth died childless, and the English, desperate for a male monarch, soon turned their attention north. In 1603 James VI of Scotland became James I of Great Britain and moved his court to London. His plan to politically unite the two countries, however, failed. For the most part, the Stewarts (now spelled Stuart) ignored Scotland from then on. Indeed,

John Knox & the Reformation

While the young Mary, Queen of Scots, was in France being raised as a Roman Catholic, the Reformation tore through Scotland. The preachings of John Knox (1510–72), pupil of the Swiss reformer Calvin, found sympathetic ears and Knox became leader of the Reformation in Scotland, and a founder of its Presbyterian church. Concerned with the sway that political rulers wielded over the church, Knox wrote *The First Blast of the Trumpet Against the Monstrous Regiment of Women*. It was an attack on three women rulers calling the shots in Scotland, England and France, and has linked his name to a hatred of women ever since.

1298–1305
Edward defeats the Scots at Falkirk, Wallace resigns as guardian and is fatally betrayed.

1314
Robert the Bruce wins a famous victory over the English at the Battle of Bannockburn.

1328
Treaty of Northampton gives Scotland independence, with Robert I, the Bruce, as king.

when Charles I (r 1625–49) succeeded James, he couldn't be bothered to travel north to Edinburgh to be formally crowned as king of Scotland until 1633.

Covenanters & Civil War

Civil war strangled Scotland and England in the 17th century. Arrogant attempts by Charles I to impose episcopacy (the rule of bishops) and an English liturgy on the Presbyterian Scottish Church set off public riots in Edinburgh. The Presbyterians believed in a personal bond with God that had no need of mediation through priests, popes and kings. On 28 February 1638 hundreds gathered in Greyfriars Kirkyard to sign a National Covenant affirming their rights and beliefs. Scotland was divided between the Covenanters and those who supported the king.

In the 1640s, civil war raged in England between the Royalists and Oliver Cromwell's Parliamentarians. Although there was an alliance between the Covenanters and the English parliament against Charles I, the Scots were appalled when the Parliamentarians executed the king in 1649. They offered his son the Scottish Crown provided he signed the Covenant and renounced his father, which he did. Charles II (r 1649–85) was crowned at Scone on 1 January 1651 but was soon

Gravestones in Greyfriars Kirkyard (p77)
PHOTOGRAPHER: JONATHAN SMITH

1371

Last of Bruce dynasty dies, succeeded by Stewarts who rule for next three centuries.

1488–1513

Scottish Renaissance produces intellectual climate that is fertile ground for the rise of Protestantism.

1513

James IV invades northern England, but is defeated at the Battle of Flodden.

The Best Historic Sites

forced into exile by Cromwell, who invaded Scotland and captured Edinburgh.

After Charles II's restoration in 1660, he reneged on the Covenant; episcopacy was reinstated and hardline Presbyterian ministers were deprived of their churches. Charles' brother and successor, the Catholic James VII/II (r 1685–89), made worshipping as a Covenanter a capital offence.

James had converted to Catholicism but as long as his Protestant daughter Mary was next in line a lid was kept on the simmering pot of religious conflict. When his second wife, however, gave birth to a son (a Catholic heir to the throne) in 1688, things erupted. Parliament called for James's Protestant son-in-law, William of Orange, to invade from the Netherlands, and James was forced into exile.

James' daughter, Mary, and her husband William (1689–1702), reigning jointly, restored the Presbyterian structure in the church and kicked out the bishops, but the political and legal functions of the church were subject to parliamentary control.

Union With England

The civil wars left the country and its economy ruined. Anti-English feeling ran high: William was at war with France and was using Scottish soldiers and taxes – many Scots, sympathetic to the French, disapproved. This feeling was exacerbated by the failure of an investment venture in Panama (the so-called Darien Scheme, designed to establish a Scottish colony in the Americas), which resulted in widespread bankruptcy in Scotland.

The failure of the Darien Scheme made it clear to the wealthy Scottish merchants and stockholders that the only way they could gain access to the lucrative markets of developing colonies was through union with England. The English parliament favoured union through fear of Jacobite sympathies in Scotland being exploited by its enemies, the French.

On receiving the Act of Union in Edinburgh in 1707, the chancellor of Scotland, Lord Seafield – leader of the parliament that the Act of Union abolished – is said to have murmured under his breath, 'Now there's an end to an auld sang'. Robert Burns later castigated the wealthy politicians who engineered the union in characteristically stronger language: 'We're bought and sold for English gold – such a parcel of rogues in a nation!'

1560

Scottish parliament creates a Protestant Church that is independent of Rome and the monarchy.

KARL BLACKWELL

1567

Mary Queen of Scots is deposed and thrown in prison; she is executed in 1587.

Bonnie Prince Charlie

The Jacobite rebellions of the 18th century sought to restore a Catholic Stuart king to the British throne. James Edward Stuart (Jacobite is derived from the Latin word for James), known as the Old Pretender, was the son of James VII/II. With French support he arrived in the Firth of Forth with a fleet of ships in 1708, but was seen off by English men-of-war. The earl of Mar led another Jacobite rebellion in 1715 but his campaign fizzled out soon after the inconclusive Battle of Sheriffmuir.

The Old Pretender's son, Charles Edward Stuart – better known as Bonnie Prince Charlie or the Young Pretender – landed in Scotland for the final uprising. Raised in France, he had little military experience, didn't speak Gaelic and had a shaky grasp of English. Nevertheless, after rallying an army of Highlanders at Glenfinnan, he marched southwards and captured Edinburgh in September 1745. He got as far south as Derby in England, but success was short-lived; a Hanoverian army led by the duke of Cumberland harried him all the way back to the Highlands, where Jacobite dreams were finally extinguished at the Battle of Culloden in 1746.

Bonnie Prince Charlie's flight after Culloden is legendary. He lived in hiding in the remote Highlands and islands for months before being rescued by a French frigate. His narrow escape from Uist to Skye, dressed as Flora MacDonald's maid, is the subject of the Skye Boat Song.

The Best Castles

1 Edinburgh Castle (p65)

2 Stirling Castle (p170)

3 Urquhart Castle (p280)

4 Dunvegan Castle (p236)

5 St Andrews Castle (p187)

6 Blair Castle (p204)

IN FOCUS HISTORY

The Highland Clearances

In the aftermath of the Jacobite rebellions, Highland dress, the bearing of arms and the bagpipes were outlawed, and the Highlands came under military control. The clansmen, no longer of any use as soldiers and uneconomical as tenants, were evicted from their homes and farms by the Highland chieftains to make way for sheep. A few stayed to work the sheep farms; many more were forced to seek work in the cities, or to eke a living from crofts (small holdings) on poor coastal land. Men who had never seen the sea were forced to take to boats to try their luck at herring fishing, and many thousands emigrated to North America, Australia and New Zealand in the late-18th and 19th centuries.

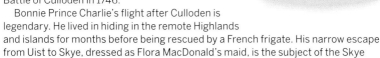

1603
James VI of Scotland inherits the English throne, becoming James I of Great Britain.

1707
Act of Union joins England and Scotland under a single parliament, sovereign and flag.

1745–46
Jacobite rebellion sees Bonnie Prince Charlie invade Scotland, ends in defeat at Battle of Culloden.

The Industrial Revolution

The development of the steam engine ushered in the Industrial Revolution. The Carron Ironworks near Falkirk, established in 1759, became the largest ironworks and gun factory in Britain, and the growth of the textile industry saw the construction of huge weaving mills in Lanarkshire, Dundee, Angus and Aberdeenshire. The world's first steamboat, the *Charlotte Dundas,* sailed along the newly opened Forth and Clyde Canal in 1802, and the world's first sea-going steamship, the *Comet,* was launched on the Clyde in 1812.

Glasgow, deprived of its lucrative tobacco trade following the American War of Independence (1776–83), developed into an industrial powerhouse, the 'second city' of the British Empire (after London). Cotton mills, iron and steelworks, chemical works, shipbuilding yards and heavy-engineering works proliferated along the River Clyde in the 19th century, powered by the coal mines of Lanarkshire, Ayrshire, Fife and Midlothian.

The main gate of Stirling Castle (p170)
PHOTOGRAPHER: SEAN CAFFREY

1740s–1830s

Edinburgh declines in political importance, but cultural and intellectual life flourishes during Scottish Enlightenment.

Late 18th-19th century

Industrial Revolution – Scotland becomes world leader in shipbuilding and marine engineering.

1914–1932

Scottish industry slumps during WWI, collapses in its aftermath; 400,000 emigrate between 1921 and 1931.

North Sea Oil & Devolution

Scotland largely escaped the devastation wrought by WWII on the industrial cities of England. Indeed, the war brought a measure of renewed prosperity to Scotland as the shipyards and engineering works geared up to supply the war effort. But the postwar period saw the collapse of shipbuilding and heavy industry, on which Scotland had become over-reliant.

The discovery of North Sea oil in 1970 fuelled dreams of economic self-sufficiency, and led to increasing nationalist sentiment in Scotland. The Scottish Nationalist Party (SNP) developed into a major force in Scottish politics.

In 1979 a referendum was held on whether to set up a directly elected Scottish Assembly. Fifty-two per cent of those who voted said 'yes' to devolution, but the Labour prime minister decided that everyone who didn't vote should be counted as a 'no'. By this devious reasoning, only 33% of the electorate had voted 'yes', so the Scottish Assembly was rejected.

From 1979 to 1997 Scotland was ruled by a Conservative government in London for which the majority of Scots hadn't voted. Separatist feelings, always present, grew stronger. Following the landslide victory of the Labour Party in May 1997, another referendum was held on the creation of a Scottish parliament. This time the result was overwhelmingly and unambiguously in favour.

Elections to the new parliament took place on 6 May 1999 and the Scottish parliament convened for the first time on 12 May in Edinburgh, with Labour's Donald Dewar, who died in office the very next year, becoming First Minister.

The Best Historical Museums

1 National Museum of Scotland (p83)

2 Museum of the Isles (p229)

3 Skye Museum of Island Life (p238)

4 War & Peace Museum (p239)

5 Highland Folk Museum (p287)

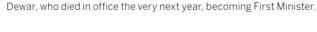

1941–45
Clydebank blitzed by German bombers in 1941; by 1945 workforce is employed in heavy industries.

1970s
Discovery of oil in North Sea brings prosperity to Aberdeen and Shetland Islands.

1999–2004
Scottish parliament convened in 1999; new parliament building opened by the Queen in October 2004.

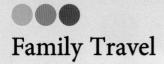

Family Travel

The Jacobite Steam Train (p299)

ARCHWHITE/A

Scotland is a great place for a family holiday. There are plenty of things to keep the young ones occupied, from wildlife parks and outdoor activities to top-notch museums with interactive hands-on exhibits. Many tourist towns and national parks organise events and activities for kids, and even local museums usually make an effort with an activity sheet or child-focused information panels. Tourist offices are a great source for information on child-friendly attractions.

Accommodation

Children are generally well received all over Scotland, but accommodation can sometimes be a headache. Not all hotels and guest houses are happy to accept younger children (especially those at the boutique end of the market), so check their policy before you book. Many places quote a price per person rather than per room; look for B&Bs that advertise 'family rooms' (which usually sleep two adults plus one or two children) and you'll get better value.

In places that are happy to accept children, kids under a certain age can often stay free in their parents' room, and child-friendly facilities, including cots, are provided.

Eating Out

Many restaurants (especially the larger ones) have highchairs and decent children's menus. However, a lot of more upmarket places can prove distinctly chilly if you turn up with a young family.

A lot of pubs are family friendly and some have great beer gardens where kids can run around and exhaust themselves while you enjoy lunch and a quiet pint. However, be aware that many Scottish pubs, even those that serve bar meals, are forbidden by law to admit children under 14; even in family-friendly pubs (ie those in possession of a Children's Certificate), under-14s are only admitted between 11am and 8pm, and only when accompanied by an adult.

Feeding & Changing Baby

Breastfeeding in public remains mildly controversial in the UK, but if done discreetly is usually considered OK. In 2005 the Scottish Parliament passed legislation safeguarding the freedom of women to breastfeed in public, so if anyone tries to stop you, quote the law at them!

On the sticky topic of dealing with nappies (diapers) while travelling, most big museums, galleries and visitor centres have baby-changing facilities, though you probably won't be terribly impressed with the facilities in motorway service stations and city-centre public toilets.

For more advice, see www.babygoes2.com and www.travelforkids.com.

IN FOCUS FAMILY TRAVEL

Things To Do

Weather is usually the big deciding factor when it comes to a successful family holiday. This being Scotland, expect some rainy days! Pack waterproofs and umbrellas,

Need to Know

- **Changing facilities** Available in most shopping centres, major museums and attractions
- **Cots** Usually provided in better hotels, but rare in B&Bs
- **Health** Standards similar to most Western nations; no special innoculations need
- **Highchairs** Common in chain restaurants and fast-food places, but ask elsewhere
- **Kids' menus** As above for highchairs
- **Nappies (diapers)** Sold in every supermarket
- **Strollers** Widely accepted on most public transport
- **Transport** Child discounts and family tickets (usually two adults plus two kids) widely available

The Harry Potter Connection

If your kids are fans of the Harry Potter movies, then impress them with a visit to locations where many of the scenes were shot. Here are a few:

○ **Jacobite Steam Train** (p299) The locomotive that stars as the Hogwarts Express

○ **Glen Nevis** (p297) Background to the quidditch match in *Philosopher's Stone*

○ **Glenfinnan Viaduct** (p299) Railway viaduct is the setting for the flying-car sequence in *Chamber of Secrets*

○ **Glen Coe** (p288) Hagrid's Hut in *Prisoner of Azkaban* was built just outside Glencoe village

For more details check out www.scotlandthemovie.com.

and always have a 'Plan B' that involves retreating to an indoor location. Locals are well used to this, and even outdoor attractions such as national parks have visitor centres and indoor exhibitions to keep young minds occupied when it's pouring down outside.

It's well worth asking in tourist offices for local family-based publications as a source of ideas. The *List* magazine (www.list.co.uk), available at newsagents and bookshops, has a section on children's activities and events in and around Glasgow and Edinburgh. A good online resource is www.dayoutwiththekids.co.uk.

See Edinburgh for Kids, p97, for more on the capital city. See also Lonely Planet's *Travel with Children,* by Brigitte Barta et al.

Highland Culture

Tug-of-war at the Braemar Gathering (p208)

JONATHAN SMITH

The distinctive culture of the Scottish Highlands – from bagpipes and Highland dance to the swing of the kilt and the spectacle of Highland games – has its origins in the clan system that was remorselessly crushed following the Jacobite rebellion of 1745. The playing of pipes and the wearing of Highland dress remained illegal until the revival of interest in all things Highland in the 19th century.

Highland Games

The origins of Scotland's Highland games are lost in the mists of time. It is thought that trials of strength among clansmen were staged following military musters, and these impromptu contests were formalised in the early 19th century when Highland culture was romanticised by Britain's high society.

The traditional roster of events has changed little since those days, typically including piping and dancing competitions, alongside demonstrations of physical prowess such as tossing the caber (heaving a tree trunk into the air), throwing the hammer and putting the stone. Many games also include athletic events such as running and jumping.

Highland games attract locals and tourists alike, and are held in Scotland throughout the summer, not just in the

The Best Highland Games

Highlands. You can find dates and details of games held all over the country on the Scottish Highland Games Association website (www.shga.co.uk).

Highland Dancing

Highland dancing today is a fiercely competitive and athletic discipline, popular not only in Scotland but in places with large immigrant Scottish communites such as Canada, the USA and Australia.

The earliest written records of Highland dancing date back to the 15th century, with descriptions of probably the best-known Highland dance, the Sword Dance. In this, the dancer hops and steps nimbly between the blades of a pair of crossed swords, a discipline that may have emerged as practice for the fancy footwork necessary in a hand-to-hand swordfight.

Another well-known dance, the Highland Fling, is thought to have its origins in a dance of celebration performed by clansmen following success in battle.

Bagpipes

Highland soldiers were traditionally accompanied into battle by the skirl of the pipes, and the Scottish Highland bagpipe is unique in being the only musical instrument ever to be classed as a weapon of war. The playing of the pipes was banned – under pain of death – by the British government in 1747 as part of a scheme to suppress Highland culture in the wake of the Jacobite uprising of 1745. The pipes were revived when the Highland regiments were drafted into the British Army towards the end of the 18th century.

The bagpipe consists of a leather bag held under the arm, kept inflated by blowing through the blowstick; the piper forces air through the pipes by squeezing the bag with the forearm. Three of the pipes, known as drones, play a constant note (one bass, two tenor) in the background. The fourth pipe, the chanter, plays the melody.

Ceilidhs

The Gaelic word ceilidh (pronounced kay-lay) means 'visit'. A ceilidh was originally a social gathering in someone's house after the day's work was over, enlivened with storytelling, music and song. These days, a ceilidh usually means an evening of traditional Scottish entertainment including music, song and dance, often held in a village hall. The local tourist office or pub will usually have details of any events taking place.

Shinty

Shinty (camanachd in Gaelic) is a fast and physical ball-and-stick sport similar to Ireland's hurling, with more than a little resemblance to clan warfare. It's an indigenous Scottish game played mainly in the Highlands, and the most prized trophy is the Camanachd Cup. The cup final, held in September, is a great Gaelic get-together.

Tartan

The oldest surviving piece of tartan – a patterned woollen textile now made into everything from kilts to key rings – dates back to the Roman period. The Falkirk Tartan is a piece of cream and brown cloth found with a hoard of Roman coins dating from around AD 320; it is on display in the National Museum of Scotland (p83) in Edinburgh.

Today tartan is popular the world over, and beyond – astronaut Al Bean took his MacBean tartan to the moon and back. Particular setts (tartan patterns) didn't come to be associated with particular clans until the 17th century, although today every clan, and indeed every Scottish football team, has one or more distinctive tartans.

The Kilt

The original Scottish Highland dress was not the kilt but the plaid – a long length of tartan cloth wrapped around the body and over the shoulder. The wearing of Highland dress was banned after the Jacobite rebellions but revived under royal patronage in the 19th century. George IV and his English courtiers donned kilts for their visit to Scotland in 1822.

During the same century, Sir Walter Scott – novelist, poet and dedicated patriot – did much to rekindle interest in Highland culture. By then, however, many of the old setts had been forgotten, and as a result some tartans are actually Victorian creations. The modern kilt only appeared in the 18th century and was reputedly invented by Thomas Rawlinson, an Englishman!

Kilts don't have pockets, so kilted Scotsmen keep their beer money in a sporran, a pouch made of leather or animal skin that hangs in front of the kilt, suspended from a chain around the waist.

Exploring Your Scottish Roots

Many visitors to Scotland take the opportunity to do some detective work on their Scottish ancestry. One of the best guides is *Tracing Your Scottish Ancestry* by Kathleen B Cory.

The **Scotland's People Centre** (0131-314 4300; www.scotlandspeoplehub.gov.uk; 2 Princes St, Edinburgh; ⌚9am-4.30pm Mon-Fri) provides access to the main records used in Scottish genealogical research – the Statutory Registers of births, marriages and deaths (1855 to the present), the Old Parish Registers (1533–1854) and the 10-yearly census returns from 1841 to 1901. Daily search fee is £10.

The **Scotland's People Website** (www.scotlandspeople.gov.uk) allows you to search the records online (pay-per-view).

The Scottish Flag

Scottish football and rugby supporters can never seem to make up their minds which flag to wave – the Saltire or the Lion Rampant.

The Saltire, or St Andrew's Cross – a diagonal white cross on a blue ground – is one of the oldest national flags in the world, dating from at least the 12th century. Originally a religious emblem – St Andrew was crucified on a diagonal cross – it became a national emblem in the 14th century. According to legend, white clouds in the form of a saltire appeared in a blue sky during the battle of Nechtansmere between Scots and Saxons, urging the Scots to victory. It was incorporated in the Union Flag of the UK following the Act of Union in 1707.

The Lion Rampant – a red lion on a golden-yellow ground – is the Royal Banner of Scotland. It is thought to derive from the arms of King William I the Lion (r 1143–1214), and strictly speaking should only be used by a Scottish monarch. It is incorporated in the British Royal Standard, quartered with the three lions of England and the harp of Ireland.

Writers & Artists

The Royal Scottish Academy (p82), Edinburgh

JONATHAN SMITH

In the world of literature, Scotland packs a punch well above its diminutive weight. Its national poet, Robert Burns, is known and celebrated all over the world, his works translated into dozens of languages. Walter Scott and RL Stevenson are almost as widely read, as are contemporary novelists such as Ian Rankin and Iain Banks. Scottish artists are less well known, but have carved out a niche within the British art world.

Robert Burns

Best remembered for penning the words of 'Auld Lang Syne', Robert Burns (1759–96) is Scotland's most famous poet and a popular hero whose birthday (25 January) is celebrated as Burns Night by Scots around the world.

Burns was born in 1759 in Alloway to a poor family who scraped a living gardening and farming. At school he soon showed an aptitude for literature and a fondness for the folk song. He later began to write his own songs and satires. When the problems of his arduous farming life were compounded by the threat of prosecution from the father of Jean Armour, with whom he'd had an affair, he decided to emigrate to Jamaica. He gave up his share of the family farm and published his poems to raise money for the journey.

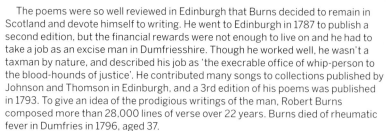

The poems were so well reviewed in Edinburgh that Burns decided to remain in Scotland and devote himself to writing. He went to Edinburgh in 1787 to publish a second edition, but the financial rewards were not enough to live on and he had to take a job as an excise man in Dumfriesshire. Though he worked well, he wasn't a taxman by nature, and described his job as 'the execrable office of whip-person to the blood-hounds of justice'. He contributed many songs to collections published by Johnson and Thomson in Edinburgh, and a 3rd edition of his poems was published in 1793. To give an idea of the prodigious writings of the man, Robert Burns composed more than 28,000 lines of verse over 22 years. Burns died of rheumatic fever in Dumfries in 1796, aged 37.

Burns wrote in Lallans, the Scottish Lowland dialect of English that is not very accessible to the Sassenach (Englishman), or foreigner; perhaps this is part of his appeal. He was also very much a man of the people, satirising the upper classes and the church for their hypocrisy.

Many of the local landmarks mentioned in the verse-tale 'Tam o'Shanter' can still be visited. Farmer Tam, riding home after a hard night's drinking in a pub in Ayr, sees witches dancing in Alloway churchyard. He calls out to the one pretty witch, but is pursued by them all and has to reach the other side of the River Doon to be safe. He just manages to cross the Brig o'Doon, but his mare loses her tail to the witches.

The Burns connection in southern Scotland is milked for all it's worth and tourist offices have a *Burns Heritage Trail* leaflet leading you to every place that can claim some link with the bard.

Sir Walter Scott

In 1787 Robert Burns was introduced to a 16-year-old boy at a social gathering in the house of an Edinburgh professor. The boy grew up to be Sir Walter Scott (1771–1832), Scotland's greatest and most prolific novelist. The son of an Edinburgh lawyer, Scott lived at various New Town addresses before moving to his country house at Abbotsford, south of Edinburgh.

Scott's early works were rhyming ballads, such as *The Lady of the Lake*, while his first historical novels – Scott effectively invented the genre – were published anonymously. He almost singlehandedly revived interest in Scottish history and legend in the early 19th century, and was largely responsible for organising King George IV's visit to Scotland in 1822. Plagued by debt in later life, he wrote obsessively – to the detriment of his health – in order to make money, but will always be best remembered for classic tales such as *Waverley, The Antiquary, The Heart of Midlothian, Ivanhoe, Redgauntlet* and *Castle Dangerous*.

Robert Louis Stevenson

Along with Scott, Robert Louis Stevenson (1850–94) ranks as Scotland's best-known novelist. Born at 8 Howard Pl in Edinburgh into a family of famous lighthouse engineers, Stevenson studied law at Edinburgh University but was always intent on pursuing the life of a writer. An inveterate traveller, but dogged by ill health, he finally settled in Samoa in 1889, where he was revered by the natives as 'Tusitala' – the teller of tales. Stevenson is known and loved around the world for those tales: *Kidnapped, Catriona, Treasure Island, The Master of Ballantrae* and *The Strange Case of Dr Jekyll and Mr Hyde*. The Writers' Museum in Edinburgh (see p69) celebrates the work of Burns, Scott and Stevenson.

Sir Arthur Conan Doyle

Sir Arthur Conan Doyle (1859–1930), the creator of Sherlock Holmes, was born in Edinburgh and studied medicine at Edinburgh University. He based the character of

Holmes on one of his lecturers, the surgeon Dr Joseph Bell, who had employed his forensic skills and powers of deduction on several murder cases in Edinburgh. There's a fascinating exhibit on Dr Bell in Edinburgh's Surgeons' Hall Museums (see p79).

Iain Banks

One of Scotland's most successful contemporary authors, Iain Banks (1954–) is also one of its most prolific. Banks burst onto the Scottish literary scene with his dazzling debut novel *The Wasp Factory* (1984), a macabre but compelling exploration of the inner world of Frank, a strange and deeply disturbed teenager.

Banks' most enjoyable books include *Complicity* (1993), a gruesome and often hilarious thriller, and *The Crow Road* (1992), a warm, witty and moving family saga. The latter provides one of Scottish fiction's most memorable opening sentences: 'It was the day my grandmother exploded.'

Ian Rankin

The Edinburgh-based crime novels of Ian Rankin (1960–), featuring the hard-drinking, introspective detective inspector John Rebus, are sinister, engrossing mysteries that explore the darker side of Scotland's capital city. Rankin's novels are filled with sharp dialogue, telling detail and three-dimensional characters; he attracts a growing international following (his books have been translated into 22 languages). Rankin seems to improve with every book – the final Rebus novel, *Exit Music* (2007), is one of his best. In *The Complaints* (2009) he created a new and completely different character, Malcolm Fox, a cop who investigates other cops.

The Scottish Colourists

In the early 20th century the Scottish painters most widely acclaimed outside of the country were the group known as the Scottish Colourists – SJ Peploe, Francis Cadell, Leslie Hunter and JD Fergusson – whose striking paintings drew on French postimpressionist and Fauvist influences. Peploe and Cadell, active in the 1920s and '30s, often spent the summer painting together on the Isle of Iona, and reproductions of their beautiful landscapes and seascapes appear on many a print and postcard.

The Edinburgh School

In the 1930s a group of modernist landscape artists called themselves the Edinburgh School. Chief among them were William Gillies (1898–1978), Sir William MacTaggart (1903–81) and Anne Redpath (1895–1965). Following WWII, artists such as Alan Davie (1920–) and Sir Eduardo Paolozzi (1924–2005) gained international reputations in abstract expressionism and pop art.

The Best Art Galleries

1 National Gallery of Scotland (p81)

2 Royal Scottish Academy (p82)

3 Gallery of Modern Art (p129)

4 Kelvingrove Art Gallery & Museum (p140)

5 Burrell Collection (p148)

6 Hunterian Art Gallery (p132)

IN FOCUS WRITERS & ARTISTS

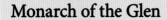

Monarch of the Glen

If asked to think of a Scottish painting, many people picture *Monarch of the Glen,* a romanticised portrait of a magnificent Highland red deer stag by Sir Edwin Landseer (1802–73). Landseer was not a Scot but a Londoner, though he did spend a lot of time in Scotland, leasing a cottage in Glen Feshie and visiting the young Queen Victoria at Balmoral to tutor her in drawing.

The painting was commissioned in 1850 for the refreshment rooms in the House of Lords in London, but ended up being sold to Dewar's whisky distillery, where it became a trademark of Glenfiddich single malt.

Contemporary Artists

Among contemporary Scottish artists the most famous – or rather notorious – are Peter Howson and Jack Vettriano. Howson (1958–), best known for his grim portraits of Glasgow down-and-outs and muscular workers, hit the headlines when he went to Bosnia as an official war artist in 1993 and produced some disturbing and controversial works. *Croatian and Muslim,* an uncompromising rape scene, sparked a debate about what was acceptable in a public exhibition of art. More recently his nude portraits of Madonna – the pop icon, not the religious one – garnered even more column inches in the press. His work is much sought after and collected by celebrities such as David Bowie and Madonna herself. You can see examples of Howson's work at Glasgow's Gallery of Modern Art (p129).

Jack Vettriano (1954–) was formerly a mining engineer, but now ranks as one of Scotland's most commercially successful artists. An entirely self-taught painter, his work – realistic, voyeuristic, occasionally sinister and often carrying a powerful erotic charge – has been compared to that of the American painters Edward Hopper and Walter Sickert. You can see reproductions of his work in coffee-table books and posters, but not in any Scottish art gallery. The Scottish art establishment looks down its nose at him, despite – or perhaps because of – the enormous popularity of his work.

Flavours of Scotland

A display of Scottish whiskies

MARTIN MOOS

Traditional Scottish cookery is all about comfort food: solid, nourishing fare, often high in fat and carbohydrates, that would keep you warm on a winter's day spent in the fields or out fishing, and sweet treats to come home to in the evening. Scotland's traditional drinks – whisky and beer – have found a new lease of life in recent years, with single malts being marketed like fine wines, and a new breed of microbreweries springing up all over the country.

Scotch Whisky

'Love makes the world go round? Not at all! Whisky makes it go round twice as fast.'

Whisky Galore, Compton Mackenzie
(1883–1972)

Scotch whisky (always spelt without an 'e' – whiskey with an 'e' is Irish or American) is Scotland's best-known product and biggest export. The spirit has been distilled in Scotland at least since the 15th century.

Malt whisky is distilled from malted barley – that is, barley that has been soaked in water, then allowed to germinate for around 10 days until the starch has turned into sugar – while grain whiskies are made from other cereals, usually wheat, corn or unmalted barley.

A single malt is a whisky that has been made with malted barley and is the product of a single distillery. A pure (vatted) malt is a

The Best Single Malt Whiskies

1 Bowmore (Islay)

2 Macallan (Speyside)

3 Highland Park (Island)

4 Bruichladdich (Islay)

5 Springbank (Campbeltown)

6 Talisker (Island)

mixture of single malts from several distilleries, and a blended whisky is a mixture of various grain whiskies (about 60%) and malt whiskies (about 40%) from many different distilleries.

A single malt, like a fine wine, somehow captures the essence of the place where it was made and matured – a combination of the water, the barley, the peat smoke, the oak barrels in which it was aged, and (in the case of certain coastal distilleries) the sea air and salt spray. Each distillation varies from the one before, like different vintages from the same vineyard.

A good malt whisky can be drunk neat, or preferably with a little water added. To appreciate the aroma and flavour to the utmost, a measure of malt whisky should be cut (diluted) with one-third to two-thirds as much spring water (still, bottled spring water will do). Ice, tap water and (God forbid) mixers are for philistines. Would you add lemonade or ice to a glass of Chablis?

Haggis

Scotland's national dish is often ridiculed because of its ingredients, which admittedly don't sound promising – the finely chopped lungs, heart and liver of a sheep, mixed with oatmeal and onion and stuffed into a sheep's stomach. However, it tastes surprisingly good.

Haggis should be served with *champit tatties* and *bashed neeps* (mashed potatoes and turnips), with a generous dollop of butter and a good sprinkling of black pepper.

Although it's eaten year-round, haggis is central to the celebrations of 25 January, in honour of Scotland's national poet, Robert Burns. Scots worldwide unite on Burns Night to revel in their Scottishness. A piper announces the arrival of the haggis and Burns' poem 'Address to a Haggis' is recited to this 'Great chieftan o' the puddin-race'. The bulging haggis is then lanced with a dirk (dagger) to reveal the steaming offal within, 'warm, reekin, rich'.

Vegetarians (and quite a few carnivores, no doubt) will be relieved to know that veggie haggis is available in some restaurants.

Smoked Fish

Scotland is famous for its smoked salmon, but there are many other varieties of smoked fish – plus smoked meats and cheeses – to enjoy. Smoking food to preserve it is an ancient art that has recently undergone a revival, but this time it's more about flavour than preservation.

There are two parts to the process – first the cure, which involves covering the fish in a mixture of salt and molasses sugar, or soaking it in brine; and then the smoke, which can be either cold smoking (at less than 34°C), which results in a raw product, or hot smoking (at more than 60°C), which cooks it. Cold-smoked products include traditional smoked salmon, kippers and Finnan haddies. Hot-smoked products include *bradan rost* ('flaky' smoked salmon) and Arbroath smokies.

Arbroath smokies are haddock that have been gutted, beheaded and cleaned, then salted and dried overnight, tied together at the tail in pairs, and hot-smoked over oak or beech chippings for 45 to 90 minutes. Finnan haddies (named after

Scottish Ales

The increasing popularity of real ales has seen a huge rise in the number of specialist brewers and microbreweries springing up all over Scotland. They take pride in using only natural ingredients, and many try to revive ancient recipes, such as heather- and seaweed-flavoured ales.

Here are a few of our favourites:

◦ **Cairngorm Brewery** (www.cairngormbrewery.com)
◦ **Isle of Skye Brewery** (www.skyebrewery.co.uk)
◦ **Orkney Brewery** (www.sinclairbreweries.co.uk)
◦ **Williams Bros** (www.fraoch.com)

the fishing village of Findon in Aberdeenshire) are also haddock, but these are split down the middle like kippers, and cold-smoked.

Kippers (smoked herring) were invented in Northumberland, in northern England, in the mid-19th century, but Scotland soon picked up the technique, and both Loch Fyne and Mallaig are famous for their kippers.

Oat Cuisine

The most distinctive feature of traditional Scottish cookery is the abundant use of oatmeal. Oats (*Avena sativa*) grow well in the cool, wet climate of Scotland and have been cultivated here for at least 2000 years. Up to the 19th century, oatmeal was the main source of calories for the rural Scottish population. The farmer in his field, the cattle drover on the road to the market, the soldier on the march, all would carry with them a bag of meal that could be mixed with water and baked on a griddle or on hot stones beside a fire.

Long despised as an inferior foodstuff, oatmeal is enjoying a return to popularity as recent research has proved it to be highly nutritious (high in iron, calcium and B vitamins) and healthy (rich in soluble fibre, which helps to reduce cholesterol).

The best-known Scottish oatmeal dish is, of course, porridge, which is simply rolled oatmeal boiled with water. A lot of nonsense has been written about porridge and whether it should be eaten with salt or with sugar. It should be eaten however you like it – as a child in the 1850s, Robert Louis Stevenson had golden syrup with his.

Oatcakes are another traditional dish that you will certainly come across during a visit to Edinburgh, usually as an accompaniment to cheese at the end of a meal. A mealie pudding is a sausage-skin stuffed with oatmeal and onion and boiled for an hour or so. Add blood to the mixture and you have a black pudding. Skirlie is simply chopped onions and oatmeal fried in beef dripping and seasoned with salt and pepper; it's usually served as a side dish. Trout and herring can be dipped in oatmeal before frying, and it can be added to soups and stews as a thickening agent. It's even used in desserts – toasted oatmeal is a vital flavouring in cranachan, a delicious mixture of whipped cream, whisky and raspberries.

Flora & Fauna

The Scottish red deer

DAVID

Scotland can boast the best wildlife-watching in Britain – from the majestic sea eagle to the iconic red deer, its roar reverberating among the hills during the autumn rut. The countless islands moored offshore, pounded by the raging North Atlantic Ocean, are havens for species hunted to extinction centuries ago in habitats further south. Whales and dolphins patrol the seas, and the remote archipelagos of the northeast are sanctuaries for seabird breeding colonies of extraordinary magnitude.

The Land

Scotland's mainland can be neatly divided into three. The southern Uplands, ranges of rounded hills covered with grass and heather and bounded by fertile coastal plains, extend south from Girvan in Ayrshire to Dunbar in East Lothian.

The central Lowlands lie in a broad band stretching from Glasgow and Ayr in the west to Edinburgh and Dundee in the east. This area is underlaid by sedimentary rocks, including the beds of coal and oil shale that fuelled Scotland's industrial revolution. Though it's only a fifth of the nation by land area, most of the country's industry, its two largest cities and 80% of the population are concentrated here.

Another great geological divide – the Highland Boundary Fault – runs from Helensburgh in the west to Stonehaven on the east coast, and marks the southern edge of the Scottish Highlands. These hills – most of their summits around the 900m to 1000m mark – were deeply dissected by glaciers during the last Ice Age, creating a series of deep, U-shaped valleys, including the long, narrow sea lochs that are such a feature of the west Highland scenery.

Despite their pristine beauty, the wild, empty landscapes of the western and northern Highlands are artificial wildernesses. Before the Highland Clearances many of these empty corners of Scotland supported sizable rural populations.

Offshore, some 800 islands are concentrated in four main groups; the Shetlands, the Orkneys, the Outer Hebrides and the Inner Hebrides.

The Water

It rains a lot in Scotland – some parts of the western Highlands get over 4½ metres of it a year – so it's not surprising there's plenty of water about. Around 3% of Scotland's land surface is fresh water; the numerous lochs, rivers and burns form the majority of this, but about a third is in the form of wetlands: the peat bogs that form so much of the Highland and island landscape.

But it's the salt water that really shapes the country. Including the islands, there's over 10,000 miles of Scottish coast: a tortuous, complex, shoreline that doubles back on itself at the slightest opportunity.

Animals

Britain's largest land animal, the red deer, is present in large numbers, as is the (more common) roe deer. You'll see them if you spend any time in the Highlands – some are quite content to wander down the village street in the evening and crop at the lawns.

Otters are found in most parts of Scotland, around the coast and along salmon and trout rivers. The best places to spot them are in the northwest, especially in Skye. The piers at Kyle of Lochalsh and Portree are otter 'hot spots', as the otters have learned to scavenge from fishing boats.

Scotland is home to 75% of Britain's red squirrel population; they've been pushed out in most of the rest of the country by the dominant grey squirrels, introduced from North America. The mountain hare dwells in high mountain environments, and swaps a grey-brown summer coat for a pure-white winter one.

Of course, most of the animals you'll see will be in fields or getting in your way on single-track roads. Several indigenous sheep varieties are still around, smaller and stragglier than the purpose-bred supermodels we're used to. Other emblematic domestic animals include the gentle Highland cow with its wide horns and shaggy reddish-brown coat.

The waters off Scotland's north and west coasts are rich in marine mammals. Dolphins and porpoises are fairly common, and in summer, minke whales are regular visitors. Orcas, too, are occasionally sighted. Seals are

The Salmon's Journey

One of Scotland's most thrilling sights is the flash of rippling silver as a salmon leaps up a fast-flowing cascade. The salmon's life begins in early spring, hatching in a gravel stream bed in a remote Scottish glen. The salmon fry stay in the river for a couple of years until they are big enough to head downstream and out to sea. After several years feeding and growing in the North Atlantic, they eventually return home to reproduce, unerringly finding the river of their birth.

The Best Wildlife Encounters

1 Ospreys, Loch Garten (p287)

2 Sea eagles, Skye (boxed text, p250)

3 Minke whales, Mull (boxed text, p251)

4 Bottlenose dolphins, Moray Firth (p269)

5 Reindeer, Aviemore (p287)

6 Wildcats, Kincraig (p287)

widespread – both the Atlantic grey (identified by its roman nose) and the common seal (with a shorter, dog-like face) are often seen along the coasts and especially in the islands.

Birds

Scotland has an immense variety of birds. For birdwatchers, the highlight of a visit to Scotland is the chance to see the mighty white-tailed sea eagle, Britain's biggest bird of prey. Reintroduced to the western seaboard after having been hunted to extinction, they once again patrol the skies high above Skye and Mull.

The majestic osprey (also absent for most of the 20th century) nests in Scotland from mid-March through to September, after migrating from West Africa. There are around 200 breeding pairs and you can see nesting sites throughout the country, including at Loch Garten. Other birds of prey too, such as the golden eagle, buzzards, peregrine falcon and hen harrier, are now protected and their populations are slowly recovering.

The ptarmigan (a type of grouse) is a native of the Scottish mountains, seldom seen below 700m, with the unusual feature of having feathered feet. It is the only British bird that plays the Arctic trick of changing its plumage from mottled brown in summer to dazzling white in winter, to blend in with the snowfields. In heavily forested areas you may see a capercaillie, a black, turkey-like bird that is the largest of all British birds.

Plants & Trees

Although the thistle is Scotland's national flower, more characteristic are the Scottish bluebell (harebell), carpeting native woodlands in spring; and heather, whose tiny pink and purple flowers emerge on the moors in August. Vivid pink rhododendrons are an introduced species but grow vigorously here, and bright-yellow gorse also flowers in May and June.

Only 1% of Scotland's ancient woodlands – which once covered much of the country – survive, and these are divided into small parcels across the land. Managed regeneration forests are slowly covering more of the landscape – especially in the Highlands. Some 1.3 million hectares of tree cover (17% of the land area) now exists; not a huge figure, but an improvement on what it was. About a third of this is controlled by the government's Forestry Commission (www.forestry. gov.uk), which, as well as conducting managed logging, dedicates large areas of it to sustainable recreational use. The vast majority of this tree cover is coniferous, and there's a plan to increase it to 25% of land area by 2050.

Golf

Golfers on the Old Course (p194), St Andrews

MARTIN MOOS

Scotland is the home of golf. There are more than 550 golf courses here – that's more per capita than in any other country. The sport is hugely popular and much more egalitarian than in other countries, with lots of affordable, council-owned courses. There are many world-famous championship courses too, of course, from Muirfield in East Lothian, and Turnberry and Troon in Ayrshire, to Carnoustie in Angus and St Andrews Old Course in Fife.

Origins of the Game

The oldest documentary evidence of a game of golf being played dates from 1456, referring to Bruntsfield Links in Edinburgh. The game itself is much older – depending on which version you believe, it may have its origins in Roman times, or in medieval China, or it may have been invented in Scotland in the 12th century; some sources claim it was introduced to Scotland from the Low Countries.

Whatever its origins, there is no denying that golf was first systematised and given a set of official rules in Scotland in the 18th century. The country is home to the world's oldest golf course, its oldest golf club and the sport's governing body (except for the USA and Mexico, where the PGA holds sway), the Royal and Ancient Golf Club of St Andrews.

The Best Golf Courses

1 Ailsa Course, Turnberry

2 Kingsbarns Golf Links, Fife

3 Kings Golf Course, Gleneagles

4 Carnoustie Golf Links, Angus

5 St Andrews Old Course, Fife

Leith Links

Although St Andrews claims seniority in having the oldest golf course in the world, it was at Leith Links in 1744 that the first official rules of the game were formulated by the Honorable Company of Edinburgh Golfers – these 13 rules formed the basis of the modern game. Back then, the game was played over five holes, each being around 400 yards. Rule No 9 gives some insight into the 18th-century sport – 'If a ball be stop'd by any person, Horse, Dog or anything else, the Ball so stop'd must be played where it lyes'. The original document is in the National Library of Scotland and the Honorable Company is now the famous Muirfield Golf Club.

St Andrews

St Andrews is the headquarters of the game's governing body, the Royal and Ancient, and the location of the world's oldest and most famous golf course, the Old Course. The earliest written evidence of golf being played on the links at St Andrews dates from 1552, but the present course layout took form in the 1860s when Old Tom Morris had a hand in its design. One of the course's many unusual features is its double greens: seven of the greens have two holes each. And then there's the Road Hole, the 17th – probably the most famous golf hole in the world – where the hazards include a hotel, a stone dyke and a tarmac road (all of which are in play).

For details on playing the Old Course, see p194.

The Open Championship

Scotland not only has the world's oldest golf course, but gave birth to the first of golf's major competitions, the Open Championship (better known as simply the Open), the only one of which is held outside the USA. Founded in 1860, it was held at Prestwick in Ayrshire for its first decade. Today it takes place over the weekend of the third Friday in July, and is hosted in rotation at a number of links courses in Scotland and England, but every five years it returns to the Old Course at St Andrews (next time is 2015).

In the realm of professional golf, Colin Montgomerie (1963–) has been Scotland's top golfer for over 15 years, consistently finishing in the top five in international tournaments, and ranking second in the world at the peak of his careeer. In the 2005 Open Championship at St Andrews, Montgomerie was runner-up to Tiger Woods, and he lost the 2006 US Open by a single shot – he is widely regarded as the best golfer never to have won a major tournament.

Playing Golf in Scotland

VisitScotland publishes the *Official Guide to Golf in Scotland*, a free annual brochure listing course details, costs and clubs with information on where to stay. Some regions offer a Golf Pass (http://golf.visitscotland.com/golf-passes), costing between £40 and £120 for five days (Monday to Friday), which allows play on a range of courses. Most clubs, be they obscurely local or internationally famous, are open to visitors – details can be found at www.scotlands-golf-courses.com.

Survival
Guide

St Giles Cathedral (p72), Edinburgh
PHOTOGRAPHER: KARL BLACKWELL

A-Z
Directory

●●●●

Accommodation

Scotland provides a comprehensive choice of accommodation to suit all visitors. In this book accommodation choices are flagged with price indicators, based on the cheapest accommodation for two people in high season:

ACCOMMODATION PRICE INDICATORS

£	up to £50
££	from £50 to £130
£££	£130 and over

For budget travel, the options are campsites, hostels and cheap B&Bs. Above this price level is a plethora of comfortable B&Bs and guesthouses (£25 to £40 per person per night). Midrange hotels are present in most places, while, for high-end lodgings (£50-plus per person a night) there are some superb hotels, the most interesting being converted castles and mansions, or chic designer options in cities.

If you're travelling solo, expect to pay a supplement in hotels and B&Bs, meaning you'll often be forking over 75% of the price of a double for your single room.

Almost all B&Bs, guesthouses and hotels (and even some hostels) provide breakfast; if this is not the case, then it is mentioned in individual reviews throughout this book.

Prices increase over the peak tourist season (June to September) and are at their highest in July and August. Outside of these months, and particularly in winter, special deals are often available at guesthouses and hotels. Smaller establishments will often close from around November to March, particularly in more remote areas. If you're going to be in Edinburgh in the festival month of August or at Hogmanay (New Year), book as far in advance as you can – a year if possible – as the city will be packed.

Tourist offices have an accommodation booking service (£3 to £4, local and national), which can be handy over summer. However, note that they can only book the ever-decreasing number of places that are registered with **VisitScotland** (www.visitscotland.com /accommodation). There are many other fine accommodation options which, mostly because of the hefty registration fee, choose not to register with the tourist board. Registered places tend to be a little pricier than non-registered ones.

B&BS & GUESTHOUSES

B&Bs are a Scottish institution. At the bottom end you get a bedroom in a private house, a shared bathroom and a fry-up (juice, coffee or tea, cereal and cooked breakfast – bacon, eggs, sausage, baked beans and toast). Midrange B&Bs have en suite bathrooms, TVs in each room and more variety (and healthier options) for breakfast. Almost all B&Bs provide hospitality trays (tea- and coffee-making facilities) in bedrooms. An excellent option is the farm B&B, which offers traditional Scottish hospitality, huge breakfasts and a quiet rural setting – good for discharging urban grit. Pubs may also offer cheap (and sometimes noisy) B&B and can be good fun.

Guesthouses, often large converted private houses, are an extension of the B&B concept. They are normally larger and more upmarket than B&Bs, offering quality food and more luxurious accommodation.

HOSTELS

Numerous hostels offer cheap accommodation and are great centres for meeting fellow travellers – in Scotland the

---

Book Your Stay Online

For more accommodation reviews by Lonely Planet authors, check out hotels.lonelyplanet. com/Scotland. You'll find independent reviews, as well as recommendations on the best places to stay. Best of all, you can book online.

standard of facilities is generally very good. The more up-market hostels have en suite bathrooms in their dorms, and all manner of luxuries, giving them the feel of hotels if it weren't for the bunk beds.

Hostels have facilities for self-catering, and many provide internet access and can usually arrange activities and tours.

From May to September and on public holidays, hostels – even the remote rural ones – can be booked out, sometimes by large groups, so phone in advance.

INDEPENDENT & STUDENT HOSTELS

There are a large number of independent hostels, most with prices around £10 to £16. Facilities vary considerably, but some of the best are listed in this book and because they are aimed at young backpackers, they can often be great places to party. The free *Independent Backpackers Hostels Scotland* guide (www.hostel-scotland.co.uk), available from tourist offices, lists over 100 hostels in Scotland, mostly in the north.

SCOTTISH YOUTH HOSTEL ASSOCIATION

The **SYHA** (☎ 0845 293 7373; www.syha.org.uk) has a network of decent, reasonably priced hostels and produces a free booklet available from SYHA hostels and tourist offices. There are more than 60 to choose from around the country, ranging from basic walkers' digs to mansions and castles. You've got to be a member of Hostelling International (HI) to stay, but nonmembers can pay a £2 supplement per night that goes towards the £10 membership fee. Prices vary according

to the month, but average around £16 to £18 per adult in high season.

Most SYHA hostels close from mid-October to early March but can be rented out by groups.

HOTELS

There are some wonderfully luxurious places, including rustic country-house hotels in fabulous settings, and castles complete with crenellated battlements, grand staircases and the obligatory rows of stag heads. Expect all the perks at these places, often including a gym, a sauna, a pool and first-class service. Even if you're on a budget, it's worth splashing out for a night at one of the classic Highland hotels, which function as community centres, including the local pub and restaurant.

In the cities, dullish chain options dominate the midrange category, though there are some quirkier options in Glasgow and Edinburgh.

Increasingly, hotels use an airline-style pricing system, so it's worth booking well ahead to take advantage of the cheapest rates. The website www.moneysaving expert.com has a good guide to finding cheap hotel rooms.

Some online discount sites:

www.hotels.com

www.laterooms.com

www.lastminute.com

www.priceline.co.uk

SELF-CATERING ACCOMMODATION

Self-catering accommodation is very popular in

Scotland and staying in a house in a city or cottage in the country gives you an opportunity to get a feel for a region and its community. The minimum stay is usually one week in the summer peak season, three days or less at other times.

We've only listed limited self-catering options in this guide. The best place to start looking for this kind of accommodation is the website of **VisitScotland** (www.visitscotland.com), which lists numerous self-catering options all over Scotland. These options also appear in the regional accommodation guides available from tourist offices.

Expect a week's rent for a two-bedroom cottage to cost from £160 in winter, and up to £280 July to September.

The following are other places to search:

CKD Galbraith (☎ 0131-556 4422; www.ckdgalbraith. co.uk) Offers a wide range of self-catering accommodation, from cottages to castles.

Cottage Guide (www .cottageguide.co.uk) Lots of Scottish cottages to browse online.

Ecosse Unique (☎ 01835-822277; www.uniquescotland .com) Offers furnished holiday homes all over the country.

Landmark Trust (☎ 01628-825925; www.landmarktrust.org .uk) A building-preservation charity that restores historic buildings and lets them out as accommodation.

Practicalities

○ Leaf through Edinburgh's *Scotsman* newspaper or Glasgow's *Herald,* over 225 years old.

○ Have a giggle at the popular Labour-influenced tabloid, the *Daily Record,* or try the *Sunday Post* for rose-tinted nostalgia.

○ BBC Radio Scotland (AM 810kHz, FM 92.4-94.7MHz) provides a Scottish point of view.

○ Watch BBC1 Scotland, BBC2 Scotland and ITV stations STV or Borders. Channel Four and Five are nationwide channels with unchanged content for Scotland.

○ Use the metric system for weights and measures, with the exception of road distances (in miles) and beer (in pints). The pint is 570mL, more than the US version.

○ In Scotland you can't smoke in any public place with a roof and that is at least half enclosed. That means pubs, bus shelters, restaurants and hotels – basically, anywhere you might want to.

Activities

Scotland is a brilliant place for outdoor recreation and has something to offer everyone, from those who enjoy a short stroll to full-on adrenaline junkies. Although hiking, golf, fishing and cycling are the most popular activities, there is an astonishing variety of things to do.

Most activities are well organised and have clubs and associations that can give visitors invaluable information and, sometimes, substantial discounts. **VisitScotland** (www.visitscotland.com) has information on most activities. Its website has useful pages on fishing, golf, skiing, cycling and adventure sports.

Detailed information can be found in the regional chapters throughout this guide. Some other useful sources:

Fishing Seasons and permits vary according to locality. Permits can usually be obtained at the local tackle shop.

Cycling There are many excellent routes throughout the country. **Sustrans** (www .sustrans.org.uk) is the first place to go for information.

Golf *The Official Guide to Golf in Scotland* is published by VisitScotland and can also be browsed on its website.

Walking Lonely Planet's *Walking in Scotland* is a comprehensive walker's resource.

Birdwatching The **Royal Society for the Protection of Birds** (www.rspb.org.uk) should be any birdwatcher's first port of call.

Business Hours

Shops open at least 9am to 5.30pm Monday to Friday and most open Saturday too, with late-night shopping usually until 8pm Thursday in the cities. A growing number also open Sunday, typically 11am to 5pm. In the Highlands and islands Sunday opening is restricted, and it's common for there to be little or no public transport.

In this guide, specific opening hours are only listed if they differ markedly from the following:

Banks 9.30am to 4pm Monday to Friday, plus some are open 9.30am to 12.30pm Saturday.

Cafes 10am to 5pm; in large towns and cities some open for breakfast from about 7am. If licensed, they may stay open for dinner, too.

Nightclubs 10pm to 4am Thursday to Saturday.

Post offices 9am to 5.30pm Monday to Friday, 9am-12.30pm Saturday.

Pubs & Bars 11am to 11pm Monday to Thursday, 11am to 1am Friday and Saturday, 12.30pm to 11pm Sunday; lunch is served noon to 2.30pm, dinner 6pm to 9pm daily.

Restaurants Lunch noon to 2.30pm, dinner 6pm to 9pm or 10pm; in small towns and villages the chippy (fish-and-chip shop) is often the only place to buy cooked food after 8pm.

●●○●

Customs Regulations

Travellers arriving in the UK from other EU countries don't have to pay tax or duty on goods for personal use, and can bring back as much EU duty-paid alcohol and tobacco as they like. However, if you bring in more than the following, you'll probably be asked some questions: 3200 cigarettes, 400 cigarillos, 200 cigars, 3kg of smoking tobacco, 10L of spirits, 20L of fortified wine (eg port or sherry), 90L of wine and 110L of beer. Those under 17 years cannot import any alcohol or tobacco. There are different allowances for tobacco products from the newer EU member countries, though (such as Estonia, Poland, Hungary, Latvia, Lithuania, Slovakia, the Czech Republic and Slovenia) – check the website of **HM Customs and Excise** (www.hmrc.gov .uk) for further details.

Travellers from outside the EU can bring in, duty-free:

○ 200 cigarettes *or* 100 cigarillos *or* 50 cigars *or* 250g of tobacco

○ 4L of still table wine

○ 1L of spirits *or* 2L of fortified wine

○ 60mL of perfume

○ £300 worth of all other goods, including gifts and souvenirs.

Anything over this limit must be declared to customs officers on arrival.

For details of restrictions and quarantine regulations, see the customs website.

●●○●

Discount Cards

HISTORIC SITES

Membership of Historic Scotland (HS) and the National Trust for Scotland (NTS) is worth considering, especially if you're going to be in Scotland for a while. Both are nonprofit organisations dedicated to the preservation of the environment, and both care for hundreds of spectacular sites. Throughout this guide the abbreviations HS and NTS are used to indicate places that are under the care of these organisations. You can join up at any of their properties.

Historic Scotland (HS; 0131 668 8600; www.his toric-scotland.gov.uk) A year's membership costs £40.50/76 per adult/family, and gives free entry to HS sites (half-price entry to sites in England and Wales). Also offers short-term Explorer membership – three days out of five for £22, seven days out of 14 for £31.50.

National Trust for Scotland (NTS; ☎ 0131-243 9300; www.nts.org.uk) A year's membership of the NTS, costing £46/76 for an adult/

Climate

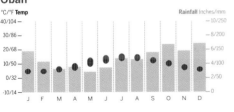

Edinburgh
°C/°F **Temp**   Rainfall Inches/mm

Inverness
°C/°F **Temp**   Rainfall Inches/mm

Oban
°C/°F **Temp**   Rainfall Inches/mm

family offers free access to all NTS and National Trust properties (in the rest of the UK).

HOSTEL CARDS

If travelling on a budget, membership of the **Scottish Youth Hostel Association/Hostelling International** (SYHA/HI; ☎ 0845 293 7373; www.syha.org.uk) is a must (annual membership over/under 16 years is £10/free, life membership is £100).

SENIOR CARDS

Discount cards for those over 60 years are available for train travel (see 354).

STUDENT & YOUTH CARDS

The most useful card is the International Student Identity Card (ISIC), which displays your photo. This can perform wonders, including producing discounts on entry to attractions and on many forms of transport.

There's a global industry in fake student cards, and many places now stipulate a maximum age for student discounts or substitute a 'youth discount' for 'student discount'. If you're under 26 but not a student, you can apply for the Euro/26 card, which goes by various names in different countries, or an International Youth Travel Card (IYTC) issued by the **International Student Travel Confederation** (ISTC; www.istc.org). These cards are available through student unions, hostelling organisations or youth travel agencies.

Electricity

120V/60Hz

Food

In this guide eating choices are flagged with price indicators, based on the cost of an average main course from the dinner menu:

EATING PRICE INDICATORS	
£	up to £9
££	from £9 to £18
£££	£18 and over

Note though that lunch mains are often cheaper than dinner mains, and many places offer an 'early bird' special with lower prices (usually available between 5pm and 7pm). See p342 for restaurant opening hours, and the Flavours of Scotland chapter (p331) for information about tucking into Scottish cuisine.

Gay & Lesbian Travellers

Although many Scots are fairly tolerant of homosexuality, overt displays of affection aren't wise if conducted away from acknowledged 'gay' venues or districts – hostility may be encountered.

Edinburgh and Glasgow have small but flourishing gay scenes. The website www.gayscotland.com and the monthly magazine *Scotsgay* (www.scotsgay.com) keep gays, lesbians and bisexuals informed about gay-scene issues.

Health

While Scotland has excellent health care, prevention is the key to staying healthy while travelling in the country. A little planning before departure, particularly for pre-existing illnesses, will save trouble later. Bring medications in their original, clearly labelled containers. A signed, dated letter from your physician describing your medical conditions and medications, including generic names, is also a good idea. If carrying syringes or needles, be sure to have a physician's letter documenting their medical necessity. Carry a spare pair of contact lenses and glasses, and take your optical prescription with you.

INSURANCE

If you're an EU citizen, a European Health Insurance Card (EHIC), available from health centres or, in the UK, post offices, covers you for most medical care. EHIC will not cover you for non-emergencies, or emergency repatriation. Citizens from non-EU countries should find out if there is a reciprocal arrangement for free medical care between their country and the UK. If you do need health insurance, make sure you get a policy that covers you for the worst possible case, such as an accident requiring an emergency flight home. Find out in advance if your insurance plan will make payments directly to providers or reimburse you later for overseas health expenditures.

RECOMMENDED VACCINATIONS

No jabs are required to travel to Scotland

MIDGES & CLEGS

The most painful problems facing visitors to the Highlands and islands are midges and clegs. The midge is a tiny, 2mm-long blood-sucking fly. Midges are at their worst during the twilight hours and on still, overcast days. They proliferate from late May to mid-September, but especially from mid-June to mid-August – which unfortunately coincides with the main tourist season. Cover up, particularly in the evening; wear light-coloured clothing (midges are attracted to dark colours); and most importantly, use a reliable insect repellent containing DEET or DMP.

The cleg, or horse fly, is 13mm long and slate-grey in colour. A master of stealth, it loves to land unnoticed on necks and ankles, and can give a painful bite (it can even bite through hair or light clothing). Unlike midges, they are most active on warm, sunny days and are most common in July and August.

Insurance

Travel insurance not only covers you for medical expenses, theft or loss, but also for cancellation of, or delays in, any of your travel arrangements.

Lots of bank accounts give their holders automatic travel insurance – check if this is the case for you.

Always read the small print carefully. Some policies specifically exclude 'dangerous activities', such as scuba diving, motorcycling, skiing, mountaineering and even trekking.

There's a variety of policies and your travel agent can give recommendations. Make sure the policy includes health care and medication in the countries you may visit on your way to/from Scotland. See left for advice on health insurance.

You may prefer a policy that pays doctors or hospitals directly rather than forcing you to pay on the spot and claim the money back later. If you have to claim later, make sure you keep all documentation. Some policies ask you to call back (reverse charges) to a centre in your home country where an immediate assessment of your problem is made.

Not all policies cover ambulances, helicopter rescue or emergency flights home. Most policies exclude cover for pre-existing illnesses.

Worldwide travel insurance is available at www.lonelyplanet .com/travel_services. You can buy, extend and claim online anytime – even if you're already on the road.

Internet Access

If you're travelling with a laptop, you'll find a wide range of places offering a wi-fi connection. These range from cafes to B&Bs and public spaces.

Accommodation and eating and drinking options with wi-fi have the 🛜 symbol in the listing. Wi-fi is often free, but some places (typically, upmarket hotels) charge.

There are some increasingly good deals on pay-as-you-go mobile internet from mobile network providers.

If you see the @ symbol, then the place has an internet terminal.

If you don't have a laptop, the best places to check email and surf the internet are public libraries – almost every town and village in the country has at least a couple of computer terminals devoted to the internet, and they are free to use, though there's often a time limit.

Internet cafes also exist in the cities and larger towns

and are generally good value, charging approximately £2 to £3 per hour.

Many of the larger tourist offices across the country also have internet access.

Legal Matters

The 1707 Act of Union preserved the Scottish legal system as separate from the law in England and Wales.

Police have the power to detain, for up to six hours, anyone suspected of having committed an offence punishable by imprisonment (including drugs offences). They can search you, take your photo and fingerprints, and question you. You are legally required to provide your correct name and address – not doing so, or giving false details, is an offence – but you are not obliged to answer any other questions. After six hours, the police must either formally charge you or let you go.

If you are detained and/or arrested, you have the right to inform a solicitor and one other person, though you have no right to actually see the solicitor or to make a telephone call. If you don't know a solicitor, the police will inform the duty solicitor for you.

The government can now detain foreigners suspected of terrorist activities, without charge, for a period of 28 days.

If you need legal assistance, contact the **Scottish Legal Aid Board** (☎ 0131-226 7061; www.slab.org.uk; 44 Drumsheugh Gardens, Edinburgh).

Possession of a small amount of cannabis is punishable by a fine, but possession of a larger amount of cannabis, or any amount of harder drugs, is much more serious, with a sentence of up to 14 years in prison. Police have the right to search anyone they suspect of possessing drugs.

A maximum blood-alcohol level of 35mg/100mL when driving is allowable.

The following legal minimum ages apply in Scotland: 18 years for drinking alcohol, smoking and voting; 17 years for driving.

Travellers should note that they can be prosecuted under the law of their home country regarding age of consent, even when abroad.

Maps

If you're about to tackle Munros, you'll require maps with far greater detail than the maps in this guide, or the ones supplied by tourist offices. The Ordnance Survey (OS) caters to walkers, with a wide variety of maps at 1:50,000 and 1:25,000 scales. Alternatively, look out for the excellent walkers' maps published by Harveys; they're at scales of 1:40,000 and 1:25,000.

Money

The British currency is the pound sterling (£), with 100 pence (p) to a pound. 'Quid' is the slang term for pound.

Three Scottish banks issue their own banknotes, meaning there's quite a variety of different notes in circulation. They are legal tender in England too, but you'll sometimes run into problems changing them. They are also harder to exchange once you get outside the UK.

Euros are accepted in Scotland only at some major tourist attractions and a few upmarket hotels – it's always better to have sterling cash. For exchange rates and information on general dining and accommodation costs, see p49.

ATMS

ATMs (called cashpoints in Scotland) are widespread and you'll usually find at least one in small towns and villages. You can use Visa, Master-Card, Amex, Cirrus, Plus and Maestro to withdraw cash from ATMs belonging to most banks and building societies in Scotland.

Cash withdrawals from some ATMs may be subject to a small charge, but most are free.

CREDIT CARDS

Visa, MasterCard, Amex and Diners Club cards are widely recognised, although some places will charge for accepting them (generally for small transactions). Charge cards such as Amex and Diners Club may not be accepted in smaller establishments. Credit and credit/debit cards like Visa and MasterCard are more widely accepted, but smaller B&Bs may not take cards.

MONEYCHANGERS

Be careful using bureaux de change; they may offer good exchange rates but frequently levy outrageous commissions and fees. The best-value place to change money in the UK is at post offices, but only the ones in larger towns and cities offer this service. Larger tourist offices also have exchange facilities.

TIPPING

Tip 10% in sit-down restaurants, but not if there's already a service charge on the bill.

In very classy places they may expect closer to 15%.

Service is at your discretion: even if the charge is added to the bill, you don't have to pay it if you feel service has been poor.

Don't tip in pubs: if the service has been exceptional over the course of an evening, you can say 'have one for yourself'.

Tip taxi drivers in cities around 10%, or just round up.

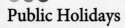

Public Holidays

Although bank holidays are general public holidays in the rest of the UK, in Scotland they only apply to banks and some other commercial offices.

Scottish towns normally have four days of public holiday, which they allocate themselves; dates vary from year to year and from town to town. Most places celebrate St Andrew's Day (30 November) as a public holiday.

General public holidays:
New Year 1 & 2 January
Good Friday March or April
Christmas Day 25 December
Boxing Day 26 December

Telephone

The famous red telephone boxes are a dying breed now, surviving mainly in conservation areas. You'll mainly see two types of phone booths in Scotland: one takes money (and doesn't give change), while the other uses pre-paid phone cards and credit cards. Some phones accept both coins and cards. Payphone cards are widely available.

The cheapest way of calling internationally is to buy a discount call card; you'll see these in newsagents, along with tables of countries and the number of minutes you'll get for your money.

MOBILE PHONES

Codes for mobile phones usually begin with ☑07. The UK uses the GSM 900/1800 network, which covers the rest of Europe, Australia and New Zealand, but isn't compatible with the North American GSM 1900. Most modern mobiles, however, can function on both networks – check before you leave home though.

International roaming charges can be prohibitively high, and you'll probably find it cheaper to get a UK number. This is easily done by buying a SIM card (around £10 including calling credit) and sticking it in your phone. Your phone may be blocked by your home network though, so you'll have to either get it unblocked, or buy a pay-as-you-go phone along with your SIM card (think £50).

Pay-as-you-go phones can be recharged by buying vouchers from shops.

PHONE CODES & USEFUL NUMBERS

Dialling the UK Dial your country's international access code then ☑44 (the UK country code), then the area code (dropping the first 0) followed by the telephone number.

Dialling out of the UK The international access code is ☑00; dial this, then dial the code of the country you wish to call.

Making a reverse charge (collect) international call Dial ☑155 for the operator. It's an expensive option, but not for the caller.

Area codes in Scotland Begin with ☑01xxx, eg Edinburgh ☑0131, Wick ☑01955.

Directory Assistance There are several numbers; ☑118500 is one.

Mobile phones Codes usually begin with ☑07.

Free calls Numbers starting with 0800 are free; calls to 0845 numbers are charged at local rates.

Time

Scotland is on GMT/UTC. The clocks go forward for 'summer time' one hour at the end of March, and go back at the end of October. The 24hr clock is used for transport timetables, but plenty of folk still struggle to get the hang of it.

TIME DIFFERENCE BETWEEN SCOTLAND & MAJOR CITIES

Paris, Berlin, Rome	1hr ahead
New York	5hr behind
Sydney	9hr ahead Apr-Sep, 10hr Oct, 11hr Nov-Mar.
Los Angeles	8hr behind
Mumbai	5½hr ahead, 4½hr Mar-Oct
Tokyo	9hr ahead, 8hr Mar-Oct

Tourist Information

The Scottish Tourist Board, known as **VisitScotland** (☏ 0845 225 5121; www.visitscotland.com; info@visitscotland.com; Ocean Point One, 94 Ocean Dr, Leith, Edinburgh EH6 6HJ), deals with inquiries made by post, email and telephone. You can request, online and by phone, regional brochures be posted out to you online.

Most larger towns have tourist offices that open 9am or 10am to 5pm Monday to Friday, and on weekends in summer. In small places, particularly in the Highlands, tourist offices only open from Easter to September. Details of tourist offices can be found throughout the guide.

Travellers with Disabilities

For many travellers with disabilities, Scotland is a strange mix of user-friendliness and unfriendliness. Most new buildings are accessible to wheelchair users, so modern hotels and tourist attractions are fine. However, most B&Bs and guesthouses are in hard-to-adapt older buildings, which means that travellers with mobility problems may pay more for accommodation. Things are constantly improving though.

It's a similar story with public transport. Newer buses have steps that lower for easier access, as do trains, but it's wise to check before setting out. Tourist attractions usually reserve parking spaces near the entrance for drivers with disabilities.

Many places such as ticket offices and banks are fitted with hearing loops to assist the hearing-impaired; look for the symbol of a large ear.

A few tourist attractions, such as Glasgow Cathedral, have Braille guides or scented gardens for the visually impaired.

VisitScotland produces the guide *Accessible Scotland* for wheelchair-bound travellers, and many tourist offices have leaflets with accessibility details for their area. Regional accommodation guides have a wheelchair-accessible criterion.

Many regions have organisations that hire wheelchairs – contact the local tourist office for details. Many nature trails have been adapted for wheelchair use.

For more information:

Historic Scotland (HS; ☏ 0131-668 8600; www.historic-scotland.gov.uk) Has a free leaflet outlining access and facilities at HS properties, and also produces a large-print version of the HS promotional brochure.

Royal Association for Disability & Rehabilitation (RADAR; ☏ 020-7250 3222; www.radar.org.uk; Information Dept, 12 City Forum, 250 City Rd, London EC1V 8AF) Excellent; publishes a guide (£10) on travel in the UK and has an accommodation website.

Holiday Care Service (☏ 0845 124 9971; www.holidaycare.org.uk) Publishes regional information guides (£5) to Scotland and can offer general advice.

Disabled Persons Railcard (www.disabledpersons-railcard.co.uk) Discounted train travel (see p354).

Visas

If you're a citizen of the EEA (European Economic Area) nations or Switzerland, you don't need a visa to enter or work in Britain – you can enter using your national identity card.

Visa regulations are always subject to change, so it's essential to check with your local British embassy, high commission or consulate before leaving home. Currently, if you're a citizen of Australia, Canada, New Zealand, Japan, Israel, the USA and several other countries, you can stay for up to six months (no visa required), but are not allowed to work.

Nationals of many countries, including South Africa, will need a visa: for more info, see www.ukvisas.gov.uk.

British immigration authorities have always been tough; dress neatly and carry proof that you have sufficient funds with which to support yourself. A credit card and/or an onward ticket will help.

Women Travellers

Women travelling alone are highly unlikely to have problems in Scotland, though there are still a few pubs where you'll turn heads if you walk in alone. Cosmopolitan city pubs and most rural pubs are fine – you'll get a pretty good idea as soon as you open the door.

The contraceptive pill is available only on prescription; however, the 'morning-after' pill (effective against conception for up to 72 hours after unprotected sexual intercourse) is available over the counter at chemists.

Transport

Getting There & Away

 AIR

There are direct flights to Scottish airports from England, Wales, Ireland, the USA, Canada, Scandinavia and several countries in western and central Europe. From elsewhere, you'll probably have to fly into a European hub and catch a connecting flight to a Scottish airport – London, Amsterdam, Frankfurt and Paris have the best connections. If flying from North America, it's worth looking at Icelandair, which often has good deals to Glasgow via Reykjavik.

AIRPORTS

Scotland has four main international airports of its own: Aberdeen, Edinburgh, Glasgow and Glasgow Prestwick. A few short-haul international flights land at Inverness and Sumburgh, while London is the main UK gateway for long-haul flights.

 LAND

BUS

Buses are usually the cheapest way to get to Scotland from other parts of the UK. The main operators:

Megabus (www.megabus.com) One-way fares from London to Glasgow from as little as £5.50 if you book well in advance (up to eight weeks).

National Express (www.gobycoach.com) Regular services from London and other cities in England and Wales to Glasgow and Edinburgh.

Climate Change & Travel

Every form of transport that relies on carbon-based fuel generates CO_2, the main cause of human-induced climate change. Modern travel is dependent on aeroplanes, which might use less fuel per mile per person than most cars but travel much greater distances. The altitude at which aircraft emit gases (including CO_2) and particles also contributes to their climate change impact. Many websites offer 'carbon calculators' that allow people to estimate the carbon emissions generated by their journey and, for those who wish to do so, to offset the impact of the greenhouse gases emitted with contributions to portfolios of climate-friendly initiatives throughout the world. Lonely Planet offsets the carbon footprint of all staff and author travel.

Scottish Citylink (www .citylink.co.uk) Daily service between Belfast and Glasgow and Edinburgh via Stranraer ferry.

CAR & MOTORCYCLE

Drivers of EU-registered vehicles will find bringing a car or motorcycle into Scotland fairly easy. The vehicle must have registration papers and a nationality plate, and you must have insurance. The International Insurance Certificate (Green Card) isn't compulsory, but it is excellent proof that you're covered. If driving from mainland Europe via the Channel Tunnel or ferry ports, head for London and follow the M25 orbital road to the M1 motorway, then follow the M1 and M6 north.

For rules of the road, speed limits etc, see p352.

TRAIN

Travelling to Scotland by train is usually faster and more comfortable than the bus, but more expensive. Taking into account check-ins and travel time between city centre and airport, the train is a competitive alternative, time wise, to air travel on the London to Edinburgh route.

East Coast (www.eastcoast .co.uk) Trains between London Kings Cross and Edinburgh (four hours, every half-hour).

Eurostar (www.eurostar.com) It is possible to travel from Paris or Brussels to London in around two hours on the Eurostar service. From St Pancras it's a quick and easy change to Kings Cross or Euston for trains to Edinburgh or Glasgow. Total journey time from Paris to Edinburgh is about eight hours.

First ScotRail (www.scotrail .co.uk) Runs the **Caledonian Sleeper**, an overnight service connecting London Euston with Edinburgh, Glasgow, Stirling, Perth, Dundee, Aberdeen, Fort William and Inverness.

National Rail Enquiry Service (08457 484 950; www.nationalrail.co.uk) Timetable and fares info for all UK trains.

Virgin Trains (www.virgin trains.co.uk) Trains between London Euston and Glasgow (4½ hours, hourly).

Getting Around

Public transport in Scotland is generally good, but it can be costly compared with other European countries. Buses are usually the cheapest way to get around, but also the slowest. With a discount pass, trains can be competitive; they're also quicker and often take you through beautiful scenery.

Traveline (0871 200 2233; www.travelinescotland .com) provides timetable info for all public transport services in Scotland, but can't provide fare information or book tickets.

 AIR

Most domestic air services are geared to business needs, or are lifelines for remote island communities. Flying is a pricey way to cover relatively short distances, and only worth considering if you're short of time and want to visit the Hebrides, Orkney or Shetland.

Flying in Style

Loch Lomond Seaplanes (www .lochlomondseaplanes .com) operates Scotland's only seaplane passenger service, offering flights on demand from Glasgow to Oban (March to November, sea conditions permitting). Flights depart from the River Clyde next to Glasgow's Science Centre, and take only 25 minutes to reach Oban Bay; a return flight costs £169.

AIRLINES IN SCOTLAND

Eastern Airways (www .easternairways.com) Flies from Aberdeen to Stornoway and Wick.

Flybe/Loganair (www.logan air.co.uk) The main domestic airline in Scotland, with flights from Glasgow to Barra, Benbecula, Campbeltown, Islay, Kirkwall, Sumburgh, Stornoway and Tiree; from Edinburgh to Inverness, Kirkwall, Sumburgh, Stornoway and Wick; from Aberdeen to Kirkwall and Sumburgh; and from Inverness to Kirkwall, Stornoway and Sumburgh. It also operates inter-island flights in Orkney and

Shetland, and from Barra to Benbecula.

Orkney to Shetland and from Aberdeen to Shetland.

Hebridean Air (www.hebrideanair.co.uk) Flies from Connel airfield near Oban to the islands of Coll, Tiree, Colonsay and Islay.

 BICYCLE

Scotland is a compact country, and travelling around by bicycle is a perfectly feasible proposition if you have the time. Indeed, for touring the islands a bicycle is both cheaper (in terms of ferry fares) and more suited to their small size and leisurely pace of life. For more information, see http://cycling.visitscotland.com.

 BOAT

CalMac (www.calmac.co.uk) Serves the west coast and islands. Comprehensive timetable booklet available from tourist offices.

CalMac Island Hopscotch More than two dozen tickets giving reduced fares for various combinations of crossings; these are listed on the website and in the CalMac timetables booklet.

CalMac Island Rover Ticket allowing unlimited travel on CalMac ferries, £48.50/70 for a foot passenger for eight/15 days, plus £232/348 for a car or £116/175 for a motorbike. Bicycles travel free with a foot passenger's ticket.

Northlink Ferries (www.northlinkferries.co.uk) Ferries from Aberdeen and Scrabster (near Thurso) to Orkney, from

 BUS

Scotland is served by an extensive bus network that covers most of the country. In remote rural areas, however, services are more geared to the needs of locals (getting to school or the shops in the nearest large town) and may not be conveniently timed for visitors.

First (www.firstgroup.com) Operates local bus routes in Aberdeen, Greater Glasgow, Edinburgh and southeast Scotland.

Royal Mail postbuses (www.postbus.royalmail.com) Minibuses, or sometimes four-seater cars, driven by postal workers delivering and collecting the mail – there are no official stops, and you can hail a postbus anywhere on its route. Although services have been cut severely in recent years, it's still the only public transport in some remote parts of Scotland.

Scottish Citylink (www.citylink.co.uk) National network with comfy, reliable buses serving all main towns. Away from the main roads, you'll have to switch to local services.

Stagecoach (www.stagecoachbus.com) Operates local bus routes in many parts of Scotland.

Traveline (0871 200 2233; www.travelinescotland.com) Up-to-date timetable information.

BUS PASSES

Scottish Citylink offers discounts to students, SYHA members and holders of the **NEC Smartcard** (www.youngscot.org), which gives discounts all over Scotland and Europe. Holders of a National Entitlement Card, available to seniors and disabled people who are UK citizens, gives free bus travel throughout the country.

The **Scottish Citylink Explorer Pass** offers unlimited travel on Scottish Citylink services within Scotland for any three days out of five (£35), any five days out of 10 (£59) or any eight days out of 16 (£79). Also gives discounts on various regional bus services, on Northlink and CalMac ferries, and in SYHA hostels. Can be bought in the UK by both UK and overseas citizens. It is not valid on National Express coaches.

 CAR & MOTORCYCLE

Scotland's roads are generally good and far less busy than in England, so driving's more enjoyable. However, cars are nearly always inconvenient in city centres.

Motorways (designated 'M') are toll-free dual carriageways, limited mainly to central Scotland. Main roads ('A') are dual or single carriageways and are sometimes clogged with slow-moving trucks or caravans; the A9 from Perth to Inverness is notoriously busy.

Life on the road is more relaxed and interesting on the secondary roads (designated 'B') and minor roads (undesignated), although in the Highlands and islands there's the added hazard of suicidal sheep wandering onto the road (be particularly wary of lambs in spring).

At around £1.17 per litre (equivalent to more than US$8 per US gallon), petrol is expensive by American or Australian standards; diesel is about 3p per litre more expensive. Prices tend to rise as you get further from the main centres and are over 10% higher in the Outer Hebrides (around £1.27 a litre). In remote areas petrol stations are widely spaced and sometimes closed on Sunday.

DRIVING LICENCE

A non-EU licence is valid in Britain for up to 12 months from time of entry into the country. If bringing a car from Europe, make sure you're adequately insured.

HIRE

Car rental is relatively costly and often you'll be better off making arrangements in your home country for a fly/drive deal. The international rental companies charge from around £140 a week for a small car (Ford Fiesta, Peugeot 106); local companies, such as **Arnold Clark** (www.arnoldclarkrental.co.uk), start from £26 a day or £128 a week.

The main international hire companies:

Avis (www.avis.co.uk)

Budget (www.budget.co.uk)

Europcar (www.europcar.co.uk)

Hertz (www.hertz.co.uk)

Thrifty Car Rental (www.thrifty.co.uk)

Tourist offices have lists of local car-hire companies.

The minimum legal age for driving is 17 but to rent a car, drivers must usually be aged 23 to 65 – outside these limits special conditions or insurance requirements may apply.

If planning to visit the Outer Hebrides, Orkney or Shetland, it'll often prove cheaper to hire a car on the islands, rather than pay to take a rental car across on the ferry.

ROAD RULES

The *Highway Code*, which is widely available in bookshops, details all UK road regulations. Vehicles drive on the left; front-seat belts are compulsory and if belts are fitted in the back seat, then they must be worn too; the speed limit is 30mph in built-up areas, 60mph on single carriageways and 70mph on dual carriageways; you give way to your right at

Road Distances (miles)

	Aberdeen	Dundee	Edinburgh	Fort William	Glasgow	Inverness	Kyle of Lochalsh	Mallaig	Oban	Scrabster	Stranraer
Dundee	70										
Edinburgh	129	62									
Fort William	165	121	146								
Glasgow	145	84	42	104							
Inverness	105	131	155	66	166						
Kyle of Lochalsh	188	177	206	76	181	82					
Mallaig	189	161	180	44	150	106	34				
Oban	180	118	123	45	94	110	120	85			
Scrabster	218	250	279	185	286	119	214	238	230		
Stranraer	233	171	120	184	80	250	265	232	178	374	
Ullapool	150	189	215	90	225	135	88	166	161	125	158

Single-track Roads

In many country areas, and especially in the Highlands and islands, you will find single-track roads that are only wide enough for one vehicle. Passing places (usually marked with a white diamond sign, or a black-and-white striped pole) – are used to allow oncoming traffic to pass. Remember that passing places are also for overtaking – check your rear-view mirror often and pull over to let faster vehicles pass if necessary. Be aware that it's illegal to park in passing places.

roundabouts (traffic already on the roundabout has right of way). Motorcyclists must wear helmets.

It is a criminal offence to use a hand-held mobile phone or similar device while driving; this includes while you are stopped at traffic lights, or stuck in traffic, when you can expect to be moving again at any moment.

The maximum permitted blood-alcohol level when driving is 35mg/100mL; to stay under this level, drink no more than one pint of beer or one glass of wine.

Traffic offences (illegal parking, speeding etc) usually incur a fine for which you're allowed 30 to 60 days to pay. In Glasgow and Edinburgh the parking inspectors are numerous and operate without mercy – never leave your car around the city centres without a valid parking ticket, or you risk a hefty fine.

TOURS

There are lots of companies in Scotland offering all kinds of tours, including historical, activity-based and backpacker tours. It's a question of picking the tour that suits your requirements and budget. More companies are listed in destination chapters under Tours.

Classique Tours (www.classiquetours.co.uk) Bus tours of the western isles in vintage 1950s coaches, departing from Glasgow and staying in atmospheric country hotels.

Haggis Adventures (www.haggisadventures.com) Backpackers tours, with

longer options taking in the Outer Hebrides or Orkney.

Heart of Scotland Tours (www.heartofscotlandtours.co.uk) Specialises in minicoach day tours of central Scotland and the Highlands, departing from Edinburgh.

Hebridean Princess (www.hebridean.co.uk) Luxury cruises around the west coast of Scotland, the Outer Hebrides and the Orkney and Shetland islands (HM the Queen chartered this ship for her summer holiday in 2010).

Macbackpackers (www.macbackpackers.com) Minibus tours for backpackers, using hostel accommodation, from Edinburgh to Loch Ness, Skye, Fort William, Glencoe, Oban and Stirling.

Mountain Innovations (www.scotmountain.co.uk) Guided activity holidays and courses in the Highlands; walking, mountain biking and winter mountaineering.

Rabbie's Trail Burners (www.rabbies.com) Oneto five-day tours of the Highlands in 16-seat minibuses with professional driver/guide.

Scot-Trek (www.scot-trek.co.uk) Guided walks for all levels; ideal for solo travellers wanting to link up with others.

🚃 TRAIN

Scotland's train network extends to all major cities and towns, but the railway map has a lot of large, blank areas in the Highlands and the Southern Uplands where you'll need to switch to bus or

car. The **West Highland line** from Glasgow to Fort William and Mallaig, and the **Inverness to Kyle of Lochalsh line** are two of the world's most scenic rail journeys.

National Rail Enquiry Service (☎ 08457 484 950; www.nationalrail.co.uk) For info on train timetables.

ScotRail (www.scotrail.co.uk) Operates most train services in Scotland; website has downloadable timetables.

COSTS & RESERVATIONS

Train travel is more expensive than the bus, but usually more comfortable: a standard return from Edinburgh to Inverness is about £55 compared with £26 on the bus.

Reservations are recommended for intercity trips, especially on Fridays and public holidays; for shorter journeys, just buy a ticket at the station before you go. On certain routes, including the Glasgow–Edinburgh express, and in places where there's no ticket office at the station, you can buy tickets on the train.

Children under five travel free; those five to 15 usually pay half-fare. On weekends on some intercity routes you can upgrade a standard-class ticket to 1st class for £3 to £5 per single journey – ask the conductor on the train.

Bikes are carried free on all ScotRail trains but space is sometimes limited. Bike reservations are compulsory on certain train routes, including the Glasgow–Oban–Fort William–Mallaig line and the Inverness–Kyle

353

of Lochalsh line; they are recommended on many others. You can make reservations for your bicycle from eight weeks to two hours in advance at main train stations, or when booking tickets by phone (☎ 0845 755 0033).

There are several types of ticket; in general, the further ahead you can book the cheaper your ticket will be.

Advance Purchase Book by 6pm on the day before travel; cheaper than Anytime.

Anytime Buy any time, travel any time, no restrictions.

Off Peak There are time restrictions (you're not usually allowed to travel on a train that leaves before 9.15am); relatively cheap.

DISCOUNT CARDS

Discount **railcards** (www .railcard.co.uk) are available for people aged 60 and over, for people aged 16 to 25 (or mature full-time students), and for those with a disability (☎ 0845 605 0525, text phone 0845 601 0132). The Senior Railcard (£26), Young Persons Railcard (£26) and Disabled Persons Railcard (£18) are each valid for one year and give one-third off most train fares in Scotland, England and Wales. Fill in an application at any major train station. You'll need proof of age (birth certificate, passport or driving licence) for the Young Persons and Seniors railcards (proof of enrolment for mature-age students) and proof of entitlement for the Disabled Persons Railcard.

TRAIN PASSES

ScotRail has a range of good-value passes for train travel. You can buy them at BritRail outlets in the USA, Canada and Europe, at the British Travel Centre in Regent St, London, at train stations throughout Britain, at certain UK travel agents and **ScotRail Telesales** (☎ 0845 755 0033) and online at www.scotrail.co.uk. Note that Travelpass and Rover tickets are not valid for travel on certain (mainly commuter) services before 9.15am weekdays.

Central Scotland Rover Covers train travel between Glasgow, Edinburgh, North Berwick, Stirling and Fife; costs £33 for three days' travel out of seven.

Freedom of Scotland Travelpass Gives unlimited travel on all Scottish train services (some restrictions), all CalMac ferry services and on certain Scottish Citylink coach services (on routes not covered by rail). It's available for four days' travel out of eight (£114) or eight days out of 15 (£153).

Highland Rover Allows unlimited train travel from Glasgow to Oban, Fort William and Mallaig, and from Inverness to Kyle of Lochalsh, Aviemore, Aberdeen and Thurso; it also gives free travel on the Oban/Fort William to Inverness bus, on the Oban–Mull and Mallaig–Skye ferries, and on buses on Mull and Skye. This pass is valid for four days' travel out of eight (£74).

Behind the Scenes

Author Thanks

NEIL WILSON

Many thanks to all the helpful and enthusiastic staff at TICs throughout the country, and to the many travellers I met on the road who chipped in with advice and recommendations. Thanks also to Carol Downie, and to Andrew Henderson, Steven Fallon, Russell Leaper, Amy Hickman, Erlend Tait and Pamela Tait. Finally, thanks to co-author Andy and to the ever-helpful and patient editors and cartographers at Lonely Planet.

Acknowledgments

Climate map data adapted from Peel MC, Finlayson BL & McMahon TA (2007) 'Updated World Map of the Köppen-Geiger Climate Classification', *Hydrology and Earth System Sciences*, 11, 163344.

Illustrations p70-1, p94-5 and p178-9 by Javier Zarracina.

Cover photographs: Front: Eilean Donan Castle, Sean Caffrey/Lonely Planet Images. Back: Edinburgh as seen from Calton Hill, Sean Caffrey/Lonely Planet Images. Many of the images in this guide are available for licensing from Lonely Planet Images: www.lonelyplanetimages.com.

This Book

This 1st edition of *Discover Scotland* was coordinated by Neil Wilson, and researched and written by Neil Wilson and Andy Symington. This guidebook was commissioned in Lonely Planet's London office, and produced by the following:
Commissioning Editors Clifton Wilkinson, Errol Hunt, Glenn van der Knijff
Coordinating Editor Ali Lemer
Coordinating Cartographer Csanad Csutoros
Coordinating Layout Designer Wibowo Rusli
Managing Editors Bruce Evans, Liz Heynes
Managing Cartographers Amanda Sierp, Herman So
Managing Layout Designers Indra Kilfoyle, Celia Wood
Assisting Editors Trent Holden, Anna Metcalfe, Susan Paterson, Kate James
Assisting Cartographers Julie Dodkins, Jennifer Johnson
Cover Research Naomi Parker
Internal Image Research Sabrina Dalbesio
Thanks to Shahara Ahmed, Judith Bamber, Melanie Dankel, Janine Eberle, Ryan Evans, Chris Girdler, Laura Jane, Yvonne Kirk, Nic Lehman, John Mazzocchi, Wayne Murphy, Trent Paton, Piers Pickard, Malisa Plesa, Mazzy Prinsep, Averil Robertson, Lachlan Ross, Mik Ruff, Lyahna Spencer, Laura Stansfeld, Juan Winata

NOTES

Index

000 Map pages

Z

000 Map pages

How to Use This Book

These symbols will help you find the listings you want:

- ◉ Sights
- ❶ Activities
- ◒ Courses
- ❺ Tours
- ✿ Festivals & Events
- 🛏 Sleeping
- ✕ Eating
- ☕ Drinking
- 🎭 Entertainment
- 🛍 Shopping
- ℹ Information/ Transport

Look out for these icons:

- **FREE** No payment required
- ✔ A green or sustainable option

Our authors have nominated these places as demonstrating a strong commitment to sustainability – for example by supporting local communities and producers, operating in an environmentally friendly way, or supporting conservation projects.

These symbols give you the vital information for each listing:

- ✆ Telephone Numbers
- ⊙ Opening Hours
- P Parking
- ⊖ Nonsmoking
- ❄ Air-Conditioning
- @ Internet Access
- ⬚ Wi-Fi Access
- ⊠ Swimming Pool
- ✒ Vegetarian Selection
- ⬚ English-Language Menu
- ⬚ Family-Friendly
- ⬚ Pet-Friendly
- ⬚ Bus
- ⬚ Ferry
- M Metro
- S Subway
- ⊖ London Tube
- ⬚ Tram
- ⬚ Train

Reviews are organised by author preference.

Map Legend

Sights
- ◉ Beach
- ◬ Buddhist
- ◉ Castle
- ◉ Christian
- ◉ Hindu
- ◉ Islamic
- ◉ Jewish
- ❶ Monument
- ⊕ Museum/Gallery
- ◉ Ruin
- ◉ Winery/Vineyard
- ◉ Zoo
- ◉ Other Sight

Activities, Courses & Tours
- ◉ Diving/Snorkelling
- ◉ Canoeing/Kayaking
- ◉ Skiing
- ◉ Surfing
- ◉ Swimming/Pool
- ◉ Walking
- ◉ Windsurfing
- • Other Activity/ Course/Tour

Sleeping
- ◉ Sleeping
- ◉ Camping

Eating
- ✕ Eating

Drinking
- ◉ Drinking
- ◉ Cafe

Entertainment
- ◉ Entertainment

Shopping
- ◉ Shopping

Information
- ◉ Post Office
- ℹ Tourist Information

Transport
- ◉ Airport
- ◉ Border Crossing
- ◉ Bus
- ⊕ Cable Car/ Funicular
- ◉ Cycling
- ◉ Ferry
- Ⓜ Metro
- ◉ Monorail
- Ⓟ Parking
- Ⓢ S-Bahn
- ◉ Taxi
- ◉ Train/Railway
- ◉ Tram
- ⊙ Tube Station
- Ⓤ U-Bahn
- • Other Transport

Routes
- Tollway
- Freeway
- Primary
- Secondary
- Tertiary
- Lane
- Unsealed Road
- Plaza/Mall
- Steps
-)=(Tunnel
- Pedestrian Overpass
- Walking Tour
- Walking Tour Detour
- Path

Boundaries
- International
- State/Province
- Disputed
- Regional/Suburb
- Marine Park
- Cliff
- Wall

Population
- ◉ Capital (National)
- ◉ Capital (State/Province)
- ◉ City/Large Town
- ◉ Town/Village

Geographic
- ◉ Hut/Shelter
- ◉ Lighthouse
- ◉ Lookout
- ▲ Mountain/Volcano
- ◉ Oasis
- ◉ Park
-)(Pass
- ◉ Picnic Area
- ◉ Waterfall

Hydrography
- River/Creek
- Intermittent River
- Swamp/Mangrove
- Reef
- Canal
- Water
- Dry/Salt/ Intermittent Lake
- Glacier

Areas
- Beach/Desert
- Cemetery (Christian)
- Cemetery (Other)
- Park/Forest
- Sportsground
- Sight (Building)
- Top Sight (Building)

Our Story

A beat-up old car, a few dollars in the pocket and a sense of adventure. In 1972 that's all Tony and Maureen Wheeler needed for the trip of a lifetime – across Europe and Asia overland to Australia. It took several months, and at the end – broke but inspired – they sat at their kitchen table writing and stapling together their first travel guide, *Across Asia on the Cheap*. Within a week they'd sold 1500 copies. Lonely Planet was born.

Today, Lonely Planet has offices in Melbourne, London and Oakland, with more than 600 staff and writers. We share Tony's belief that 'a great guidebook should do three things: inform,' educate and amuse'.

Our Writers

NEIL WILSON

Coordinating Author, Edinburgh, Stirling & Northeast Scotland, Skye & the Islands, Inverness & the Highlands Neil was born in Scotland and save for a few years spent abroad has lived there most of his life. A lifelong enthusiasm for the great outdoors has inspired his hiking, biking and sailing expeditions to every corner of the country. Memorable moments on his latest research trip included watching the sunset light up the hills of Applecross from a campsite high on Skye's Trotternish Ridge, and sighting two golden eagles thermalling over the wilds of central Mull. Stumbling across the magnificent menu at the Dores Inn near Inverness was an added bonus. Neil has been a full-time author since 1988 and has written more than 50 guidebooks for various publishers, including Lonely Planet's Encounter guide to his home town of Edinburgh. Neil also wrote the Plan Your Trip, Scotland in Focus and Survival Guide chapters.

Read more about Neil at:
lonelyplanet.com/members/neilwilson

ANDY SYMINGTON

Glasgow, Stirling & Northeast Scotland, Skye & the Islands, Inverness & the Highlands Andy's Scottish forebears make their presence felt in a love of malt, a debatable ginger colour to his facial hair and a love of wild places. From childhood slogs up the M1 he graduated to making dubious road trips around the firths in a disintegrating Mini Metro and thence to peddling whisky in darkest Leith. Whilst living there, he travelled widely around the country in search of the perfect dram; now resident in Spain, he continues to visit very regularly.

Read more about Andy at:
lonelyplanet.com/members/andy_symington

Published by Lonely Planet Publications Pty Ltd
ABN 36 005 607 983
1st edition – May 2011
ISBN 978 1 74220 286 0
© Lonely Planet 2011   Photographs © as indicated 2011
10 9 8 7 6 5 4 3 2 1
Printed in China